Business
and Management
Education in
Transitioning and
Developing Countries

Business
and Management
Education in
Transitioning and
Developing Countries
A Handbook

Foreword by Ben L. Kedia

John R. McIntyre
Ilan Alon
Editors

M.E.Sharpe
Armonk, New York
London, England

From John R. McIntyre: To Simone and Tim, always at my side

From Ilan Alon: To my Kareen

Car

Library of Congress Cataloging-in-Publication Data

Business and management education in transitioning and developing countries : a handbook /
[edited by] John R. McIntyre and Ilan Alon.
   p. cm.
Includes bibliographical references and index.
ISBN 0-7656-1504-5 (hardcover : alk. paper)
  1. Business education—Developing countries. 2. Business education—Former
communist countries. 3. Management—Study and teaching—Developing countries.
4. Management—Study and teaching—Former communist countries. I. McIntyre, John R.
II. Alon, Ilan.

HF1191.B85 2005
650′.071′11722—dc22   2004027436

Contents

Part III. Transitioning Europe and Central Asia

Part IV. Latin America

Part V. Africa and Near East

List of Tables, Figures, and Appendices

Tables

Figures

Appendices

Foreword

Adequately preparing future generations of managers, executives, and entrepreneurs is a challenge for all societies. For transitioning and developing countries, the issues are magnified by the lack of professional education infrastructure and of a tradition of educating for the private sector. Harnessing professional education to economic development objectives is indeed a precondition to narrow the egregious gaps with more developed societies. Business education is a nascent phenomenon in many of these markets where economic elites have been heretofore trained overseas. The choices made by developing and transitioning countries have included sending future managerial elites to advanced industrialized countries' business schools or "importing" ready-made Western-style business programs and curricula to meet the demand for training at the local level. The national need for managerial talent, fast-changing demographics, and evolving market dynamics more than justify a scholarly review and analysis of a policy area now identified as critical by scholars, policy makers, and business executives.

This edited volume by John R. McIntyre and Ilan Alon is the result of a research conference held at the Georgia Institute of Technology, November 6–7, 2003. It makes a worthy contribution to the literature of management and business education in developing and transitioning economies, as broadly defined by the World Bank. It is an area over which much anecdotal experience has accumulated but it lacks a much deeper and systematic analysis. This second specialized text on the same topic area by the editors brings together experienced scholars and practitioners to focus on a choice of regions and countries that at once face unique training challenges and offer innovative new responses. It is hoped that the knowledge contained in this volume will benefit business education policy makers and practitioners in making better choices and finding optimal solutions to meet their professional education and economic development goals in a globalizing economy.

The chapters, selected through a review process, cover a variety of topics ranging from successful pedagogical models, needs analysis in the light of a rapidly changing environment, successful and transferable organizational models of the business education enterprise to course content and curricula, as well as cross-cultural lessons. However, these models, course content, and curricula will have to be modified in view of the local needs and economic and political environments of different countries in which business organizations are embedded.

A uniquely indigenous professional business education system, based on best practices and lessons, will ensure a steady, high quality, and motivated pool of talent. Domestic qualified managerial talent—mastering both the local and international business environments—is a precondition to attracting job-creating foreign direct investment, reducing the brain drain, securing greater shares of global markets with attendant supply chains, ensuring continuous productivity gains, and, finally, generating strong export sectors for growth and diversification.

Ben L. Kedia
Wang Chair Professor in International Business
Director, Center for International Business Education
University of Memphis, Memphis, Tennessee

Acknowledgments

The book is the culmination of work that extends beyond the efforts of the primary editors. We wish to acknowledge the participation, review, and support of the following individuals: Abraham M. George, founder and president, the George Foundation and chairman, eMedexOnline LLC; Mauricio Cardenas, professor of international management, Tec de Monterrey, Mexico; H.E. Jose Octavio Bordon, ambassador of Argentina to the United States of America, and former executive director, Social and Economic Development Program—a joint initiative of the Government of Argentina and the Inter-American Development Bank; David L. McKee, professor of economics, Kent State University, president of the International Academy of Business Disciplines; David M. Currie, professor of economics and finance, Crummer Graduate School of Business, Rollins College; James Johnson, associate professor of international business, Crummer Graduate School of Business, Rollins College; Craig M. McAllaster, dean and professor of management, Crummer Graduate School of Business, Rollins College; R. Reeves-Ellington, professor emeritus, Binghamton University; Rich Lee, assistant professor of English, SUNY Oneonta; Saul Klein, Lansdowne Professor of International Business, University of Victoria; Sergio Postigo, Cátedra Karel Steuer de Entrepreneurship, Universidad de San Andrés, Argentina; Raj Agrawal, professor of economics and international business, Institute for Integrated Learning in Management, New Delhi, India; Shaomin Li, professor of management, Old Dominion University; Michael R. Bowers, professor of marketing, Crummer Graduate School of Business, Rollins College; Barry R. Render, professor of management science and operations management, Crummer Graduate School of Business, Rollins College; Cecilia McInnis-Bowers, professor of marketing and international business, Rollins College; Dr. Robert G. Hawkins, past president of the Academy of International Business, professor emeritus of economics and management, past dean of the Ivan Allen College, Georgia Tech; Francis Ulgado, associate professor of international marketing and faculty director, Georgia Tech CIBER; Alka Citrin, assistant professor of marketing, College of Management, Georgia Tech; Rajesh Chakrabarti, assistant professor of international finance, College of Management, Georgia Tech; Lee Caldwell, professor of strategy and associate dean, College of Management; Mark Ballam, associate director, Georgia Tech CIBER; David Bruce, professor of international business, Institute of International Business, Georgia State University; Vera Ivanaj, associate professor of strategy, University of Metz, France; Silvester Ivanaj, associate professor of information technology management, ICN Graduate School of Management, Nancy, France; Sonia Gatchair, graduate research assistant, Georgia Tech and Tracy Wooten, instructor of English, University of Central Florida.

In addition to the individuals above, the following institutions were instrumental in making this book a reality: the College of Management's Dean Office, Georgia Tech, Atlanta, Georgia; the Georgia Tech Center for International Business Education and Research; the U.S. Department of Education CIBER Programs; the Crummer Graduate School of Business, Rollins College; AGL Resources, Inc.; the Consulate General of Argentina in Atlanta and the Embassy of Argentina in Washington, DC; and World Times, Inc.

Introduction

This specialized edited text presents a collection of reflections on the directions and choices facing both public and private sectors in building and strengthening business education in developing economies around the world. The countries under review account not only for most of the world's population but also for most of the world's growth in trade, investment, and production in years to come. Despite their relatively less developed market conditions and socioeconomic infrastructures, ranging from the deep structural problems of Africa to the rapid and required adaptation to European Union norms by Baltic countries, they all have made noteworthy strides in modernizing their business educational institutions, sometimes partnering with Western business schools, sometimes innovating on their own, and all the while imitating and adapting best practices, as justified by rapidly evolving global and regional markets. China, by virtue of its size and rates of economic growth, endowed with characteristics of both a developing and transitioning economy, deserves special attention. It is addressing gaps in its professional business education delivery system and experimenting with a variety of models.

We divide the book into six sections:

Part I   Indian Subcontinent
Part II   Russian Federation
Part II   Transitioning Europe and Central Asia
Part IV   Latin America
Part V   Africa and Near East
Part VI   China

By providing broad-spectrum perspectives on multiple regions, the book fills an important void in the international business education literature and offers an understanding of the varied conditions, opportunities, and threats that define the development of business and management education in select and representative developing and transitioning market economies.

Part I. Indian Subcontinent

We start by looking at India, the world's largest democracy, and a growing superpower regionally. Chapter 1, by Vipin Gupta, Kamala Gollakota, and Ancheri Sreekumar, deals with quality in business education in the Indian context. Because of pent-up demand for business education and liberalization of the education sector, there has been rapid growth in business and management education. However, the rapid growth and proliferation of business schools has led to the emergence of some schools of dubious quality—and business education has come under scrutiny. Outside of the United States, India now trains the largest number of MBAs, awarding about 75,000 degrees annually. The Indian government liberalized the business education market over the 1990s, resulting in a rapid growth of business schools offering programs at both undergraduate and graduate levels. The authors find that Indian business schools have sought to replicate the U.S.-based organizational, pedagogical, curricula, industry-interface, and academic research models, but are struggling to introduce several adaptations that take into consideration differences in the work culture system. In their chapter, the authors describe the shift from a commerce focus to a management focus in popular business education, the status of contemporary business education, broad issues and challenges, and implications for the academic quality dialogue.

Chapter 2, building on the previous assessment, and written by Vipin Gupta and Kamala Gollakota, highlights governance of publicly funded business schools, an area that is currently debated in India. The authors explore the accountability of publicly funded institutions providing business education in India by examining the current debate relating to issues accessibility and affordability of India's premier business schools—the Indian Institutes of Management. They suggest that, as these institutions see a larger role for themselves and make the necessary changes, they will be able to better address the regulatory challenges and further their founding missions.

Chapter 3, by V.P. Wani, T.K. Garg, and S.K. Sharma, continues the discussion on Indian education by focusing on the largely successful international technology dimensions. The authors discuss the importance of training engineers as entrepreneurs in order to launch successful product innovation. Prior to the liberalization of the economy, the entrepreneur in India worked in a protected economic environment with very little attention to productivity improvement, research and development, and innovation, resulting in unprogressive industrial ventures in this sector. However, changing economic policy posed challenges for this entrepreneurial sector. Training for technical innovation and improvement in productivity, production processes and systems, and effective technology management are now needed and demanded. For this reason, the authors argue that engineers, as entrepreneurs, can be the best option. The chapter explores this educational strategy and the steps for inculcating an innovative entrepreneurship ethos among engineers, so that they can face the challenges of sustainable development of the small-scale sector in India.

In chapter 4, Raj Agrawal discusses the internationalization of the curriculum as a prerequisite for enhancing the competitiveness of India globally. According to the author, the major challenge of all education is to develop an efficient and proactive quality-oriented education system, which fine-tunes itself regularly to meet the changing demands of globalization. This is something many business schools all over the world are struggling to achieve. The internationalization of the curriculum is the most important component of pedagogy. An internationalized curriculum is relevant also for students going offshore. Business schools have to consciously consider the knowledge demands of the country if they are to play a leading role in making India compete effectively in the twenty-first century. There is a need to bring the institutions of higher learning together, to give impetus to new curriculum developments, which are rooted in the sociocultural context of India but adjustable to the demands global markets. Undergraduate curricula in business schools should be based on identifying major business issues in response to the new opportunities and challenges of globalization. The undergraduate program (BBA) that was introduced by Indian universities some years ago to fulfill the emerging corporate expectations follows a curriculum patterned after the MBA and is not linked to the need profiles of first-line positions in the leading sectors. The main issue is that the trainees are often young with little work experience; the feeling is that management should be taught to older people with work experience. Agrawal explores the undergraduate degree, espouses a corporate orientation, and develops curricula and delivery systems that are market oriented and tailored to the Indian context. The curriculum has been linked with employability in new businesses. Major sectors, where most commercial or frontline jobs are opening have been identified. Required competencies and skills at the undergraduate level have been linked with the emerging needs of these sectors in the proposed curricula design.

Shifting focus from India to Nepal, in chapter 5, Alfred Rosenbloom and Bijay K.C. examine management education for the "high country." Nepal is a country often overlooked in the world's business and management literature, and it is easy to see why. Nepal is geographically situated between China and India, two of the world's biggest emerging markets, which dwarf Nepal in size and scope. Yet within this tiny, tradition-bound, Himalayan kingdom management education is flourishing. The authors fulfill two goals in their chapter: (1) providing a brief, historical overview of management education in Nepal, and (2) describing how successful curricular innovation in management education is a direct response to the evolving needs of Nepali businesses for expertly educated managers. Throughout, the chapter stresses that when MBA programs are entrepreneurial and innovative, they can survive and thrive, even in a national environment that is in political flux. To illustrate these ideas, the chapter highlights the innovative vision and curriculum of the Kathmandu School of Management, Kathmandu University.

The lesson learned from the Indian subcontinent is that successful modifications of business curricula are not only advisable but also necessary, in order for business schools to add value to their respective communities and their needs. While imitation is a first step toward modernization, the unique characteristics of the subcontinent require an evaluation of the environment and appropriate organizational responses.

Part II. Russian Federation

In chapter 6, Leo Paul Dana covers entrepreneurship training across postcommunist Europe, including Albania, Belarus, Bosnia and Herzegovina, Estonia, Hungary, Lithuania, the former Yugoslav Republic of Macedonia, Moldova, Poland, Russia, Serbia and Montenegro, Slovakia, Slovenia, and Ukraine. Due to the breadth of his chapter, it is positioned first as a lead-in to the most influential country in the region, Russia. Of the countries covered in the text, recently privatized, transitional economies provide a particularly fascinating backdrop for the development of entrepreneurship. While certain skills, not deemed necessary in the West, can be useful in a postcommunist economy, entrepreneurship training can nevertheless be most rewarding. This chapter reports findings of the author's recent study of entrepreneurship training across a selection of East European nations. The research took place in 2003. Findings reveal that there is often a mismatch between market demands and skills available in the workforce. The workforce needs retraining in skills that are in demand. Consequently, the technical content of courses needs to be adapted to changes in the economy. As the economy of a nation becomes increasingly complex, marketing and financial functions will mature and become more specialized. Training will be required to help managers solve new problems of planning, distribution, and transportation. A difficulty, however, is that educational initiatives are fragmented and often undertaken without a full grasp of the rapid changes these historically planned economies are undergoing.

In chapter 7, Galina G. Preobragenskaya and Robert W. McGee explore the recent development of accounting education in Russia. Accounting is the key function that will ensure accountability of the firm's management to the stakeholders and identify risk areas for correction. Russia is in the process of converting its accounting system from the old Soviet model to one that resembles the systems found in developed market economies. The country is adopting international financial reporting standards but with a distinct Russian flavor. To make the transition successful, it is necessary to transform accounting education. Present practitioners must be educated in the new accounting standards system, and a new generation of accountants must master its demanding mechanics. This chapter reviews the relevant accounting education literature and summarizes the results of interviews of accounting educators conducted in Russia during the summer of 2003.

In chapter 8, Scott G. Dacko presents research examining key skills developed in a major Russian business program relative to the same key skills in United Kingdom (UK) and American business school programs. Nine key skills, including analytical skills, written and oral communication, computer skills, and risk taking, are examined in the Russian, UK, and American contexts to determine to what extent differences exist between what participants believe are currently emphasized in the programs as well as what participants believe should be emphasized. A survey of participants in these programs finds that a Russian management program emphasizes the development of many key skills to significantly different degrees relative to U.K. and American programs. In general, it is found in the study that Russian, U.K., and American students have significantly different views in two areas: first, in their views on the extent to which key skills are actually being developed in their business programs, and second, in their views on preferences for skills that should be developed in their business programs. For example, Russian students perceive a need for relatively greater overall emphasis on developing computer skills and oral communication skills, when compared to the views of U.K. students. When comparing Russian programs to both American and U.K. programs, it is found that American programs tend to place less emphasis on developing oral communication skills relative to either Russian or U.K. business programs. In addition, Russian students see a need for greater emphasis on developing leadership and interpersonal skills, although to a lesser extent than that desired by U.K. students. These and other findings support the view that Russian students have significantly different needs and expectations than Western business school students. These needs must be understood and met if (1) student satisfaction is to be maintained or increased by teachers and academicians from any country, and (2) business program competitiveness is to be maintained and enhanced.

The Russian Federation resembles the Indian continent in at least one aspect: Universities must adapt to changing conditions as these markets are changing. However, business and management needs differ; student expectations are diverse; and the skills and abilities needed for success differ in significant ways.

Part III. Transitioning Europe and Central Asia

Transitioning markets in Europe and Central Asia have been largely affected by Russia. In chapter 9, X. Dai Rao and Liza Rybina explore business education practices in the former Soviet Republic of Kazakhstan where the Soviet style of education based on centralized democracy and Marxist theory prevailed for many years. With the collapse of this system and theory, many republics have found themselves in the category of "developing countries." The models that are currently being used in national and government-funded universities to teach business education are similar to those used in the 1950s in America and Europe; however, this is beginning to change, as a consumer culture with access to cable television exposes a new generation of Kazakhstanis to consumerism and capitalism. The chapter explores a range of theories pertaining to what is being taught, how it is being delivered, and whether it has any impact on the economy. Significant differences between the type of institutions and their capacity to absorb foreign faculties' input, and the ability of students to pay the resultant escalating tuition are considered. Such issues, among others, are directly affecting who is "winning" the race in transitioning from historical central planning to the norms of capitalism in a former Soviet republic.

Chapter 10 features the work of Sharon V. Thach, Serhiy Gvozdiov, and Galen Hull on entrepreneurial behavior in another key and emblematic post-Soviet country—Ukraine. This chapter is a case study of the Lviv Institute of Management (LIM), an entrepreneurial venture in western Ukraine that was launched with sharply limited resources in an environment not particularly conducive to educational experimentation, but nevertheless grew through innovation and skillful deployment and select application of initially small resources. Established as a private management training institution in 1990, it was among the first Western-style business schools in the former Soviet Union. The case history describes LIM's entrepreneurship in the acquisition, development, and use of resources as a private institution; its ability to attract and mold students into entrepreneurs and its mission to model the behavior taught. It also profiles LIM's partnership with two American universities: Tennessee State University (TSU) and Lincoln University (Missouri). In October 2000, a two-year United States Agency for International Development (USAID) grant entitled "Developing Business Management Capacities for Private Sector Development" was awarded. Its goal was to enhance management-training capabilities in each of the three participating institutions, while promoting private sector relations between Western Ukraine and the U.S. partnership. The activities consisted of twenty-three faculty and staff exchanges, including intensive courses in marketing and management, adapting materials and concepts to create new courses, and collaborative research resulting in a paper accepted for publication in a leading American scholarly journal. With assistance from TSU faculty, a survey of LIM's impact on the Ukrainian economy was conducted. The partnership resulted in lasting personal and professional ties that exemplify how business educational change can be institutionalized in transitioning economies coming out of a central planning tradition.

Chapter 11, by Vytautas Pranulis and Audra I. Mockaitis, discusses international business education in Lithuania, using the case study of the Vilnius University Master of International Business Program. As in the previous chapters, the authors acknowledge that universities in Central and Eastern Europe have, over the past decade, begun revising existing programs of study to reorient them to changing market demands. The chapter presents a relatively new master's program in international business at Vilnius University in Lithuania, including information on its content, goals, tasks, admissions procedures, and student turnover. The Master of International Business Program, introduced in 2001 is designed to develop the knowledge and skills necessary for a dynamic globalized business environment, and its aims and objectives emphasize the attainment of both theoretical and practical knowledge. The aim of the program is to obtain an optimal balance between functional and interpersonal aspects in the implementation of distance learning courses. A survey of prospective students revealed that of the graduate-level business programs offered by the university, this program was the primary choice. Recent graduates of the program also evaluated the program rather favorably. Business education in Lithuania has come a long way since the 1990s, with a shift away from narrower technical to the more general business and management disciplines. Many of the programs have been heavily influenced by Western principles of education, and have borrowed from European and U.S. education. However, it is apparent that modules and programs cannot be copied directly from Western countries and applied identically. The current needs of future executives must be built into the definition of pacing change, curricular contents, delivery modes, evaluation. It is obvious that business education in Lithuania, considering the size of the Lithuanian market and its entry into the European Union, will be rapidly internationalized. The pending question is how best to achieve the goals and how to assess the competitiveness of these relatively new programs.

In chapters 12 and 13, Robert W. McGee reflects on accounting education trends in Armenia and Bosnia and Herzegovina, respectively. The USAID and various other governmental and nongovernmental organizations have been expending resources in developing countries for decades to improve the infrastructure of their economies. In recent years, several projects have aimed at reforming the accounting and financial reporting systems of several countries, most notably in Eastern Europe and the former Soviet Union. Chapter 12 summarizes the accounting education segment of the USAID Accounting Reform Project in Armenia, discusses the history and culture of Armenia, and delves into a discussion of the major aspects of accounting education reform. Education reform included replacing the accounting curriculum of all the major universities and institutes in Armenia as well as training existing certified accountants and auditors and enterprise accountants. Accounting training was provided for other groups as well. There is also some discussion of the new certification model, which closely parallels the Association of Chartered Certified Accountants model, and some of the implementation problems that arose during the reform process. In chapter 13, the problem of proper educational preparation and experience for professors expected to teach the new curriculum is discussed in the context of Bosnia and Herzegovina.

This section concludes with chapter 14, by Vera Ivanaj, Silvester Ivanaj, and Palok Kolnikaj, who offer a longer term critical perspective on the unique case of Albania, at once a Balkan and a European country with a heterogeneous population and a long history of economic and political isolation. The business education system reforms and innovations undertaken in the wake of regime change and economic reorganization appear at first mired in obstacles and deeply embedded within existing public structures. But the beneficial influence of external forces provides needed stimulus to launch new business educational initiatives. The authors assess the pace of changes and the likelihood of success.

The challenges facing countries in transition and particularly the countries that were under Soviet rule are similar to the ones facing the Russian Federation at present. In addition, some of these countries have lesser stature and resources to deal with critical shortages, exacerbating the situation.

Part IV. Latin America

The globalization phenomenon and geographic proximity to the North American markets compel Latin American business students to be prepared adequately to function in an increasingly interdependent and dynamic regionalized economy. Shifting social, legal, economic, political, and technological constraints pose different challenges to business colleges in Latin America. Understanding the educational implications of the internationalization process requires faculty with a global mindset. Business education in Latin America aiming to satisfy the demand of business students to garner the skills to cope with the forces that govern tomorrow's world economy. A combination of corporate overseas internships and study abroad programs, and, more important, a solid business curriculum should allow them to become more effective, problem-solving individuals. Jaime Ortiz expertly discusses issues related to the internationalization of business education in Latin America in chapter 15.

Narrowing the field of investigation, in chapter 16, Sergio Postigo and Maria Fernanda Tamborini and in chapter 17, Sergio Postigo, Donato Iacobucci, and Maria Fernanda Tamborini present a single country perspective —Argentina—in the context of entrepreneurship education. Their discussions can be contrasted with the analysis of Dana in chapter 6 which reviews entrepreneurship in postcommunist Europe. Chapter 16 argues that the emergence of entrepreneurship in developing countries is critical because it functions as a paramount agent of change, and that universities play a linchpin role in shaping entrepreneurship by availing future entrepreneurs of a knowledge base and "organizational incubation." Recent research in Latin American countries found that half of the most dynamic entrepreneurs have a university degree.

Chapter 17 builds on the information on Argentinean entrepreneurship education and contrasts it with the practices of a developed country in the European Union—Italy. This comparison can be telling because in the information age, new ventures founded by graduates are expected to play a critical role in the emergence of knowledge-based firms. The aim of the chapter is to analyze the influence of different contexts—developed and developing countries in the image that students have about entrepreneurs; the influence of social background on the motivation to become an entrepreneur; and the perception about what positive or negative factors affect the creation of new ventures. The cases analyzed are San Andrés University in Argentina and Ancona University in Italy. Interestingly, there are more similarities than differences between Argentinean and Italian students in their perception of entrepreneurship. The social background of the students plays a major role in the propinquity to become entrepreneurs while country specificity has little impact on it. Remarkable similarities between the two groups of students are also found in the reasons for creating their own firm. The perceived obstacles in starting up their own firm are also largely similar: Both groups emphasize the risk and the lack of funding, in substantial agreement with the findings of the Global Entrepreneurship Monitor project.

Moving to Chile in chapter 18, Maria-Teresa Lepeley presents a unique perspective on business education as a transitioning market itself. In the early

1970s, developing countries in Asia and Latin America started to drift apart from centralized or socialistic economies and began experimenting with market systems to improve growth and welfare.

Part V. Africa and the Near East

In chapter 19, the World Bank's Guy Pfeffermann, drawing on substantial program implementation leadership, reflects on business education in developing countries with reference to Africa, an economically underdeveloped region of the world, and suggests that business schools can contribute in significant ways to the process of economic development in societies with structural problems. The chapter details how well-designed business education contributes not only to individual achievement but also to higher societal aspirations—what is generally termed "development." While the chapter is intended to apply to the whole of the developing world, it is particularly focused on Africa, and has a practical slant, drawing on recent work undertaken, initiatives launched, and research performed by the World Bank Group and related organizations. To seek some answers to what business school education may contribute, three questions are asked: First, what is the role of enterprise in reducing poverty? Second, how do business schools serve the needs of society? Third, how can business education be strengthened?

Focusing on Sub-Saharan Africa and Uganda, in chapter 20, Romie F. Littrell and Peter Baguma present results of a research project investigating subordinates' preferences for explicit leader behavior there, and compare the results to those from other geocultural areas. The authors suggest that development of Africa by indigenous peoples has been slowed or prevented by poor or nonexistent management training. In consequence, the public sector is often mismanaged; and success in private enterprise is hindered by a lack of well-trained senior and middle managers capable of competently operating in modern business, government, and economic systems.

In chapter 21, continuing in the same vein, Jan-Erik Jaensson and Lettice Rutashobya introduce a joint venture project between Tanzanian and Swedish universities. In 1997, the knowledge transfer project was formulated between the Faculty of Commerce and Management at the University of Dar es Salaam in Tanzania, and the Department of Business Administration at Umea School of Business and Economics in Sweden. The project received total funding of US$2.6 million from the Swedish International Development Cooperation Agency, initially for six years, then subsequently for four years, until 2007. During six years of operation, the project output has yielded some outstanding results. This project fitted well into the strategies of both organizations, where the main objective of the faculty in Tanzania was to invest in research capacity building while the strategy of the faculty in Sweden was to continue with their internationalization process and look for cooperation outside the traditional Western world universities, where they already had a saturation of links. During the first six years, substantial research capacity has been built along with the launching of a PhD program in which knowledge about doctoral training has been transferred from the Swedish organization to the Tanzanian one. The expected outputs from the project include ten PhD examinations in Tanzania, fourteen licentiate exams in Sweden, thirteen PhD supervisors from Tanzania trained during workshops in Sweden, eight postdoctoral projects conducted, conferences held each year in Tanzania, and conference papers and published articles in international journals.

Chapter 22, by Rana Ozen Kutanis and Serkan Bayraktaroglu, focuses on the change dynamics in the business curriculum of a unique Near Eastern country, Turkey. The chapter concerns educational curricula design and is set in the context of a national policy agenda to drive forward a knowledge-based economy and an enterprise society. The authors argue that university business schools are about to undergo a period of radical transformation as a result of external pressures favoring the evolution of knowledge work. They discuss entrepreneurship in the context of the Business School of Sakarya University and highlight interesting trends in university–industry collaboration over the past decade. Universities provide the qualified workforce and participate in the accumulation of scientific knowledge and technology that industry demands, along with the primary function of education. The socioeconomic impact of the higher-education sector on the economy includes three areas. First, fundamental and applied research activities of universities contribute to the stock of knowledge in the economy. Second, universities provide highly trained human resources. Third, the sector supplies ideas and inventions through technology transfer.

In chapter 23, Earl N. Caldwell II and Vanessa Gail Perry investigate how the concept of open and closed minds impacts management education in Ghana and benchmarks to the United States. The authors explore the role of dogmatism, self-esteem, and locus of control as basic beliefs useful in differentiating African and American students' learning and behavioral choices. Their correlation analysis indicates that dogmatism is positively correlated with self-esteem, locus of control, and country of origin, but not with collectivism, and that Ghanaian students with low self-esteem were more dogmatic than American students with low self-esteem. Designing business educational programs without a firm grasp of underlying cultural assumptions, values, and beliefs may lead to dysfunctional educational strategies as developing and transitioning countries diffuse business education models initially conceptualized elsewhere.

Part VI. China

Management education in China—the second largest economy in the world in purchasing power parity terms—is developing rapidly though still at a stage of relative infancy by the standards of Organization for Economic Cooperation and Development countries. There is little tradition of management education in China, with many of the extant initiatives finding historical roots in the 1980s. But the growing interdependency between the Chinese and global economies being felt around the world, with one-quarter of the world's growth in 2003 generated by China alone, means that a managerial revolution is under way. Business education is therefore a salient policy issue for China, as it reforms and opens up further under the "gaige kaifan" approach (opening up and liberalizing).

Most business education models have been imported, often taking the form of foreign business schools or Chinese academics returning home to work in a Chinese university setting. Business programs and faculties are therefore not the power centers that they are in American or even Western universities. Chinese universities have traditionally been more focused on engineering, the sciences, and sometime political economy. Given the size of China's economy, its rapid growth, and the momentum of foreign direct investment, a dazzling array of management programs in China—from private local ventures to internationally accredited operations—has emerged. As of 2004, some eighty-seven Chinese universities had been awarded the designation of "experimental MBA institutions" by the State Council. Among the more prestigious can be included: Fudan, Qinghua, Renmin, Xi'an Jiaotong Universities. On the whole, there are as many as 150 MBA programs offered in China either as a foreign MBA degree in association with Chinese universities or without any formal association with a Chinese university. A number of them are offered in Chinese with local faculty, in a lower fee category. A unique organizational and pedagogical experiment, the China Europe International Business School, deserves special mention as an experiment in the making.

Chapter 24, by Jonatan Jelen and Ilan Alon, addresses the distance learning dimension of business education in China. The information technology sector is without a doubt one of the major drives in transitioning economies such as China. Distance learning is a strategy that may allow the closing of some critical gaps. The authors explore four strategies to respond to the burgeoning demand for business education services in China: overseas education, local education, adaptation, and reconfiguration of Chinese universities' business education departments and distance education. They develop an analytical framework to assess the proper response to the ambitious Chinese business educational challenges.

In chapter 25, the focus shifts to a critical dimension of business education for a globalizing China: professional marketing education. Ilan Alon and Le Lu review the shortage in qualified workers and the lack of available training and identify educational lags and pedagogical strategies to address them. The authors review the assumptions underlying modern business education and the challenges facing marketing and business education China, and suggest problem-solving strategies.

Part I

Indian Subcontinent

1

Quality in Business Education

A Study of the Indian Context

*Vipin Gupta, Kamala Gollakota,
and Ancheri Sreekumar*

Business education has its origins in the late nineteenth century in the United States. Currently 250,000-plus undergraduate degrees and 100,000-plus graduate degrees in business are awarded in the United States every year by more than 1,200 accredited colleges and universities. In recent years, the United States has seen a 10 percent annual growth in nondegree executive education programs, with revenues exceeding $3 billion (Pfeffer and Fong 2002: 78). Similar trends are seen worldwide—business education has spread rapidly in Europe, Asia, and Latin America. The rapid growth and proliferation of business schools has led to the emergence of some schools of dubious quality—and business education has come under scrutiny. Pfeffer and Fong (2002), in their controversial paper "The End of Business Schools? Less Success than Meets the Eye," contended that graduates with a business education are no more successful than leaders without the degree, for success is a function of what a person can do. Does it then make sense for the potential students to bear the cost of an MBA education that often tops $175,000, including tuition and lost salaries? Similar issues were raised in a recent paper from the consulting company Booz Allen Hamilton that derided "cookie-cutter" MBA programs that were producing look alike MBAs and not meeting businesses needs (Doria, Rozanski, and Cohen, 2003).

The goal of this article is to assess the quality of contemporary business education and to identify opportunities for further enhancement of that quality. India is an appropriate context for our study because of three factors. First, outside of the United States, India now trains the largest number of

MBAs with about 75,000 degrees annually. Second, the Indian government has liberalized the business education market over the 1990s, resulting in a rapid growth of business schools offering programs at both undergraduate and graduate levels. Third, Indian business schools have sought to replicate the U.S.-based organizational, pedagogical, curricula, industry-interface, and academic research models, but are struggling to introduce several adaptations because of the differences in the work culture system. Therefore, it would be fruitful to investigate the challenges of enhancing the quality of business education in India.

An understanding of contemporary business education in India will be incomplete without first understanding the historical context of its evolution. In the first section of our chapter, we will describe the shift from a commerce focus to management focus in popular business education. Thereafter, the quality status of contemporary business education in India is discussed. Subsequently, we discuss broad issues and challenges. Finally, research implications for academic quality dialogue are highlighted. Appendix 1.1 reviews Indian business school rankings for the most recent available year.

Historical Context and Social Status of Business Education in India

Business education has a long history in India dating back to the nineteenth century. Early business schools focused on the commercial side of business, seeking to fulfill the colonial administration needs of the British government. Their graduates joined the British government colonial bureaucracy, usually at the clerical ("babu") rank. India's first business school—Commercial School of Pachiappa Charities—was set up in 1886 in the southern city of Chennai. In 1903, the British government initiated secondary school level commerce classes at the Presidency College in Calcutta with a focus on secretarial practice/business communication (shorthand, typing, correspondence) and accounting. The first college-level business school was founded in 1913 in Mumbai (Sydenham College) and was soon followed by another in Delhi in 1920 (Commercial College, later renamed Shri Ram College of Commerce). These business colleges imparted basic skills about the principles of trade and commerce to clerks and supervisors from fields such as banking, transport, and accounting. After India's independence in 1947, business education, which was associated with "babu-ism" and therefore lacked a strong social status, started to evolve. In an attempt to enhance vocational skills, the government of India introduced commerce as a third stream of specialization at the high school level, science and arts being the other two.

Many of the graduates of the commerce stream sought apprenticeship or employment after graduating from high school, and some even joined their family businesses. Joining as an apprentice auditor at any public accounting firm was among the most popular career options for a commerce graduate. The undergraduate commerce colleges also sought to offer skills complementary to the public accounting profession, as evident in the nature of their core courses: business economics, accounting, management, banking theory, auditing, and cost accounting, all emphasizing theoretical and applied understanding of business transactions. However, even at this stage, business education (commerce) was not meant, in the eyes of the society, for the intellectually and academically talented students. Intelligent students were expected to join the science stream at the high school level and take the engineering stream at the college level in one of the Indian Institutes of Technology, universities, or other technical institutions. They then joined corporations as technical supervisors and moved up the management cadre.

A shift in the social status of business education began occurring during the 1980s. Two major forces were at play. First, competition for college level education became cutthroat as the gap in the number of admissions at the premier undergraduate programs and the number graduating from high schools grew for the science stream. Second, as companies began to grow, they began hiring commerce graduates from the colleges at the junior executive level, often backed by some in-company executive training program, as the premier engineering colleges failed to meet their growing needs for executive personnel. Consequently, society began seeing commerce education as a viable alternative passport to enter the corporate world at the executive, as opposed to the clerical, level. Many parents encouraged their children to take up the commerce stream at the high school level, with a view that their children could perform relatively well in the commerce domain and get a great corporate position without living with the intense competitive pressure to excel academically in the science streams. In addition, the social cost of commerce-related education was significantly lower than the social cost of science-related education because, unlike the latter, the former did not require laboratories and other testing facilities. Therefore, it was easier for the government and the educational institutions to meet the demand for commerce education.

Emergence of Management-Focused Business Education in India

A major development was under way: the distinction that was being made between commerce and the management aspect of business education. The focus of commerce education was on building a strong foundation about the knowledge of business transactions and processes, primarily from the economics and accounting perspectives. In contrast, management education focused on building knowledge about overall business and its various functions, given its stakeholders and the market landscape. It was felt that one needed some disciplinary background, especially in the science or commerce streams, or some work experience to effectively learn management principles. Therefore, management education was intended for the graduate and executive levels, focusing on nurturing future leaders who could lead the private and public sector organizations with a sense of social mission.

The Indian Institute of Social Science, a premier institute of higher learning focused only on graduate and doctoral programs, founded India's first management program in 1948, intending to systematically train manpower and create and spread the knowledge required for managing industrial enterprises in India. Soon thereafter, in 1949, the Catholic community founded Xavier Labor Relations Institute (XLRI) at Jamshedpur—the city of Tata Group (TISCO). TISCO had been a pioneer in progressive labor relations approaches in India, and XLRI was oriented toward developing managerial competence with a sense of social justice and values of discipline, dedication, and commitment to "Magis" (excellence in everything). The Indian Institute of Social Welfare and Business Management was set up in 1953 under the auspices of the University of Calcutta as India's first official management institute. Formed in cooperation with the business community and national and state governments, the faculty of the Institute took up the mandate to promote professionalism in the industry by undertaking several field consulting projects for the industry and the government. The primary areas of consulting included organizational development, project formulation, and socioeconomic programs.

Encouraged by the results of these early initiatives, the government applied for and obtained a grant from the Ford Foundation in 1961 to launch two Indian Institutes of Management (IIM)—one at Calcutta (West Bengal) and the other at Ahmedabad (Gujarat). This grant was focused on helping transfer American business education knowledge and models to other nations and required intensive collaboration with an American business school for facilitating the transfer of learning. The IIM at Calcutta established collaboration with the Sloan School of Management at the Massachusetts Institute of Technology for faculty and pedagogy development, and the IIM at Ahmedabad established a similar collaboration with Harvard Business School (HBS). The IIM at Calcutta adapted Sloan's incident method and laboratory training and pursued a research and teaching philosophy more focused on the quantitative and operational aspects of management. On the other hand, following HBS, the IIM at Ahmedabad pioneered the case method of teaching in India and conducted influential research oriented toward writing cases on Indian companies and context, with an emphasis on qualitative strategic integration. The mission of the IIMs was to professionalize Indian management through teaching, research, training, institution building, and consulting. They also had a mandate to professionalize vital sectors of the economy, particularly agriculture, education, health, transportation, energy, and public administration.

Growth, both in numbers and status, occurred during the 1990s. A large number of multinational companies entered India and sought to hire business graduates for their management training positions. Domestic companies also followed suit, trying to compete. Companies found that the skills of business graduates fell considerably short of the demands of the executive positions in a competitive world. In particular, commerce graduates had good accounting skills, but lacked the requisite marketing, behavioral, and operations skills. They had weak grounding in oral and written communication skills, critical thinking, and critical reading skills, as well as in information technology and teamwork skills that were becoming very relevant during the 1990s. Consequently, given the costs of training commerce graduates, companies offered huge premiums for those with an MBA degree.

As compared to the MBA program, the BBA programs demanded less qualified faculty (e.g., faculty with more limited work experience and without doctoral qualification) and offered a more captive student body (because bachelor's programs were typically three years, while the master's programs lasted only two years). As such, these programs gained popularity, offering a variety of concentrations customized to the requirements of the local industry in areas such as advertising, sales management, travel management, foreign trade, rural development, regional planning, stock exchanges, actuarial science, entrepreneurship, and business communication.

The growing popularity of the BBA programs is now creating a crisis for the positioning of the traditional undergraduate commerce degree programs. The students are increasingly giving preference to the BBA programs rather than to the commerce programs. Clarifying the role of the undergraduate commerce degree has become a major challenge because substantial academic resources are currently invested in the undergraduate commerce programs. More than 100 universities offer three-year undergraduate degrees in commerce through a large number of colleges affiliated to them, and some of them specialize just in commerce education. Forty-two universities offer Bachelor's in Commerce programs in a distance learning mode also.

Meanwhile, management institutes continued to grow. With the support of expertise developed by the pioneering IIMs, two more IIMs were founded—in Bangalore (Karnataka) in 1973 and in Lucknow (Uttar Pradesh). In the late 1990s, two additional IIMs, one at Calicut (Kerala) and the other at Indore (Madhya Pradesh), were established to further decentralize and develop management resources talent throughout India. The share of business programs in undergraduate enrolment grew from less than 15 percent in 1970 to more than 22 percent by 2000.

Quality of Business Education in India

There is a great diversity of business education in India, and it may not be meaningful to consider all types of schools in an analysis of quality. Until recently, the top business schools have functioned as role models for the rest; however, a number of business schools are striving to create their own regional or sectoral innovation niches. These quality initiatives have been partly supported by a recognition at the national policy level of a need to balance a resource allocation strategy focused on "creating islands of excellence in a mass of mediocrity" with a strategy that aids "small improvements in [a] large number of institutions" (Natarajan 2003).

Although there are many problems in making comparisons across business schools, there are some universal yardsticks for measuring quality in business education, and we will use the common ones: (1) quality of students, including the admissions process; (2) pedagogy; (3) placement; (4) faculty development; and (5) infrastructure.

Quality of Students

The quality of students entering business schools is very important to consider. As described earlier, education in commerce was not, traditionally, seen as the educational path of the brightest students. However, currently, getting accepted into a well-regarded business school is seen as very attractive career. IIMs have been ranked at the top in several surveys of b-schools in the Asia-Pacific region, and admission to any IIM is seen by most as a passport to a fast track career at the national and international levels (*Wall Street Journal Guide to B-Schools* 2003).

Each year about 125,000 aspiring candidates take the Common Admission Test or the entrance exam of the IIMs. Of these, 1,200 will be selected to join one of the IIMs. Thus, admission standards are very high. Collectively, the IIMs have been recognized as the world's number-one institutions in terms of their selectivity and the difficulty of gaining admission (*Times of India* February 19, 2003).

An interesting aspect of the selection process is the use of different admission tests and procedures by different business schools, unlike the United

States where the Graduate Management Admission Test (GMAT) is used as a standard test score. The Supreme Court of India has ruled that private educational institutions have the right to choose and select the students who can be admitted in order to maintain their unique personality, atmosphere and traditions (Goswami 2003). The merits of a common entrance test are debatable; still, there is a need to develop measures of equivalencies among scores of different admission tests so that the quality of the inputs can be isolated from the quality of the academic process while benchmarking.

A distinctive element of b-schools in India is the diversity of student profiles. Because management education is most popular at the graduate level, aspiring candidates come from a variety of academic streams such as engineering, liberal arts, science, commerce, and medicine, thereby providing a very rich interdisciplinary classroom experience. Although many of the Indian institutions give some extra weight for work experience, a majority of students are without work experience. The situation is the same in both the top-ranked and second-tier schools. This is in contrast to the United States, where traditional graduate students have at least three to four years of work experience (Zachariah 2003). Recently, though, Harvard Business School has begun accepting candidates without work experience; it now evaluates applicants on academic ability, personal characteristics, and leadership experience, where informal or formal leadership experience outside work settings is also recognized. Thus, the benefits of relating business theories to their own work experience may not take place, but there is expected to be stronger openness to learning about alternative business models.

Pedagogy

Academic quality may be enhanced not only by procuring better quality students but also by improving the quality of those students. The important question is what skills do business students need? In recent years, U.S. business schools have been criticized for not educating students in skills relevant to business. In a widely quoted report from Booz Allen Hamilton, business education has come under criticism for not training students to meet the needs of business (Doria, Rozanski, and Cohen 2003). The authors recommend more "courses in communication, leadership, human resources, psychology, and other fields that provide graduates with skills vital to effectively managing people and team-driven organizations" (Doria, Rozanski, and Cohen 2003).

The situation in India looks positive. An important feature common to most business schools in India is the mandatory summer project that students need to undertake between their first and second years. Students are expected to work with business organizations for two months at the least. This is similar to internships in the United States, except that it is required of all students. This allows schools to introduce local context into their curriculum, going beyond simply using the American textbooks and discussing Japanese principles in the name of the global content. Further, many of these schools have strived to cater to the specific needs of the local businesses by offering specific knowledge-based sectoral programs, such as by including real-world projects and forging strong interfaces with industry.

Considerable diversity exists in the pedagogical approach. The case-based and experiential approach is not universally used. In traditional business schools, the curriculum is influenced by traditional syllabi-oriented academic pedagogy. The faculty rushes through topics with a view to completing the courses and delivers lectures using the material given in the books. There is often only a limited emphasis on the development of critical and analytical reasoning and a sense of scientific inquiry, observation, problem diagnosis, and problem solving. Consequently, these graduates show deficient technical and social skills and demonstrate a theoretical and self-oriented attitude. Many companies have been concerned that graduates lack a sense of social citizenship and service. Most companies had to put "reeducation" programs in place to reorient graduates to the industry they were recruited to. Guided by the mindset in commerce-oriented programs, it was traditionally assumed that quality might be enhanced by tougher examinations, where students are asked to prepare a large number of topics. However, in reality, evaluators typically lower their expectations and award marks liberally so that the proportion of students scoring different grades more or less remains constant. Recently, there has also been an increased focus on trying to test critical application competencies, such as those involving project work. Examinations remain an important element of the curriculum, guided by a philosophy that every worthwhile activity must be reviewed, monitored, appraised, and fed back to increase efficiency and effectiveness (Natarajan 2003).

Placement

Placement is an important aspect of quality. Consistently successful placement indicates that the school is meeting the needs of industry. Top-ranked business schools have excellent placement of their graduates. Almost all the graduates from these schools get excellent jobs with extremely high salaries. Some students are even finding employment abroad.

The career focus of many schools may be seen in the efforts made by the students for the summer internship and request that the companies provide comprehensive feedback on the performance of summer interns so as to increase the chances of converting summer positions into full-time post-graduation offers. Some schools utilize psychological assessment tools to pinpoint the capabilities of enrolled students and identify promising areas of their concentration. For example, personality mapping may be used to predict that a student who is ambitious and extroverted would do better in the marketing world while one with empathy would be suitable for the Human Resource Development.

In comparing the salaries earned by top ranking MBA students and those from second tier schools, it is clear that there is a great premium for graduates from the top schools. Yet until recently, many of the schools did not have professionally manned placement departments, and in some cases, the students were responsible for promoting their schools and organizing their placements and the networking needed to establish self-employment entrepreneurial ventures.

Faculty Development

Although a majority of faculty in most Indian business schools do not have a PhD, many faculty in top ranking schools have PhDs. Further, rather than remaining purely teaching institutes, Indian b-schools have encouraged faculty to apply knowledge through extension and consulting. Such extension activities help faculty bring real life experiences to the classroom and allow b-schools to augment their resources by sharing a part of the consulting fee.

There exists a considerable gap between the desire for a comprehensive mission-based research and multifunctional, multisectoral disciplinary education and the ground realities. As mentioned earlier, faculty in most Indian b-schools do not have a doctorate degree. A typical faculty member has only an MBA or equivalent degree, usually with several years of industry experience. Limited availability of a qualified doctorate faculty is the major reason, but a concern with helping students connect to the ground realities of managerial practice has also been a paramount factor in the emphasis given to the industry experience of faculty.

An interesting aspect of business education in India is the use of practitioners to teach classes. Often, full-time faculty teach the core courses that are front-loaded into the program and that allows them to mentor the students better. The high teaching and administrative loads on the faculty in most schools makes the faculty development initiatives quite difficult. However, with increased stability in enrollments, a number of b-schools are trying to encourage faculty to write case studies and even to enroll in doctorate programs; many sponsor their faculty for conferences and training workshops.

Infrastructure

While the cost and resource limitations have made the development of infrastructure a challenge for most b-schools, the developmental banks have recently become more willing to grant loans for viable educational projects.
The typical tuition fee for b-schools in India is $2,000 per year, or $4,000 for
a two-year MBA program. If the b-school invests in excellent infrastructure,
including residence dorms, state-of-the-art classrooms, and library facilities,
backed by initiatives for faculty development, then the breakeven number of
enrollments comes to about 250 per year; which implies a tuition base of $1
million per year. By offering an additional BBA program, the numbers per
batch can be further reduced. The critical constraint remains the administration, which has to devote time to infrastructure development as well as to the
development of faculty, programs, and industry interface for placements. Most
b-schools have therefore started with only one batch of forty to fifty students
at the MBA and/or BBA level, offering only modest infrastructure and gradually building up scale, scope, and facilities.

Challenges in Business Education

The most important challenge for business education in India centers around
the fact that high quality education is limited to the top-tier schools. The
number of students graduating from these schools is minuscule compared to
the needs of the country. The fact that there is such a difference between the
top tier and next level leads to numerous problems that we will discuss below. It must, however, be noted that the second tier of business schools, especially the ones that have emerged over the past two decades, have also created
several pockets of excellence of high quality.

In our analysis of the quality of business institutes, we pointed out that the
top-tier business institutes have merit-based selection. However, to do well
in the selection, a student should have had a top-class prior education. In
most cases, such education is expensive and not affordable by the majority.
So the playing field is not even in the first place. Further, the entrance tests
are in English, which handicaps an otherwise brilliant student who has studied in rural areas and is less familiar with English. Thus, despite the merit-
based entrance exam, in reality, getting admission into the IIMs is not within
the reach of most Indians.

If indeed the quality of education in most other institutions falls short of
that at top-tier schools such as IIMs (as the premiums in starting incomes
earned by IIM graduates suggest), then one cannot expect graduates from
top-tier schools to add as much value to their workplace as they could if their

peer group also received an enhanced quality of management education.

Another problem with the big difference in quality of education leads to an elitist mentality. As institutions attain success, some become wrapped up in their reputation and lose focus on real accomplishments. This attitude rubs off on students graduating from such institutions. Often, applicants who gain admission into any of the top schools tend to view themselves in elitist terms and enact behavior such as looking down on those from second-tier schools. However, considering that most of their colleagues in the workplace will have degrees from less prestigious institutions, such an attitude will get in the way of the teamwork that is becoming increasingly important in organizations today.

There are many reasons for this wide difference in quality of business education in India. One important reason is likely to be the absence of a body that all institutions look toward to set standards—for example, the Association to Advance Collegiate Schools of Business in the United States. It must be noted that there is an apex body—the All India Council for Technical Education (AICTE)—that is responsible for defining the basic framework for quality of business education and approving entry and expansion of all institutions. There are, in practice, many problems that undermine its effectiveness.

All proposals for entry or expansion must first go through the concerned state government, in case of autonomous institutions, or through the University Grants Commission, in the case of public universities. The AICTE is responsible for giving final approval.

The AICTE requires at least 1,200 contact hours for the MBA program, in addition to six to eight weeks of summer internship and field projects, divided over two years for the full-time format and over three years for the part-time and distance learning formats. The applicants are to be admitted on the basis of a national or regional level written test to assess their aptitude and preparedness for learning management, performance in group discussions and interviews, behavioral and personality trait tests for professional aptitudes, and prior academic record and work experience. A variety of pedagogical approaches are encouraged beyond lectures, including case studies, group and individual exercises, class assignments, project work and presentations, role play, and management games. Each core faculty member is expected to teach up to six courses a year, with an additional four-course load in equivalent time devoted to research, executive development programs, academic administration, and consulting. The recommended faculty–student ratio is 1 : 60. Each institution is required to have a minimum of seven core full-time faculty members, who then serve as anchors for the part-time, visiting, or guest faculty equivalent to at least three additional full-time faculty members. A library with at least 30 journals and at least 200 titles in each of the subject areas must also be maintained. Finally, sufficient computer and instructional technology and aids are required. These criteria define the minimum entry barriers. Recently, to encourage a process of continuous review, the AICTE has also launched the National Board of Accreditation (NBA) using a benchmarking system with regard to factors such as physical infrastructure, quality of inputs, and faculty training. However, falling standards of schools approved by the AICTE has decreased its credibility. It is reported that many business schools received AICTE approval on the basis of attractive project plans, which were never implemented, so that some of them operated in very poor buildings and facilities (Raghunath 1998). The result is that most b-schools have abstained from seeking accreditation under the NBA.

A further factor limiting the popularity of what might have potentially been a national accreditation standard is the availability of substitutes. For instance, in 1998, the All India Management Association (AIMA) used International Organization for Standardization (ISO) 9000 to develop a quality assurance system known as QBS 1000. The QBS 1000 program determined and assessed b-school's quality and processes and certified their capacity across crucial and desirable parameters. The QBS 1000 system was intended to evaluate quality at 100-plus institutions associated with the AIMA (Raghunath 1998). Many other independent b-schools also found ISO an attractive option for developing and branding their institutions. But at this point, it is not clear that there is any widely used accreditation system.

Despite the lack of consistency in quality of business education, high demand for business graduates and liberalization have led to the two innovative trends—the emergence of private business schools and niche players and the increased globalization of business education.

Emergence of Private Business Schools and Niche Players

During the 1990s, buoyed by a high demand for management graduates, many private entrepreneurs set up management institutes in various parts of India. These programs were generally backed by an affiliation with some university, since only universities are allowed to grant a degree in India. However, most used the affiliation primarily as a basis to gain credibility in the marketplace and offered additional autonomous diploma programs. While the university-affiliated programs had to follow the university norms of curriculum and pedagogy, the autonomous diploma programs could be designed with full flexibility.

Many of these private business schools showed considerable dynamism in understanding the changing needs of local industry and customizing their diploma programs to those needs, thereby establishing their own niches that gained more prominence than university degrees. Illustrative specialized niches for management education include agribusiness, banking, computer and information technology, construction, cooperatives, defense, education, entrepreneurship, finance, hotel resource development, industrial relations, international business, marketing, office, pharmaceutical, police, production, project, public enterprise, public relations, total quality management, rural development, sports, telecom, tourism and travel, and transport. These niches reflect the special management needs of the specific sectors to which the b-schools have tried to cater. For instance, hospital management has become a highly popular offering in recent years. Health care is one of the largest segments of most industrial economies. The hospital management curriculum has been adapted from hotel management, as both hotel and hospital managers oversee functional areas such as front office, reception, billing, security, finance, marketing, customer relations, food and beverages, laundry, and housekeeping. In addition, training is offered in managing diagnostic and various other patient-care services that traditionally had to be managed only by senior doctors (Dhaundiyal 2002). Similarly, retail management is being offered by some b-schools. Retailing employs about 1 million people in India, but mostly in unorganized sectors. Most retail stores incur substantial losses, making professional programs highly attractive (Pradhan 2002).

Over the past few years, the central government and various state governments have recognized the entrepreneurial efforts of the private b-schools and have begun granting "deemed" or "private" university status to several private b-schools that have excellent brand names and resource infrastructure. These forces have created a very positive climate for the growth of b-schools. In 1991, there were only about 130 approved management education institutions in India, with an annual MBA intake of about 12,000 students comprised of 8,000 full-time, 3,000 part-time, and 1,000 distance education students. The number of approved institutions has now grown to approximately 1,000, with an annual MBA intake of about 75,000.

Most notable of the new institutions is the Institute of Certified Financial Analysts of India (ICFAI) University. The ICFAI's roots lay in a distance education program launched in 1985, which has since qualified 2,000-plus financial analyst graduates. In 1994, it set up the IFCAI b-school, which has since grown to nine centers all over India, namely, Ahmedabad, Bangalore, Bhubaneswar, Chennai, Gurgaon, Hyderabad, Kolkata, Mumbai, and Pune. All centers offer eight MBA programs in different areas, taught primarily by industry practitioners. In 2002, the ICFAI received private university status from the state government of Chattisgarh. It has also founded an institute for training management teachers, leading to the award of PhD degrees. It has attained third rank among b-schools set up during the post-1991 liberalization and seventh among non-IIM b-schools. With rapid growth, it already boasts 2,700 plus alumni.

The Indira Gandhi National Open University (IGNOU) is another institution that has helped extend management education to the masses. The IGNOU is an apex "open learning and distance education" institution that enrolls several thousand students in its undergraduate and graduate business education degree programs via distance learning. Recently, it also launched Gyan Darshan—the educational TV channel, and Gyan Vani—the FM radio network comprised of forty channels, for promoting business and technical education in the nation. The channels deliver course content developed by IGNOU faculty and by faculty of other institutions, such as IIMs, to students all over India, reaching even rural and other underdeveloped communities. The courses are currently delivered at no cost to the users and can be accessed by anyone with a television or a radio. Instead of the lecture method, the channels offer a mix of educational, cultural, and musical programs to inspire nonconventional students and fulfill their educational needs. The programs also offer an interactive session, allowing students from around the nation to ask questions of experts. Any b-school can provide its taped material to IGNOU for delivery of course content through these channels (Pant 2002). The IGNOU's approach has proved highly valuable in the Indian context, where education as a whole itself remains a luxury consumption item even in urban India. In urban India, the elasticity of consumption for education in the private consumption basket is 1.62, that is, a 1 percent rise in total family expenses leads to a 1.62 percent increase in education expenditure (Soman 2003).

The Emerging Role of the Global Factor

While internal efforts remain paramount in quality enhancement initiatives, the global factor is also beginning to play a role. Several overseas b-schools from the United States, the United Kingdom (UK), Ireland, Australia, and France have been prominent in India. Most of these focus on attracting Indian students to their home campuses, riding on the increased incomes of the upper middle-class segment in India and the willingness of commercial banks in India to offer loans for overseas education. Every year, about 7,000 applicants from India take the GMAT, and about 35,000 books on GMAT are sold (Chanda 2002). Many Indian b-schools have leveraged the growing interest of foreign universities in recruiting Indian students to obtain "international validation." Under this system, the foreign b-school certifies quality assurance on issues such as curriculum content, content delivery, and evaluation procedures. The level of commitment by the foreign b-school varies and ranges from provision of its own curriculum and visiting faculty to assistance in developing local curriculum and in developing local faculty resources. For instance, the Indian School of Business offers a graduate degree in business, validated by the Wharton School, Kellogg, and the London Business School. These programs allow the foreign universities to reach out to students who may be interested in visiting overseas for only one or two semesters and help the Indian b-schools harmonize their curriculum with international standards. In some cases, the foreign b-schools are also able to secure a share of tuition revenue, which is used to provide opportunities for their faculty to visit and consult in India.

Many b-schools have launched successful programs where the students cover part of their program in Indian institutions and the rest in the foreign institution overseas. The study abroad programs are less popular because most students are willing to pay the costs of overseas education only if there is an option to get jobs abroad. Therefore, most programs offer the students an option to spend a final four to twelve months with the foreign partner institution. Further, by including overseas internship as a requirement for graduation, the students become eligible to work overseas as an intern without requiring any work permit. For instance, the Institute of Management Technology, Ghaziabad, has a set up a global MBA program with Fairleigh Dickinson University in the United States. The students split their coursework between India and the United States and are required to do a six-month internship in the United States (Sablania 2002).

Many leading Indian companies—such as Tata Group, the Birla group, Madura Coats, Cargill India, Godrej, and Wipro—are giving a fillip to international initiatives by regularly bringing in overseas faculty from such institutions as Harvard, Wharton, Kellogg, and the London Business School for holding short-term classes on their sites (Bhupta and Kothari 2003). In response, some foreign business schools have launched special executive programs in India. The University of Michigan runs a two-week Global Program for Management Development in Bangalore targeted at thirty to thirty-five senior manager-level participants from a select group of thirty companies whose chief executive officers participate in another two-day program every year.

At the same time, the government of India is beginning to push India as a destination for management education, especially for students from Asia and Africa. Because of their affinity in terms of culture, climate, and, in some cases, language, Indian institutions in south India, for instance, are expected to be successful in attracting Sri Lankan students. Offering programs for executives and consulting services for companies in Asia and Africa are also seen as high growth opportunities (Bhaya 2001). These efforts have generated a keen recognition of the need to harmonize the Indian b-school system with international standards, including curriculum, the teaching-learning process, and methods of evaluation (*Economic Times* 2003a).

An interest is beginning to emerge in benchmarking and learning from the success of the Indian information technology (IT) education model for expanding overseas and catering to the lucrative corporate market. In 2003, India's software education market was $325 million. The market leader, SSI/Aptech group, had 3,200 branches of a franchise-oriented business, followed by 2,400 franchisees of NIIT. During the 2000s, SSI/Aptech's revenues from overseas centers grew at a rate of 50 percent annually. The most successful of its overseas operations is in China, where it runs 90 centers through a joint venture, formed in 2001, with an affiliate of Beijing University, with revenues of $5.6 million in 2002. It translated its English courseware used in India into Chinese and trained Chinese faculty in its Indian centers. Its biggest rivals in China include NIIT, with 100 centers, and Singapore's Informatics Holdings (*Economic Times* 2003b). The success of the IT education model in the corporate training market is also catching the attention of business schools. Tata Infotech, for instance, uses blended IT training modules that include both "off-the-shelf and customized content" for targeting both domestic as well as overseas customers (Gupta 2003). Similarly, New Horizons, the global leader in IT education, has entered the Indian market through collaboration with Shri Ram Group, with a focus on corporations seeking to develop an IT strategy and on India's booming back-office industry, which offers global firms services such as call centers and payroll processing (*Economic Times* 2003c). Such global exchange offers an excellent opportunity to Indian business schools for global brand building, global reach, and cross-pollination of ideas and academic models. However, without an appropriate governance system, an attempt to introduce global exchange could prove to be quite counterproductive, such as by creating negative country-of-origin impressions in the world.

Discussion and Conclusions

In this chapter, we reviewed the historical development of business education in India and highlighted the shift from the traditional commerce-focused programs to the new management-focused programs. We identified major parameters that are useful for evaluating the quality of business schools and evaluated Indian business schools against these standards. Our analysis leads us to believe that there are high quality business schools in India. However, these are very few. The lack of acceptable and reliable standards of accreditation has resulted in a set of elite schools resting on their reputations and a large number of schools where the lack of standards makes quality suspect.

The emergence of elitist schools may be explained by considering the power-distance dimension of national cultures. The concept of quality business education will be defined differently in different cultures. Indian culture is characterized by high power distance, and consequently high quality may denote elitism, reflecting preeminent standing among peers as ascribed by public beliefs and reinforced by cultural media, rewards, and rankings (Gupta, Hanges, and Dorfman 2002). On the other hand, in low power-distance cultures, excellence could reflect action orientation and be more a symbol of accomplishment, indicating the core mission and strategic commitment of the business school to all-around quality. The concept of quality, as defined by low power-distance cultures, is what is useful to compete in the current global economy where success needs action orientation and team work. This suggests that Indian business schools might need to change their culture and adapt to a new world economy by viewing quality more in terms of achievements than reputation. Failure to do so will result in the top-tier schools becoming increasingly elitist until they lose touch with the needs of Indian businesses.

We recommend the following as a way to further enhance business education in India:

1. It is essential that there should be reliable and widely accepted standards of accreditation of business schools in India. Either the AICTE needs to work on improving implementation (as in other facets of India, the goals and guidelines are usually in place, it is the implementation that is the problem) and building up credibility, or some other body that is more acceptable needs to provide accreditation standards. Obviously such accreditation will go well beyond ranking based on reputation or salaries of graduates and find measures that focus on the essence of business education. Such reliable and valued accreditation will go a long way toward improving the quality of less-well-known institutions. Further, institutions that currently focus on their reputation and rank will need to become more action oriented by focusing on what it is that makes business education valuable. This will help curb their tendency to elitism and allow them to retain their current high quality education.

2. Top-tier business schools have a responsibility to share their knowledge and skills with schools that might not have the same standards. This will not only raise standards, but will also allow their own graduates to be more effective in the workplace. Furthermore, top-tier schools need to change their culture from one that rests on its reputation and is elitist to one that is achievement oriented. This change in attitude is essential if their graduates are to compete in a world that values results and employees who are team players.

3. Executives need to be more concerned about the actual quality of business graduates they hire rather than be carried away by reputations.

4. Ultimately, it is up to the students to decide whether they are in busi-

Appendix 1.1

India Business School Ranking in 2002*

Rank	Institute
1	Indian Institute of Management Ahmedabad
2	Indian Institute of Management Bangalore
3	Indian Institute of Management Calcutta
4	Fore School of Management Delhi
5	XLRI Jamshedpur
6	NITIE Mumbai
7	Jamnalal Bajaj Institute Mumbai
8	Indian Institute of Management Indore
9	Indian Institute of Management Kozhikode
10	S P Jain Institute Mumbai
11	Shailesh J Mehta SoM IIT Bombay
12	Indian Institute of Foreign Trade Delhi
13	Institute of Management Tech Ghaziabad
13	XIM Bhubneshwar
14	Narsee Monjee Institute Mumbai
15	Vinod Gupta SoM IIT Kharagpur
16	University Business School Chandigarh
17	International Management Institute Delhi
17	DMS IIT Delhi
18	Indian Institute of Planning and Management Delhi
19	T A Pai Management Institute Manipal
20	Amity Business School Noida (UP)

Source: Outlook—C fore Survey, September 9, 2002.

*Rankings differ considerably across different surveys of business schools in India because of differences in methodology and differences in sample participation. Further, rankings change considerably on an annual basis because of the rapidly changing environment of business education in India. Therefore, these rankings should be considered with caution.

ness schools just for passive learning or they are also ready to meet the challenge of forcing changes in the mental attitudes of the administrators in matters that are critical for sustaining the reputation of their institutions and preserving the lifelong premiums of their learning.

There are reasons to be hopeful that business education in India will improve and be considered excellent globally. Significant improvements in the quality of business programs have occurred since liberalization in India. The existence of pockets of quality is evidence that it is possible to get high quality education in India. These schools can act as role models for others. The effort to reach out globally will also play an important role in exchanging institutional learning and in broadening the perspectives of faculty and students, which will result in the improvement of business education in India.

Increasingly, business schools in India are striving to be responsive to local needs. Research, for instance, is emerging as something that goes beyond articles, books, and publications; it should, and does, include personal and institutional introspections that enhance the quality of the learning experience in the classrooms and in industry. Such a broadened perspective is perhaps more appropriate for the diverse cultural and emerging market context of India. The use of cookie-cutter tools, borrowed from the United States, may just cause managers to introduce replicas of American business models in India. That would be a disaster, for it would hinder the development of the unique endowments of India and also erode the idiosyncratic advantages of American corporations.

References

Bhaya, A.G. 2001. "Influencing Management Practices." *Times of India*, December 3.
Bhupta M., and P. Kothari. 2003. "Back to School." *Economic Times*, February 15.
Chanda, A.K. 2002. "A Truly Indian Effort." *Times of India*, September 10.
Dhaundiyal, P. 2002. "Demand, on a High." *Times of India*, July 9.
Doria J.; H. Rozanski; and E. Cohen. 2003. "What Business Needs from Business Schools." *Strategy + business*. Available at www.strategy-business.com (accessed November 30, 2004).
Economic Times. 2003a. "Govt Moves to Make India an Education Destination." February 7.
———. 2003b. "SSI Moving to Take on NIIT." February 14.
———. 2003c. "New Horizons Plans $10 mn Indian Investment." February 19.
Goswami, U.A. 2003. "Common Entrance Tests Could Be History." *Economic Times*, January 30.
Gupta, I.D. 2003. "Tata Infotech Shifts Focus to Corp Training." *Economic Times*, January 26.
Gupta, V.; P.J. Hanges; and P. Dorfman. 2002. "Cultural Clusters: Methodology and Findings." *Journal of World Business* 37, no. 1: 11–15.
Natarajan, R. 2003. "Keynote Address." Presented at the National Seminar on Achieving Corporate Excellence in the Changing Business Environment, Bhubaneswar, India, July 20.
Outlook-C fore Survey. 2002. "Business School Rankings." September 9.
Pant, P. 2002. "Distance Education Made Easy." *Times of India*, November 29.
Pfeffer J., and C. Fong. 2002. "The End of Business Schools? Less Success than Meets the Eye." *Academy of Management Learning and Education* 1, no. 1: 78–95.
Pradhan, S. 2002. "New Openings in Retailing." *Times of India*, May 16.
Raghunath, R. 1998. "Quality Standards for Business Schools." *Financial Express*, November 25.
Sablania, R. 2002. "IMT Launches Global MBA." *Times of India*, November 12.
Soman, M. 2003. "Education and Health Are Urban Luxuries." *Economic Times*, February 2.
Times of India. 2003. "Diagnostic CAT 2003." February 19.
Wall Street Journal Guide to Top Business Schools. 2003. New York
Zachariah, C. 2003. "Quantity Battles Quality Test." *Times of India*, October 13.

2

Governance of Publicly Funded Business Schools

The Current Debate in India

Vipin Gupta and Kamala Gollakota

Over recent years, there has been an increasing demand for accountability from management education programs responding, in part, to an evolving "risk society" with its lack of trust (Trow 1998). Hedmo, Sahlin-Andersson, and Wedlin (2001) use the term "regulatory field" to characterize the dynamics of the evolving regulations. A field is held together by the "common belief" (Bourdieu 1977) in certain strategic intents, such as offering appropriate and relevant management education, though the individual actors in the field may differ in their views on how those strategic intents should be pursued and perused. The interactive relationships in a field serve to generate conformity to the shared strategic intent by assuring transparency (access to all essential information), openness (nondiscriminatory participation by all constituencies), impartiality (no privilege to one party), relevance (reflective of market and regulatory needs), and coherence (aligning conflicting contexts, perspectives, purposes, and actions). The regulatory actors emphasize a "mission" that should define management education based on the interests of their constituencies, from whom they derive legitimacy and who are the key consumers of their regulatory activities. Indeed, mission-based operation is now the fundamental element for the accountability of business programs (AACSB 2003).

In this article, we identify the areas where the regulatory field has influenced the development of academic institutions' missions by alleviating various kinds of academic barriers. Thereafter, we look at the currently debated issues of business school accountability in India.

Literature Review

The higher education system has traditionally underserved the nonmajority student pool, that is, minorities and lower-income students (Wolanin 2003). Cultural barriers, academic barriers, financial barriers, capacity barriers, quality barriers, and institutional barriers have been some of the major factors underlying this opportunity gap.

Cultural barriers. These barriers refer to social attitudes and perceptions that undermine the motivation of low-income and minority students in benefiting from the opportunities for higher business education (Wolanin 2003). For example, in the low gender-egalitarian communities, female children receive less active encouragement than male children to pursue business education (House et al. 2004). Similarly, in the high power-distance communities, underprivileged students and their parents may lack understanding of the factors critical to gaining access to and being successful in higher business education (Wolanin 2003). The U.S. data show that several forces multiply cultural barriers. First, low family income: only 21 percent of college qualified low-income high school graduates, compared with more than 60 percent of the high-income college-qualified high school graduates, complete a bachelor's degree (ACSFA 2002). Second, first-generation students (students who are first in their family to attend college) are less academically prepared to go to college, take fewer college preparatory courses, and fail to take college entrance exams (Wolanin 2003). As a result of the regulatory-driven outreach programs, first-generation students now comprise 40 percent of all undergraduate students on U.S. college campuses (Wolanin 2003).

Academic barriers. Research shows that students from low-income families and minority students have lower academic performance and grades than other students (Fitzgerald and Delaney 2002). Inadequate academic preparation is a major impediment to access to higher education. More than 70 percent of the population of India lives in rural areas (World Bank 1997). However, fewer than 5 percent of high school teachers are from rural areas. Such a system fails to provide role models for minority students, and, at the same time, does not offer majority students exposure to teachers who represent the country's diversity and changing economic landscape.

Financial barriers. Many students who are motivated and informed about their higher education options and have adequate academic preparation for higher education may not be able to afford to pay for it. Supporting the enrollment of qualified individuals who would not otherwise attend a higher education institution generates public benefits, such as higher productivity and growth, and a more just and fair society. Thus, there is a basis for public support of higher education. Research shows that grant aid is particularly well suited for low-income and minority students, who tend to be reluctant to borrow because of limited confidence in their future earning capacity and who are more likely to attend higher education when grant aid is available (Wolanin 2003). At the same time, the individuals who get access to higher education enjoy private benefits, in terms of higher earnings and higher social status, and should be responsible for bearing the costs of their education to the extent possible (Wolanin 2003). According to the U.S. Census data, the average high school graduate earned $26,059 in 2000, while the average bachelor's degree recipient earned $49,674. Over a working lifetime, this earnings gap is estimated to add up to more than $1 million. The wage premium associated with the higher education degree has been rising over time (Wolanin 2003). In light of this recognition, more than 80 percent of the federal student aid for higher education in the United States is now in the form of loans (Wolanin 2003).

Capacity barriers. The demand for higher education generally exceeds the supply. Technology-mediated distance learning programs are expected to mitigate the capacity barriers. However, until now, education technology has been used primarily as an enhancement to the educational programs, thereby adding to rather than reducing the cost of education (Wolanin 2003). In the United States, the federal government no longer plays a significant role as partner in the higher education infrastructure.

Quality barriers. Many of the places available for higher education are not necessarily of adequate quality. Quality assurance and quality improvement in higher education is driven by the accreditation system, which relies largely on self-regulation and peer review. Accreditation, usually carried out by specialized, private, nonprofit organizations, attests that the institution (1) is guided by a defined and appropriate mission, (2) has established systems under which its mission can be realized, (3) is accomplishing its mission substantially, (4) is organized, staffed, and supported so as to continue to accomplish its mission, and (5) meets the standards of academic quality (AACSB 2003). The ratio of students applying and the spots available at the most selective schools in the United States is up to nine to one; on the other hand, some of the low-end schools may not even be able to fill available spaces.

Institutional barriers. Systems for selecting and assessing participants at higher education institutions have also come under scrutiny in recent years as important sources of impediments. A growing number of research evidence in the United States is showing that women score lower than men on standardized tests that are required for admission into colleges and universities (Silverstein 2001). Further, "minorities and women may receive lower scores because the tests are not written objectively, and the questions reflect the writers' subjective and cultural experiences" (Silverstein 2001: 679). Standardized tests were expected to measure the "physical property of the brain," and it was presumed that preparation for those tests could not influence test results (Silverstein 2001). But this presumption lays shattered with professional test preparation programs such as The Princeton Review, even guaranteeing a significant score improvement (Kiehl 2000). Since only those able to afford the courses have an opportunity to improve, the standardized tests limit access to higher education for the low-income groups. In 1998, students from families whose income ranged from $10,000 to $20,000 a year averaged 171 points lower on the Scholastic Aptitude Test than students whose family income ranged from $80,000 to $100,000 a year (Silverstein 2001). In the United States, the leading business schools have increasingly shifted away from using the standardized Graduate Management Admission Test scores as a dominating criterion for admission decisions; instead the thrust is on leadership in academic, work, community, and other contexts.

In light of the above literature, we next examine the debate surrounding the role of regulatory actors and the need for an appropriate approach for addressing various academic barriers.

The Business Education Landscape in India

In 1961, with the help of a grant from the Ford Foundation, the government of India established two premier Indian Institutes of Management (IIMs)—at Calcutta and at Ahmedabad. IIM-Calcutta forged collaborative relationships with the Massachusetts Institute of Technology (MIT), while IIM-Ahmedabad collaborated with Harvard Business School (HBS). Later, between 1972 and 1997, four more IIMs were established—at Bangalore, Lucknow, Kozhikode, and Indore. Meanwhile, other business schools were being established—between 1950 and 2000, 744 institutions were established that were recognized by the All India Council for Technical Education—the government agency responsible for approving business schools and their programs. A majority of these institutions were set up in the 1990s and funded by businesses or private sponsors (Dayal 2002). By 2003, there were about 1,200 institutions offering graduate business programs in India (Gupta, Gollakota, and Sreekumar 2003).

The mission of the IIMs has been to professionalize Indian management through teaching, research, training, institution building, and consulting. They also have a mandate to professionalize vital sectors of the economy, particularly agriculture, education, health, transportation, population control, energy, and public administration. Toward this end, they have helped launch several specialized management education schools (such as Indian Institute of Forest Management), offered short-term training for the faculty members of other business schools, and delivered executive development and incorporate training programs. The two-year graduate program in management remains their flagship product, and unlike their international peers, they have not expanded into the undergraduate programs. They have also carried small doctoral programs. Graduates of the IIMs are highly regarded in industry, both domestically and internationally. The starting salaries for these graduates are at least three times greater than those for the graduate of an average business school in India. Many of the graduates have gone on to assume top management positions in prominent domestic and multinational corporations.

While the IIMs have operated as autonomous institutions since their inception, between 20 percent and 100 percent of the annual operating budget of the IIMs continues to be covered by grants from the government. Established IIMs, such as IIM-Ahmedabad and IIM-Bangalore, receive about Rs100–120 million as a grant out of a budget of Rs500 million, while newer institutions like IIM-Kozhikode receive their entire budget of Rs500 million from the government (Lakshman 2003). The Ministry of Human Resources, under whose purview education lies, has articulated a perspective that the IIMs need to take a deeper and more comprehensive leadership role in business education in the nation, holding that there is a considerable gap between what the IIMs can do to fulfill their mission and what they are actually accomplishing. IIM-Ahmedabad, for instance, has produced only about 120 doctorates over a period of more than twenty-five years. The other IIMs have produced even fewer doctorates. As a way to redirect the priorities of the core mission of the IIMs, the Ministry commanded that IIMs reduce their fee from Rs150,000 per year to Rs 30,000 per year in early 2004. The Ministry believes that by reducing the fees, which would be funded by the government, the IIMs will cease to be perceived as elite.

The Ministry's perspective needs to be seen against the backdrop of a 2001 amendment in the Constitution of India that makes elementary education a fundamental right for children and makes it legally enforceable for every child to demand free compulsory education between the ages of six and fourteen (BBC News 2001). Currently, only 59 percent of the children enrolled reach grade five in India, and 44.3 percent of those age fifteen and above are illiterate—defined as people who cannot even write their own name (Mallick 2001).

The Fee Cut Decision

The Ministry has decided to make business education more accessible by reducing the fees at the IIMs and by calling upon the private sector to also follow suit. This is partly guided by the recommendations of an independent committee that looked at fees charged by American universities, such as Harvard, Stanford, Berkeley, and California Institute of Technology, in regard to that country's per capita GNP (Raj 2004). The committee concluded that even the best American universities charge up to 30 percent of the nation's per capita GNP. Therefore, if technical education in India were as affordable as it is for American citizens, then fees in technical institutions should be approximately 30 percent of India's per capita income, or Rs 6,000 per year (Raj 2004). The Ministry believes that a reduction in the tuition fees will improve the access of millions of poor students to the premier state-funded business schools (Raj 2004).

However, the decision to cut fees apparently is based on deeper mission-related issues. At a fundamental level, a fee cut is unlikely to make the IIMs accessible to lower income groups. While the IIM student body comes largely from middle-class and upper-middle class families that earn steady incomes (Anand and Bakshi-Dighe 2003), the graduates of IIMs command a huge premium in the job market, earning upward of Rs500,000 annually, as compared to an average of Rs200,000 earned by other business graduates in India. Consequently, there is no shortage of bank loans and even scholarships to cover their educational expenses at the IIMs if families are unable to afford the tuition fees (Anand and Bakshi-Dighe 2003). Given the job premiums and easy availability of bank loans, a lower tuition fee alone is unlikely to increase the attractiveness of the IIMs to a larger pool of applicants. The Ministry's decision to cut tuition fees, and, as a result, its declared commitment to fund the shortfall under judicial oath in early 2004, is grounded on a presumption that the fee cut would lead to a fundamental change in the way IIMs have approached their mission. The Ministry believes that the fee cut would inspire the IIMs to be more focused on increasing the capacity of the students, to be better role models for the private business schools that have been established in the nation over the past ten years, and to take a more active leadership role in this process.

Every year, IIMs graduate only about 1,200 students out of a total of 75,000 business graduates in the nation (Gupta, Gollakota, and Sreekumar 2003). A large demand for business education remains unmet. About 140,000 apply for admissions to IIMs every year, and about half of them are unable to get admission to any of the business schools in India. Although there are about 1,200 business schools in India offering graduate programs, most of them do not have faculty members with relevant doctoral qualifications. A recent survey showed that while 550 out of a total of 773 full-time faculty, or 73 percent, at the top 15 business schools in India had a PhD degree, only 1,181 out of 2,361 full-time faculty, or 50 percent, at the top 100 business schools had a PhD degree in 2003 (Cosmode Management Research Center 2003). About 70 percent of Indian business schools do not even have a seven-member faculty, and generally no faculty with a PhD degree (Zachariahs 2003). The estimated current demand for PhD faculty members at the nation's business schools is 7,200 (Cosmode Management Research Center 2003). Thus, many alternative programs are not of adequate quality.

The admission process has been identified by the Ministry as one of the prime examples of how the workings of the IIMs are misaligned with their mission. Currently, the IIMs design and administer a Common Admission Test (CAT), the scores on which provide significant input into the shortlisting of the candidates. Fifty-five other business schools are affiliate members and use the scores on the CAT for their own shortlist. Each business school shortlists its own candidates, who then participate in each business school's specific compulsory group discussions and interviews with the faculty panel. Five other competing national admission tests exist that are used by various business schools.

The ministry points out that applicants spend an average of Rs 25,000 on application fees for various business schools, travel to take different examinations, and participate in group discussions and interviews. They also pay an average of Rs15,000 to various private institutions that help them prepare for the tests—on the whole, test preparation is estimated to be a Rs2 billion business. In the government's view, that is a big burden for people in a nation where the annual per capita income averages only about Rs20,000. Further, the IIMs charge Rs1,000 for each candidate taking the Common Admission Test and another Rs1,000 for the transcript, generating about Rs250 million in funds (Lakshman 2003). After incurring an expenditure of about Rs20 million, they still enjoy an annual cash flow of nearly $5 million from the Common Admission Test (Lakshman 2003).

On October 10, 2003, the Ministry decided to introduce one common entrance test in the last quarter of 2004 for admission to all management institutes in India (Ray 2003). The Ministry is also pushing to do away with the requirement of group discussions and interviews in the admission process. The Ministry is pressuring the IIMs to limit their corpus to Rs250 million so that government funds can be invested in higher-priority educational initiatives, specifically primary education (*Times of India* 2004). Therefore, it holds that the IIMs should use their earnings from management development programs and faculty consulting for making stronger contributions to higher education. The three newer IIMs—at Lucknow, Khozikhode, and Indore—have agreed to sign an agreement to limit their corpus and to take permission from the Ministry for further program development. These IIMs depend heavily on government funding and have no funds or insignificant funds in their corpus (Lakshman 2003). The three older IIMs—at Ahmedabad, Calcutta, and Bangalore—have refused to sign the agreement. The government funding constitutes only a small portion of these IIMs now, and each of them has built a corpus of about Rs 1 billion, primarily based on consulting, in-corporate training, and management development programs for industry over the years (Lakshman 2003). IIM-Ahmedabad has even indicated its willingness to phase out its dependence on Rs 100 million in annual government grants so that those funds may be applied to higher-priority primary education and to giving other institutions a chance (Ghosh 2003; *Times of India* 2004).

The IIMs do contribute significantly to the nation's education program currently, as indicated by their reputation and by the leadership role played by their alumni in the corporate, governmental, nongovernmental, and academic fields, nationally as well as internationally. The IIMs have been helping to upgrade executive skills through their management development programs. They also contribute to management skills through their faculty development programs, their membership on the boards of directors of several companies, and through their consulting roles with the private and public sectors as well as nongovernmental agencies. However, as stated earlier, the Ministry would like the IIMs to see their role in broader terms and to have an impact on the lives of a larger number of citizens.

Summary

On the whole in India, a key question guiding the role of regulatory actors has been whether the contribution of top educational institutions in the nation should at all be evaluated in terms of their accessibility and affordability. There is additional concern about whether the nation needs more MBAs— already the number of MBAs has grown more than sixfold from 12,000 in 1991 to 75,000 in 2003; and the number of approved MBA schools has risen from 130 to 1,200 in the same period (Gupta, Gollakota, and Sreekumar 2003). A policy thrust on the accessibility of business education may be seen as a factor in the subpar quality of most business schools outside the IIMs; alternatively, a policy that does not drive home the mission of accessibility has been seen by the Ministry as a factor inhibiting stronger autonomous initiatives for helping improve the quality of these business schools. Many of these business schools rely only on part-time and visiting faculty, and most have no doctoral qualified faculty members or only a few. Many of these business schools have modest and only quite basic infrastructures, including computers, libraries, classrooms, and hostel facilities. Thus, the critical issues are whether a publicly established and funded business school in a developing country should provide business education that commands a premium in the industry; whether it should respond to societal demands for mitigating cultural, academic, financial, capacity, quality, and institutional barriers only if they are offered large government grants as incentives and only if they are forced to by lawmakers; and whether it can maintain "high academic standards" in the process of meeting social needs.

Discussion

The IIMs are considered the premier schools of business in the international arena. Several regional and international agencies have rated the IIMs as providing excellent business education. IIM-Ahmedabad has been rated Asia's number-one business school, and a survey by the *Economist* rated it as forty-fifth on a list of the top-fifty business schools in the world (*Times of India* 2003). Evidence indicates that the two major stakeholders, students and employers, are happy with the performance of these IIMs. As indicated earlier, there is a massive demand for seats in the IIMs. Employers—mostly large, professionally managed companies and multinationals—vie with each other to hire the graduates from these institutions. Graduates from these institutions earn, on average, three times the amount earned by their peers from other business schools in the country. If we look at these results using the lens of microeconomic market forces, certainly these IIMs are meeting the needs of their market.

However, when we switch the lens from a microeconomic view of the educational institution and use one that incorporates a more macroeconomic as well as social perspective, the situation becomes more complex and makes the publicly funded business schools in emerging markets susceptible to regulatory interventions.

In India, at the national level, the intake of business schools to their graduate programs is only about 50 percent of the current demand from applicants. Much of this demand is from students who join multinationals and large, professional organizations. Meeting the needs of such organizations is important. However, considerable economic activity takes place at much smaller microenterprise levels in much of the developing world (Brown and Masten 1998). Individuals, families, and cooperatives are involved in various economic activities from selling fish to handicrafts. While there is no need for formal MBA education for microenterprises, certainly there is considerable need for knowledge of sound business practices. The IIMs, being the premier business schools in India and using public funds, could take a lead in helping to bridge the gap by imparting education through various outreach programs.

In addition, currently, the student body of the IIMs and most of the business schools in India is relatively homogeneous—predominantly male, urban, and from well-to-do and upper-middle-class families. Multiple barriers, as can be seen from the literature review, act to exclude many talented but poor students, and these barriers are stronger in emerging markets such as India where there are no concerted regulatory mechanisms for alleviating the barriers.

The admission processes used in the business schools in India are largely designed to predict candidates' ability to cope with the high pressure and the competitive academic environment. The fundamental premise is that individuals rely on their personal abilities to cope with the intense pressure. However, research shows that individuals vary in their pressure coping strategies—minorities, the poor, and women tend to build stronger social capital and rely on cooperative strategies for minimizing the occurrence of pressure situations and for coping with pressure situations. Not surprisingly, therefore, minority groups such as women tend to score lower on these admission tests (Silverstein 2001).

In high power-distance and low gender-egalitarian cultures, as in the case of India, men, especially those educated in the larger cities, belonging to dominant ethnic groups or from well-to-do families are likely to do better in the high-pressure situations of interviews and group discussions as well as to score higher on competitive admission tests as compared to the others (House et al. 2004). Scoring higher on the admission tests, such applicants are more likely to go through the admission process. On the other hand, those educated in the smaller cities, those from poorer families, and women are less likely to be accepted. The percentage of women taking the Common Admission Test of the IIMs hovers around 22 percent, and this percentage declines further after the selection of 5 to 15 percent of the women in the student body (John 2003). This result is in line with research (discussed in the literature review section earlier) showing that the diversity of enrolled students tends to have a strong negative relationship with the emphasis put on the admission test scores by the business schools. According to the Dean of IIM-Ahmedabad, women are deterred from applying to IIMs because of the perception that competition is so stiff (John 2003). The high difficulty and pressure levels simulated by the Common Admission Test continue to be anchored in a world of ranking, contests, and pyramid-shaped hierarchies, with fewer and fewer plum jobs as one approaches the top. The fact that modern management is increasingly based more on teamwork than on individual ability to cope with pressure is not reflected in the design of the competitive tests. The graduates of the IIMs and other business schools get better placement opportunities and are more likely to be placed in the management and leadership positions. Minorities, the poor, and women, who are more adept at consensus decision making, the use of social capital, and coopera- tive strategies, are put at an added and long-term disadvantage (Woolcock and Narayan 2000). On the whole, a heavy reliance on competitive admission tests as screening devices acts to limit the diversity of personalities, ethnicities, and gender in any institution, and to that extent limits the development of cre- ative potential and learning of all the members of that institution.

The solution here is not to introduce quotas for various ethnic, income, and gender groups. Already, the government requires 22.5 percent of the students admitted to the IIMs to be from the underprivileged scheduled castes/ scheduled tribes. Many of these students are admitted despite their low scores on the admission test, and a great majority of them find it difficult to stand up to the intensely competitive and high-pressure academic culture of the IIM classrooms.

Instead, the solution starts with better selection procedures. The easiest and simplest change is to do away with the group discussions and interviews used. Each year, several faculty members of the IIMs visit different cities and conduct group discussions and interviews with thousands of candidates. Each IIM holds its separate group discussion and interview, held in the larger cities of the nation. These mandatory group discussions and interviews are believed to be critical to the ability of the IIMs and other business schools in India to maintain stronger control over the quality and potential of the in- coming students, and thereby maintain their academic culture and sustain their credentials and reputation among the recruiters and future applicants. However, these group discussions and interviews have many unintended ef- fects. First, they add to the cost of the application process, especially for the potential applicants who work or live in the smaller cities. Second, the man- datory group discussions and interviews inadvertently focus attention on whether an applicant appears to fit the stereotype of the successful execu- tive. Deviation from the norm, which is a fundamental aspect of creativity and diversity, is rejected and further filtered down. Through its effect of thin- ning the diversity among the pool of admitted students, the admission pro- cess of the IIMs that relies significantly on the use of standardized admission tests, group discussions, and interviews, makes it more difficult for India to celebrate, promote, and sustain unity in her diversity. In the United States, very few business schools require a compulsory interview, and probably none mandate a compulsory group discussion.

An important change in the selection process might be to moderate reli- ance on the competitive admission test scores, and instead more strongly emphasize evaluating the distinctiveness and uniqueness of the learning strat- egies, developmental efforts, and leadership missions reflected by prior academic, extracurricular, and work experiences. True, the IIMs consider academic background and achievements, extracurricular activities, and postdegree work experience even now as part of their admission process; however, what is needed is a stronger and more focused priority on the uniqueness, distinctiveness, integrity, and boldness evidenced by the applicants on factors such as these. For instance, a candidate from a small city or village who has completed college with merit, has paid for the education by working at the same time as pursuing the degree, and who has shown evidence of community leadership, may significantly enhance learning on campus through helping his or her peers to gain a better appreciation of small city/rural life. Such learning would help graduates better formulate strategies for marketing and business process outsourcing in the smaller cities.

The benefits from the enhanced diversity will be greatest if the IIMs do not reduce access to the group of students currently getting through the admission process, but instead add access for a group of students who do not get through the admission process because of their divergent—though no way qualitatively inferior—experiential and learning potentials. A simple increase in the number of seats, without any development in the admissions criteria or any change in the pressure-oriented academic culture, will only intensify the competitive pressure on the admitted students for distinctions in the classrooms and for the top-paying placement positions. On the other hand, adding students with distinctive experiential and learning potentials will enhance the versatility of all the graduates, making them attractive for a broader group of positions even beyond those available currently, including better preparing them for starting up and leading their own creative, entrepreneurial ventures.

The IIMs may need to take a more proactive stance in working with the colleges to help groom high quality applicants from diverse social, gender, and economic groups. If the IIMs are preparing their graduates to better handle the opportunities for business process outsourcing and to learn world-class practices of vendor management, then a key component of the learning process has to be the development—and not just the selection—of the vendors. The IIMs may involve their students in helping to develop the college curricula, especially in the growing private education sector, and in mentoring the college students regarding how to enrich their portfolio of learning approaches through added experiences and initiatives in the community. Just as the IIMs have inadvertently been reinforcing biases against minorities, women, and the poor through their high-pressure academic culture, the nation's colleges have a no better track record in this sense. Eventually, the target should be to establish linkages with the high schools, secondary schools, and primary schools, as well as the parents, and to have active collaboration and support from corporations, nongovernmental organizations, and community leaders so that a fundamental change in academic processes might occur from the very start of the supply chain that shapes and defines the applicant pool of the IIMs. These vendor development linkages would not only enhance the quality of and accessibility for the applicant pool in the short to medium terms, but also allow the graduates the support of a more capable and creative workforce when they assume leadership positions in industry in the long term.

Another way to enhance the excellence of the IIMs, and of business education in India in general, is to develop a comprehensive and robust system of faculty development. The primary factor limiting the ability of the IIMs to take a more broad-based leadership role in the national management education system is their lack of focus on their core competencies: the research and development of management know-how and its mass dissemination. The IIMs have evolved into vertically integrated institutions, where the faculty spends a large part of the time on administrative issues related to nonacademic matters such as hostels, meals, admissions, and placement, which are either outsourced by the leading management institutions in the United States or managed by nonfaculty administrative support staff. Thus, the faculty at the IIMs get limited time to devote to "original research," bringing their original research to the classrooms or making their research available to the managers and the community, and servicing the community through outreach programs. Original research would allow the IIMs to learn about the tacit know-how of diverse communities and cultures of India and of various corporations, and to codify, develop, and disseminate knowledge about alternative practices and appropriate practices for solving various types of problems in different situations and contexts.

As a result of their involvement in low value-adding activities outside their core competencies, the IIMs have not been able to put sufficient effort into the development of management faculty, even for themselves, let alone for the rest of the nation. Even the top IIMs, such as IIM-Bangalore, suffer from a "faculty crunch" in areas such as marketing and human resources (Lakshman 2003). Though the IIMs have been willing to run faculty development programs for other institutions, such programs are of a short-term nature and do little to increase the supply of core faculty with doctorate degrees—an international prerequisite for quality higher education management education programs. At IIM-Bangalore, many of the faculty are hired for the management development programs and do not teach in the graduate program as they do not possess the requisite skills (Lakshman 2003). In contrast, the top U.S. business schools develop sufficient doctorate-qualified management faculty to cover not only their own internal requirements but also to lead the accreditation and quality improvement of other business schools that lack sufficient resources for running doctoral programs. Furthermore, the faculty who teach executive education programs are more experienced and no less qualified than those who teach in the graduate program because the former are supposed to be the mentors of the latter in the corporate world and not the other way around.

Resources for Changes and Linkages

An obvious constraint to the ability of the IIMs to take a leadership role in meeting the social and broader economic needs of the nation is the limited availability of faculty time. If one looks at faculty student ratios, the IIMs have very favorable numbers. IIM-Ahmedabad, for instance, has about 80 full-time faculty members and 500 full-time students, yielding a faculty student ratio of 1 : 6.25. In contrast, the Wharton School, as a matter of illustrative comparison, has about 275 full-time faculty members and 3,500 full-time students, yielding a faculty student ratio of 1 : 12.75. On average, each IIM faculty teaches only half the number of students taught by the faculty at the leading business schools internationally. A major factor accounting for the differentials in faculty–student ratio is the number of credits or contact hours. At the IIMs, students take 60 credits, or 600 contact hours, every year. In most international programs, the students take 30 credits, or 300 contact hours of classes, every academic year. Over a two-year period in the graduate program, the IIMs require 1,200 contact hours of classes, while the leading international business schools require only 600 to 660 contact hours of classes. Put differently, the students of IIMs spend twice the time with the faculty in the classrooms.

This raises a question: Is it worthwhile for the students to spend twice as much time in the classroom as do their international peers? True, the students in India come from two different undergraduate tracks: the four-year track in engineering and the three-year track in most other fields. In the United States, on the other hand, the undergraduate programs have a standardized four-year duration. Still, even in the undergraduate programs, the U.S. colleges require 300 contact hours per academic year. In contrast, 600 contact hours per academic year are routine in the undergraduate programs in India.

If the IIMs were to align their contact class hours with the norm used by the leading business schools internationally then that would help change the pressure-oriented academic culture and make the program accessible to double the number of students compared to the present. Currently, the IIMs are planning to double the number of students by adding more faculty and infrastructure. However, the IIMs also need to consider revising their curricula so that the number of students could be further increased without increasing faculty and infrastructure. A change at the IIMs would also help generate similar changes at other business schools in India that have followed the IIM model of a 1,200 contact hour program. Many business schools in India have gone a step beyond, instituting a 1,800 contact hour program over a two-year period.

The IIMs do not need to reduce the rigor of their program. Instead, they could use the time released from the contact class hours for incorporating more outreach and additional field projects. The outreach and field projects—for example, involving graduates in mentoring college students and school children, in advising small and family businesses, in scouting and commercializing the innovative ideas of microentrepreneurs, and in conducting joint projects with students from other business schools nationally and internationally, making use of online technology—would instill a stronger sense of leadership as well as entrepreneurship among the graduates. Often, minorities, women, and the poor have a better contextual awareness and street smartness about the developmental opportunities in their community. The shift in emphasis from a purely contact class hour-intensive curriculum to a more rounded one would allow the IIMs to make their programs more accessible and to enhance learning for their current target group of admitted students; thus the credibility of IIM graduates would be enhanced in the market.

Adopting such initiatives would be mutually reinforcing and would enhance the quality of education offered by these institutions as well as meet their broader social responsibilities. Figure 2.1 represents this process. As institutions change their selection processes to be more inclusive, they not only enrich the student body but also free up valuable faculty resources. The increased diversity of the student body itself is a source of development and learning for traditional students. By changing the curriculum to reduce contact hours between student and faculty and increase student involvement in community-based entrepreneurial projects, two purposes will be served. First, students learn by becoming closer to average Indian consumers, people that well-to-do students never encounter; second, essential outreach activities are performed. The freeing up of faculty time might be utilized in many useful ways—to direct outreach activities (further developing the faculty member) and to conduct research. Research by faculty enhances the development of faculty members and the standing of their institution, and puts them in a position to mentor faculty in other business schools in the country. The end product of these initiatives is a much better student who better understands the realities of the Indian market.

Figure 2.1   **Quality Improvement Process for Business Education in India**

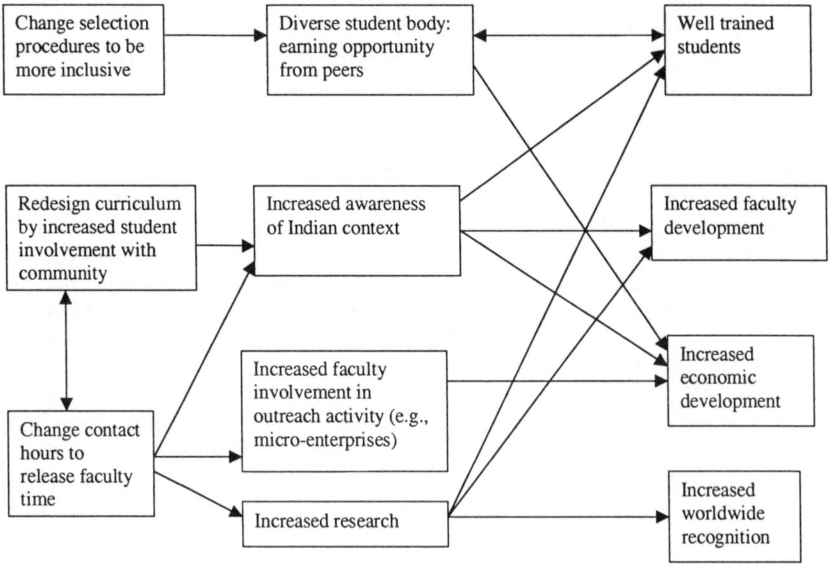

Conclusion

Publicly funded institutions like the IIMs stand at a crossroad in emerging market contexts: Do they eschew state funds and go the private autonomous route? If they choose to continue to use state funds, can they deliver what is expected of them without diluting the quality of education? Our own exploration of this issue leads us to believe that by responding to their social mission, they would actually enhance the quality of their students by putting them more in touch with the realities of the country.

References

Advisory Committee on Student Financial Assistance (ACSFA). 2002. *Empty Promises: The Myth of College Access in America.* Washington, DC.

Anand, S., and A. Bakshi-Dighe. 2003. "Mr. Joshi, We Don't Want Your Help." *Indian Express*, November 29.

Association to Advance Collegiate Schools of Business (AACSB). 2003. Eligibility Procedures and Standards for Business Accreditation. March 10. Available at www.aacsb.edu (accessed January 18, 2005).

BBC News. 2001. "India Votes on Right to Education." November 28.

Bloor, D. 1997. *Vingenstein: Rules and Institutions.* London: Routledge.

Bourdieu, P. 1977. "The Production of Belief. Contribution to an Economy of Symbolic Goods." *Media, Culture and Society* 2, no. 3: 261–93.

Brown, S., and J. Masten. 1998. "The Role of a Business School in an Emerging Country: The Case of Ghana." *Journal of Education for Business* 73, no. 5: 308–13.

"Controversial College Test Is Trying to Even the Playing Field by Rewarding 'Strivers.'" *New York Daily News*, September 5: 53.

Cosmode Management Research Center. 2003. "B-schools Short on Doctoral Faculty." *Economic Times*, September 19.

Crouse, J., and D. Trusheim. 1988. *The Case Against the SAT*. Chicago: University of Chicago Press.

Dayal, I. 2002. "Developing Management Education in India." *Journal of Management Research* 2, no. 2: 98–113.

Fitzgerald B.K., and J.A. Delaney. 2002. "Educational Opportunity in America." In *Condition of Access: Higher Education for Lower Income Students*, ed. D.E. Heller, 4–4. Westport, CT: Praeger.

Ghosh, S. 2003. "Enough! IIMA Rejects Govt Cash." *Indian Express*, December 28: 1.

Gupta, V.; K. Gollakota; and A. Sreekumar. 2003. "Quality in Business Education: A Study of the Indian Context." Paper presented at the Business Education and Emerging Market Economies: Trends and Prospects Conference, Atlanta, GA, November 7.

Hedmo, T.; K. Sahlin-Andersson; and L. Wedlin. 2001. "The Emergence of a European Regulatory Field of Management Education: Standardizing Through Accreditation, Ranking and Guidelines." Paper presented at the workshop Transnational Regulation and the Transformation of States, Stanford, CA, the Scandinavian Consortium for Organizational Research, June 22–23.

House, R.J.; P.J. Hanges; M. Javidan; P. Dorfman; and V. Gupta, eds. 2004. *Leadership, Culture, and Organizations: The GLOBE Study of 62 Societies*. Thousand Oaks, CA: Sage.

John, S. 2003. "Why Most Women Give Business Schools the Go-by?" *Times of India*, July 7.

Kiehl, S. 2000. "Golden Rule for Getting into College: Start Early—Experts: Begin Planning in Middle School." *Palm Beach Post*, October 8: 1B.

Lakshman, N. 2003. "The Battle for the B-schools." *Business Standard*, November 29.

Mallick, S. 2001. "Privatization of Education: A Boon or a Bane?" www.geocities.com/husociology/privatization.htm (accessed November 30, 2004).

Raj, Y. 2004. "IIT or IIM at Rs6,000 a Year? Panel Tells Govt to Reduce Fees." *Hindustan Times*, January 4.

Ray, J. 2003. "CAT out of IIM Hands." *Business Standard*, December 4.

Silverstein, A.L. 2001. "Standardized Tests: The Continuation of Gender Bias in Higher Education." *Hofstra Law Review* 29: 669–700.

Times of India. 2003. "IIM-A Set to Join the Ivy League." November 20.

Times of India. 2004. "IIM-A Buys MM Joshi's Formula." January 2.

Trow, M. 1998. "On the Accountability of Higher Education in the United States." In *Universities and Their Leadership*, ed. W.G. Bowen and H.T. Shapiro, 15–61. Princeton, NJ: Princeton University Press.

Wolanin, T., ed. 2003. *Reauthorizing the Higher Education Act (HEA): Issues and Options*. Washington, DC: Institute for Higher Education and Policy.

Woolcock, M., and D. Narayan. 2000. "Social Capital: Implications for Development Theory, Research and Policy." *World Bank Observer* 15, no. 2: 225–49.

World Bank. 1997. *World Development Report, 1997*. New York: Oxford University Press.

Zachariahs, C. 2003. "Quantity Battles Quality Test." *Times of India*, October 13.

3

Engineer as Entrepreneur

A Necessity for Successful Product Innovation in the Small-scale Industry Sector in India

V.P. Wani, T.K. Garg, and S.K. Sharma

Levels of industrial activity considerably affect the development and growth of the national economy. This level goes up with the increase in number of industrial ventures, that is, enterprises: An enterprise can be defined as an economic activity in which resources are processed using facilities that interact to form an organized whole. As the industrial sector is one of these core sectors, an increase in industrial ventures plays a significant role in carrying the economy forward and thereby assuming a better life for society as a whole. Thus, developing technology-based entrepreneurship will be a key element in keeping pace with the march.

The Small-scale Industry Sector in India: An Overview

A small-scale industry (SSI) sector has emerged as the most dynamic and vibrant sector in recent times and currently contributes about 40 percent of industrial production, 35 percent of total export, and provides employment for over 18.6 million persons in India (Prasad 2001). India started its process of integration with the global economy in July 1991. The government has pursued far-reaching economic and structural reforms in all sectors of economic policy, the thrust of these measures being to make the Indian economy internationally competitive.

In India, small and medium-sized enterprises (SMEs) are generally referred to as small-scale units (including tiny sectors) as defined by the criterion of scale of capital investment. This is not the case in many other countries, such as China, Japan, Germany, Indonesia, Iran, and Turkey, where the criterion for identifying small and medium-scale units is based on the number of employees (Mukharjee 2001). In India, the investment limit for small-scale units at present is Rs10 million for plant and machinery. These small enterprises serve as the seedbed of entrepreneurship based on the following features:

1. They create more employment opportunities with comparatively low capital investment.
2. The industrial unit in this sector is generally based on local resources and demands.
3. They can be located anywhere easily, resulting in horizontal growth and removal of regional imbalance.
4. The sector gives quick returns and has a shorter gestation period.
5. These units help to maintain, retain, and develop traditional skills and handicrafts.
6. These units assist large and medium industries by acting as ancillaries.

While the basic accent of India's policy for small-scale sectors has been defensive, aiming to insulate the small-scale sector from the dynamics of competitive growth, now the changing economic and liberalized scenario of this insulation has been removed. New environments for small-scale industries consist of changes emerging from ongoing processes of economic reform that conform to World Trade Organization agreements and to the fast-changing economic, technological, and information scenario. In the process, liberalized policy has posed certain challenges and provided opportunities to this sector (Vasundhara, 2000). Challenges take the form of increased competition and reduced protection due to lowering of tariffs and market-determined rates of interest. On the other hand, opportunities have come in the form of access to better technology, availability of a variety of raw materials and components, impetus to quality, efficiency, and opportunities to restructure and diversify. In the fast-changing technological environment, wherein product lifetime cycles and technology lifetime cycles are shrinking, technical entrepreneurship has assumed a central place in enterprise development and economic growth. It can make contributions to industrial development through technical innovation, that is, development and improvement of productivity and production processes. The Indian small-scale sector has constantly outperformed large industry on crucial parameters such as growth in production and employment. Numbers of units have increased from 1.94 million in 1990–91 to 3.22 million in 2000. Production has risen from Rs1,553.4 billion to Rs5,784.7 billion for the same period. Employment generation has increased from 12.53 million to 17.73 million. This sector makes significant contributions in exports, which has increased from Rs96.64 billion to Rs489.78 billion.

In spite of this development, it is a fact that the SSI sector has not developed to its fullest potential. The sector is beset with problems that have impeded such development. Widespread inefficiency is growing at increasing rates and resulting in huge losses. Inefficiency has arisen because the units in this sector have operated in sheltered markets and the majority have paid little attention to technology upgrades, quality improvement, and cost reductions over the past several decades. A policy regime of quotas, control, and licensing has given rise to an industrial unit with the singular aim of making windfall gains, irrespective of whether the individual is quality conscious or not. This has resulted in large numbers of under-par units with little scope for any improvement in the future. The changing economic environment has posed challenges to the small-scale industrial sector as a result of:

1. increased competition (both domestic and international) in most spheres of manufacturing activity, including those in rural areas;
2. increased penetration of branded consumer products in rural areas from large-scale units;
3. increased purchasing power among the rural populace;
4. increased awareness levels of consumers due to deep penetration of the media, in turn leading to
5. quality consciousness, preference for branded products, wider selections of brands/products, and
6. services to satisfy similar needs;
7. limited scope for quality price trade-offs; and
8. need for technology upgrades to meet the quality needs of consumers.

To face these challenges, entrepreneurs have to adopt innovative products/processes, and to improve productivity techniques and effective technology management for sustainability of their own units. Here, innovative approaches will provide a remedy for entrepreneurs in terms of sustainability.

Engineer as Entrepreneur

Entrepreneurship is essential for economic development and needs to be developed for the implementation of economic measures. Technology and entrepreneurship cannot be reviewed in isolation. Since invention and innovations have invariably led to growth in advanced countries, developing entrepreneurship among engineers should therefore be considered a necessary part of the normal curriculum in developing countries like India. Engineering and engineering education have undergone significant changes in the recent past. The lead times in education, in general, and engineering education, in particular, are long, and unless we plan ahead reasonably accurately, we will be unable to fulfill our obligations effectively.

Engineering as a profession demands traditional attributes such as problem-solving abilities, analytical skills, communication skills, interpersonal skills, and decision-making skills. The new millennium has imposed additional demands, such as learn-ability, a yen for lifelong learning, the ability to work as part of a team, creativity and innovation, integrative skills, interdisciplinary knowledge, and a commitment to sustainable development (Natarajan 2000). Technology should be the bedrock of engineering as well as a practical vocational arm of physics. Indeed it should be the great enabling subject that teaches children how to bring knowledge from a whole range of subjects to bear on a specific practical problem (Davies 1993). These skills, the very essence of problem solving, are essential to industry, and as such, they should provide the foundation of an engineering degree. In enterprise education, awareness should extend beyond just the classroom. It should involve outside experiences relating directly to the children themselves so they do not see education merely as core and foundation subjects. Active participation in a meaningful process is the foundation of enterprise education (Iredale 1993).

Entrepreneurship is a human, creative act. It involves finding personal energy to initiate and build an enterprise or an industrial venture rather than simply to watch, analyze, or describe one. It usually requires a vision and the passion, commitment, and motivation to transmit this vision to other stakeholders such as customers, suppliers, employees, and financial backers. It also requires a willingness to take calculated risks, both personal and financial, and then to do everything possible to influence the odds. Entrepreneurship involves building a team of people with complementary skills and talents, sensing an opportunity where others see chaos, contradiction, and confusion; and finding, marshaling, and controlling the resources (often owned by others) to pursue the opportunity.

For small-scale sectors in particular, entrepreneurship is a one-man show— owner, manager, technician, planner, everything. The success of an industrial venture evolves around the capability of an entrepreneur. Therefore, the engineer as entrepreneur, if nurtured, can be a better solution for running and managing industrial ventures in the SSI sector in an efficient way. In today's educational scenario, where unemployment levels are rising and career paths are becoming less well defined, Kelmer (1992) emphasizes a more practical approach to teaching that could foster stronger business acumen in the potential entrepreneur. Engineers who learn sufficient science and engineering acquire the capabilities to know the why and how of various theories influencing the SSI sector and can design products and services based on knowledge and skill competencies.

The engineer, through entrepreneurship, can bring the technical revolution needed to meet the challenges of emerging scenarios of globalization and liberalization with the key element of competition rather than protection (Baburao 1999). Smilor and Gill (1986) list talent, technology, capital, and know-how as the four key factors essential in the formation of new technology-based industrial ventures. Talent refers to entrepreneurs who recognize market opportunities and organize the unit to take advantage of those opportunities. Sources for talented entrepreneurs will be universities, technical institutions, technology-oriented corporations, and research laboratories. The amount of innovation in emerging technology industries holds tremendous potential for the start-up of new technology enterprises. When that talent is linked with technology, that is, when entrepreneurs recognize and then begin to promote viable ideas, the entrepreneurial process is under way. Capital provides financial resources through which the ideas of the entrepreneur can be developed, tested, and commercialized. Know-how is the ability to leverage business or scientific knowledge in linking talent, technology, and capital in emerging and expanding enterprises. It is the ability to find and utilize expertise in a variety of business and scientific disciplines to turn technological devices into marketable products. Technology entrepreneurship requires a unique synergy among talent, technology, capital, and know-how (Smilor and Feeser 1991). In today's society, it is technology that drives economy; because engineers create this technology, they are the real masters of society.

Relevance of Technical Education in Small-scale Industry Growth

Educational qualification is an asset to individuals in every field. It not only boosts confidence but also helps in solving various problems. Technical education is an added advantage for those in the engineering industry. Whether technical education helps entrepreneurs to improve their performance was the focus of a 1989 study conducted in the engineering industry, the hypothesis tested being that technical education does, indeed, improve performance (Bhatia and Sharma 1989). The study's observations are reported in Table 3.1.

Table 3.1 shows that 42.3 percent of entrepreneurs with technical qualifications appeared in significantly positive growth patterns, while 18.3 percent with general education were in this category. In negative growth, 11.5 percent of entrepreneurs with technical education and 14.6 percent of entre-

Table 3.1

Growth Patterns of Units with Entrepreneurs of General/Technical Background

Educational qualification of the entrepreneur	Growth pattern			
	Significant positive growth	Significant negative growth	Insignificant growth	Total
Technical education	42.3% (11)	11.5% (03)	46.2% (12)	100% (26)
General education	18.3% (15)	14.6% (12)	67.1% (55)	100% (82)
Total	26	15	67	108

Note: Figures in the brackets are number of cases.

preneurs with general education were found. Similarly, 46.2 percent with technical education showed stagnated growth while in the general education category the figure was 67.1 percent. This analysis demonstrates a positive relationship between technical education and entrepreneurial performance.

Apart from this, because of phenomenal growth in the number of engineering colleges and polytechnics in the private sector, the output of technical persons has increased many times. Thus, there is a rise in unemployment of technical persons every year. In this context, self-employment is the solution for the technical workforce, which will not only provide employment for them but also generate employment for others (Wani and Sharma 1999).

Due to liberalization and globalization, industry can survive on new ideas and constant product upgrades as per global standards and specifications before developing projects with venture capital support and then metamorphosing into hi-tech auxiliary units and large industries.

This philosophy provides wide scope for technocrats in the entrepreneurial field to meet the requirements and face challenges that will sustain them in a competitive market.

Do Engineering Students Possess Entrepreneurial Capabilities?

The authors conducted a survey among final year students of mechanical engineering at the Regional Engineering College, Kurukshetra. The questionnaire was prepared, explained, and administered to the students, and was intended to assess students' inclination toward self-employment/wage-employment, their entrepreneurial concepts, and their entrepreneurial capabilities.

Table 3.2

Entrepreneurial Concepts and Capabilities of Engineering Students

Year	Self-employment option of students			Wage-employment option of students		
	No. of students	Capability	Concept	No. of students	Capability	Concept
1997	22	0.5495	0.8558	22	0.5283	0.7848
1998	25	0.6735	0.8687	15	0.5844	0.8448
1999	18	0.6329	0.8888	27	0.5815	0.8281
2000	09	0.6396	0.8524	25	0.5946	0.8075

The hypothesis tested the relationship between students' entrepreneurial concepts and entrepreneurial capabilities in selecting a career option. The responses and findings are summarized in Table 3.2.

Observations

The entrepreneurial concepts and capabilities of a student have a definite effect when selecting career options.

1. The entrepreneurial concepts and capabilities of students opting for self-employment are higher than those of students selecting wage-employment.
2. The entrepreneurial capabilities of all students, irrespective of their career option, are lower than their entrepreneurial concepts.

Students opting for self-employment as a career choice have more entrepreneurial concepts and capability than students opting for wage-employment as a career choice.

Analysis

The entrepreneurial capabilities of students are not as great as their entrepreneurial concepts. Concepts are developed through theoretical lectures, whereas capabilities are developed through students' product-oriented technical-commercial and practical/industrial exposure and field experience.

The Significance of Invention and Innovation

Recent world trends reveal that exclusive research companies are being set up in the United States, Germany, and Japan based on the realization that it is more profitable to do research, obtain patents, and sell technology. Innovation is a wealth-creating activity. In India, the government has to increase funding for research and development (R&D), especially in engineering colleges with technology transfer and patent departments. Although at the national level there is a council for scientific and industrial research, at the state level we do not have such councils. Community-oriented R&D and innovation are extremely important in overcoming poverty and increasing the standard of living. It has been established that more innovation means more employment. Innovation is a dynamic process that aims at achieving or improving the competitive advantage of an industrial venture. It involves development, adoption, or improvement of any of the following: new products, services, technologies, processes, institutions, partnerships, ideas, systems, and solutions.

Entrepreneurs see opportunities to introduce radical innovations, and they act on these opportunities. Their analysis may not be complete, but they are committed to action and they learn by doing, although, often, this is an expensive lesson. Large companies in traditional industries, on the other hand, may realize that their industries are suddenly changing and that winners in the new millennium will be those who adopt the quickest process and innovate most effectively. They seem to be genetically incapable of radical commercial innovation, and they cannot bring themselves to learn by doing (Stringer 2000).

Uncertainty and Innovations

The risks of technical innovation differ from normal risks, which are insurable. Most economists, following Knight (1965), distinguish between measurable uncertainty, or risk proper, immeasurable certainty, and true uncertainty (Shackle 1955, 1961). Technical innovations are usually classified in the second category. By definition, innovations are not homogeneous classes of events, but some categories of innovation are recognizably less certain than others and less risky (Morek 2001). Knight (1965) recognized the classification of risk and uncertainty as a matter of degree, except in the extremes. Life and fire insurance, and other repetitive calculable risks, are usually cited as instances of the first type of risk, which can be dealt with in a fairly straightforward manner by the theory of statistical probability, but, even here, uncertainty can occur. The second type of risk will not be assumed by insurance companies, except by special types of financial institutions; therefore, handling this type of uncertainty involves a specific judgment in each individual instance (see Table 3.3).

The nature of uncertainty associated with innovations is such that most firms have a powerful incentive not to undertake a more radical type of product

Table 3.3

Degree of Uncertainty Associated with Various Types of Innovations

Degree of uncertainty	Type of innovations
i) True uncertainty	Fundamental research
	Fundamental innovations
ii) Very high degree of uncertainty	Radical product innovations
	Radical process innovations outside firm/ system
iii) High degree of uncertainty	Major product innovations
	Radical process innovations
iv) Moderate uncertainty	New generation of established products
v) Little uncertainty	Licensed innovations
	Imitation of product innovations
	Modification of product and process
	Early adoption of established process
vi) Very little uncertainty	New model
	Product differentiation
	Agency for established product innovations
	Late adoption of process innovation in firms
	Minor technical improvements

innovation, and they concentrate their R&D on defensive, initiative innovations, product differentiation, and process innovations (Sen, Dickinson and Driscoll 1994; Catalani and Clerico 1996). The distinction between in-house process innovation and open-market product innovation is very important. Product innovation involves technical and market uncertainty, whereas process innovation involves only technical uncertainty if it is for in-house application, and it can be minimal for minor technical improvements (Hollander 1965).

Technological Innovation

Technological innovation refers to the process by which an entrepreneur plans, implements, controls, and evaluates technical changes to create new opportunities for his unit's competitiveness and growth. It provides the performance of product and process by way of reducing cost or adding value. It may take the form of new product designs, design of new process technologies, or improvement in technological delivery systems, among others. Technological innovation will result not only from investment in physical assets but also from intangibles such as research and development, training, organization, and information systems. This reinforcement of physical investments by knowledge, resulting in technology to allow innovation, is now formally recognized in economic theory as an engine of growth. Innovation stands for new product information, knowledge, and services. It requires imagination and insight; it is more than just invention and marketing.

In the era of scientific technology management, Naik (1999) emphasizes a drive for development of creativity and innovation by academic and research institutes. Today, these institutes are concerned only with stability and security. Innovation-based industrial growth is found to be sustainable, and hence, to be a valid goal. Technology development (invention) within the country is important, but equally important is the rapid application of new technology (innovation) regardless of whether it is *swadeshi* (local) or *videshi* (foreign).

In the present economic order of technological developments, a shift in the perception of national resources has changed from natural resources to human capital (Sandhya and Mrinalini 1998). A significant factor of management for human resources is skill enhancement, which in turn is the most crucial aspect of innovation. In technology application, identifying which business idea has real commercial potential is one of the most difficult challenges that entrepreneurs face. Chan and Mauborgne (2000) recommend three tools that determine utility, price, and business model, which can help an entrepreneur to invest wisely. Revealing what makes a new idea a commercial success enables entrepreneurs to develop a coherent strategy for success in business innovation. The winds of technology are blowing very fast, and it is necessary to cope with them. Otherwise, the implications are very serious: the nation may permanently leave the twenty-first century behind. The gravity of raising the scientific and technological capability of prospective entrepreneurs is significant, and key individuals must attend to these aspects themselves. They must keep in mind that industries can achieve high goals only through scientific technology management.

Developing a Market Through Value Innovations

A systematic approach to value innovation can help an entrepreneur break away from the competitive pack. Competing head to head can be cutthroat, especially when markets are flat and growing slowly. Entrepreneurs dislike such competition and search for better alternatives. Here, instead of looking within the accepted boundaries that define how we compete, entrepreneurs can look systematically across them (see Table 3.4). In so doing, they can find unoccupied territory that represents a real breakthrough in value in that the marketplace requires a pattern of strategic thinking that differs from that used in head-to-head competition (Chan and Mauborgne 1999).

In today's dynamic business environment, the key tasks for people in charge are to innovate, improve, and deal with the unexpected. The "unexpected" takes the form of problems whose solutions can open the door to innovation and improvement. Challenged by world-class competitors, manufacturing

Table 3.4

Head-to-Head Competition vs. Creating Market Space

Conventional boundaries of competition	Head-to-head competition	Creating new market space
Industry	Focuses on rivals within its industry	Looks across suitable industries
Strategic group	Focuses on competitive position within strategic group	Looks across strategic group within its industry
Buyer group	Focuses on better serving the buyer group	Redefines the buyer group of the industry
Functional and emotional orientation of an industry	Focuses on improving price performance inline with functional and emotional orientation of its Industry	Rethinks the functional and emotional orientation of its industry
Time	Focuses on adapting to external trends as they occur	Participates in shaping external trends over time

companies in the United States have undergone a renaissance in the past decade (Bohn 2000). Emphasis was formerly on built-in quality, elimination of waste, and faster throughputs. But attention quickly turned upstream to product development, where Japanese companies were outperforming their U.S. competitors on nearly every front. The key to Japanese success and U.S. industry weakness was the integration of product design and manufacturing process design with marketing, purchasing, finance, and other business functions (Sobek, Liker, and Ward 1998).

Significance of Technology Application in Small- and Medium-sized Enterprises

Worldwide industrial restructuring with flexible manufacturing practice is perceived in terms of a shift from the mass production of standardized product to more flexible innovative systems that can respond to fast-changing markets. Technology-based structural changes that emphasize quality and specialized products have brought small- and medium-sized enterprises (SMEs) on the scene again. Japan, Italy, and West Germany are capable of withstanding economic crisis better than the United States and the United Kingdom as they are switching to flexible manufacturing systems (Ashok 1994). In these countries, the role of SMEs has been significant. In Italy, the clustering of firms has helped them to gain the capabilities needed to innovate products and processes to enter markets independently. In Japan, though SMEs existed, emphasis has been given to restructuring existing firms to cater to the needs of large firms. In Japan, the role of SMEs as supplier/subcontractor to larger firms is very significant. Through this, they are gaining expertise in technological and organizational innovations. West Germany's SMEs can create a niche in the machine tool industry. The decentralized production system and breakup of markets opens a wide range of opportunities for the SMEs to operate.

In India, SMEs traditionally do no research. They make profits mostly by improving marketing and management, saving taxes, and importing technology (Naik 1996). Innovation in technology by and large is not seen as a means of increasing profit. Many industries depend on foreign collaboration for diversification and progress rather than on any academic or research institution within the country. In spite of these odds, small-scale industrial sectors have made significant contributions. This sector produces more than 7,500 different products and contributes to 40 percent of gross manufacture; directly or indirectly, it contributes to 45 percent of total export (Tuteja 2000).

Managing New Product Innovation

In advanced manufacturing technology, innovation plays an important role in competitive strategy. It not only affects the structure of organization but also can provide additional flexibility and capability in manufacturing complex products and can respond more effectively to changes in demand (Matani 1999). There are many useful steps that, if followed, can lead to the successful implementation of change, for example, advanced manufacturing technology (AMT) systems. Figure 3.1 suggests that seven important stages for successful implementation of change are needed.

**Strategies: Developing an Entrepreneurial Vision
Among Engineers**

It is a fact that, with proper education and training provided to an individual who has entrepreneurial zeal, sustainable entrepreneurship can be developed. This was established when Khursheed (1999) carried out an experiment in two towns of Andhra Pradesh in collaboration with India's Small Industry Extension Training Institute, where young businessmen were given an orientation course to stimulate imagination and the trainees displayed active behavior, worked long hours, and started new ventures.

It is universally known that the education and training of potential entre-

Figure 3.1   **The Seven Stages of Successful Change Implementation**

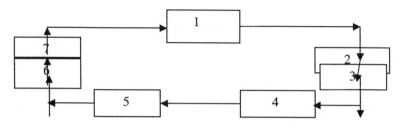

1. Determining the need and desire for change
2. Preparing alternative plans—subject to adjustment
3. Analyzing impacts and reactions—possibility of resistance and rejection of change
4. Making a final decision—after comparison of various strategies of implementation
5. Establishing time table—developing degree of complexity of change to be implemented
6. Communicating the change
7. Implementing the change—continuous evaluation is an integral part of this step

preneurs has a significant bearing on the successful pursuit of entrepreneurship. Yet questions arise. What training inputs are needed for potential entrepreneurs? An entrepreneur of the SME sector has to discharge the twin functions of "entrepreneur" and multifaceted "manager," so it is necessary for them:

- to be highly knowledgeable, possessing vision and dynamism;
- to be fully aware of the different schemes/incentives offered and procedures involved;
- to understand the different laws, regulations, and procedures in the establishment of a unit;
- to develop entrepreneurial vision, attitude, and motivation, and to understand what behavioral competencies are important for successful entrepreneurship;
- to understand the importance of submitting to financial discipline;
- to be educated about the stages of enterprise growth, and to learn how to face uncertainty and competition;
- to understand how to forge good relations with different individuals and organizations involved in industrial development;
- to learn how to seize an opportunity and conduct market surveys in preparing project cum feasibility reports; and
- to be fully capable of know-how, that is, to know how to marshal and utilize knowledge as well as resources in an effective way for the success of an industrial venture.

Figure 3.2   **Basis for Entrepreneurship Development Model**

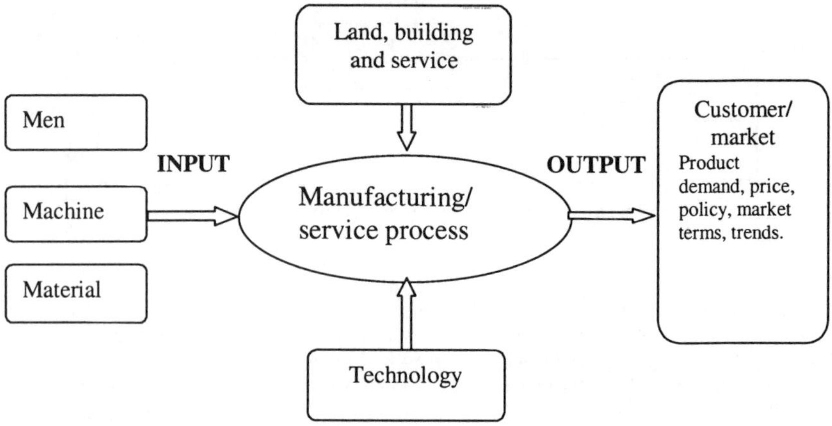

Figure 3.2 represents an industrial venture based on entrepreneurship, as discussed above.

Figure 3.2 shows that inputs for an industrial venture are men, machine, material, land, building, and technology. Manufacturing/service operation is carried out in land and building of the unit, where services are also input and are responsible for operation of the unit. Manufacturing or service operation is carried out at the unit location. The product/service to be produced/provided should meet market requirements. So the prospective entrepreneur, who will be responsible for running the unit, should be well aware of these inputs, the services required, manufacturing/service processes, technology involved, and the market/end user, that is, the customers, requirements, market trends, and so on. Entrepreneurship development programs should incorporate these factors. The proposed entrepreneurship development programs in technical institutions can be categorized in five phases as detailed in Table 3.5.

In the context of globalization and liberalization, industries respond to emerging calls for quality assurance as well as cost-effective strategies of production. The management of new enterprises and establishments must therefore respond to the challenges of managing technology growth and innovation. This challenge of growing competition has necessitated a high degree of application capability and innovation spirit among entrepreneurs. Entrepreneurs can initiate innovation by seizing opportunities in changing situations through discovering how to:

- make sure that all innovations are appealing to customers and meet high quality standards;

Table 3.5

**Proposed Entrepreneurship Development Program for
Engineering Institutions**

Phases of Programme	Focus to be made on	Input/Action during program
Selection of right prospective entrepreneur	The entrepreneur	Entrepreneurial characteristics and capability test of student then input
Motivation for encouraging towards entrepreneurship	The entrepreneur	Awareness about incentives, avenues, and schemes in the field, interaction with entrepreneurs followed by visit to their unit. Achievement motivation program
To start the unit	Venturing process: steps in marshalling resources and product/market assessment	Industrial potential survey, market survey for assessment of product demand, market terms and conditions. Preparation, presentation of techno-economic feasibility projects report followed by group discussion
To run the unit	Running a business/ venture; awareness of internal and external factors affecting units performance	In plant study, interactions with the successful/unsuccessful entrepreneurs. Giving open-end problem in industrial training as exercise. Report preparation involving the techno-commercial aspects and presentation
To expand the unit	Unit, market, customer	Case study, written report, formal presentation, and discussion

- build innovation from planning to communication to feedback systems;
- find paradigms to remain on the cutting edge of change;
- study the past, analyze the present, and forecast the needs of tomorrow's customer;
- establish a shared vision involving everyone in fostering and achieving important innovations; and
- synthesize opportunities in the marketplace with organizational capabilities and stockholders' needs.

What Technical Institutions Can Do

Engineering, technological, and research institutions have a surplus of intellectual cream, and these organizations are a significant constant source of new ideas. On the foundation of proven theories and established scientific knowledge, fresh endeavors should provide some impetus to recognizing and using sparks of excellence from students and faculty working on different projects. Technical research institutions should not only confine themselves to invention but also expand toward innovation. Organizations, apart from the production of novel and useful ideas, have to accept responsibility for the adoption of these ideas and their implementation. There is a need to transfer technology from the laboratory to industry, as has been successfully done in the case of agricultural universities and dairy research institutes, resulting in the green and white revolutions, respectively, in India. The workshop/laboratory facilities of technical institutions are of good quality and precision. In this context, it is important for teachers to understand how to apply the knowledge in the field because it is they who deliver knowledge and its practical application in industry to the students.

The aims of students seeking admission to technical institutions are (1) wage-employment, (2) self-employment, and (3) higher studies for research. The majority of students prefer wage-employment, and few are interested in self-employment. This is due to a lack of awareness among students about entrepreneurial avenues and various government schemes for encouraging self-employment in small-scale industrial sectors. In turn, this is due to a lack of awareness among teachers resulting from ineffective industry-institute interaction. Effective industry-institute interaction not only will educate faculty but also will be helpful in recognizing the problems of the industrial sector. A good example of this is the Silicon Valley project conceived by Fredrick Terman of Stanford University, California, in 1948. At that time, Terman noted that if Western industry and Western industrialists were to serve their own enlightened and long-range interests effectively, they would have to cooperate with universities, and, whenever possible, strengthen them with financial and other assistance.

Technical institutions should develop their curricula from an occupational and vocational perspective to develop (1) diagnostic skills, (2) computer handling skills, (3) management skills, and (4) awareness of national and international standards and quality control operations. These capabilities are equally important for self-employment and wage-employment for students. They are prerequisites for being a successful entrepreneur as well as an intrapreneur.

Recommendations

In the changing world economy, partnerships among industry, research, and academia are necessary to generate an innovative workforce for sustainable industrial development in India.

Indian industry (especially SMEs) is suffering from a deficiency of "innovation and technology transfer"; a technopreneur can be helpful in reducing this deficiency.

Technology transfer mechanisms in engineering institutions can work, as they have in agricultural universities and dairy research institutes, where technology is transferred to the field, which has resulted in the green and white revolutions in India. These can work as invention and innovation centers for SMEs.

Increased networking is necessary between research institutions, technical institutions, and industry to develop technologies that are required by and suitable to the SMEs. Encouragement and promotion of venture capital facilities for first-generation technical entrepreneurs is needed.

The manufacturing industry has to place more emphasis on products, not necessarily only in the price context but also on products that have to compete in the marketplace on additional features such as performance, reliability, speed of delivery, and customer service.

The innovative nature of a product and its appeal with respect to necessity in allocating resources for the development of innovative product must be tested for suitability to the marketplace and performance in relation to competitor's product.

Conclusion

As competition becomes more knowledge based, it is becoming imperative for Indian industries to effectively develop and deploy their knowledge-generating assets. In changed scenarios, many entrepreneurs feel it is necessary to be technologically innovative, and therefore to realize the need to provide a more central strategic role in their R&D functions.

For effective integration of research with mainstream business activities, it is necessary to build linkages between R&D and an organization's vision, strategies, customers, and stakeholders. Only then will it be possible to use research as a source of innovative business ideas for sustainable industrial development.

In the small-scale engineering industry, entrepreneurial success and failure depend not only on what entrepreneurs know but also on what they can do with what they know. Since they are often dealing in areas of uncertainty and change, their comfort and insight with respect to intuitive judgments and actions are as important as their deliberative decisions and implementation. Strategies for developing entrepreneurial values among engineers can be useful in building technical entrepreneurs for successful product innovation, effective industry-institute interaction, faculty exposure to industry, entrepreneurial awareness of the faculty, and effective utilization of infrastructures available at engineering institutes. In a nutshell, it will be helpful in developing effective engineers as per the requirements of industry either in wage-employment or in self-employment for successful product innovation in the small-scale sector.

References

Ashok, J. 1994. "Role of SMEs in a Modern Economy and Related Technological Problems: A Review." In *Technical Entrepreneurship: Content and Parameter*, ed. Vinayshil Gautam, 14–22. New Delhi: Allied.

Baburao, G. 1999. "Promotion of Technical Entrepreneurship: Role of Humanities and Social Sciences." *Journal of Engineering Education*, 7–11.

Bhatia, B.S., and R.K. Sharma 1989. "Entrepreneurial Performance in a Developing Economy: A Case Study of Punjab." In *Entrepreneurship Development in India*, ed. Sami Uddin, 177–90. Delhi: Mittal.

Bohn, R. 2000. "Stop Fighting Fires." *Harvard Business Review* 78, no. 4: 83–91.

Catalani, M.S., and G.F. Clerico. 1996. "Decision-Making Structures: Dealing with Uncertainty Within Organizations." New York: Springer Verlag.

Chan, K.W., and R. Mauborgne. 1999. "Creating New Market Space." *Harvard Business Review* (January–February): 83–93.

———. 2000. "Knowing a Winning Business Idea When You See One." *Harvard Business Review* (September–October): 129–38.

Davies, G. 1993. "Meeting the Needs of the Society It Serves." *Education + Training* 35, no. 5: 17–24.

Dickinson, David G.; Michael J. Driscoll; and Somnath Sen. 1996. "Risk and Uncertainty in Economics: Essays in Honor of James L. Ford." *The Economic Journal* 106, no. 436: 769.

Hollander, S. 1965. *The Sources of Increased Efficiency: A Case Study of DuPont Rayon Plants*. Cambridge: Massachusetts Institute of Technology Press.

Iredale, N. 1993. "Enterprise Education in Primary Schools." *Education + Training* 35, no. 4: 22–29.

Kelmer, J.H. 1992. "Business Plans for Teaching Entrepreneurial Behavior." *Education + Training* 34, no. 1: 30–32.

Khursheed, B. 1999. "Small Entrepreneurial Education: Approach and Methodology." *Abhigyan* 17, no. 4: 35–44.

Knight, F.H. 1965. *Risk Uncertainty and Profit*. New York: Harper and Row.

Matani, A.G. 1999. "Managing New Product Innovations." *Industrial Engineers Journal* 28, no. 4: 21–23.

Morek, J.D. 2001. "Innovation Sources and Strategies." *International Journal of Technology Management* 21, nos. 5/6: 612–27.

Mukharjee, N. 2001. "World Trade Organization and Small and Medium Enterprises from a Developing Country's Perspective. A Study of Indian Small-scale Industries." *Laghu-Udyog* 25–26: 36–48.

Naik, B.M. 1996. "Innovation and Technology Transfer Practices and Policies in Germany: Lessons of Experience." *Indian Journal of Technical Education* 19, no. 3: 3–10.

————. 1999. "Technology Management Making India More Competitive." *Indian Journal of Technical Education* 22, no. 3: 24–27.

Natrajan, R. 2000. "Keynote Address." Paper presented at the National Seminar on New Perspectives and Prospects for Technical Education, College of Engineering, Trivandrum, India, January 7.

Prasad, C.S. 2001. "The Third Census of SSI Units." *Laghu-Udyog* 25–26: 14–20.

Sandhya, G.D., and N. Mrinalini. 1998. "Industrial Training, Skill Development and Innovation." *Productivity* 39, no. 2: 221–25.

Shackle, G.L.S. 1955. *Uncertainty in Economics and Other Reflections.* Cambridge: Cambridge University Press.

————. 1961. *Decision Order and Time in Human Affairs.* Cambridge: Cambridge University Press.

Smilor, R.W., and H.R. Feeser. 1991. "Chaos and the Entrepreneurial Process: Patterns and Policy Implications for Technology Entrepreneurship." *Journal of Business Venturing* 6: 165–72.

Smilor, R.W., and M.D. Gill. 1986. *The New Business Incubator: Linking Talent, Technology, Capital, and Know-how.* Lexington, MA: Lexington Books.

Sobek, D.K.; J.K. Liker; and A.C. Ward. 1998. "Another Look at How Toyota Integrates Product Development." *Harvard Business Review* 76, no. 4 (July–August): 36–48.

Stringer, R. 2000. "How to Manage Radical Innovation." *California Management Review* 42, no. 4: 70–88.

Terman, Fredrick E., Professor of Stanford University, California. 1948. Well known as the Father of Silicon Valley (while supporting the cause of forging links between university and industry).

Tuteja, S.K. 2000. "Institutional Support for Technological Acquisition and Skill Upgradation for Micro-, Small-, and Medium-scale Enterprises." *Laghu-Udyog Samachar*, 24-25: 10–18.

Vasundhara, R. 2000. "Taking SSI Towards the New Millennium: Message of Hope." *Laghu-Udyog* 24–25: 3–8.

Wani, V.P., and S.K. Sharma. 1999. "Technocrat an Entrepreneur: Avenues." Paper presented at the national seminar on Recent Trends in Manufacturing Systems, at MHT, Pinjore, India.

4

Undergraduate Curriculum in India

The Corporate Context

Raj Agrawal

The major challenge of business education at the undergraduate level is to develop an efficient and proactive corporate-oriented curriculum that fine-tunes itself regularly to meet the changing demands of business. This is something many business schools are struggling to achieve.

In India, management education programs are currently limited to the post-graduate level and prepare students to assume managerial positions in industry. More than 900 All India Council for Technical Education (AICTE)/ university-approved postgraduate diploma in management (PGDM)/master of business administration (MBA) programs in the country are enough to fulfill the demand for such positions in industry. While managerial vacancies are thus well provided for, there is no appropriate program to cater to the upsurge expected in the first-line commercial positions in the burgeoning service industry.

Various preliminary studies also showed that the developed world would experience a shortage of professional manpower due to aging and low population growth rates. To make up for the shortage, developed countries will compete to attract the right kind of skill sets—either through migration or outsourcing. India is uniquely placed to optimize the gains arising from these new opportunities.

The major remote services, where most of these opportunities are emerging, are primarily in sectors like information technology (IT) services, IT-enabled services, telemedicine, e-learning, tourism, health care services, and education services. Other services include accounting, auditing, bookkeeping, architectural services, urban planning and landscape architectural services, medical and dental services, services provided by midwives, nurses, and hospital services, construction and engineering services, computer-related services, consultancy services related to the installation of computer hardware, software implementation services, data processing services, database services and other computer-related services, insurance and insurance-related services, banking and other financial services, hotel and restaurant services (including catering), travel agency and tourist operators services, and maritime transport services (All-India Management Association 2003).

These opportunities will simultaneously demand new skill sets primarily at the undergraduate level in frontline jobs or commercial jobs in the services sector. Undergraduate management education programs—such as the bachelors in business administration (BBA), the bachelors in business management (BBM), and others—were introduced by Indian universities some years ago to fulfill such needs, and they follow a curriculum patterned after MBA subjects. Neither program curriculum is linked to the need profiles of first-line positions in the corporate world. Our initial investigations also reveal that traditional BBA and BBM programs have disappointed bright and dynamic youngsters as they fail in linking to the competency needs of business and industry. The prevailing quality, orientation, and standards of most BBA and BBM programs have not led to corporate employability.

The issue here is that these students are teenagers, and we already have the sense that management education should be imparted to older people with work experience. There is a need to provide a good undergraduate degree, but one oriented toward developing a commercial and managerial mindset, not another version of a postgraduate management program (MBA). Therefore, in curriculum design, the focus should be on fulfilling corporate needs. Curriculum design may include a range of functional specializations and sectoral modules as electives, using a cafeteria approach so students can be molded in line with profiles of employment opening up for graduates.

Objectives

The major objectives of study based on the current business environment are identified as follows:

1. to make a dispassionate assessment of the current status of the prevailing undergraduate business education programs in many Indian universities and institutions; and
2. to assess the current structure of undergraduate program course structure and reorient it to serve the need of frontline commercial jobs in the corporate world by obtaining the opinions of business experts.

At the level of undergraduate business education itself, students should receive a broad business-based management education. After completing the program, students are expected to have a good understanding of the economic, social, cultural, legal, and political framework within which businesses and individuals operate, as well as to become sensitized to the drives and demands of employability in current business scenarios. Curriculum design should focus on these aspects.

Besides offering an undergraduate-level business education, education should contribute to personal growth, build a large number of marketable skills, enhance career prospects, and create productive options for the future.

Functional specialization modules should be developed in close collaboration with senior business executives. These should be an integral part of the entire program. Specialization modules should provide an opportunity to students for integrated work with industry and business, on the one hand, and teaching by industry experts, on the other. Actual projects should also be carried out with the support of corporations.

Curriculum design will be different from that of the existing university and institution BBA/BBM programs in terms of:

1. specializations in line with industry and business needs;
2. industry-interfaced projects;
3. foundation skills such as communication, language, presentation, and so on; and
4. modular approaches of awarding diplomas with total credits earned.

Hypothesis

Ensuring the development of an appropriate curriculum for sound business education is an important requirement. New courses have to be added, and old courses that are no longer relevant have to be deleted in order to cater to the needs of emerging sectors. It is not out of context to mention here that a good number of universities and institutions have a tendency to pursue the same course structure for a long time without upgrading it.

Most of the curricula in Indian universities and institutes are designed with an emphasis on forward integration approaches (Pritam 2002). By forward integration approaches, we mean that general, business, and specialization courses are identified and distributed in various terms or semesters. These are not identified and integrated by assessing current corporate and business needs. This approach represents a traditional model of curriculum design. In most of the curricula, we find that in the first semester, foundation courses such as Quantitative Methods and Economics are taught, and in subsequent semesters, integrative courses like Operation Research and Strategic Management are included; finally, specialization and application-oriented courses are taught.

In the past decade, global and domestic business environments have changed rapidly. Issues related to business have changed. There has been a complete paradigm shift. The kinds of skills and competencies required to operate in this dynamic global environment are different than those of earlier eras. Most of the time, these courses do not match the skills and competencies required by corporations. For example, students learn marketing whether they develop competencies or not. The delivery mechanism of these competencies is also based on traditional methods such as classroom teaching, teacher- and memory-centered approaches, limited use of industry experts, no use of corporate labs, and so on (Natrajan 2002). It has generally been felt that such methods do not provide practical knowledge, hardly allow any early interaction with companies, and often include theoretical expertise that is outdated (Sivaramakrishna and Ramesh, 2000). Initial investigations also reveal that industry is often an unwilling partner of management education, and this is applicable not only in Indian cases but also at the global level.

In curriculum design, instead of adopting the prevailing forward integration approach, there is a need to evolve to a backward integration approach. In backward integration, identifying the major issues of business is inevitable. First, privatization and the emergence of the World Trade Organization are current issues that affect Indian businesses. Second, competency and skills should be identified and linked with business issues in accordance with changing corporate requirements. Corporations have also changed or are changing with the domestic and global business environments. Third, major competencies and skills that have been identified should be incorporated in curriculum design. The backward integration approach discussed above would be more appropriate in this dynamic global environment and would also ensure that the emerging needs of corporations are met by business education.

Research Design and Methodology

The study includes all companies in sectors such as IT services, IT-enabled services, telemedicine, e-learning, tourism, health care services, auditing, bookkeeping services, data processing services, database and other computer-related services, insurance and insurance-related services, banking and other financial services, hotel and restaurant services (including catering), travel agency and tourism operation services, maritime transport services, and fast-moving consumer goods sectors.

In the first instance, a cross-section of 650 companies was taken, covering

Table 4.1

Study Sample

Sample	Companies	Sample size
1	Insurance	40
2	Banking	80
3	Travel related	40
4	Information technology related	150
5	Hospitality related	100
6	Fast-moving consumer goods	150
7	Others like sports, leisure, and so on	90

different emerging business areas—insurance, banking, fast-moving consumer goods, tourism operators, hotels and restaurants, and transport were selected from private and public limited companies. The sample size of the study is given in Table 4.1. In the second stage, a cross-section of senior executives, such as senior human resource development managers and production executives, were selected to participate in a survey to identify the skills considered to be most important.

The Delphi technique was used primarily on experts from business to identify a set of necessary initial skills and competencies.

The process was completed in two stages. In the first stage, through discussion with like-minded experts, a list of skills and competencies was prepared. In the second stage, by conducting a brainstorming session, only skills and competencies related to the needs of corporations were selected in preparing the questionnaire.

The questionnaire was based on a ten-point scale designed to focus on ranking listed skills needed for a frontline position (office/executive) in the services and industrial sector. The identified skills were divided into two parts: (1) general skills and (2) knowledge-based skills or competencies. In the cover letter itself, it was made very clear that BBA program design would be developed to fulfill the needs of large numbers of frontline commercial jobs expected to open up in the emerging service sector. Conducting personal interviews and relying on personal contacts also helped in the collection of data. The empirical aspect forms the most important feature of the study. The questionnaire and personal interviews constituted the major tools of data collection for the present study.

Observations and Findings

The responses and observations received from the cross-section of 356 companies are shown in Table 4.2. Skills and competencies are ranked in terms

Table 4.2

Rankings of General Skills by Companies

Sample	General skills	Ranking	Total response
1	English communication	2	170
2	Competence in information technology	3	140
3	Workforce management	5	125
4	Negotiation skill	11	70
5	Troubleshooting	12	20
6	Conceptual skills	10	84
7	Planning skills	9	90
8	Organizational skills	8	110
9	Monitoring skills	7	118
10	Control skills	6	122
11	Motivation	1	200
12	Decision making	4	135

Table 4.3

Knowledge-based Skill Rankings

Sample	Knowledge-based skills	Ranking	Sample size of companies
1	Product sales	4	300
2	Accounting/finance	3	275
3	E-business	2	275
4	Export/import	7	300
5	Marketing of services	1	275
6	Starting small scale business	5	300
7	Public relations/event management	6	300

of total response. The ranking of various skills by corporations highlights the need to integrate these basic skills.

The rankings of knowledge-based competencies are exhibited in Table 4.3; we can conclude that the new and emerging areas are where these new competencies are required and they should be included in the design of BBA-level curricula.

The major findings of the survey in terms of requisite skills, competencies, and specialization were integrated into the development of a curriculum. Specialization modules were selected from the sectors that have shown high growth potential in the past five years. These sectors are hospitality, e-business, small businesses, services, and international business.

Curriculum design was divided into three stages: (1) inclusion of requisite skills, (2) knowledge and competencies, and (3) specialization modules. This approach is known as backward integration.

The first year is divided into two semesters and the curriculum strongly emphasizes development of the required skills. For developing motivation skills, which were given top ranking in the survey, additional courses, for example, Introduction to Humanities, were included in the first year. To further keep teenagers motivated, proper care was taken to include industry-interfaced projects with the support of corporations, in the belief that students' involvement in industry-oriented projects will provide sufficient motivation and work orientation from the very beginning.

Other ranked preferences were English communication and IT-related skills. For developing English communication skills, courses like English Composition, English as a Second Language, and Communications were introduced. For IT-related skills, both theoretical and lab-oriented courses were included in the first year. In sum, major skill-oriented papers were introduced in the first year. This approach is different from the traditional university curriculum where the initial major emphasis has been on knowledge-based papers. The proposed curriculum design here can be benchmarked with the traditional university-based BBA curriculum.

In the second and third years, major competency-based courses as well as six specialization modules according to the needs and expectations of the corporate world were introduced. These modules accord well with the contemporary issues of business and have shown a high growth potential in the past few years. It is also expected that major commercial and frontline jobs are opening in these areas, and corporations expect BBA degrees to include these areas that provide the requisite skills and competencies. Specialization modules for these sectors include e-business, international business, hospitality business, marketing management, services business, and entrepreneurship and small businesses. This is one of the most innovative findings of the entire study. The introduction of specialized modules in accordance with market requirements is a major innovation of the proposed curriculum for undergraduate students as well as an important departure from the traditional curricula used by various universities and institutions. Based on the findings and observations of the study, an innovative approach to new curriculum design for undergraduate segments in most business schools in India has been proposed. In the new curriculum, the major emphasis is on developing new sets of skills, relevant competencies, and specialized modules in accordance with corporate requirements.

Recommended Pedagogy and Curriculum

Academic Years, Semesters, and Credit

The program should comprise six semesters spread over three to four years and should include forty-two courses. There should be twenty-eight general and business courses. From six specialization modules, students should se- lect ten courses. For effective industry interface, students should do two in- dustry-interfaced projects consisting of four courses. Each course consists of four credits, and consists of thirty-two to thirty-four sessions, each seventy minutes in duration. Each credit is equivalent to eight to nine sessions, and the total number of credits for the program is 168. The credit distribution was benchmarked with the most prestigious BBA programs abroad, such as the London Business School, University of Bradford (UK), Northwood Uni- versity (United States), Thames Valley University, and London University. The parity in credit equivalence may facilitate credit transfer from one insti- tute to another, even at the international level. From the second year onward, students have to choose ten electives from two of the six specialization streams offered.

Completion of ten electives, five each from two specialization streams, will lead to dual specialization.

The distribution of courses in each semester is given in Table 4.4.

Specialization Modules

The program is enriched by specialization modules that will bring better employability to corporations in emerging sectors. Specialization modules provide an opportunity for students to evaluate theory in a corporate con- text, thus fulfilling the objective of providing a broad and integrative in- vestigation of management. An illustrative list regarding the intention and specific inputs of modules are given in Table 4.5. Faculty members in close collaboration with industry and business would specifically develop these by taking into consideration the need to employ BBA students at a rela- tively younger age.

Projects

Two industry projects will be carried out simultaneously with teaching dur- ing the second and third years. These projects should be completed before the student is admitted to take term-end examinations during the fourth and sixth semesters.

Conclusions

Based on the above observations, discussions, and findings, it can be con- cluded that education in India, as in much of the world, is undergoing a transitional phase. Teaching methodologies have changed. Curricula and

Table 4.4

Distribution of Courses by Semester

Year	Semester no.	General and business courses + specialization courses
First year	1	7
	2	7
Industry Interfaced Project I	During the second year	2
Second year	3	4+2
	4	4+2
Industry Interfaced Project II	During the third year	2
Third year	5	3+3
	6	3+3

Weight of subjects	No. of subjects	Percent
Foundation subjects	14	37
Business subjects	14	37
Specialization subjects	10	26
Total	38	100

First year

S. No.	Semester I	Semester II
1	English Writing	English Verbal
2	Introduction to I.T.	Computer Application Lab -I
3	Business Math	Business Statistics
4	Understanding of Business Organizations	Micro Economics
5	Macro Economics	Accounting II (Cost Accounting)
6	Accounting I (Financial Accounting)	Project Writing
7	Introduction to Humanities (Psychology & Sociology)	Communication

Industry interfaced project—2 courses (general stream)

Second year

S. No.	Semester III	Semester IV
1	Concepts of Operations (Manufacturing & Services)	Management of Operations (Manufacturing & Services)
2	Principles of Marketing	Financial Management I
3	Business & Social Environment	Organizational Behavior
4	Business Application of Software & Lab. Work	Marketing Management
5	Elective I from modules	Elective III from modules
6	Elective II from modules	Elective IV from modules

Industry interfaced project—2 courses (specialization stream)

Third year

S. No.	Semester V	Semester VI
1	Financial Management II	Business Strategy
2	Human Resource Management	Entrepreneurship
3	Business Law	International Business
4	Elective V from modules	Elective VIII from modules
5	Elective VI from modules	Elective IX from modules
6	Elective VII from modules	Elective X from modules

Table 4.5 **Specialization Modules**

1	2
Marketing Management Modules • Advertising and Brand Management • Direct Marketing • Distribution Channel Management • Marketing Research • Marketing of Services • Marketing on the Internet • Sales Management	**E-Business Modules** • Data Communication and Networking • Database Management • Systems Analysis and Design Methodologies • Web Technologies • Management of Information Technology • Fundamentals of E-Commerce
3	4
International Business Modules • Export and Import Policies and Procedures • Export Costing and Financing • International Logistics Management • International Marketing • Foreign Exchange Management • Import Management • Formation of an Export Company	**Entrepreneurship and Small Business Modules** • Government Business Interface • Small Business Marketing • Financing of Small Business • Entrepreneurial Development • New Enterprise Management • Small Business Environment and Management
5	6
Hospitality Business Modules • Principles of Travel and Tourism Operations • Introduction to the Hospitality Industry • Foundation of Tourism • Tourism Enterprises (Operations and Human Resources) • Tourism Marketing • Adventure and Sports Management	**Services Business Modules** • Financial Services • Retailing • Transport • Health Care Services • Entertainment Services • Corporate Public Relations

delivery systems are the key drivers in this highly competitive climate. Curricula should be designed to take into account the existence of parallel yet converging global and domestic business environments. It should also be linked with employability in the new business sectors of emerging economies. Identifying the major sectors where most commercial or frontline jobs are opening and undergraduate segments that best fulfill their requirements is exemplified in the curricular design presented.

References

All-India Management Association and Boston Consulting Group. 2003. *India's New Opportunity, 2020—Report of High Level Strategic Group*, 8.

Natrajan, N. 2002. Address. Presented at the All-India Council for Technical Education, New Delhi, November 29.

Pritam, S. 2002. "Keynote Address." Presented at the seventh Directors Conclave organized by the All-India Management Association in collaboration with the Narsee Monjee Institute of Management Studies, November 29.

Sivaramakrishna, K., and K. Ramesh. 2000. "Technical Education and the New Millennium: Role of HRD Interventions." In *Delivering Service Quality*, ed. M. Raghavachari and K.V. Ramani, 296. New Delhi: Macmillan.

5

Management Education in Nepal

A View from the High Country

Alfred Rosenbloom and Bijay K.C.

Nepal is a small, landlocked country that straddles the Himalayan mountain range in south Asia. To its north, Nepal shares a common border with China, and to its south, it shares a common border with India. India and China dwarf Nepal in both scale and scope. As a result, Nepal is often overlooked when talking about Asia, in general, and south Asia, more specifically. Numerous examples exist of Nepal's "invisibility" in the academic and professional business/management literature. One current illustration will suffice. In the World Economic Forum's most recent *Global Competitiveness Report* (Porter, Schwab, and Cornelius 2003), Nepal is omitted in the large appendix of country profiles. A review of the global management literature reveals a similar pattern. Few if any books or articles explore the special management issues and challenges relative to Nepal. This chapter begins to fill in that gap.

This chapter is specifically about management education in Nepal—how it developed and how various Nepali institutions of higher learning have responded to the evolving needs of Nepali businesses for expertly educated managers. The chapter weaves together two ideas throughout: that market needs should be the essential driver of management program development and that those management programs, which are entrepreneurial and innovative, have the best chance of surviving and thriving long term. No discussion of Nepali higher education and business practices, though, can be meaningful without also discussing Nepal's cultural and economic relationship with India. This topic is also discussed in the chapter.

Nepal's Economy

Historically, Nepal has been an agriculture-based society and continues to be so even today. Like many countries with emerging economies, Nepal has a dual economy. It has an industrialized, highly competitive and congested modern sector, centered in the country's capital, Katmandu, and it has an underdeveloped, slow-growth, subsistence economy across the rest of the country. More than 80 percent of the country's population earns a living through agriculture. As a result, 40 percent of Nepal's GNP comes from agriculturally based industries, such as grain, jute, sugar cane, and tobacco (*CIA World Factbook* 2003). Consistent with an economy that is agriculturally based, Nepal has a low unemployment rate. The Asian Development Bank (ADB) estimates a national unemployment rate of only 2 percent. The ADB also estimates that unemployment increases to 7 percent in cities (Asian Development Bank 2003).

Nepal shares a common border with India. As befits a nation of traders, Nepal has had a longstanding economic relationship across this border (Zivetz 1992). Today, India is Nepal's largest trading partner and accounts for 40 percent of Nepal's exports and imports (World Bank 2001: 239). Because the Nepal-India border is somewhat porous, both goods and people move freely across it. The Nepali rupee is pegged to the Indian rupee. The Indian rupee officially can be used to purchase goods and services in Nepal, although Nepali merchants are often reluctant to do so. The Nepal-India relationship is further solidified through a common religion. Both countries are predominantly Hindu. Yet Nepal is the only country in the world to officially declare itself as a Hindu state. Cooperation between the two countries is further solidified through language. Hindi and Nepali are very closely related. And finally, some of Nepal's leading business houses have their origins in India, where their families were part of the large Marwari merchant and trading caste of Rajasthan.

Nepal also happens to be one of the poorest countries in the world. Average per capita income is about US$220. The World Bank states that "Nepal is the 12th poorest country in the world and the poorest in South Asia" (World Bank 2002: 1). Poverty is endemic. As a result, Nepal receives substantial support from international aid agencies for a large variety of economic and social development projects. Many international aid and development agencies have their headquarters in Katmandu.

Attempts to diversify Nepal's economic base and to improve over productivity have met with mixed success. Nepal has a large carpet export industry, but the carpet industry, just as the garment and pashmina shawl industries, has experienced recent declines due to market oversaturation coupled with declines in global economic demand. Recent developments in computer information technology, though, are bright signs of progress. Information technology (IT) is helping Nepal develop a vital, growing, and international IT sector. Governmental policies to stimulate industrial growth have also produced mixed results. Both tax and infrastructure reforms are progressing. Yet banking reform is urgently needed (Khatiwada 2002). In 2001, two of the country's leading banks, Nepal Rastra Bank and Nepal Bank Ltd., were "technically insolvent" (i.e., they were bankrupt). These two banks control 60 percent of the country's total banking assets. Thus, the banks' poor financial positions are serious threats to the country's overall macroeconomic stability. Efforts to improve the efficiency and integrity of Nepal's civil service have likewise moved slowly. Corruption is a major, ongoing, public issue. Governmental decision making is slow and is often highly politicized. Privatization efforts progress in fits and starts.

Finally, Nepal continues to be challenged by a grassroots, Maoist uprising. For the past several years, the Marxist-Leninist party of Nepal has been waging a people's war against the national government. National public strikes, called *bandhs*, are frequent and can last up to a week. During a *bandh*, all public and private enterprises (including schools and universities) are closed. This Maoist insurgency not only threatens national security but also diminishes Nepal's economic vitality. The ongoing threat of *bandhs* has sharply reduced tourism in Nepal, which accounts for 10 percent of Nepal's nonagricultural GDP.

Development of Management Education

Management education in Nepal is of relatively recent origin. Yet any attempt to understand the progress Nepal has made in terms of management education must begin with a brief overview of the country's higher education landscape. In 2003, there were five universities in Nepal: Tribhuvan University, Katmandu University, Pokhara University, Mahendra Sanskrit University, and Purbanchal University. All these universities, except Mahendra Sanskrit, grant degrees in business. In 2003, besides the constituent campuses of these universities, four management institutes under the private sector also provided master-level programs in management. These institutes are affiliated with various universities and offer master of business administration (MBA) and executive MBA programs.

Tribhuvan University

Tribhuvan University was Nepal's first university. It was established only in 1959. (Historians note, though, that Nepal's first institution of higher education, Tri-Chandra College, was established in 1918.) Tribhuvan University is a large, multicampus, national university that enrolled about 150,000 students in 1998. Students can take classes either on its main campus in Katmandu or in 61 constituent or 191 affiliated campuses across the country. Clark Kerr would call Tribhuvan University a "multiversity" (Kerr 1995). The university offers 1,079 courses at the bachelor's level and over 1,000 courses at the master's level (see www.tribhuvan-university.edu.np) and has both undergraduate and graduate programs in business. Tribhuvan grants both Bachelor and Master of Business Studies degrees and has recently started offering a four-year Bachelor in Business Administration degree.

Tribhuvan University has played a vital role in the development of management education in Nepal. Management education started in Nepal in the form of commerce education in 1954 when the government established a commerce department in the then government-run Tri-Chandra College. Tribhuvan University offered a postgraduate-level degree in commerce education in 1961. Nepal's historical relationship with India is further evidenced in its higher education system, especially with Tribhuvan University. Because of its close relationship with India, it was quite natural, for Tribhuvan administrators and faculty to look to India for both curricular models and faculty when the university was first founded. For its initial humanities and social sciences curriculum, Tribhuvan University patterned itself on Patna University in India. Indeed, initially, Patna University even conducted final examinations for all Tribhuvan University courses. Today, the university administers it own examinations.

As commerce education was based on the model then prevalent in India, which itself leaned heavily toward the British system, it had no clear-cut objectives regarding its role in the process of nation building and did not respond to the needs of the nation. It also lacked future direction. The influence of Indian curricular models is also seen in Tribhuvan's initial management curriculum. Agrawal directly acknowledges this relationship: historically, "the structure of business discipline was copied from the Indian universities and, in line with their tradition, [was] known by the name of commerce education in Nepal" (1974: 83).

The graduates so produced were regarded as inferior to other graduates and criticized for their lack of performance. In a seminar on Commerce Education in Nepal, organized by the Federation of Nepalese Industry and Commerce in 1968, many deficiencies of commerce education were pointed out (as cited in Pradhananga 1982). Businessmen and administrators complained that graduates lack the skills needed to carry out their jobs although the standard is no different from that of other disciplines classed as liberal (Ojha 1969). Despite the criticisms, the number of students studying commerce increased because commerce education was considered less tough in comparison to other disciplines such as science and economics and it provided opportunities for jobs in specialized areas such as accounting. By 1970 there were fifteen colleges providing commerce education in the country.

In 1971 the government made radical changes in the education system of the nation and introduced the National Education System Plan. The new education plan was a milestone in the history of management education in the sense that it departed from traditional commerce education to business administration, and many new courses with emphasis on developing managerial skills and knowledge were introduced into the curriculum. The Institute of Business Administration, Commerce, and Public Administration was established under Tribhuvan University, and students were awarded the degree of business administration and commerce. Despite the change, management education did not see any fundamental improvement and was not much different from the old commerce education in many respects, including the teaching methods adopted, the size of the class, teaching materials, and so on. As a majority of the teachers were commerce degree holders they could not understand the spirit of the new system and lacked the expertise and knowledge to treat the courses differently. The objectives of the institute were definitely lofty and laudable, but the implementation of the programs was poor and faulty. The institute was renamed the Institute of Management in 1976, but things did not change. Rather, a state of confusion existed because the institute emphasized that it was providing management education in place of the old commerce education while the business community and outsiders were not willing to accept this as management education as it did not impart the skills and knowledge necessary for a good manager. The situation became worse as some of the strengths of the old commerce education were also lost. A serious discussion took place among members of the Faculty Board of the institute on this issue in 1982, and the board decided in favor of offering two streams of business education simultaneously—Business Administration and Business Studies.

The pedagogical legacy of India is deeply ingrained cross the entire university. Pedagogy across all disciplines is very formal and lecture oriented. Students sit in large lecture halls, dutifully transcribing lecture notes delivered by the faculty. There is almost no interaction between faculty and student, other than the one-way communication of lecture information. This is also true in terms of management education. Management education at both the bachelor's and master's levels tends to be very theoretical. Emphasis is given to a detailed, theoretical understanding of each business discipline. In turn, exams require students to repeat, verbatim, large blocks of theory. For the student, rote memorization becomes the primary means of success in passing the exams. The consequence of this is enormous for Nepal. It has meant, generally, that there is a mismatch between business needs and Tribhuvan business graduates, and this has been a longstanding imbalance. Agrawal acknowledges this point: "The present curriculum [at Tribhuvan University] does not prepare students for lifelong careers, nor does it provide them with an understanding and appreciation of the challenges and problems faced by the developing nation. Consequently, Commerce graduates desperately look for a clerical job in the bureaucracy; and, if successful they wait in the hope of getting one. In the meantime, they swell the ranks of the educated unemployed" (Agrawal 1974: 84). Indeed, the current evolution of Nepal's economy has only accentuated this labor gap. With the entrance of more multinational corporations into Nepal, the development of more information, computer, and knowledge-based industries in Nepal, the growing sophistication of Nepali business houses themselves, and the need to reform major sectors of the Nepali economy like banking, the skills and abilities that Nepali businesses say they now need from business graduates are often not represented in the skill set of Tribhuvan alumni.

Kathmandu University

Katmandu University was founded in 1991 as "an autonomous, not-for-profit, nongovernmental public institution" and was created through private initiative. The University's main campus is in Dhulikhel, a small town fifteen miles east of Kathmandu. Its first program of study was in its School of Science in 1992, but its second program was in business. In 1993, Kathmandu University founded its School of Management (KUSOM). Recognizing that the business, commercial, and policy center of the country is located in the nation's capital, the School of Management is located in Kathmandu. KUSOM grants an MBA and an executive master of business administration (EMBA); its first MBA class enrolled in 1993, while its first EMBA class enrolled in 2001.

Purbanchal University

Purbanchal University was established in 1995 with the objectives of providing higher education in the country in a decentralized manner and expanding the opportunities of higher education in the country. The prime minister is the chancellor of the university, and the pro-chancellor is the minister for education. The vice chancellor is the academic and administrative head of the university. The university was incorporated under the Purbanchal University Act in 1994, and its first senate meeting was held in June 1996, during which it was decided to develop the university as a full-fledged institution of higher learning devoted to achieving high academic standards. At present, it functions as a teaching-cum-affiliating university with two constituent campuses and thirty-nine affiliated colleges. The university offers a wide range of programs, mostly through its affiliated colleges; the programs include computer application information technology, computer engineering, civil engineering, agriculture, electronics and communications, business administration, commerce, sociology, arts, mass communications and journalism, education, law, and fashion design. The university is located in Biratnagar in the eastern part of Nepal on 545 hectares of degenerating forest land. The university relies mainly on government funding to meet its financial requirements.

Pokhara University

Pokhara University, founded in 1996, is the newest university in Nepal. The central office of the university is located in Pokhara, Kaski district, in the Western Development Region of Nepal. It was founded not only to serve the country's western region but also to further privatize Nepali higher education. Pokhara University offers undergraduate and graduate degree programs in business as well as degrees in hotel management and so on.

The university's long-term viability, however, is questionable. In May 2003, the university faced a crushing budget deficit. Of the Rs19.1 million budgeted by the government for university operations, only Rs1.1 million had been dispersed. As a result, all building and program development has been suspended. Faculty have not been paid. The university's ultimate fate is uncertain (Neupane 2003).

Innovation at the Kathmandu University School of Management

The Kathmandu University School of Management represents an entirely different model of management education in Nepal. In particular, there is an entrepreneurial ethos that permeates everything the school does. As a professional school, KUSOM has been able to gauge and respond to market needs as they develop. Many aspects of KUSOM's approach to management education have been innovative for Nepal, but five will be highlighted here. They are:

- Mission
- Curriculum
- Pedagogy—action learning and summer projects
- Local case development
- Social responsibility

Mission

From its very inception, KUSOM had a different educational philosophy
from that of Tribhuvan University. As publicly stated, KUSOM's mission
and goals are to:

- Prepare individuals aspiring to a career in business, social, development, and public organization management as a profession
- Develop and support practicing managers for their professional enrichment and career advancement
- Enhance the managerial capability of practicing managers for better
  performance and effectiveness
- Assist organizations in planning and implementing changes in various
  functional areas of management and help them to improve their managerial practices and organizational performance, and
- Develop a base of management knowledge relevant to the country and
  share it with organizations for improving the quality of management
  (School of Management 1998: 1).

KUSOM's mission, then, is to prepare expertly qualified business managers
who can both understand and use the most reliable analytic tools in finance,
accounting, management, marketing, and information systems to make sound
business decisions in a wide variety of organizations—and who can combine
a sensitive understanding of Nepali business tradition with world class management practice. In short, KUSOM aims to develop a cadre of *practical*
business professionals who can incorporate management's best practices in
the day-to-day operations and decision making of Nepali businesses of all
kinds.

The mission statement links KUSOM directly with the Nepali labor market.
Nepali businesses and nongovernmental organizations all need professional
managers, and KUSOM's mission is to produce them. This tight linkage with
the emerging and evolving needs of Nepali businesses/organizations means
that both curriculum and pedagogy must be practical. And, indeed, they are.
KUSOM's guiding MBA philosophy is to develop "practicing, professional
managers rather than theorists; [to develop] generalists rather than technicians";
and to instill within all students the values of "entrepreneurial managers" (School
of Management 1998: 2). Curriculum and pedagogy support this approach.
The fact that KUSOM graduates are well placed in Nepali organizations indicates that KUSOM's MBA program meets the needs of the business community and other organizations. The graduates work for various firms, including
banks, finance companies, manufacturing enterprises, trading enterprises, in-

Table 5.1

MBA Curriculum Overview, Katmandu University School of Management

Foundation courses	Financial Accounting
	Macroeconomics
	Managerial Economics
	Managerial Communication
	Data Management
Management core	Operations Management
	Financial Management I
	Financial Management II
	Marketing Management I
	Marketing Management II
	Organizational Behavior
	Human Resource Management
	Business Environment
	Corporate Laws
	Management Information System
Capstone courses	Entrepreneurial Management
	International Business
	Strategic Management
Concentration	Elective courses (4)
Summer project	

ternational agencies, and nongovernmental organizations. Many KUSOM graduates have also established their own enterprises or joined family business. KUSOM has in fact created a market for MBAs in Nepal.

Curriculum

KUSOM's curriculum is modeled on an American MBA (see Table 5.1). As is readily seen, KUSOM requires traditional MBA courses in accounting, economics, management, marketing, and management information systems. Students must also choose a course concentration. Concentrations in finance, marketing, and human resources management are available.

Reflecting innovative, forward thinking course options, students can choose from three additional electives: Total Quality Management (TQM), Econometrics, and Knowledge Management. The TQM course is especially innovative in the context of Nepal. Historically, many Nepali businesses have been run on an intuitive, trial-and-error basis. Large fluctuations in product quality often result. Nepali consumers are skeptical about local products. KUSOM recognized, early on, that if Nepali businesses were to improve their domestic as well as international competitive standing, quality assurance measures would have to be in place. Nepali businesses need TQM, and multinational corporations demand it.

Similarly, KUSOM recognized that Nepal, like many countries, is experiencing an economic shift. Increasingly, computers and information technology are becoming important in the Nepali economy. Knowledge workers are increasingly needed in Katmandu. Thus, the course in Knowledge Management reflects this forward thinking.

Pedagogy

Curriculum innovation would mean nothing if KUSOM's pedagogy had continued to mirror Indian models. Here, two innovations are central: (1) the school's emphasis on action learning across the curriculum and (2) student summer projects. Action learning goes right to the core of what is different about KUSOM. Across the entire curriculum, emphasis is placed on the intensive, practical application of learning. This goal of creating involved, practical, and competent business professionals is expressed both inside and outside the classroom.

In each course, the faculty makes a concerted effort to engage students in their learning. This is done through a variety of pedagogical techniques. On the one hand, Harvard cases are used to focus student learning on critical, complicated business decisions. An integral part of the case method (as is well known) is a combination of team and class discussions, which take place at KUSOM across the curriculum. On the other hand, KUSOM places great emphasis on participative or active learning. The aim of active learning is to transform the student from being a passive recipient of knowledge (as in the lecture-only teaching approach) into an active, engaged individual who assumes responsibility for his or her own learning. In class, small group assignments are common at KUSOM. This not only makes learning alive but also creates a dynamic class environment.

Finally, there are summer projects. KUSOM's MBA curriculum spans two years. The curriculum is divided into four semesters, with a mandatory summer project linking the end of the first year with the beginning of the second. Summer projects serve several purposes: (1) Summer projects allow students to apply the knowledge gained during the MBA's first year in a real world setting. (2) They let students experience firsthand the realities of Nepali businesses. As is often the case in countries with emerging economies, textbook "theories" need adaptation to make them "work" in Nepal. This type of practical, albeit short-term, experience is invaluable in sensitizing students to the real challenges that confront Nepali businesses. (3) Summer projects require students to work in teams. This enables students to develop greater confidence in using this important business skill. (4) Every summer project is written up and formally presented to the business involved. Eventually, each project is catalogued and made available in the KUSOM library. (It should be noted that summer projects are not catalogued until five years after completion. This is done to encourage business participation in the process by reassuring a business that sensitive and confidential information will be protected for five years.)

Local Case Development

One of the greatest challenges in delivering meaningful management education in countries with emerging markets is the issue of case examples. Like most developing countries, Nepal is underrepresented in the world case literature. Culturally and economically, Nepal differs greatly from the countries most often represented in business texts. Students constantly ask how a theory, principle, or case has meaning in the context of Nepal. This is a valid question, and it goes to the heart of one of the greatest challenges for management education in emerging markets—how to balance the desire to give students techniques, tools, and ideas that work effectively in industrialized countries (which thus serve as models of how things *should* work or be done) against the everyday reality that (except for multinational companies) Nepali businesses and organizations often face operational and organizational climates that are very different from the organizations studied.

KUSOM's response is to actively encourage the development of local, Nepal-based cases. The long-term goal is to develop a broad-based case library dealing with the critical issues Nepali businesses face. As noted above, including summer projects in the KUSOM library is a first step toward illustrating the range of problems and solutions that local Nepali businesses confront. In addition, KUSOM encourages all faculty to develop local Nepali-based cases as well. A few local cases have been developed already, yet many more need to be written.

Social Responsibility

As noted in this chapter's discussion of the Nepali economy, corruption is an exceptionally important national and business policy issue. As will be noted in the conclusion, corruption and the political instability created by the Maoist insurgency are probably the greatest external threats to continuing progress in management education. Yet, quite specifically, KUSOM states that one of the MBA's guiding principles is to develop "socially responsible managers who value ethics in business" (School of Management 1998: 6). KUSOM's innovative response to the challenge of ethical leadership is twofold. First, it takes great care in faculty hiring, and second, it has numerous student inter-action sessions with Nepali chief executive officers (CEOs) and executives. Rather than just limiting itself to cases or texts that present various ethical dilemmas and issues, KUSOM hires faculty who specifically believe in right, moral, business conduct. Faculty communicate to students that they have twin responsibilities: to perform well and always to make sound ethical deci-sions. The student's personal career depends on the former; the country's continued development depends on the latter. Additionally, students get to meet, talk with, and hear about business "realities" through interaction ses-sions with CEOs and other business executives. These sessions educate stu-dents on both the challenges businesses face and on the personal dilemmas that individuals can confront. Overall, KUSOM's goal is to acknowledge that Nepali business students are privileged and that with this privilege come responsibilities both to self and to country.

Management Education in Nepal: The Road Ahead

Perhaps the biggest challenge to management education in Nepal is the po-litical instability created by the Maoist rebellion. Without doubt, this insur-rection creates uncertainty for investors and operational instability for every business in the country (Asian Development Bank 2003). The effects of the Maoist revolt trickle down and seep even into the classroom. With the con-stant threat and realization of national strikes (*bandhs*), universities are closed and education is halted. Continuity in learning is disrupted. In a nation that teeters on the brink of chaos, the normalcy of everyday living belies the apprehension that lies just beneath the surface. The Malaysian proverb serves best here: "Just because the water is calm does not mean that there are no crocodiles underneath."

On a smaller scale, Nepal may soon be experiencing market saturation for both MBA and EMBA programs. Nepal is a small country. The 2001 Census estimated the country's total population at 23.21 million. Of that total, 1.1 million live in Katmandu, the primary market for MBA and EMBA pro-grams. While no one knows the actual market size for management educa-tion, one can be assured that it is very small. With real growth averaging about 2.5 percent per annum, expanding and new business formation is rela-tively low. Thus, when new private schools enter the market, competitive pressure is placed on existing institutions. The challenge for schools like KUSOM is to maintain their competitive advantage in an increasingly com-petitive marketplace.

Finally, at the Cancun Ministerial Trade Conference held in September 2003, Nepal's accession to the World Trade Organization (WTO) was approved. This puts Nepal in line to be the WTO's 148th member country. Clearly, competitive pressures on Nepal substantially increase with its entry into the WTO. As a partner in the global trading system, Nepali businesses will now have global opportunities for exports, but they also will face intense pressures to compete. Just as Nepali goods can flow out to world markets, products and services from the world can flow in. Sound strategic management, coupled with a global vision and a sound grounding in financial and operational decision making, become more important than ever. This, in turn, requires managers who can think globally, act locally, and manage effectively. The need for educated, professional managers in all sectors of the Nepali economy is now greater than ever. Management education in Nepal must continue to develop if it is to fulfill this need.

References

Agrawal, G. 1974. *Higher Education for Business in Developing Nations: A Proposed Model for Nepal*. Katmandu: Center for Economic Development and Administration.

Asian Development Bank. 2003. *Economic Outlook 2003: Nepal*. Available at www.adb.org/Documents/Books/ADO/2003/nep.asp (accessed December 2, 2004).

CIA World Factbook. *Country Profile: Nepal*. Available at www.cia.gov/cia/publications/factbook/geos/np.html (accessed December 2, 2004).

Khatiwada, Y. 2002. "Banking Sector Reforms for Nepal: Implications for Corporate Governance." In *Corporate Governance in Nepal*, ed. J. Adams, B. Maskay, and S. Tulandhar, 20–29. Katmandu: Center for Development and Governance.

Kerr, C. 1995. *The Uses of the University*. 4th ed. Cambridge: Harvard University Press.

Neupane, K. 2003. "Pokhara University in Dire Financial Crisis." *Katmandu Post*, May 23. Available at www.nepalnews.com.np/contents/englishdaily/ktmpost/2003/may/may23/local.htm (accessed December 2, 2004).

Ojha, J.C. 1969. "The Planning of Management Education in Nepal." *Nepal Review* (November).

Porter, M.; K. Schwab; and P. Cornelius. 2003. *The Global Competitiveness Report, 2002–2003*. New York: Oxford University Press.

Pradhananga, U.B. 1982. "Management Education in Tribhuvan University." Kathmandu: Research and Management Forum Limited.

School of Management. *M.B.A. Program*. [Brochure]. Katmandu, Nepal. Author United Nations Development Programme. 1998. *Nepal Human Development Report*. Available at www.undp.org.np/publications/nhdr98/Chapter5.pdf (accessed December 2, 2004).

Tribhuvan University. Available at www.tribhuvan-university.edu.np.

World Bank. 2002. *Nepal Development Forum: Economic Update 2002*. Available at http://lnweb18.worldbank.org/SAR/sa.nsf/Attachments/rpt/$File/econnp.doc (accessed December 2, 2004).

————. 2001. *World Development Report: Building Institutions for Markets.* New York: Oxford University Press.

Zivetz, L. 1992. *Private Enterprise and the State in Modern Nepal.* Madras: Oxford University Press.

Part II

Russian Federation

6

Entrepreneurship Training in Postcommunist Europe

Leo Paul Dana

Recently privatized, transitional economies provide a particularly fascinating backdrop for the development of entrepreneurship. In the words of Birzulis, "MBA courses teach their pupils that business is a dicey, dynamic world where anything can happen. But no amount of seminars and lectures can prepare the budding entrepreneur for the surprises awaiting them in the post-communist environment" (2002: 20).

Much has been written about privatization; a survey of empirical studies on privatization was compiled by Megginson and Netter (2001). As well, there is considerable literature about how the pace of privatization affects unemployment (Bolton and Roland 1992; Estrin 1994; Frydman, Rapaczynski, and Earle 1993; Hughes and Hare 1992; Ivy 1996; Murrell 1993; Seibert 1992; Simoneti 1993; Wilson 1992). Where privatization has taken place rapidly, many people have been pushed to self-employment (Meager 1992). Where privatization and downsizing of state-owned enterprises causes mass unemployment, there is often a mismatch between market demand and skills available in the workforce. The workforce needs retraining in skills that are in demand. Certain skills, that are not deemed necessary in the West, can be very useful in a postcommunist economy. Entrepreneurship training can be most rewarding.

In transitional economies, three schools of thought have emerged with regard to entrepreneurship training. One opinion is that entrepreneurship must be taught and encouraged. The second is that entrepreneurship must evolve on its own. The third is that entrepreneurship should be allowed to develop gradually, only as a complement to state-owned firms.

China and Vietnam are examples of countries that have implemented models of gradual transition, tolerating private enterprise as a complement to the centrally planned state sector, but not as a replacement (Dana 1999b, 2002). Kruft and Sofrova (1997) emphasized the gradualism. In China, the government allows some entrepreneurs to function outside the planned sector, while other aspects of the economy remain under state control; the rich literature includes Beamish (1993), Chau (1995), Chow, Clement, and Tsang (1995), Dana (1998, 1999a, 2002), Dandridge and Flynn (1988), Fan, Chen, and Kirby (1996), Lombardo (1995), McMillan and Naughton (1992), Overholt (1993), Peng (2000), Shirk (1993), Siu and Kirby (1995), Wei (2001), and Williams and Li (1993). Similarly, Vietnam introduced some free enterprise policies without rejecting socialism, as discussed by Dana (1994a, 1994b, 2002), Litvack and Rondinelli (1999), Peng (2000), Ronnås (1996), and Tan and Lim (1993); the result is gradual transition involving a complementarity between state firms operating under a system of centralization and the small business sector operating independently.

This chapter reports findings of the author's recent study of entrepreneurship training across a selection of East European nations. The research took place in 2003. Methodology included open-ended interviews with consultants, entrepreneurs, and government officials. Interviews typically lasted between two and three hours. Some respondents asked to be paid. Content validity was enhanced with triangulation (Patton 1982, 1987, 1990).

Albania

The Women's Center, in Tirana, is an important organization that encourages the participation of women in entrepreneurship. Recognizing the need for networking (Aldrich, Rosen, and Woodward 1987; Aldrich and Zimmer 1986; Birley 1985), the Women's Center provides such opportunities as well as providing documentation, information, assistance, training, and access to experts and specialists. Courses offered by the Women's Center include: Start Your Business and Improve Your Business. The Albanian Economic Development Agency also provides individuals with basic knowledge. Yet, formal entrepreneurship training, in Albania, is in its infancy stage.

Belarus

With funding from the United States, the Belarus Small-Scale Privatization Project was launched in 1993. This project introduced a mechanism for auction-based privatization, along with amendments to the Privatization Law and the State Privatization Program. This resulted in the privatization of over 1,000 enterprises. A problem, however, is that this did not come with a training package. Managers of privatized firms are often the same people who excelled in a communist economy, but who have little training about doing business in a market-driven environment. The government has since requested support from the United Nations Development Programme (UNDP). Fighting growing poverty through small and medium-scale enterprises is an important area of UNDP support, and women in this country have been targeted for entrepreneurship training.

Novikova, Petrovskaia, and Daniltchenko (1999) identified the following obstacles to small business development in Belarus: the lack of government stimulation; the lack of financing; the lack of subsidies; the lack of loans; and the lack of credits. In addition, I would argue that the lack of entrepreneurship training has been a problem.

Bosnia and Herzegovina

Civil war interrupted the process of privatization in Bosnia and Herzegovina, and most of the formerly state-owned industry was damaged during interethnic fighting. Much entrepreneurship here takes place in the parallel economy. O'Driscoll, Holmes, and Kirkpatrick (2001) reported that estimates place the level of black market activity at 40 percent to 60 percent; covert activities include the trafficking of stolen cars and export of prostitutes.

Entrepreneurs interviewed by the author suggested that the state is not doing as much as other countries to promote legitimate value-adding entrepreneurship here. In fact, much entrepreneurship promotion is organized and paid for by external sources. During 2002, the UNDP made possible a Youth Enterprise Program in the Brcko District. This is focused on encouraging entrepreneurship among people who are between the ages of eighteen and thirty. Three components provide training: business mentoring, advisory services, and microcredit finance. The training and business advisory services are free of charge. The mentoring and financing operate on a cost recovery basis.

In December 2002, the Canadian Center for Entrepreneurship and Development cohosted a ten-day entrepreneur-training course teaching women to become entrepreneurship trainers. The Swiss Development Corporation contributed funding. A second component was organized to train trainers in 2003, initiated by a multidonor initiative managed by the Small and Medium Enterprise Department of the World Bank Group and the International Finance Corporation. CARE International also supports self-employment and job creation by small and medium enterprises through financial assistance.

Estonia

As discussed by Blawatt (1995), the Estonian government believes that the entrepreneur and a supportive environment are the keys to a successful economy. A Law on State Aid to Enterprises came into effect in 1994, providing government funds to small and medium enterprises in Estonia; to qualify for financial assistance, a firm had to have fewer than eighty employees, and its turnover could not exceed EEK15 million. This law is no longer in force. Instead, the Law of Competition regulates state aid to enterprises, and such aid to small and medium enterprises in Estonia is limited to training courses and consulting support.

In 1995, the Nordic Council of Ministers supported an Export Development Program for Estonian companies. This was a joint effort that included the participation of the Helsinki School of Economics and the Trade Council of Iceland, as well as local talent. After the training sessions, each participant was required to develop an export-marketing plan. The Estonian Chamber of Commerce and Industry decided to become involved in subsequent programs.

A large variety of export training and consulting options are offered by the Estonian Chamber of Commerce and Industry, by the Estonian Trade Council, by universities, and by training enterprises. Enterprise Estonia is a foundation that provides business training, counseling, and start-up grants to new ventures; it also offers grants to growing small and medium enterprises interested in staff training and research and development.

Hungary

A state initiative launched in 1990, the Hungarian Foundation for Enterprise Promotion fosters the establishment of small and medium enterprises and helps existing ones to stay profitable. The mission of the foundation is to provide long-term training for prospective and active entrepreneurs, thus promoting the professional and market-related development of small and medium enterprises. In 1991, the Foundation began setting up rural enterprise development centers, and a national network was soon assisting entrepreneurs in all counties. There are now about 100 contact points for entrepreneurs.

The chambers of commerce in Hungary are also promoting entrepreneurship. According to Hungarian law, the role of chambers of commerce includes vocational training and business development.

Lithuania

Lithuania has been very successful in creating an environment that supports local entrepreneurs. Under the authority of the Ministry of Economy, the

Lithuanian Development Agency for Small and Medium Enterprises was established in 1996. Its purpose is to stimulate the start-up rate of Lithuanian small and medium enterprises; to increase their competitiveness and their survival rate; to increase the level of information technology (IT) literacy among them; and to promote job creation.

The Lithuanian Development Agency for Small and Medium Enterprises developed a Web site (www.svv.lt) that has been serving as an active portal of information for entrepreneurs. Topics include setting up a business, funding opportunities, investment, labor relations, exporting, importing, and customs, and other taxes.

A program called the Formation of a Favorable Service Infrastructure for Small and Medium Businesses implements development projects to improve the skills of first-time entrepreneurs. Supported by the government, the program also provides entrepreneurs accessibility to information.

The Law on Small and Medium Business Development came into effect in 2003. This legislation redefined a medium enterprise as an independent firm with fewer than 250 employees and an annual income not exceeding LTL138 million, or total assets with a book value not exceeding LTL93 million. As well, a small enterprise was redefined as an independent firm with fewer than 50 employees and an annual income not exceeding LTL24 million, or the book value of its assets not exceeding LTL17 million. The amendment redefined a microenterprise as an independent firm with fewer than 10 employees and an annual income not exceeding LTL7 million, or the book value of its assets not exceeding LTL5 million. The legislation provides small and medium enterprises with financial assistance, including tax relief, access to loans on favorable terms, provision of guarantees, credit insurance, reimbursement of certain cash outlays, and subsidies for job creation. In addition, it provides for advisory services, training, and the establishment of business centers and incubators.

The Former Yugoslav Republic of Macedonia

Citing the fact that the National Enterprise Promotion Agency failed to obtain support from various institutions and ministries, the state proposed the establishment of an Entrepreneurship Support Coordinative Council, consisting of representatives from a variety of relevant ministries, agencies, banks, and trade unions. The state also suggested that a central Entrepreneurship Agency would be more effective than was the National Enterprise Promotion Agency. The new program involves financial and other support. It focuses on four areas: the creation of institutional infrastructure for the promotion of entrepreneurship; the establishment of an economic environment favorable for the start-ups of new ventures; entrepreneurship promotion; and financial support. Interviewees told the author that entrepreneurship training was "not necessary here, because entrepreneurs already know what to do."

As noted by the Ministry of Economy in 2002, the promotion of entrepreneurship has been less than adequate. Those who have lived abroad often become successful entrepreneurs, but these represent a minority of Macedonians. Therefore, it could be beneficial to establish large-scale work-abroad/sojourn programs in this country, as have been organized by Israeli organizations in Romania. Encouraging more Macedonians to sojourn abroad could thus enable more individuals to accumulate working capital, and, more important, to experience a free enterprise market-oriented economy. This may facilitate the acquisition of the skills necessary in a small business.

Moldova

In 1997, business people met in Moldova's capital city, Chişinău, to discuss a variety of issues related to small business; this resulted in the establishment of the Small Business Association of Moldova, with branches across the country. Here, entrepreneurs learn from one another.

In January 2002, BIZPRO Moldova, a project of economic growth through small and medium enterprise development, launched the Entrepreneurs Hotline Program, funded by the United States Agency for International Development (USAID). This involved the establishment of hotlines, in cooperation with business associations in Balti, Cahul, and Chişinău. From January 15 until July 1, hotline operators tutored 2,600 entrepreneurs, half of whom were sole proprietors, while four-fifths of the others represented microenterprises. Almost a quarter of the calls pertained to tax regulations. A fifth of the calls referred to business registration and the launch of new ventures.

Today, several organizations promote entrepreneurship in Moldova. The Microfinancing Alliance of Moldova, for example, prepares educational materials of use to entrepreneurs. Small numbers of formal sector entrepreneurs operate in all the major centers. Their businesses, however, are not always popular, as their prices are often high. In Balti, for instance, there is a small, privately owned grocery called Pet Shop (nothing to do with pets); on any given day, business is slower than one might expect, considering that there are few food stores in Balti, which is a major metropolitan area of Moldova. Not surprisingly, formal entrepreneurship, as it is known in the West, is not very common in this country; individuals often lack the enterprise, culture, and education required to become entrepreneurs in the formal sector.

Poland

The Polish Craft and Small Business Association was established before World War II and has been active ever since then. The association includes 484 guilds as well as 26 regional chambers of crafts and small and medium enterprises. Its mandate includes vocational training.

On January 1, 1990, Poland embarked on its Big Bang shock therapy model of transition as many price and monetary restrictions were abandoned. As prices rose by 80 percent that month, Crook described the reforms as "frighteningly bold" (1990: 4). The Balcerowicz Plan was aimed at stabilizing the economy while creating a free market. Reform liberalized prices, enacted comprehensive privatization measures, and created the Ministry for Ownership Changes, charged with overseeing the process of privatization. The Ministry for Ownership Changes was given a very specific mandate, including the launch of training courses.

The Polish Agency for Enterprise Development was launched on January 1, 2001, as the successor to the Polish Foundation for Promotion and Development of Small and Medium Enterprises. The mission of this agency, which is financed by the state budget, is to participate in the implementation of economic development programs with an emphasis on supporting small and medium enterprises. The agency provides advisory services to entrepreneurs and provides them with grants for managerial training. The agency collects information that is of possible use to entrepreneurs, administers databases, and conducts analyses. It also prepares and publishes documentation in accordance with its mandate to disseminate knowledge and to facilitate access to information.

Russia

As was the case elsewhere across the Soviet Union, perestroika and glasnost during the 1980s brought a variety of changes to Russia. Khamidulin reported, "Perestroika offers more opportunities for people everywhere" (1988: 5). Perestroika even provided opportunities in the covert sector. In 1988, several publications introduced the word "mafia" into Russian to describe the organized crime networks involved in embezzlement, extortion, bribery, black-market profiteering, and drug trafficking (Keller 1988).

In contrast to the situation in Poland, where state enterprises were restructured while still in state hands, business establishments in Russia were seeing little restructuring; this was true even among privatized firms as subsidies continued distorting the Russian economy (Belyanova and Rozinsky 1995). Boycko and Shleifer (1994) explained that most enterprises were being managed by preprivatization teams who lacked the interest to initiate significant changes. Aoki (1995) confirmed that privatized firms were doing as little restructuring as was the case among state-owned enterprises. Vamosi summarized the situation: "In other words, the same administrative technology, the same physical frames and the same 'old' culture prevail!" (2003: 195).

With finance from the Russian Federal Science and Technology budget, in 1994 Russia established the Fund for Assistance to Small Innovative Enterprises. Yet, the lack of managerial competence appears to have limited the growth of such enterprises. Zhuplev and colleagues (1998) found that although network skills were important for Russian entrepreneurs, people gave little value to people skills; the study concluded that Russia was making far less progress than Kazakhstan in developing entrepreneurship.

Radaev (1993) reported that the typical small-scale businessman in Russia is an educated man, often with an engineering or technical background. Yet, Hisrich and Gratchev (1995) found that despite their technical education, these people are often lacking business skills.

An empirical study by Robinson and colleagues (2001) identified mindset as a source of problems challenging the small business sector.

"Gorbachev observed that to achieve glasnost and perestroika, Russian culture would have to change" (Behrman and Rondinelli 1999: 10). Almost two decades since the launch of perestroika, a fact that has become evident in Russia is that structural changes to the economy are relatively easy to orchestrate when compared to changes in culture and human nature, that is, the attitudes that comprise paradigms regarding salient aspects of life. The processes involved in changing one's mindset differ significantly from the decrees used by the Russian president to initiate and regulate changes to the market economy.

In the case of Russia, the greatest difficulty in converting from a centralized economy to a free-market economy has *not* been the lack of technical knowledge of designing, engineering, and building products. Russia has a highly educated workforce with a much higher proportion of college-educated people per capita than Western countries. Western travelers to the country can easily encounter numerous unemployed or underemployed engineers. A lack of experience with the firm-type economy, as it works in the West, is an important barrier in the development of enterprising culture across Russia. There is, admittedly, a lag in the retraining of older managers in the practical application of business skills and knowledge in the emerging new market economy.

Serbia and Montenegro

The State Union of Serbia and Montenegro is a loose confederation, and entrepreneurship promotion here is conducted at the local level. Montenegro and Serbia have different approaches to entrepreneurship issues.

Montenegro's 2003 Privatization Plan emphasized the protection of ownership rights, economic freedom, and the national treatment of foreigners; this has had an amazing impact. The privatization process has already brought significant foreign investments to Montenegro, and the benefits are not limited to inflow of new capital; investors are introducing new technologies, implementing training programs for employees, and contributing to the creation of a new business environment. A large portion of the revenues from privatization are used for financing new small and medium enterprise loan programs.

The Serbian strategic plan for the period 2003 to 2008 calls for the creation of an environment favorable to entrepreneurs and to small and medium enterprises. The body in charge of economic policy for the development of small and medium enterprises is the Ministry of Economy and Privatization. This ministry has two sectors: one is for the development of small and medium enterprises and the other for private entrepreneurship. The primary player in implementing the strategy for the development of small and medium enterprises and entrepreneurship during the period from 2003 to 2008 is the Agency for the Development of Small and Medium Enterprises and Entrepreneurship in Belgrade. Founded in 2001, the mission of this agency is to aid, advise, assist, and protect the development and interests of the small and medium enterprise sector.

Other participants in the strategy for the development of small and medium enterprises and entrepreneurship during the period from 2003 to 2008 include: the Ministry of Agriculture and Waterpower Engineering; the Ministry of Economic Relations with Foreign Countries; the Ministry of Education and Sport; the Ministry of Finance and Economy; the Ministry of Labor and Employment; the Ministry of Science, Technology, and Development; the Ministry of State Administration and Local Self-Government; and the Ministry of Trade, Tourism, and Services.

Slovakia

On September 27, 2000, Slovakia approved several guarantee and credit programs to assist small and medium enterprises. Simultaneously, the state approved the following programs to promote small and medium enterprises up to the year 2005: The Education and Training Program for Small and Medium Enterprises and the Education, Training, and Advice Program for Selected Groups of Potential and Start-up Entrepreneurs.

Slovenia

As pointed out by Glas (1998), the development of small and medium enterprises in Slovenia is synonymous with entrepreneurship promotion. The

National Employment Office developed two streams of entrepreneurship assistance. One option involved a program of training, coaching, and financial assistance, while the alternative was limited to financial assistance only.

Ukraine

In 1992, the government of Ukraine invited the International Finance Corporation to launch a small-scale privatization project. Funded by USAID, this project eventually helped privatize over 50,000 firms across Ukraine. There were delays, however, as the privatization of small enterprises, planned for 1993, did not materialize. The privatization of small enterprises finally began in 1994. With financing from the United Kingdom's Know How Fund, as well as from USAID, the International Finance Corporation managed a business development project with centers across Ukraine assisting small firms with training and information.

Nevertheless, there is still a lack of entrepreneurship trainers, as incentives to teach here have been few. Consider a university professor's monthly income in recent years: the equivalent of about $100. After paying rent, heat, and light, as well as public transportation, little remains for food and clothing. At the end of some months, the government claimed not to have money to pay salaries, and professors had to survive without pay.

Implications for Educators

Where entrepreneurial spirit exists, new venture programs may further enhance the environment for entrepreneurship, as is the case in the United States. However, in a transitional society with little experience of legitimate entrepreneurship, education should first focus on encouraging an entrepreneurship-friendly ideology. Where a vibrant entrepreneurial class is absent, this absence may be due to the public policy environment or to the lack of social norms that affect propensity for entrepreneurship and the nature of enterprise. Štulhofer discussed the distrust of the state, distrust of banks, and distrust of legal institutions, especially among the elderly (1999).

Due to the rationalization of jobs during transition, and in the absence of appropriate retraining, many people have become self-employed, often in informal or covert activities. After decades of central planning that considered entrepreneurship to be criminal, the concepts underlying entrepreneurship are not fully understood, and there is confusion as legitimate entrepreneurship is confused with illegal transactions. It would be beneficial, therefore, for educators to promote acceptance of entrepreneurship as a legitimate value-adding activity. As was stated by Child and Czeglédy, "In the context of something as fundamental as the transformation of Eastern Europe, managerial learning extends to the redefinition of the tasks themselves and of the goals which they reflect" (1996: 176.)

A problem appears to be that much education in transitional economies has focused on managerial content and methods, while trainees might expect to be told what procedures to follow (Kenny and Trick 1995). Emphasis should be placed on values as well as technical content. In the absence of the values related to sustainable long-term entrepreneurship—such as asceticism, frugality, thrift, and work ethic (Weber 1904–5)—managerial skills are not being put to optimal use.

Across Eastern Europe, there is often a mismatch between market demand and skills available in the workforce. The workforce needs retraining in skills that are in demand. Consequently, the technical content of courses needs to be adapted to changes in the economy. As the economy of a nation becomes increasingly complex, marketing functions will mature and become more specialized. Training will be required to help managers solve new problems of planning, distribution, and transportation. A difficulty, however, is that educational initiatives are fragmented.

References

Aldrich, H.E.; B. Rosen; and W. Woodward. 1987. "The Impact of Social Networks on Business Foundings and Profit in a Longitudinal Study." *Frontiers of Entrepreneurship Research* (Babson Park, MA: Babson College): 154–68.

Aldrich, H.E., and C. Zimmer. 1986. "Entrepreneurship Through Social Networks." In *The Art and Science of Entrepreneurship*, ed. D.L. Sexton and R.W. Smilor, 3–24. Cambridge, MA: Ballinger.

Aoki, M. 1995. "Controlling Insider Control: Issues of Corporate Governance in Transition Economies." In *Corporate Governance in Transitional Economies*, ed. Masahiko Aoki and Hyung-Ki Kim, 3–29. Washington, DC: World Bank.

Beamish, P. 1993. "The Characteristics of Joint Ventures in the People's Republic of China." *Journal of International Marketing* 1, no. 2: 29–48.

Behrman, J.N., and D.A. Rondinelli. 1999. "The Transition to Market-oriented Economies in Central and Eastern Europe: Lessons for Private Enterprise Development." *Global Focus* 11, no. 4: 1–13.

Belyanova, E., and I. Rozinsky. 1995. "Evolution of Commercial Banking in Russia and the Implications for Corporate Governance." In *Corporate Governance in Transitional Economies*, ed. Masahiko Aoki and Hyung-Ki Kim, 185–214. Washington, DC: World Bank.

Birley, S. 1985. "The Role of Networks in the Entrepreneurial Process." *Journal of Business Venturing* 1: 107–18.

Birzulis, P. 2002. "Go Directly to Sleaze, Do Not Pass Morality." *Baltic Times* 7, no. 300 (March 28): 20.

Blawatt, K.R. 1995. "Entrepreneurship in Estonia: Profiles of Entrepreneurs." *Journal of Small Business Management* 3, no. 2 (April): 74–79.

Bolton, P., and G. Roland. 1992. "Privatization in Central and Eastern Europe." *Economic Policy* 15 (October): 276–309.

Boycko, M., and A. Shleifer. 1994. "What's Next? Strategies for Enterprise Restructuring in Russia." *Transition* 5 (November–December): 8–9.

Chau, S.S. 1995. "The Development of China's Private Entrepreneurship." *Journal of Enterprising Culture* 3, no. 3 (September): 261–70.

Child, J., and A.P. Czeglédy. 1996. "Managerial Learning in the Transformation of Eastern Europe: Some Key Issues." *Organization Studies* 17, no. 2: 167–79.

Chow, K.W. W.K. Clement, and E. Tsang. 1995. "Entrepreneurs in China: Development, Functions and Problems." *International Small Business Journal* 1: 63–77.

Crook, C. 1990. "A Survey of Perestroika." *Economist*, April 28: 1–24.

Dana, L.P. 1994a. "A Marxist Mini-Dragon? Entrepreneurship in Today's Vietnam." *Journal of Small Business Management* 32, no. 2 (April): 95–102.

———. 1994b. "Economic Reform in the New Vietnam." *Current Affairs* 70, no. 11 (May) (University of Sydney, Australia): 19–25.

———. 1998. "Small Business in Xinjiang." *Asian Journal of Business and Information Systems* 3, no. 1: 123–36.

———. 1999a. "Entrepreneurship as a Supplement in the People's Republic of China." *Journal of Small Business Management* 37, no. 3 (July): 76–80.

———. 1999b. *Entrepreneurship in Pacific Asia: Past, Present and Future.* Singapore, London, and Hong Kong: World Scientific.

———. 2002. *When Economies Change Paths: Models of Transition in China, the Central Asian Republics, Myanmar, and the Nations of Former Indochine Française.* Singapore, London, and Hong Kong: World Scientific.

Dandridge, T.C., and D.M. Flynn. 1988. "Entrepreneurship: Environmental Forces Which Are Creating Opportunities in China." *International Small Business Journal* 6, no. 3: 34–41.

Estrin, S. 1994. "Privatization in the Transitional Economies of Central and Eastern Europe: Issues and Progress." *Business Strategy Review* 5, no. 4: 81–96

Fan, Y.; N. Chen; and D. Kirby. 1996. "Chinese Peasant Entrepreneurs: An Examination of Township and Village Enterprises in Rural China." *Journal of Small Business Management* 34, no. 4 (October): 72–76.

Frydman, R.; A. Rapaczynski; and J.S. Earle, eds. 1993. *The Privatization Process in Central Europe.* Budapest: Central European University Press.

Glas, M. 1998. "Eastern Europe: Slovenia." In *Entrepreneurship—An International Perspective,* ed. A.J. Morrison, 108–24. Oxford: Heinemann.

Hisrich, R.D., and M.V. Gratchev. 1995. "The Russian Entrepreneur: Characteristics and Prescriptions for Success." *Journal of Managerial Psychology* 10: 3–9.

Hughes, G., and P. Hare. 1992. "Industrial Restructuring in Eastern Europe." *European Economic Review* 36: 670–76.

Ivy, R.L. 1996. "Small Scale Entrepreneurs and Private Sector Development in the Slovak Republic." *Journal of Small Business Management* 34, no. 4 (October): 77–83.

Keller, B. 1988. "In the New Russia, New Greed: Growing Private Sector Brings Crime and Corruption." *International Herald Tribune,* July 26.

Kenny, B., and B. Trick. 1995. "Reform and Management Education: A Case from the Czech Republic." *Journal of East-West Business* 1, no. 1: 69–96.

Khamidulin, E. 1988. "It's Only the Beginning." *Moscow News* 27, no. 3327 (July 3): 5.

Kruft, A.T., and A. Sofrova, A. 1997. "The Need for Intermediate Support Structures for Entrepreneurship in Transitional Economies." *Journal of Enterprising Culture* 5, no. 1 (March): 13–26.

Lombardo, G.A. 1995. "Chinese Entrepreneurs: Strategic Adaptation in a Transitional Economy." *Journal of Enterprising Culture* 3, no. 3 (September): 277–92.

Litvack, J.I., and D.A. Rondinelli, eds. 1999. *Market Reform in Vietnam: Building Institutions for Development.* Westport, CT: Quorum.

McMillan, J., and B. Naughton. 1992. "How to Reform a Planned Economy: Lessons from China." *Oxford Review of Economic Policy* 8: 130–42.

Meager, N. 1992. "The Fall and Rise of Self-employment (Again): A Comment on Bögenhold and Staber." *Work, Employment and Society* 6, no. 1 (March): 127–34.

Megginson, W.L., and J.M. Netter. 2001. "From State to Market: A Survey of Empirical Studies on Privatization." *Journal of Economic Literature* 39, no. 2: 321–89.

Murrell, P. 1993. "Privatization's Harms: Economics in Eastern Europe." *Current* 349: 34–39.

Novikova, S.I.; L.M. Petrovskaia; and A.V. Daniltchenko. 1999. "Analysis of Small Business Development in the Countries in Transition: A Case of Belarus." Paper presented at the International Conference of the International Council for Small Business, Naples.

O'Driscoll, G.P.; K.R. Holmes; and M. Kirkpatrick. 2001. *2001 Index of Economic Freedom.* Washington, DC: Heritage Foundation and New York: *Wall Street Journal.*

Overholt, W.H. 1993. *The Rise of China: How Economic Reform Is Creating a New Superpower.* New York: W.W. Norton.

Patton, M.Q. 1982. "Qualitative Methods and Approaches: What Are They?" In *Qualitative Methods for Institutional Research,* ed. E. Kuhns and S.V. Martorana, 3–16. San Francisco: Jossey-Bass.

———. 1987. *How to Use Qualitative Methods in Evaluation.* Newbury Park, CA: Sage.

———. 1990. *Qualitative Evaluation and Research Methods.* Newbury Park, CA: Sage.

Peng, M.W. 2000. *Business Strategies in Transition Economies.* Thousand Oaks, CA: Sage.

Radaev, V. 1993. "Emerging Russian Entrepreneurship: As Viewed by the Experts." *Economic and Industrial Democracy* 14: 55–77.

Robinson, P.B.; A.U. Ahmed; L.P. Dana; G.R. Latfullin; and V. Smirnova. 2001. "Towards Entrepreneurship and Innovation in Russia." *International Journal of Entrepreneurship and Innovation Management* 1, no. 2: 230–40.

Ronnås, P. 1996. "Private Entrepreneurship in the Nascent Market Economy of Vietnam." In *Reforming Asian Socialism: The Growth of Market Institutions,* ed. J. McMillan and B. Naughton. Ann Arbor: University of Michigan Press.

Seibert, H., ed. 1992. *Privatization.* Tübingen: Mohr.

Shirk, S. 1993. *The Political Logic of Economic Reform in China.* Berkeley: University of California Press.

Simoneti, M. 1993. "A Comparative Review of Privatization Strategies in Four Former Socialist Countries." *Europe-Asia Studies* 45: 79–102.

Siu, W.S., and D.A. Kirby. 1995. "Marketing in Chinese Small Business: Tentative Theory." *Journal of Enterprising Culture* 3, no. 3 (September): 309–42.

Štulhofer, A. 1999. "Between Opportunism and Distrust: Socio-cultural Aspects of the Underground Economy in Croatia." In *Underground Economies in Transition:*

Unrecorded Activity, Tax, Corruption and Organized Crime, ed. E.L. Feige and K. Ott, 43–63. Aldershot, UK: Ashgate.

Tan, C.L., and T.S. Lim. 1993. *Vietnam: Business & Investment Opportunities*. Singapore: Cassia.

Vamosi, T. 2003. "The Role of Management Accounting in a Company in Transition from Command to Market Economy." *Journal of Small Business and Enterprise Development* 10, no. 2: 194–209.

Weber, M. 1904–5. *Die protestantische Ethik und der Geist des Kapitalismus*. Archiv fur Sozialwissenschaft und Sozialpolitik (20–21); translated in 1930 by Talcott Parsons, *The Protestant Ethic and the Spirit of Capitalism*. New York: George Allen and Unwin.

Wei, L. 2001. "Incentive Systems for Technical Change: The Chinese System in Transition." *International Journal of Entrepreneurship & Innovation Management* 1, no. 2: 157–77.

Williams, E.E., and J. Li. 1993. "Rural Entrepreneurship in the People's Republic of China." *Entrepreneurship, Innovation, and Change* 2, no. 1: 41–54.

Wilson, P. 1992. "Czechoslovakia: The Pain of Divorce." *New York Review of Books* 39: 69–75.

Zhuplev, A.V.; F. Kiesner; A.B. Kozhakmetov; T.W. Liang; and A. Konkov. 1998. "Traits of Successful Business Owners: A Comparative Study of Entrepreneurs in Singapore, the USA, Russia and Kazakhstan." *Journal of Enterprising Culture* 6, no. 3: 257–68.

7

Recent Developments in Accounting Education in Russia

Galina G. Preobragenskaya
and Robert W. McGee

Accounting has been going through rapid changes in Russia ever since the Russian Finance Ministry decided to replace the country's centrally planned accounting system with a market-based system in the early 1990s. A whole generation of accounting practitioners had to change to a new system they knew nothing about—1.5 million, according to one estimate (Smirnova, Sokolov, and Emmanuel 1995). There were no textbooks or educational materials available in the Russian language. There were no teachers to teach the new system. Universities had to start teaching the new system to a new generation of students, but their professors had never studied the new system they were being asked to teach.

A decade has passed since the changes were initiated. There are now some accounting materials available in the Russian language that practitioners, students, and professors can refer to, but the quantity and quality of these publications leave something to be desired. Some accounting practitioners have learned the new rules while others have not. Some professors are now teaching International Financial Reporting Standards to their students while others continue to teach the old accounting system they learned decades ago as students. In short, the movement to reform accounting education has been a mixed success. Although progress has been made in the past decade, much work remains to be done. This article focuses on university accounting education in Russia.

Review of the Literature

Much has been written about accounting reform in transition economies in general (Wallace 1993) and about Central and East European countries in particular (Richard 1998; Kemp and Alexander 1996; Garrod and McLeay 1996; Jermakowicz and Rinke 1996; Rolfe and Doupnik 1995). Some articles and book chapters have focused on accounting reform in specific East European countries and former Soviet republics, including Armenia (McGee 1999a, 1999b), Belarus (Pankov 1998; Sucher and Kemp 1998), the Czech and Slovak Republics (Zelenka, Seal, and Sucher 1996; Seal, Sucher, and Zelenka 1995), Hungary (Borda and McLeay 1996; Boross et al. 1995), Lithuania (Mackevicius, Aliukonis, and Bailey 1996), Poland (Adams and McMillan 1997; Krzywda, Bailey, and Schroeder 1995, 1996), Romania (Roberts 2001; King, Beattie, and Cristescu 2001), Slovenia (Turk and Garrod 1996) and Uzbekistan (Crallan 1997).

Several studies have been made of accounting reform in Russia. Enthoven and colleagues (1998) wrote a book covering accounting, auditing, and taxation in Russia. Enthoven (1992, 1999) has also written about accounting reform in Russia in general. Shama and McMahan (1990) discussed how perestroika was likely to change the nature of accounting in Eastern Europe and the former Soviet Union. Preobragenskaya and McGee (2003) wrote of recent changes in auditing. Ramcharran (2000) wrote about the need for accounting harmonization regarding Russian banks. The International Center for Accounting Reform in Moscow has published a number of studies on accounting reform in Russia, including *Accounting Reform Recommendations* (2000), and also has a newsletter on the topic.

Most studies have discussed the transformation process in transition economies or the adoption and implementation of market-based financial reporting rules. However, a few authors have written specifically about accounting education in transition economies. Lin and Deng (1992) review the history and the then current situation of accounting education in China and make suggestions for the development and reform of Chinese accounting education. However, their study is more than ten years old, and much has changed in Chinese accounting education since then. Chan and Rotenberg (1999) provide more recent information. However, their article is concerned mostly with other aspects of Chinese accounting and only touches on accounting education in China. The International Federation of Accountants (IFAC) published a study paper (IFAC 2000) on accounting education in developing countries and published guidelines for implementation of IFAC educational standards (2001). These IFAC publications have been used to provide guidance to educational leaders in several transition economies.

A few studies have addressed accounting education in Eastern Europe and the former Soviet republics. McGee has studied accounting education reform in Armenia (2003a) as well as in Bosnia and Herzegovina (2003b). Enthoven and colleagues (1998) devote a short chapter to accounting education in Russia in their book on accounting, auditing, and taxation in Russia. However, their study is mostly an overview and was published in 1998. Much has changed since then.

Smirnova, Sokolov, and Emanuel (1995) have published a more comprehensive study of Russian accounting education, which provides a good summary of the state of accounting education shortly after the transition process began. Kobrak (1991) discusses the rapid increase in demand for Western accounting textbooks after the Russian Ministry of Finance decided to adopt International Accounting Standards (IAS) in the early 1990s. Other articles discuss some of the weaknesses in Russian accounting education (Anonymous 1994), the benefits to be gained by educational exchange programs (Coyle and Platonov 1998), and certified investment management analyst certification (Anonymous 2001).

Methodology

After reviewing the literature on accounting reform in transition economies and accounting education in Eastern Europe and the former Soviet republics, the authors developed a tentative list of questions to ask Russian accounting educators. A sample of accounting educators representing state universities and the private sector was then selected and contacted. Interviews were scheduled and held during the summer of 2003 in Moscow, St. Petersburg, and elsewhere. Interviews were held at the following organizations:

- Deloitte & Touche, Moscow office [www.deloitte.com]
- KPMG, Moscow office [www.kpmg.ru]
- KPMG, St. Petersburg office [www.kpmg.ru]
- PricewaterhouseCoopers, Moscow office [www.pwcglobal.com/ru]
- Ajour, a Russian auditing and consulting firm, Moscow [www.ajour.ru]
- PKF (MDK), a Russian auditing and consulting firm, St. Petersburg office [www.mcd-pkf.com]
- Independent Directors Association, Moscow [www.nand.ru]
- MDM Group, Moscow [www.mdmgroup.ru]
- St. Petersburg State Polytechnic University [www.spbstu.ru]
- St. Petersburg State Railway University (a.k.a. Petersburg State Transport University) [www.pgups.ru]
- Timiryazev Agricultural Academy, Moscow [www.timacad.ru]

- Hock Accountancy Training, Moscow office [www.hocktraining.com]
- State University of Omsk [www.omsu.omskreg.ru]
- Kazan State Finance Economic Institute [www.ksfei.ru]

Although many of the interviews were held in Russia's cultural capital (St. Petersburg) and political capital (Moscow), the authors did not want to limit the information-gathering process to the two most economically advanced cities in Russia because doing so might result in a biased sample, so some interviews were conducted in more typical Russian cities (Omsk and Kazan) as well. This turned out to be a good decision, since accounting education, the level of accounting sophistication, and the attitude toward the need for accounting proved to be different once one leaves Russia's two main cities.

University Education

The number of Russian universities that teach accounting students has increased in the past ten years. Many universities that never before offered accounting courses are offering full educational programs in accounting. From Table 7.1, it can be seen that 26.7 percent of the universities in Russia now teach accounting. This percentage may not seem very high by American standards since, in America, practically all universities offer accounting courses. But this percentage is much higher now in Russia than it was ten years ago, and it is likely to increase even more in the years to come.

Table 7.1 includes data from four Russian cities and Russia as a whole. Moscow and St. Petersburg are included because they are the two main cities in Russia. But they are not typical. That is why the authors decided to also include two more typical Russian cities—Omsk and Kazan—in the table. Each of these typical Russian cities has populations greater than 1 million. In this chapter they represent the rest of Russia. One reason Omsk was chosen is because it is the home city of one of the authors, which made it a convenient place to conduct interviews. Kazan was chosen because it is a typical Russian city and also because one of the authors had to be in Kazan on business, which made it convenient to conduct interviews.

According to the law on education, only those universities that receive state accreditation for certain educational programs (accredited programs) have a right to issue State Diplomas (certificates of degree). Only 47.2 percent of the Russian universities that offer accounting courses have this accreditation.

The percentage of Russian universities offering accounting courses is lower than the percentage observed for American and Western European universi-

Table 7.1

Russian Universities Offering Accounting, 2002

	Omsk	Kazan	St. Petersburg	Moscow	All Russia
1. Total number of universities	28	27	108	243	1,898
2. Universities offering accounting courses	6	6	25	53	506
3. Percentage of universities offering accounting courses	21.4%	22.2%	23.1%	21.8%	26.6%
4. Universities offering accounting courses that have state accreditation	2	5	10	30	239
5. Percentage of universities offering accounting that are accredited	33.3%	83.3%	40%	56.6%	47.2%

Source: www.edu.ru.

ties, partly because traditionally, Russia has had many institutes devoted to just a few subjects in some specialty area. Usually, the area of specialty did not include accounting. As these institutes began to adopt the name "university" for prestige reasons, they more or less maintained their prior curriculum. If they did not offer accounting courses before the name change, they did not offer accounting courses after the name change either. Furthermore, as was previously mentioned, accounting was not a prestigious or popular major under the Soviet regime. It was only after perestroika and the opening up of the Russian economy to the market system that accounting became popular as well as increasingly important.

Of the 506 universities that offer accounting courses, 174 (34.5%) are private. The rest are state universities. Most of the 174 private universities were founded within the past fifteen years or so, after perestroika started.

University education in Russia is much different than university education in the United States. Whereas in the United States students have a large selection of electives to choose from, Russian accounting students have practically no choice in the courses they take. Once they choose to enroll in the accounting program, almost all courses are mandatory. They have few elective options.

The law on high and postuniversity education establishes the rules for the following higher education programs: bachelor's degree (four years), specialist (five years), and master's degree (six years). At present, less than 10 percent of all Russian universities offer bachelor's and master's degree programs in accounting. The majority of universities offer the five-year specialist program. There are several reasons. For one, the five-year apprenticeship has been widely used in Russia for several decades, and it is the program with which Russian employers are most familiar. Moreover, a student with only a bachelor's degree will not be as marketable as someone who completes a five-year program.

The six-year apprenticeship with the master's degree is not advantageous for universities because university budgets provide only for the five-year program. In most cases, the state will not provide funding for the sixth year, so universities have little economic incentive to offer six-year master's programs. In addition, employers do not place much extra value on the master's degree, so students have little incentive to study for an additional year.

During the course of the interviews, it was discovered that the main reasons why students decide to continue their education for the sixth year are that:

- In the case of getting a postgraduate education, some courses taken as part of the master's program are counted as postgraduate hours;
- Students who plan to work abroad find that having the master's degree makes them more marketable than just the specialist degree; and
- An extra year of study provides an additional delay from the army.

Thus, at Saint Petersburg State Polytechnic University, for example, only 20 percent of their graduates continue studying for the sixth year.

In this chapter we discuss students who major in accounting and who choose accounting as a profession. However, many universities that do not offer an accounting major offer accounting courses to managers, engineers, and others and provide introductory accounting courses to their students. The number of students studying accounting has risen dramatically in recent years. The rate of increase for accounting students is greater than the rate of increase for total students studying in universities, which means that accounting students comprise a larger percentage of the total student population now than was the case a few years ago. Table 7.2 shows that the number of students studying accounting increased by 82.6 percent from 1998 to 2001 as compared to an increase in the general student population of only 43.3 percent.

From Table 7.2 we can also see that, in Russia in 2001, 40.7 percent of students were paying for their education and 66.1 percent of accounting students were paying for their education. It may seem strange that such statistics are even compiled since, in American universities, practically all students pay at least some tuition. But on the other hand, in some West European countries university education is free. In some countries, the government even gives students a stipend for living expenses. That is one reason why students in some West European countries take so long to graduate.

Table 7.2

Growth in the Number of Students Studying Accounting in Russian Universities, 1998–2001

	1998	1999	2000	2001
1. All students in all universities (thousands)	3,347.2	3,728.1	4,270.1	4,797.4
2. Increase compared to prior year with 1998	11.4%	14.5%	12.3%	43.3%
3. Tuition paying students (thousands)	728.7	1021.3	1468.3	1954.6
4. Percentage of students who pay tuition	21.8%	27.4%	34.4%	40.7%
5. Number of accounting students (thousands)	155.1	187.9	241.4	283.2
6. Increase compared to prior year with 1998	21.1%	28.4%	17.3%	82.6%
7. Tuition-paying accounting students (thousands)	69.9	98.8	148.8	187.2
8. Percentage of accounting students who pay tuition	45.1%	52.6%	61.6%	66.1%

Source: www.edu.ru

The situation in Russia is changing. Whereas university education used to be free or almost free, there is now a trend to charge tuition at least to some students. Tuition is especially important for the many private universities that are popping up all over Russia, but it is also important for state universities because the government cannot provide all the funding that universities need to continue operating.

One reason for the increase in the number of students studying accounting is that they are willing and able to pay tuition. This has enabled Russian universities to expand their accounting curriculum, and it is one reason why some universities that formerly did not offer accounting courses are now offering them. One explanation for why the percentage of accounting students paying tuition is higher than the percentage of students in general who pay tuition is because accounting has become a more prestigious profession. Students are more willing to pay for such an education.

An accounting education is also one of the most expensive in Russia. On average it is about US$1,000–1,200 per year, which may seem low by American standards, but for Russia it is a tidy sum. In Omsk, only courses in international business and law are more expensive. Such a segmented tuition policy may seem strange to American educators insofar as American universities charge the same amount per credit hour regardless of which major a student chooses, but in Russia, market forces have more influence on the level of tuition charged.

The Syllabus

In order to discuss the accounting education that Russian students receive, it is necessary to look at the syllabus. In 2000 the Higher Education Ministry approved the State Educational Standard for the specialty "Accounting, Analysis, and Audit," which provides guidelines on preparing specialists for the qualification of "economist." The main provisions of that standard are outlined below. According to the standard, the primary categories of a graduate's professional activities include the following: transaction accounting and analysis; revision; auditing; consulting; controlling; and methodological work. Applicants for entrance to the university need a secondary education or secondary professional education. The Fundamental Educational Program (FEP) includes curriculum, programs of the discipline, and programs for educational and practical training. The program consists of a federal discipline component, a regional (university) component, some disciplines of the students' choice (elective courses), and some additional courses. The course is divided into the following categories:

- General Humanities and Social Economics Disciplines
- General Mathematics and Natural Science Disciplines
- General Professional Disciplines
- Special Disciplines
- Additional Courses

The period of study for the day program of the Fundamental Educational Program is 260 weeks and consists of:

- Theoretical study (including scientific research, practical class training, and exams), 186 weeks
- Practical training (in real companies), 16 weeks
- The final state exam, including work on a diploma project, not less than 11 weeks
- Vacations (including 8 weeks after-diploma vacation), not less than 47 weeks

The maximum load for a student cannot exceed 54 hours per week, including auditorium work time that should not be more than 27 hours per week. Universities are supposed to develop an FEP, using the Standard as the base. Specialization subjects are supposed to provide deep knowledge of certain kinds of businesses such as bank accounting, accounting for nonprofit organizations, accounting for state organization, and so on. Actual control and policies are established by the universities. The weight of grades given for interim results should not be less than 40 percent of the total grade. The remaining 60 percent is for the final examination. The main form of exam is a written test (not less than 70–75% of total tests). The grading scale is set by the university, but for the final grade, scores must be converted into "excellent," "good," "satisfactory," and "unsatisfactory."

Universities have the flexibility to change the weighting of hours among the various categories by 5 percent. The contents of the General Humanities and Social Economics Disciplines category are set by each university, but must include the following:

- Foreign languages—not less than 340 hours
- Physical training—not less than 408 hours
- Russian history and philosophy

At least 50 percent of the full-time professors must have the PhD. The final attestation includes the Diploma Project and the State Exam. Topics of Diplomas are determined by university departments. The State Exam includes questions about accounting, auditing, and analysis. The State Exam is given by an examining board, which includes university representatives, professors from other universities, and local authorities. The head of the board is usually from another university or is a business professional.

Table 7.3 shows the ten subjects to which accounting majors devote the most time and the least time at St. Petersburg State Polytechnic University.

From Table 7.3, it can be seen that several of the subjects having the least amount of time devoted to them are accounting. International Standards of Audit (ISA) has a mere 48 hours devoted to it. International Accounting Standards is studied for only 85 hours, although the Russian Finance Ministry has declared that Russian enterprises must follow IAS as of January 1, 2004, a full year before European Union countries are required to adopt IAS. Finance, Financial Statements and Analysis, and the Theory of Accounting are each allocated a mere 102 hours, even though they are included in the major.

Why are so few hours devoted to these very important subjects? The interviews conducted as part of this research uncovered several explanations. One reason mentioned before is the lack of teaching staff. It is difficult to find people who are qualified to give lectures in these subjects, especially outside of Russia's two main cities. Most potential accounting professors are in Moscow and St. Petersburg because that is where most of the sophisticated accounting is done. There is less demand for expertise on IAS and ISA outside of these two cities. There is grassroots demand for IAS and ISA expertise only among the large Russian enterprises that want

Table 7.3

Hours Devoted to the Top Ten and Lowest Ten Subjects

Rank	Discipline	Hours	%
	Top 10		
1	Foreign languages	510	6.2
2	Information science	459	5.6
3	Physical training	408	5.0
4	Mathematics	391	4.8
5	Theory of economics	357	4.3
6	Financial accounting	306	3.7
7	Logistics	306	3.7
8	Cost accounting, budgeting for different industries	297	3.6
9	Class training (a case study of accounting of an enterprise activity)	264	3.2
10	Concepts of modern natural science	255	3.1
	Lowest 10		
1	International standards of audit	48	0.6
2	Vital function safety and protection of labor	68	0.8
3	International accounting standards	85	1.0
4	Russian history	85	1.0
5	Finance	102	1.2
6	Financial statements and analysis	102	1.2
7	Pricing	102	1.2
8	Insurance	102	1.2
9	The theory of accounting	102	1.2
10	Marketing	102	1.2

to attract foreign capital, and those firms are located mostly in Moscow and St. Petersburg.

Another reason involves economics. It was learned during the course of the interviews that accounting professors are twice as expensive as professors in other disciplines. Increasing the number of hours devoted to accounting subjects increases the university's costs, and there is pressure to keep costs down.

Another reason is the transformation in the structure of Russian universities. In Soviet times, most institutions of higher education were called institutes rather than universities. These institutes specialized in teaching just a few subjects. There is now a tendency to change the name from institute to university for reasons of prestige. With the name change comes a change in emphasis in the curriculum. These former institutes that are now universities have to teach more subjects but in less depth. There is now more emphasis on general subjects and less emphasis on whatever subject the student chooses for a major.

Other Aspects of Accounting Education

In the above example, 60.8 percent of all hours are devoted to class lessons. This percentage may be broken down into lectures (24.5%), auditorium lessons (27.7%), and laboratory practice (8.6%). The remaining 39.2 percent is devoted to self-study.

Society's (and clients') assessment of an accountant's professionalism is based on his or her knowledge of the laws, instructions, and provisions they have learned using those textbooks, as well as what they have learned from their other university classes. Likewise, the universities attempt to meet market demand by producing graduates who have these characteristics and knowledge bases.

In general, it is optimal if an accountant (or even a student) can remember all the laws and is able to refer to a certain paragraph of instructions while analyzing a transaction. But there are major problems with this approach because Russian laws and instructions change so rapidly that much of what students learn is outdated by the time they graduate, and a high percentage of the normative documents that students have learned to use have become outdated.

Again, it should be emphasized that not *all* Russian textbooks fit this description; it is only the most widely used textbooks and the ones most likely to be found in university libraries that fit this description. As a consequence of this situation, many Russian professors develop their own textbooks and manuals and use them as the basis for teaching their students. Thus, as in many universities, Kazan State Finance Economic Institute, one of the most prestigious economic universities in Kazan, gives students the opportunity to study accounting using their professor's textbook (Kulikova 1999).

Because textbooks are expensive and students cannot afford them, Russian accounting students generally do not buy new textbooks as is so often done in the United States and Western Europe. Instead, they go to the library and use whatever textbooks they can find. In some cases, universities have ways to subsidize the cost of student texts. That is the case for the Timiryazev Agricultural Academy in Moscow, for example. The Agricultural Ministry provides funds to subsidize the cost of textbooks so that a text might cost students just 60 rubles ($2).

Concluding Comments

It will take time for market economy logic to gain the upper hand over the still prevalent top-down system Russia has had for several generations. Instead of using accounting as a means of control for socialist property and as a tool for fulfilling a plan, users and providers of accounting information will have to see accounting as a tool for management decision making and control at the enterprise level. It will take time for accounting textbooks to reflect this new reality as well. Although several Western accounting textbooks have been translated into Russian, these books are generally unobtainable outside of Russia's two major cities. Furthermore, the American examples in those texts do not always closely correspond to the Russian situation.

Sadly, the quality of Russian textbooks has declined during the past three generations. After the communist revolution, accounting texts began with V. Lenin quotations and contained inserts from the latest Communist Party Congress decree, but did not include definitions of capital, profit, and the main accounting equation. It is a sad state of affairs, considering that prerevolutionary accounting texts were at the level of those in Western market economies. They included not just theoretical chapters but also exercises and cases intended to motivate students go think, analyze, and make decisions. They led students from the start of a transaction to the financial statements, taking into consideration the main user of accounting information and the purpose of accounting (Lihachev 1918).

There is a cultural dimension in Russian accounting that cannot easily be changed merely by issuing decrees or passing laws. Russian accounting is not based on concepts or principles. It is based on rules. The Russian mentality after generations of communist central planning is focused on instructions and rules, not principles. When Russian accountants encounter a problem, they do not think of how accounting principles can be used to arrive at a solution. They look for some written rule, instruction, or law that addresses the issue. It is difficult to change this legalistic and formalistic approach to accounting.

There is still the widespread perception that accounting information is used primarily by tax officials and is of little use to enterprise managers or potential investors. This attitude is also the result of the prior system and will change only slowly, with the passage of time. The new generation of accountants must learn how to make decisions based on accounting principles and professional judgment and must focus more on what is important to external users. The mentality of both students and professors must change in this regard before accounting education can achieve results approximating those of the more developed Western countries.

We have attempted to cover all the major factors that affect accounting students and graduates as they prepare to be professional accountants. What can be said to summarize the research and interviews? One interesting point is that the interviewees disagreed widely regarding the state of Russian accounting education. Some were quite optimistic and thought Russian accounting education was quite good and was improving rapidly. Others were pessimistic and thought that Russian accounting education was at a very low level. Some of those interviewed thought that graduates had a good knowledge of accounting, while others thought the level of their knowledge left much to be desired.

Both of these views have some merit. Much depends on where the student studies and who the student's professors are. Those who study accounting in Moscow or St. Petersburg have a higher probability of having professors who have actually read and used the International Financial Reporting Standards (IFRS) because universities outside of these two cities take a different approach and have a different attitude about the need to teach IFRS. Professors from other Russian cities are not as well prepared or knowledgeable, and the level and quality of materials available to students is not as good.

Generally, the interviewees who were knowledgeable about IFRS were more negative about the current state of Russian accounting education than were those who had merely heard about IFRS but had never read them. It is reasonable to expect that the quality of accounting education will eventually improve in the regions outside of Moscow and St. Petersburg, but this improvement in the quality of accounting education will be a bottom-up, market-driven phenomenon rather than a top-down, decree–driven one. Accounting education in Russia will improve as more high quality materials become available and as more accounting graduates gain experience and return to the universities to share their experience with the younger generation.

References

Adams, C.A., and K.M. McMillan. 1997. "Internationalizing Financial Reporting in a Newly Emerging Market Economy: The Polish Example." *Advances in International Accounting* 10: 139–64.

Anonymous. 2001. "Accountants in Russia Gain International Skills." *Financial Management*, 44 (April).

Anonymous. 1994. "Tanya Bondarenko Seeks American Education." *Baylor Business Review*, 12, no. 1: 12–14.

Borda, M., and S. McLeay. 1996. "Accounting and Economic Transformation in Hungary." In *Accounting in Transition: The Implications of Political and Economic Reform in Central Europe*, ed. Neil Garrod and Stuart McLeay, 116–40. London and New York: Routledge.

Boross, Z.; A.H. Clarkson; M. Fraser; and P. Weetman. 1995. "Pressures and Conflicts in Moving Towards Harmonization of Accounting Practice: The Hungarian Experience." *European Accounting Review* 4, no. 4: 713–37.

Chan, M.W.L., and W. Rotenberg. 1999. "Accounting, Accounting Education, and Economic Reform in the People's Republic of China." *International Studies of Management and Organization* 29, no. 3: 37–53.

Coyle, W.H., and V.V. Platonov. 1998. "Insights Gained from International Exchange and Educational Initiatives Between Universities: The Challenges of Analyzing Russian Financial Statements." *Issues in Accounting Education* 13, no. 1 (February): 223–33.

Crallan, J. 1997. "Accounting Reform in the CIS." *Management Accounting* 34 (January).

Enthoven, A.J.H. 1992. "Accounting in Russia: From Perestroika to Profits." *Management Accounting* 74, no. 4: 27–31.

———. 1998. *Accounting, Auditing, and Taxation in the Russian Federation: 1998 Study.* Montvale, NJ: Institute of Management Accountants, and Richardson, TX: Center for International Accounting Development, University of Texas.

———. 1999. "Russia's Accounting Moves West." *Strategic Finance* 81, no. 1: 32–37.

Garrod, N., and S. McLeay, eds. 1996. *Accounting in Transition: The Implications of Political and Economic Reform in Central Europe.* London and New York: Routledge.

International Center for Accounting Reform. 2000. *Accounting Reform Recommendations.* Moscow: International Center for Accounting Reform. Available at www.icar.ru (accessed December 7, 2004).

International Federation of Accountants. 2000. Assistance Projects in Accountancy Education and Development. A Study Based on the Experience of IFAC Member Bodies. Study Paper. New York: International Federation of Accountants. Available at www.ifac.org (accessed December 7, 2004).

———. 2001. Strategy for Implementation of IFAC International Education Guideline No. 9: "Pre-qualification Education, Tests of Professional Competence and Practical Experience of Professional Accountants." A Task Force Report of the International Association for Accounting Education and Research (IAAER). New York: International Federation of Accountants. Available at www.ifac.org (accessed December 7, 2004).

Jermakowicz, E., and D.F. Rinke. 1996. "The New Accounting Standards in the Czech Republic, Hungary, and Poland vis-à-vis International Accounting Standards and European Union Directives." *Journal of International Accounting Auditing & Taxation* 5, no. 1: 73–88.

Kemp, P., and D. Alexander. 1996. "Accountancy and Financial Infrastructure in Central and Eastern European Countries." *European Business Journal* 8, no. 4: 14–21.

King, N.; A. Beattie; and A-M. Cristescu. 2001. "Developing Accounting and Audit in a Transition Economy: The Romanian Experience." *European Accounting Review* 10, no. 1: 149–71.

Kobrak, F. 1991. "Is There an Accounting Textbook Market in the New Soviet Union?" *Publishers Weekly*, September 29: 43–44.

Krzywda, D.; D. Bailey; and M. Schroeder. 1995. "A Theory of European Accounting Development Applied to Accounting Change in Contemporary Poland." *European Accounting Review* 4, no. 4: 625–57.

———. 1996. "The Impact of Accounting Regulation on Financial Reporting in Poland." In *Accounting in Transition: The Implications of Political and Economic Reform in Central Europe*, ed. Neil Garrod and Stuart McLeay, 61–92. London and New York: Routledge.

Kulikova, L.I. 1999. *Financial Accounting*, 2d ed. Kazan.

Law on Education. 1992. No. 3266–1, July 10.

Law on High and Postuniversity Education, No. 125-FZ, August 22, 1996.

Lihachev, V.N. 1918. *30 Lessons in Double Entry Bookkeeping*, 4th ed. Moscow: K.I. Tihimirov's Trade House.

Lin, Z., and S. Deng. 1992. "Educating Accounting in China: Current Experiences and Future Prospects." *International Journal of Accounting* 27, no. 2: 164–77.

Mackevicius, J.; J. Aliukonis; and D. Bailey. 1996. "The Reconstruction of National Accounting Rules in Lithuania." In *Accounting in Transition: The Implications of Political and Economic Reform in Central Europe*, ed. Neil Garrod and Stuart McLeay, 43–60. London and New York: Routledge.

McGee, RW. 1999a. "The Problem of Implementing International Accounting Standards: A Case Study of Armenia." *Journal of Accounting, Ethics & Public Policy* 2, no. 1: 38–41. Available at www.ssrn.com (accessed December 7, 2004).

———. 1999b. "Certification of Accountants and Auditors in the CIS: A Case Study of Armenia." *Journal of Accounting, Ethics & Public Policy* 2, no. 2: 338–53. Available at www.ssrn.com (accessed December 7, 2004).

———. 2003a. "Reforming Accounting Education in a Transition Economy: A Case Study of Armenia." In *Succeeding in a Turbulent Global Marketplace: Changes, Developments, Challenges and Creating Distinct Competencies*, ed. Erdener Kaynak and Talha D. Harcar, 139–46. Hummelstown, PA: International Management Development Association. Available at www.ssrn.com (accessed December 7, 2004).

———. 2003b. "Educating Professors in a Transition Economy: A Case Study of Bosnia and Herzegovina." In *Succeeding in a Turbulent Global Marketplace: Changes, Developments, Challenges and Creating Distinct Competencies*, ed. Erdener Kaynak and Talha D. Harcar, 155-62. Hummelstown, PA: International Management Development Association. Available at www.ssrn.com (accessed December 7, 2004).

Pankov, D. 1998. "Accounting for Change in Belarus." *Management Accounting* (London) 76, no. 10: 56–58.

Preobragenskaya, G.G., and R.W. McGee. 2003. "The Current State of Auditing in Russia." In *Business Research Yearbook: Global Business Perspectives*, ed. Jerry Biberman and Abbass F. Alkhafaji, vol.10, 499–503. Saline, MI: McNaughton & Gunn. Available at www.ssrn.com (accessed December 7, 2004).

Ramcharran, H. 2000. "The Need for International Accounting Harmonization: An Examination and Comparison of the Practices of Russian Banks." *American Business Review* 18, no. 1: 1–8.

Richard, J. 1998. "Accounting in Eastern Europe: From Communism to Capitalism." *International Accounting*, ed. In Peter Walton, Axel Haller, and Bernard Raffournier, 295–323. London: International Thomson Business Press.

Roberts, A. 2001. "The Recent Romanian Accounting Reforms: Another Case of Cultural Intrusion?" In *Transitional Economies: Banking, Finance, Institutions*, ed. Yelena Kalyuzhnova and Michael Taylor, 146–66. Basingstoke, UK and New York: Palgrave.

Rolfe, R.J., and T.S. Doupnik. 1995. "Accounting Revolution in East Central Europe." *Advances in International Accounting* 8: 223–46.

Seal, W.; P. Sucher; and I. Zelenka. 1995. "The Changing Organization of Czech Accounting." *European Accounting Review* 4, no. 4: 659–81.

Shama, A., and C.G. McMahan. 1990. "Perestroika and Soviet Accounting: From a Planned to a Market Economy." *International Journal of Accounting* 25: 155–69.

Smirnova, I.A.; J.V. Sokolov; and C.R. Emmanuel. 1995. "Accounting Education in Russia Today." *European Accounting Review* 4, no. 4: 833–46.

Sucher, P., and P. Kemp. 1998. "Accounting and Auditing Reform in Belarus." *European Business Journal* 10, no. 3: 141–47.

Turk, I., and N. Garrod. 1996. "The Adaptation of International Accounting Rules: Lessons from Slovenia." In *Accounting in Transition: The Implications of Political and Economic Reform in Central Europe*, ed. Neil Garrod and Stuart McLeay, 141–62. London and New York: Routledge.

Wallace, R.S.O. 1993. "Development of Accounting Standards for Developing and Newly Industrialized Countries." *Research in Third World Accounting* 2: 121–65.

Zelenka, I.; W. Seal; and P. Sucher. 1996. "The Emerging Institutional Framework of Accounting in the Czech and Slovak Republics." In *Accounting in Transition: The Implications of Political and Economic Reform in Central Europe*, ed. Neil Garrod and Stuart McLeay, 93–115. London and New York: Routledge.

8

Developing Key Skills in Russian Business Education

A Comparison Between U.K. and American Business Programs

Scott G. Dacko

Accountability for developing transferable skills in business education has received growing attention in recent years as business schools face increasing competition, student demands, and scrutiny from governing bodies (Melton 1997). Individuals pursuing a business education at an institution of further education—whether via a four- or five-year undergraduate degree or a master of business administration (MBA)—rely on their institution to develop key skills useful in their careers. Obtaining a business education involves developing strong analytical and written communication skills, as well as gaining an up-to-date, theoretical, and practical knowledge of business on an international basis.

To date, the focus on understanding the degree of skill development in a business education has mainly been with American business programs (Porter and McKibbin 1988) rather than non-U.S. programs, including those in Western and Eastern Europe. As a result of the ongoing expansion of the free enterprise system in Russia and the continuing popularity of business programs worldwide, the number of Russian students enrolled in management and business education programs in Russia is now higher than ever before. For business schools worldwide, technologies are also being leveraged to provide even greater student access to teaching resources (Daniel 1996; Knapp and Glenn 1996; Tiffin and Rajasingham 1995). In the increasingly global world of business education, a vital set of issues is therefore raised: To what extent do Russian programs emphasize the development of key skills for business students differently than non–Russian programs such as those in the United Kingdom and the United States? What gaps in skill development are perceived by these management and business education students—within these programs and relative to Western programs? Given the increasingly prevalent role of technology in a business education, how might technology be used to fill these gaps in a program of business education and produce graduates with greater sets of skills? Are there some skills that are being better developed in Russian management programs? These issues will be addressed in this chapter. The implications are increasingly important to educational administrators, academicians, and students. Even staff members who clearly excel as both teachers and researchers (Andre and Frost 1997) may not necessarily be emphasizing the development of appropriate skills if preoccupied with developing a curriculum content for students in any single country of the world.

Skills Developed in Management Programs

The concern with skill development in business education has led to a growing interest in studying the extent of skill development in business schools. In 1998, the American Association of Collegiate Schools of Business (AACSB) conducted a major survey examining nine key skills and personal characteristics developed in MBA programs to determine the extent to which they were emphasized and should be emphasized (Porter and McKibbin 1988). Specifically, students were asked to indicate the extent to which their programs were emphasizing the development of the following key skills and personal characteristics:

1. analytical;
2. computer;
3: decision making;
4. initiative;
5. leadership/interpersonal;
6. oral communication;
7. planning/organizing;
8. risk taking; and
9. written communication.

In summarizing the researcher's findings, development of analytical skills topped the list, with 62 percent of the respondents indicating "emphasized very much." Decision making and planning/organizing were next with 51 percent each, followed by written communication (42%), oral communication (28%), leadership/interpersonal (26%), initiative (21%), and computer skills (14%). Risk taking was at the bottom with an 8 percent rating. To be sure, the constituents of these programs, including faculty and deans, would like to see greater emphasis placed on developing all of these skills (Porter and McKibbin 1988). The growing popularity of business programs worldwide and in Eastern Europe in particular now raises the question of whether participants in Russian management and business education programs are developing similar key skills and to a greater or lesser extent than their Western counterparts.

A study of the management and business education program at a leading Russian and European business school was performed as a means to address the issues in this research and enable comparisons of skill development emphasis in U.K. and American business schools. In the following section, the methodology employed is described, followed by a discussion of the results and the curriculum and educational technology implications for business education in Russia.

Method

A major survey of management and business education program participants in Russia and the United Kingdom was conducted. All participants were near the very end of their final year of their school's business program. In Russia, participants were near completion of a five-year program in a leading private institute. In the United Kingdom, participants were near completion of a year-long MBA degree program at a leading European university. Both programs enroll students of strong academic and business potential. The U.K. sample consisted of currently enrolled full time participants, with each receiving a survey by e-mail at a time near the end of the academic program. The Russian sample consisted of students in their final year enrolled in an advanced course open to all students at the school, with each receiving a paper survey completed in class.

All participants were asked to respond to questions in two major areas. First, participants were asked to indicate on a scale of 1 (emphasized very little) to 6 (emphasized very much) the degree to which each of the following skills and personal characteristics were *currently emphasized* in their business program: analytical, computer, decision making, initiative, leadership/interpersonal skills, oral communication, planning/organizing, risk taking, and written communication. Second, participants were asked to indicate on the same scale the degree to which each of the same skills *should* be emphasized in their business program. As supplemental information, participants

Table 8.1

A Comparison of Emphases on Skill Development: Russian Five-Year Management Program vs. U.K. MBA Program

	Responses on a scale of 1 (emphasized very little) to 6 (emphasized very much)					
Skill	Currently emphasized			Should be emphasized		
Development Area	Russian program	U.K. program	Differentials significance	Russian program	U.K. program	Differentials significance
Oral communication	4.62	4.05	(.026)**	5.44	5.01	(.031)**
Planning/organizing	4.23	3.99	(.322)	4.81	4.75	(.793)
Written communication	3.89	4.18	(.293)	4.58	4.34	(.337)
Decision making	3.69	3.87	(.487)	5.19	5.12	(.711)
Initiative	3.62	3.54	(.757)	4.96	4.77	(.405)
Computer	3.62	2.57	(.000)***	5.50	3.99	(.000)***
Leadership/ interpersonal	3.39	3.78	(.127)	4.62	5.08	(.051)*
Analytical	2.92	4.18	(.000)***	5.15	4.96	(.374)
Risk taking	2.80	2.56	(.372)	3.88	3.94	(.814)

$*p < .1, **p < .05, ***p < .01.$

were asked an open-ended question to indicate any areas of interest in their program, as well as their age, sex, and nationality. Russian students were given the complete survey in the Russian language, with the survey back-translated into English to ensure proper translation. In making comparisons with current skill emphases in U.S. business programs, survey data from the AACSB study on American programs (Porter and McKibbin 1988) was used.

Results

Of the U.K. participants, 108 out of 133 replied to the surveys, which is a response rate of 81 percent. Surveys were completed by 62 percent, or 26 out of 42, of the Russian participants. The average ages of U.K. and Russian participants were thirty-two and twenty, respectively; 28 percent and 75 percent, respectively, were female, and 43 percent and 100 percent, respectively, claimed to be of the nationality in the location of the business school.

Table 8.1 shows the numerical results for the Russian and U.K. business programs as well as the indications of the degree of significance of differences among the findings when comparing the two programs. The table is useful for showing the magnitudes of the values indicating degree of emphasis on skill development for the business programs. The skills in the table are arranged from highest to lowest emphasis in the Russian business program. The results indicate that the highest current emphases in the Russian program are on developing oral communication skills as well as planning and organizing. Written communication, decision making, initiative, computer, and leadership/interpersonal skills receive only moderate emphasis. Analytical and risk-taking skills receive relatively little development emphasis.

The U.K. program places a high overall emphasis on analytical and written communication skills development, closely followed by oral communication, planning and organizing, decision making, leadership/interpersonal skills, and initiative. Computer and risk-taking skills receive relatively little development emphasis. Focusing on those areas identified to be significantly different between programs, it can be seen that the Russian program places significantly greater current emphasis on oral communication and computer skills and significantly less emphasis on analytical skill development. At the same time, Russian program participants perceive a need for greater future emphasis on developing both oral communication skills and computer skills. Russian participants also see a need for greater emphasis on developing leadership/interpersonal skills, but to a significantly lesser degree than their U.K. counterparts. Students in both programs would like to see significantly greater emphasis on developing all skills ($p = .000$ for all), with analytical and computer skills being in need of the greatest improvement for the Russian program in particular.

To enable further comparison between the Russian and U.K. programs, Table 8.2a shows the results for the Russian program in terms of the percentage greater or lesser skill development emphasis relative to the U.K. program. Percentages are calculated based on scaled responses. Table 8.2b shows the results in terms of the perceived need for greater emphasis on skill development by participants *within* each program. Again, percentages are calculated based on scaled responses. The differences between the degree that skills are currently emphasized and the degree that the skills should be emphasized is highly significant for both programs. Participants in each program indicate development of *all* skills should receive *greater* emphasis ($p = .000$) with the exception of written communication skill development in the United Kingdom, where the difference is not significant ($p = .216$).

Finally, Table 8.2c shows the survey results in a form enabling comparison with American business school data and show the percentage of respondents indicating a high skill development emphasis. Results of data collected on bachelor of business administration (BBA) and MBA programs in business schools nationwide (Porter and McKibbin 1988) show the percentage of respondents indicating a high *current* emphasis on developing each of the nine key skills. Data for the emphases that *should* be given to skill development in the American programs are not available. The results of Table 8.2c suggests that American business programs are, in general, placing relatively

Table 8.2a

Business Skill Development Emphasis of the Russian Five-Year Management Program: Actual and Desired (Percentage of Respondents)

Skill development area	Skills currently emphasized	Should be emphasized
Computer	40.7***	37.8***
Oral communication	14.0**	8.6**
Risk taking	9.2	(1.4)
Planning/organizing	6.0	1.2
Initiative	2.1	4.0
Decision making	(4.6)	1.4
Written communication	(7.1)	5.5
Leadership/interpersonal	(10.5)	(9.1)**
Analytical	(30.1)***	3.9

$*p < .1, **p < .05, ***p < .01.$

Table 8.2b

Business Skills Perceived as Important: Comparing Russian and U.K. MBA Program Participants (Percentage of Respondents)

Skill development area program	Russian five-year management program	U.K. MBA
Analytical	43.3	15.8
Computer	34.3	35.6
Decision making	28.9	24.4
Risk taking	28.0	35.2
Initiative	27.1	25.7
Leadership/interpersonal	26.7	25.8
Oral communication	15.2	19.2
Written communication	15.1	3.9
Planning/organizing	12.0	16.2

$*$All differences between current and desired emphases are significant at $p = .000.$

---

greater emphasis on developing analytical and decision-making skills, whereas the Russian management program places relatively greater emphasis on developing oral communication skills. Relative to the U.K. MBA program, the Russian program also places greater current emphasis on developing computer skills, and relative to both the U.K. and American programs, the Russian program places relatively less emphasis on developing leadership/interpersonal skills.

A comparison of the desired emphases on skill development for both the Russian and U.K. programs demonstrates strong similarities. The Russian

Table 8.2c

Skill Development Emphases: A Comparison with American Business School Programs

(Percent of respondents indicating a high emphasis on skill development by responding on the upper 1/3 of the scale; 1 to 6 scale for European survey, 1 to 3 scale for American survey)

Skill development area	Current emphasis				Should be emphasized*	
	Russian 5-year mgmt. program	U.K. MBA program	U.S. MBA program	U.S. BBA program	Russian 5-year mgmt. program	U.K. MBA program
Oral communication	61.5	40.7	28	38	92.0	75.9
Planning/organizing	46.2	34.3	51	46	61.5	63.9
Written communication	34.6	49.1	42	44	61.5	48.1
Decision making	23.1	30.6	51	55	88.5	82.4
Computer	23.1	2.8	14	18	88.5	31.5
Leadership/ interpersonal	15.4	31.5	26	35	65.4	73.1
Initiative	15.4	20.4	21	28	73.1	63.9
Analytical	7.7	45.5	62	51	88.5	72.2
Risk taking	7.7	4.6	8	11	34.6	26.9

*Data for American programs is not available.

and U.K. programs match very closely on the desired emphases with the exception of written communication and computer skills, where Russian students see a need for a greater increase in emphasis on developing these skills than do U.K. students.

Clearly, the possibilities for introducing new or revised courses and new educational technologies to address the gaps between current and desired skill development emphasis, both within and across programs, and across country borders, have never been greater than they are today. In particular, business education institutions offering participants a computer-enhanced education as part of their business education can increasingly draw upon many new methods to meet students' increasingly demanding program expectations. For example, some Russian business programs are developing courses offered to Russian students via computer conferencing, where the instructor is situated at a business school outside of Russia. Offering and encouraging Russian student access to the World Wide Web can provides numerous opportunities for greater development of many of the skills examined in this chapter.

Skill Development Implications for Russian Business and Management Education

The above findings are discussed and explained in greater detail in this section with the aim of identifying curriculum and educational technology opportunities to emphasize skill development in Russian business and management program education to a greater degree. The order of discussion is from highest to lowest perceived need for greater emphasis on skill development, corresponding to the order appearing in Table 8.2b.

Analytical Skills

Russian students believe that their business education program places relatively little emphasis on developing analytical skills within their program: overall, participants perceive a 43 percent increase in needed emphasis on analytical skill development. Compared to a U.K. MBA program (Table 8.2a), the Russian program emphasizes analytical skill development 30 percent less. U.S. business programs emphasize analytical skill development to a great extent and more than any other skill in U.S. MBA programs (Table 8.2c). Perhaps it is a relatively greater traditional reliance on lecture attendance over critical analysis of numerous written cases that leads to greater emphasis on understanding factual knowledge over the application of models and frameworks to analyze business scenarios. Or perhaps it is the Russian program's relatively reduced student access to computers and advanced reading materials that limits opportunities for students to learn at a greater level of detail and achieve a deeper understanding of the usefulness and applicability of analytical business models and methods. Given the complexities of many business situations and the need for managers to have sound analytical skills to make sense of these complexities, immersion in controlled scenarios of varying scope and difficulty—through that afforded by numerous computer simulations today—may be useful in further developing students' analytical skills. Integrating the use of increasingly accessible personal computer (PC)-based or Web-based computer simulations of business scenarios, such as MARKSTRAT or AutoSim, into core courses may go far in exposing students to scenarios in which they can apply and sharpen their analytical skills and see the results of their analytical learning in an accelerated manner. Clearly, providing students with further resources and tools to engage in greater degrees of critical and independent thinking can only act to facilitate the development of each student's analytical skills.

Computer Skills

On average, Russian students perceive a need for 34 percent greater emphasis on computer skill development—yet at the same time, they perceive their program to be providing 41 percent greater current emphasis on computer skill development compared to U.K. MBA students. A key reason for this view is that the Russian business education program requires formal and ongoing coursework in computing technologies, whereas the U.K. program has no formal computer coursework and assumes students learn as needed throughout the program. Thus, explicit attention to computer skill development is clearly a strength of the Russian program, yet improvement is also desired by the students.

Considerable variation in Russian business program resources and communications infrastructure reliability are clearly challenges that raise issues of available and reliable access to computer equipment and software for greater computer skill development. To the extent that a Russian program can provide and require student access to a standard PC and/or the Internet or World Wide Web, students will be in a greater position to develop their computer and/or Internet skills via assignments involving computer software and hardware (Jana 1999). Student course assignments involving the use of standard statistical software packages, business simulations (e.g., MARKSTRAT or AutoSim), and CD-ROM-based multimedia business education software (Roberts, Shaw, and Grigg 1999) become increasingly realistic. Furthermore, to the extent that students have the opportunity to visit other, more computer-intensive universities through student exchange programs for foreign language learning—an activity that is increasingly common—opportunities for developing computer software and hardware training can be potentially integrated.

Decision Making

On average, students in the Russian management program perceive a need for a 29 percent increase in emphasis on decision making skill development, where the current and desired emphasis on developing decision-making skills is similar to that of a U.K. MBA program. Perhaps the common views of these students reflect a similar focus on management decision making and problem solving throughout each program's curriculum. One way to increase emphasis on developing decision-making skills is to offer an actual course on decision making in business. Some U.S. business schools offer and require a course in Problem Formulation and Decision Making to aid in students' understanding of decision making and increase their confidence in making business decisions. Developing and offering such a course as an elective or short course may do much to increase needed emphasis on students' decision-making skills, which are currently emphasized to a great extent in U.S. programs.

Technologically, increased use of computer simulations can also significantly enhance development of decision-making skills (Sparkes 1984), particularly when students are able to retrace the steps of their decision-making processes and evaluate their mistakes, as is the case in student use of simulations at some U.S. business schools today. Russian students with access to a standard PC or the World Wide Web can clearly benefit from participating in such business simulations by enhancing development of management decision-making skills. In addition, independent business research projects involving decision making using Web-based data can further benefit decision making skill development in an unstructured setting (Henry 1994).

Risk Taking

Russian students believe that their management program needs to provide an average 28 percent increase in emphasis on risk taking skill development—again similar to the views of U.K. MBA student counterparts. In all programs—Russian, U.K., and U.S.—the current emphasis on risk taking is very low. How can risk taking skill development receive more emphasis in business programs? Is the problem that risk taking among students is not sufficiently rewarded in a business program? Or is it that the "safe" environment of a business school setting imposes a formidable impediment to creating and implementing scenarios where risks can be "realistically" understood and experienced by students? Both may be potential impediments. Clearly, students could benefit from explicitly learning others' theories and models of the risk-taking process. Many books on the subject may be found, including *The Art of Personal Risk Taking* (Byrd 1974), which qualitatively discusses managerial risk taking. Quantitatively, greater use of computer-based assessments and exams that provide feedback on risk evaluations (e.g., statistical probabilities) can further help in developing students' risk-taking skills. More explicit attention to risk taking in one or more current program courses is also possible through the additional use of computer-based business simulations. Participation in computerized business simulations, where students can internalize tradeoffs in taking action with varying degrees of uncertainty or imperfect information and acquiring better information at a price, can do much to facilitate the development of student skills in risk taking.

Initiative

Russian students view the development of the personal characteristic of initiative as needing an average 27 percent increase in emphasis in the Russian management program—a view that is similar to that expressed by students in the U.K. MBA program. Developing personal initiative to "make things happen when things normally wouldn't happen" is clearly beneficial and likely reflects students' need to grow in their ability to become self-starters in all aspects of their careers. As it is the view of all students that initiative as a personal characteristic should receive greater emphasis, opportunities must therefore be sought for involvement in a variety of activities that may cater to the individual interests of participants. Exploring independent business consultancy opportunities and conducting independent library or online research and data collection are examples of areas that could reinforce the role of initiative in successfully accomplishing goal-oriented tasks while developing skills in other areas as well.

Leadership/Interpersonal Skills

Leadership/interpersonal skill development is also perceived by Russian students as needing an average 27 percent increase in emphasis—again, similar to the views expressed by U.K. MBA students. As shown in Table 8.1, however, the relative emphasis that is desired for developing leadership/interpersonal skills among Russian students is significantly lower when compared to the views of U.K. MBA students. Such a result may reflect the fact that Russian students are less likely than their U.K. and U.S. counterparts to be preparing for business career opportunities where leadership skills are as critical (e.g., business formation and participation in entrepreneurial and business networking ventures). Nevertheless, opportunities must be explored to further develop leadership/interpersonal skills in all programs. Such skills are often developed in small groups throughout a business program. Feedback on small groups from some students suggests, however, that "the natural leaders stay leaders and the natural followers stay followers." Opportunities for further developing leadership and interpersonal skills can therefore include more explicit attention to the process of and approaches to leadership and interpersonal interaction. Phasing in a compulsory course on human resource management and leadership, for example, can assist in developing leadership and interpersonal skills. In some U.S. business programs, students have been required to read course books including *Coping with Difficult People* (Bramson 1981) and *The Art of Self-Leadership* (Manz 1981). Formally requiring small group leadership responsibilities on a rotational basis and/or offering formal and anonymous feedback may also facilitate development of these skills.

Given that all business students are to a great extent developing leadership and interpersonal skills via their growing knowledge of management, human resources, and marketing methods (including approaches for customer interaction), opportunities increasingly exist for leveraging leadership/interpersonal skill development through the use of business scenarios and simulations. Scenarios and simulations of customer sales negotiations or sales force motivation, for example, can be increasingly effective tools in the future to the extent that they reflect some of the complexities of human nature in confined business settings. Some business schools are developing computer network facilities to enable class-wide communication with students and/or an instructor at other business schools. Thus, participation in and/or moderation of online forums (Hammond 1998) and chat sessions could be used to approximate aspects of leadership in interpersonal interaction. Lesser technology-intensive approaches can include videotaping student leadership training sessions to evaluating student progress and videotaping sessions aimed at improving students' interviewing skills.

Oral Communication

According to Russian students, oral communication skill development currently receives the most attention in their management program. Still, Russian students believe they can also benefit from an average increase of 15 percent greater emphasis. Relative to both U.K. and U.S. business programs, this is clearly another area of strength of the Russian management program, since neither U.K. nor U.S. programs emphasize oral communication skill development as much as Russian programs do. Not only do some Russian business education programs require oral examinations in various courses, many programs also offer language courses that can help improve not only language but overall speaking skills. Clearly oral examinations, where the emphasis is on assessing knowledge gained during a course, are another way to assess oral communication skills. In most Western business school programs, however, oral communication skills are most clearly observed during in-class student presentations. Russian business school programs may, therefore, benefit from the increased use of such teaching methods to provide students with further practice. Business students can also benefit from formal training and feedback on oral communication skills from experienced facilitators early in their program—a practice adopted by some U.S. business schools. Such schools have small oral communication skills centers with videotaping equipment and library resources staffed by knowledgeable professionals. The programs require students to achieve basic speaking competency through training and an assessed speaking opportunity, either before a single instructor or an entire class.

Other, lower-cost solutions also exist and include audiotape recording of student presentations and the encouragement of opportunities for students to collect verbal data for marketing research projects (e.g., recorded personal interviews). For programs providing easy access to the Internet, participation in online chat sessions may also simulate the experience of oral communication, but this is, of course, dramatically different in dynamics than presenting one's case face to face and before a live audience.

Written Communication

While Russian students perceive that written communication skills development receive a high current emphasis, they also think these skills need significantly (15%) greater emphasis. U.K. students, on the other hand, perceive written communication skill development as receiving adequate attention and see no need for greater emphasis. Perhaps it is the fact that Russian students must often communicate not only in Russian but in at least one other foreign language as well that draws greater interest and attention to their developing effective written business communication skills. Clearly, with written communication, there exist many opportunities to develop synergies with other skills to be developed. For example, summarizing in writing the decisions made in computerized business simulations can facilitate developing skill in written communication as well as business decision making. For programs providing students with Web and e-mail access, e-mail exchanges (Hulme 2000) and chat session (Hammond 1998) participation can further develop both writing and computer skills. Requiring the periodic drafts of written reports can develop planning and organizing skills. For all of these teaching initiatives, providing students with more comprehensive feedback on their current level of written communication skill will do much to increase the skills' emphasis with Russian business students.

Planning/Organizing

Another personal characteristic that currently receives a high degree of development emphasis in the Russian business and management program is planning/organizing. One benefit of many business programs that offer semistructured assignments is that they require a significant personal effort in planning and organizing, and, through student practice in planning, can do much to develop planning and organizing skills. Nevertheless, Russian students perceive the development of these skills as needing an average 12 percent greater emphasis. The scope of skill in planning and organizing can be quite broad and is likely to include time management, establishing individual work priorities, and developing and implementing plans and approaches for small group projects. Given that many U.K. and U.S. business schools offer seminars on time management and developing priorities, it is possible that similar seminars could be developed and made available to Russian business students. A short course or seminar on these methods may prove quite beneficial in providing planning and organizing guidance, concepts, and tools to students to help them in their role as future managers. To facilitate development of skills in project planning and implementation, it is possible that instruction could also be provided to students on project management methods and techniques. For example, evaluating the benefits of new personal organization or project management software may be a feasible learning activity for students with computer access.

In the preceding discussion, the key skills developed in a Russian business and management programs have been examined. Comparisons with U.K. and U.S. programs have been made, and many potentially viable curriculum- and educational technology-based approaches have been presented. Clearly, these approaches suggest that greater emphasis can be placed on the development of each of the nine key skills, not only within Russia, but also to a greater extent within the United Kingdom and the United States. In the following section, overall conclusions are drawn concerning business education in Russia and recommendations for future research are made.

Conclusions and Future Research

This chapter has examined the extent to which a Russian business and management education program emphasizes the development of nine key skills and personal characteristics. Significant differences within the Russian program and between U.K. and U.S. programs are observed. The results of the study find that Russian, U.K., and U.S. students not only differ in their views of the degree of current emphasis on developing certain skills, but participants in the programs also differ on the degree of emphasis that should be placed on developing certain skills. For example, in comparison to U.K. students, Russian students perceive a need for relatively greater overall emphasis on developing computer and oral communication skills. U.S. programs tend to place less emphasis on developing oral communication skills relative to either Russian or U.K. business programs. Russian students see a need for greater emphasis on developing leadership/interpersonal skills, but to a lesser extent than U.K. students. These findings support the view that Russian students have a different set of needs and expectations than do Western business school students. These needs and expectations must be understood and met if student satisfaction is to be maintained or increased by teachers and academicians from any country (Hodgson 1994). Country and cultural differences such as these suggest the need for greater discussion and sharing of methods and approaches among business academicians—including the effective use of educational technologies—to develop skills in business students increasingly originating from geographic locations around the globe.

In addition to curriculum-based approaches, a set of technology-based approaches have also been proposed as means to achieving greater emphasis on developing key skills and personal characteristics. The proposed approaches are those with characteristics that, increasingly, are able to provide considerable leverage to development of the particular skills relative to the often scarce resources of time, effort, and money. Russian business and management education programs are becoming increasingly computerized, and to the extent that program administrators can economically build in teaching capabilities that enable the technology to facilitate development of key skills among students, time constraints can potentially be removed from time-constrained business teachers.

A discussion of the role of curriculum- and technology-based approaches in developing key skills in a Russian management program is not complete without a discussion of issues of implementation. Overall, it can also be argued that business academicians involved in any management program, including a Russian business education program, must give more explicit, rather than implicit, attention to skill development. With greater explicit attention to skill development, business teachers will be better able to establish more comprehensive teaching objectives (Bligh, Jacques, and Piper 1975), adopt appropriate technological approaches and media (Garger 1999; Heinich, Molenda, and Russell 1989), offer needed supporting facilities, and develop appropriate instructional packages (Laurillard 1993). By explicitly discussing skills and personal characteristics, students in a Russian business education program can also begin to gage their own level of understanding of these skills. Students will have the opportunity to formally learn and question the effectiveness of various individual and collective teaching approaches to a wide range of skills and personal characteristics.

Drummond, Nixon, and Wiltshire note in their study of problems of implementing good practices for developing personal transferable skills that just telling institutions and individuals about what they should be doing is insufficient to produce the desired outcomes (1999). Instead, the authors argue, more meaningful and widespread progress will be made through "sector-wide development programs" that *support* people in making things happen, not telling them what should happen. Programs for evaluating new educational technologies with respect to their appropriateness in enhancing skill development are therefore desirable and have been found to be effective (Littlejohn, Stefani, and Sclater 1999), whereas implementation without appropriate support mechanisms can lead to unacceptably high failure rates. Considerable upfront thought, effort, and planning will likely be required for appropriate transfers of knowledge to occur (Koch and Fisher 1998), but the ongoing costs are likely to be small in comparison—especially relative to the result of increasing student, staff, and business profession satisfaction.

Overall, a process-oriented approach to integration of curriculum modifications and technology-enhanced skill development learning experiences into a Russian program curriculum appears to be most desirable. Curriculum planning is often a nonlinear process in the social science of business education. Outcomes related to proficiency in key skills and development of desirable personal characteristic development are not always separable from their learning processes. Given the view that a business education is a complex yet invigorating process, Russian business program teaching staff can also facilitate developing key skills and personal characteristics of their students via students' increased participation in and responsibility for their own curriculum development and design.

Issues to be addressed in future research include determining: (1) the extent to which students and staff in Russian and other business education programs perceive a need for tradeoffs in the approaches aimed at enhancing the development of these key skills, and (2) the extent to which both students and staff in Russian and other programs are likely to perceive increased/decreased overall time and workload demands if the ultimate aim is a greater overall emphasis on developing key skills. Finally, gathering views on skills development from managers in Russian businesses and making comparisons with the views of managers in U.K. and U.S. businesses will further close the gap on addressing appropriate skill development in business education programs in Russia, Eastern Europe, and elsewhere.

References

Bligh, D.; D. Jacques; and D. Piper. 1975. *Seven Decisions When Teaching Students.* Exeter: EUTS.

Bramson, R.M. 1981. *Coping with Difficult People.* New York: Bantam Doubleday Dell.

Byrd, R.E. 1974. *A Guide to Personal Risk Taking.* New York: AMACOM.

Daniel, J.S. 1996. *Mega-Universities and Knowledge Media: Technology Strategies for Higher Education.* London: Kogan Page.

Drummond, I.; I. Nixon; and J. Wiltshire. 1999. "Personal Transferable Skills in Higher

Education: The Problems of Implementing Good Practice." Working paper, Universities of Hull and Newcastle.

Garger, E.M. 1999. "Goodbye Training, Hello Learning." *Workforce* 78, no. 11 (November): 35–40.

Hammond, M. 1998. "Learning Through On-line Discussion: What Are the Opportunities for Professional Development and What Are the Characteristics of On-line Writing?" *Journal of Information Technology for Teacher Education* 7, no. 3: 331–46.

Heinich, R.; M. Molenda; and J.D. Russell. 1989. *Instructional Media and the New Technologies of Instruction.* New York: Macmillan.

Henry, J. 1994. *Teaching Through Projects.* London: Kogan Page.

Hodgson, B. 1994. *Key Terms and Issues in Open and Distance Learning.* London: Kogan Page.

Hulme, M. 2000. "Intercultural E-mail Exchange—Educational Prospects and Problems." *Computer Education* 94: 14–18.

Jana, R. 1999. "Getting the Most out of Online Learning." *InfoWorld* 21, no. 37 (September 13): 13.

Knapp, L.R., and A.D. Glenn. 1996. *Restructuring Schools with Technology.* London: Allyn and Bacon.

Koch, J.V. and J.F. Fisher. 1998. "Higher Education and Total Quality Management." *Total Quality Management* 9, no. 8 (December): 659–68.

Laurillard, D. 1993. *Rethinking University Teaching: A Framework for the Effective Use of Educational Technology.* New York: Routledge.

Littlejohn, A.; L. Stefani; and N. Sclater. 1999. "Promoting Effective Use of Technology, the Pedagogy, and the Practicalities: A Case Study." *Active Learning* 11 (December): 27–30.

Manz, C.C. 1981. *The Art of Self-leadership.* New York: Prentice Hall.

Melton, R. 1997. *Objectives, Competences, and Learning Outcomes.* London: Kogan Page.

Porter, L.W., and L.E. McKibbin. 1988. *Management Education and Development: Drift or Thrust into the 21st Century?* New York: McGraw-Hill.

Andre, R., and P.J. Frost, eds. 1997. *Researchers Hooked on Teaching.* London: Sage.

Roberts, G.; D. Shaw; and N. Grigg. 1999. "The Multimedia Marketing Experience: A Qualitative Study." *Active Learning* 11 (December): 9–15.

Sparkes, T. 1984. "Pedagogical Differences Between Media." In *The Role of Technology in Distance Education,* ed. A.W. Bates, ch. 18. New York: St. Martin's Press.

Tiffin, J., and L. Rajasingham, L. 1995. *In Search of the Virtual Class: Education in an Information Society.* New York: Routledge.

Part III

Transitioning Europe and
Central Asia

9

Business Education in the Former Soviet Union Republic of Kazakhstan

A Former Dean's Perspective

X. Dai Rao and Liza Rybina

The Paradigmatic Approach to Business Education

Neither of the co-authors was around when business first started being taught at universities, but both of us have been taught by professors who were. One such professor is C.L. Abercrombie, now professor emeritus at the University of Memphis. He was one of the first business professors in North America and, like most in his cohort, came from a background in industry. When he first became a university professor, there were a wide variety of professors who believed a wide variety of models for how the discipline should be taught. Professor Abercrombie (no one ever used his first name, out of respect for the long history and amount of his experience) used to tell stories fondly recounting the history of business and business education and when universities first began to offer courses and programs in business administration. Most of the models being used at that time had their foundations in the paradigms of scientific enquire. Some professors believed that business should be taught from an empirical perspective, in order to establish the discipline as more "serious" and "scientific" compared to others who wanted to take a more "applied" approach (Abercrombie 1989).

Those professors who labeled themselves as empiricists felt there was one Truth that we were on a journey to discover, thus their lectures were presented in a very authoritarian manner, with *the* truth being told about how business should be done. However, those who labeled themselves phenomenologists felt that there were many truths, and thus many ways of doing business, and their classes took a more exploratory approach to figuring out what method was best used in business under which circumstance, and the way the class was conducted was a more relaxed and exploratory environment, with options to select from in completing assignments or other forms of assessment (Tidwell 1999).

Thus, as the overall discipline of business followed in the paths of paradigms, so too did the presentation of material in the classroom. These trends were also reflected in the type of research that was encouraged or discouraged at various business departments, some preferring a more empirical approach while others preferred more phenomenological approach.

Each of theses two ends of the paradigmatic spectrum (and all options in between, such as the critical theorists) had their main aspects upon which they differed in how business models developed over time, and how they were taught in the classroom:

- Ontological
- Epistemological
- Methodological

Ontological deals with where the knowledge comes from, its origins. For example, in marketing, many believe that the discipline arose from economics and the study of supply and demand; however, others believe that a consumer orientation first started in the human factors domain when airplanes were redesigned during World War II to suit the pilots' needs. Regardless of supply and demand and economic theory, those "consumer" needs played an important role in the outcome of the war, which was the business at hand (Tidwell et al. 1996).

Epistemological refers to how you know something, or to the nature of knowledge. Typically this refers to what the truth is rather than where it came from. For example, most economists believe consumers are rational beings, and thus some marketers follow this belief. However, others from a psychology background believe consumers are irrational and seek to explain this irrational behavior (Tidwell 1999).

Methodology, on the other hand, is how you test what you know to determine whether it is true or not. The empiricists tend to use experimental designs to prove causality, controlling for all extraneous variables. Phenomenologists, however, believe that these are many truths, and they exist within the mind of the researcher and in the context of what is being studied. Anthropologists, such as Russell Belk, studying modern-day consumer culture in the context of ancient rituals and rites, tend to use the emic and etic perspectives to get an overall view of how the truth is perceived from all viewpoints. In his series of studies on the Aboriginal peoples of Australia and how they integrate past and present consumer products, he investigated this phenomenon from many views. And he teaches in much the same way as he conducts his research, changing roles with his students and engaging them in his research as colleagues, as teaching becomes a mutually rewarding experience for all concerned (Belk 1995).

Many professors, such as Belk, use a sophisticated technique called triangulation. Triangulation is when you take several methods from several paradigms and test to see whether or not they all produce the same conclusions, and most doctoral theses and dissertations in business over the past ten years, throughout the world, have used this technique to satisfy supervisors and committee members, who tend to come from different paradigmatic backgrounds. Most committee members have one paradigm they prefer a student to use and have strong biases against the others, so it is in the best interest of the graduate student to use this methodology to ensure a positive outcome and expeditious progress through his or her course of study (Tidwell 1999).

Temporal Trends and Practices

Prior to 1950, business education at universities was primarily embedded in the empiricist school of thought and was emerging from a legal and economic perspective. At vocational schools, however, the applied approach was taken, with business skills being taught to all who wanted a career, for example, in legal or administrative services (Abercrombie 1989). However, World War II challenged everyone's assumptions about life, and this included how the business discipline was being taught (Abercrombie 1989). Many people challenged the rational and empiricist approach to teaching business and began integrating many other schools of thought, from psychology to anthropology and sociology, into the content and process of business teaching (Abercrombie 1989). Thus, 1950 to 1980 was an age of experimentation and testing of limits at many business schools, where multidisciplinary topics and methods of teaching emerged. Professors from psychology and sociology became members of the business faculty, and a unique combination of thought emerged (Abercrombie 1989).

However, at the same time, accreditation procedures for business education were developing, and by 1980 those who wanted to join the "club" were required to curtail their more creative curriculum tendencies as strict guidelines were established in the name of "quality" (Association to Advance Collegiate Schools of Business [AACSB], www.aacsb.edu). Some individu-

als from disciplines related to, but not offered in, business schools or departments were not allowed to take courses in the business school if they were
undergoing accreditation, which put undue restrictions on individuals and
the overall development of business education in the name of quality. For
example, at the University of Memphis, students in consumer psychology
and social psychology related to overall trends in the marketplace, and individual purchase attitudes and behavior were removed from courses in which
they enrolled in order to ensure an overall "quality" in the business discipline and permit them to enter the ranks of schools accredited under the
AACSB guidelines (Tidwell 1993).

Individuals that had been allowed to take a wide variety of business courses
in the early 1980s were not allowed to enroll in any business courses by the
late 1980s and had to get permission from the dean to sit in and audit classes
(unofficially, of course) even for the courses that they were going to be teaching once they finished their degrees, such as those majoring in consumer
psychology (a multidisciplinary degree combining computer science, cogni-
tive psychology, and marketing). Thus, we would like to label 1980 to 2000
the "bureaucratic" years, with the content and process of business teaching
being scrutinized through standards and benchmarking in a process of con-
forming to what everyone else was doing, or rather not doing. Academic
freedom was challenged as course syllabi were required to meet certain standards, and even the models of international education that had once been
respected and revered were giving up their individuality to "join the club"
(Tidwell 1993).

Presently, there is an increased awareness of the way business is taught
throughout the world but there appears also to be an overall lack of respect
for diversity and an underlying assumption that each of our own models is
the correct one. Instead of increasing our overall appreciation of the historical developments that have produced these differences, we seem willing to
trim around the edges to try to make everyone conform to certain standards,
which will restrict the overall development of the discipline. How we teach
business and what we teach are intricately linked to one another, and we
must retain "quality" without sacrificing our creativity and diversity, both as
institutions in curriculum development and as instructors in individual syllabi, course design, and delivery. I believe all accreditation bodies—local,
regional, national, and international—should carefully examine this issue
for all those who have undergone accreditation. All those business schools
who have gone through this process should ask themselves what they gave
up in order to join the club, and those contemplating membership in the club
should carefully consider the overall benefits and sacrifices that they will
have to make in the name of quality and standardization. Cloning should not

be a concept that business education implements, as diversity is what encourages creativity, and this is what started businesses in the first place.

Cultural Traditions

The Soviet Model

Education in the Soviet Union was one of the best in the world, with the highest overall quality standards and specific procedures followed for curriculum development, course content, and all assessment criteria (for a complete historical review, see Dailey and Cardozier 1997). To a degree unheard of in other countries, the centralized government ensured that universities taught only what the labor market needed. For example, economics majors were trained especially to major in the socialist form of economics based on how many economists would be needed by the time of graduation. Under this system, they ensured that all universities were doing the same thing and studying a certain content that conformed to the rhetoric of the day. Thus, this is not unlike what the AACSB was attempting to do with its accreditation procedures in the early 1980s in the United States.

Students rise at the beginning of class, no one is allowed to talk, come late, or leave early. Discipline and control are maintained by the professor to ensure maximum efficiency in delivery of the lecture material with the fewest number of interruptions. Final exams are given orally to all students with completely randomized questions being asked of each student for a subset of the total set of test questions that have been thoroughly covered in tutorials or workshops, which are held each week for each lecture delivered. The overall methods of business education were based on traditional teaching methods introduced by Peter the Great (Avis 1987; Dunstan 1987; Holmes 1991; Kirschenbaum 2001).

The Post-Soviet Model

The overall educational system under the Soviet Union has not disappeared with the collapse of the government system (Gershunsky 1993). Remnants of the past are far more likely than not to survive, with people uncertain of which parts to retain and what to jettison (Holmes, Read, and Voskresenskaya 1994). A variety of options are being considered, but each change takes a long lead time to consider and debate and test because overall decision-making autonomy has not been taught to the majority of the people in positions of authority who are able to make the changes (Dailey and Cardozier 1997; Jones 1994). Discussions of groups, debates, opinions, and evaluations take months and sometimes years in order to effect even the most minor of changes

(Zouev 1999). However, this can also be said about university bureaucracies throughout the world. Resistance to change is a human quality, regardless of which form of government prevails or how much individuals have been taught to make empowered individual decisions (Tidwell et al. 1996).

In many of the former Soviet republics, such as Kazakhstan, the Soviet style of education based on centralized democracy and Marxist theory has prevailed for many years, and with the collapse of this system, many republics have found themselves now in the category of "developing countries." The models currently being used in national and government funded universities to teach business education are similar to those used in the 1950s in America and Europe; however, this is beginning to change as a consumer culture with access to cable television begins to teach a new generation of Kazakhstanis about capitalism and materialism.

The haves and the have-nots have returned to the former Soviet republics with all the flamboyance of its former bourgeoisie and proletariat class distinctions. The wealthy seek material gratification and can afford to send their children to the most expensive universities, while the poor suffer and dream of attending any college or university, one day or one generation to come. The wealthy can afford to have their children learn the most modern and Western methods of doing business, while the poor learn 1950s economics wrapped in a Soviet-system style of delivery. Although the economy is classified as "developing," Kazakhstan has modern plumbing facilities, the most advanced science in the world (leading in aerospace technology; recall that the Soviet Union was the first in space, and those institutions were/are located in Kazakhstan). According to the classical definitions of "developing economies," the former Soviet republics meet many of the criteria of "developed" countries; however, the biggest difference lies in the overall distribution systems and level of production.

During Soviet times, the system was so elaborately linked that it was like the five blind ladies and the elephant, with each holding only a small part of the elephant and no one grasping the entire picture; no one is able to determine that it is an elephant, much less teach it how to stand on its hind legs. Thus, even though the concept of the Commonwealth of Independent States was/is a good one, with free trade across all former Soviet republic borders, overall production and distribution systems have not been coordinated well enough to maintain the level of production in the glory days of the Soviet Union. Assembly lines stand still, agricultural machinery rusts, and people go hungry making homemade bread and milking their cows by hand, selling the bread and milk door to door trying to eke out a living.

While the wealthy are able to come into the largest retail chain for electronic appliances in all of Kazakhstan and buy top quality products from around the world, the poor dream of even owning a telephone manufactured after 1950. Thus, I go to the local university and teach for the maximum wage of $200 per month for a full professor with many publications, so I can provide a Western approach to teaching international economics, from a marketing perspective, and international business, from a marketing perspective, because a consumer orientation is an alien concept to the university, businesses, and the government. Asking people what they want instead of telling them what they can or should have is a completely different approach that is simply unknown and misunderstood.

Eastern Models

Kazakhstan is also looking at the significant changes in China and its higher education system, as well as its entry into the World Trade Organization (WTO) and the impact of its Special Economic Zones. This will be compared to the sudden application and influx of capitalist perspectives in Kazakhstan, as the two countries have many features in common and have similar ambitions and goals, although different approaches to these through business education.

Confucianism + Communism

Confucius teaches respect for other human beings and respect for society, a pacifist approach, and a code of honor that goes far beyond any Western philosophy's notion of positive outcomes for followers. Combined with Communism, which is a system of egalitarian government, one can see why China has been successful at integrating and maintaining its system of government. However, the government wanted to test to see whether a modified form of capitalism could be added to this effective mix of philosophies and began what is known as "Special Economic Zones." The idea sprang forth after it was agreed with Great Britain to return Hong Kong to the mother country. How would the People's Republic of China (PRC) manage such a different culture of rampant capitalism in Hong Kong, without any prior knowledge of managing capitalist ventures? At the same time, universities began teaching business education in a way that would allow future communist leaders to become effective business leaders in these new areas.

Capitalism + Communism

Through the Special Economic Zones, the Chinese were able to establish strict control over the effects of capitalism and manage their potential integration into their communist government system. Studies at all major universities involved examinations and close scrutiny of the effects of capitalism. It led to the establishment of the first stock exchange in China. Students and practitioners joined hands in the development of business education, with an ever-increasing focus on communication, prompting millions to learn English, German, and French as second languages in primary schools to prepare for new ventures.

Special programs of business education and research institutes were established and actively sought collaboration with institutions around the world. Conferences began to be hosted in China by Chinese universities and research institutes, for example, with thousands of students and professors coming to absorb the theories and carefully consider which ones would work with the currently approved philosophies of Confucianism and Communism. This carefully considered strategy and slow pondering and examination of the phenomenon of capitalism is what earned the respect of the international community and eventually allowed the PRC entry into the WTO. To this day, integration continues in a slow and steady way in an attempt to prevent, control, and monitor the pitfalls of capitalism that so many countries are having enormous problems dealing with—such as homelessness and hunger, who is entitled to education, water, and medicine—with many socialist governments going broke and unable to carry the burden and many capitalist governments unwilling to care for the poor.

Business schools need to cover corporate citizenship and a more socialist or communistic approach to capitalism, as it appears as though the extremes have been taught in the universities throughout the world to the detriment of those societies who focused only on capitalism. Conscience needs to enter the business education system.

Western Models

East European

East European models are akin to the models used in the Soviet Union. The promotional systems of academic rank and how many years it takes to become a full professor are identical. East German practices and the strong links to West German businesses formed after the fall of the Berlin Wall have a very strong presence in Kazakhstan, and the business models found in universities derive from these practices.

North American

Business models from the North American continent are used only by private universities in Kazakhstan and run so opposite to what students expect that many students have difficulty adapting to the system. Basic principles of consumer orientation are so foreign to students that several lectures with concrete examples of how this must be done in practice are required. Marketing is still viewed as demand economics, with people factors as number-driven variables, and emphasis on how to produce enough things to meet targets and supply people, generally not taking into account what will make them happy. A production concept reigns in all businesses except the multinational corporations, which have headquarters in Western capitalist countries. Only students who have had some experience with these companies can fully comprehend what is being taught in the business classes, using the American models of business education based on a combination of market share and customer satisfaction.

British Commonwealth Countries

Models in the British Commonwealth nations are much more like the current post-Soviet style of education, and because of the socialist background, are often more comfortable to students. Research-only master and doctoral degree approaches, with little or no coursework, are also practiced in Kazakhstan universities. Strong links between the European Union and its funding bodies have provided for many university start-ups and are teaching a softer form of capitalism to students, based on lecture and tutorial-style presentations in undergraduate courses.

The Kazakhstan Experience

*Teaching at a Western-Style University Without
Partners Abroad*

Business students attending a Western-style university in Kazakhstan are confused because they have nothing with which to compare the quality of education. They try to compare it to the way other universities teach business and do not understand when faculty try to explain that it is not the way it is done at *this* place. Teachers are just as confused because teaching strategies used in other countries do not work in Kazakhstan. The common knowledge that students accumulate from living in a capitalist country by the time they arrive at a university in those countries is not present in Kazakhstan. The administration also has difficulty adapting to the evolving situation; with rampant cheating, plagiarism, and payments being received for grade inflation at almost all other universities, administrators have a difficult time explaining to parents that the student must attend class and work harder in order to improve grades because a large donation to the building fund will not work. Western models of business are being taught, and the procedures and methods being used by administrators and faculty reinforce the content of the courses at every turn.

Teaching at an International University with Partners Abroad

Universities with partners abroad who are successful with exchange programs also have more overall success in teaching business from these experience-based models because the students and faculty go and experience what is being taught firsthand. Students return with confidence and a common knowledge base that makes their classroom concepts come alive in ways that the students could not grasp before. Administrators have an easier time with students, as the overall culture reflects the business models being taught and the overall organizational culture gradually comes to reflect this as well.

Teaching at a Kazakh National University Without Partners Abroad

The faculty are still teaching the way they always have and teaching the same content they have always taught. Administrators are still administrating in the ways they always have. A few lines have been added to the course content and a few deleted to ensure that the rhetoric of old is not blatant and the new rhetoric is being embraced; however, academic integrity is a problem, and student plagiarism and openly cheating on quizzes and exams is the norm. Collectivism and communism have been taken to new heights in terms of collectivist knowledge, with replies to quizzes sometimes being discussed in groups of five or six openly in front of the instructor. In a weekly quiz, for example, in a class of thirty students, no less than ten students are given a zero for cheating and those are just the ones who are noisy and obvious enough to be caught.

Lectures on foreign countries are being taught right out of books by professors who have never been out of the country. International business, for example, is being tutored by people who have no business experience and have never been outside the country. Thus, the curriculum is neither international nor business oriented as any Western-style university would define it. Professors ought to spend far more time with junior faculty explaining the differences between the pedantic, procedural, task-related knowledge currently taught (i.e., how to write a contract proposal to an international corporation) and the underlying pedagogical theory required to determine what the needs of firms are and how students should be prepared. Currently the latter is missing. A mix of scientific and economic calculations are taught, and rote-learning is stressed to the point of putting students to sleep, but everything else in the middle, which forms the basis of a true market economy, is somehow strangely missing thus far.

Conclusions

Business education in Kazakhstan is a myriad of past, present, and future ambitions and goals, and it is implemented in different ways based on the choice of overseas affiliations, and reflecting in the resulting educational experience vast differences in cultural, historical, governmental, institutional, and leveraging paradigmatic contacts. It is, in short, a veritable pedagogical laboratory for contending business education models as innovation gradually overtakes entrenched ways and painfully allows for adjustments.

References

Abercrombie, C.L. 1989. "History of Business and Business Education." Lecture presented at the University of Memphis, Memphis, TN.

Avis, G., ed. 1987. *The Making of the Soviet Citizen.* New York: Croom Helm/Methuen.

Belk, R. 1995. "Career Strategies in Business Education." Seminar at Charles Sturt University, Bathurst, NSW Australia.

Dailey, M.T., and V.R. Cardozier. 1997. *Higher Education in Russia.* Available at http://studentorgs.utexas.edu/heaspa/library/rus.htm.

Dunstan, J., ed. 1987. *Soviet Education Under Scrutiny.* Glasgow: Jordanhill College.

Gershunsky, B. 1993. *Russia in Darkness: On Education and the Future.* San Francisco: Caddo Gap Press.

Holmes, L. 1991. *The Kremlin and the Schoolhouse: Reforming Education in Soviet Russia, 1917–1931.* Bloomington: Indiana University Press.

Holmes, B.; G. Read; and N. Voskresenskaya. 1994. *Russian Education: Tradition and Transition.* New York: Garland.

Jones, A., ed. 1994. *Education and Society in the New Russia.* Armonk, NY: M.E. Sharpe.

Kirschenbaum, L. 2001. *Small Comrades: Revolutionizing Childhood Education in Russia, 1917–1932.* New York: Routledge-Falmer.

Lee, D.C. 1988. *The People's Universities of the U.S.S.R.* New York: Greenwood.

Tidwell, P.M. 1993. Interview conducted for the student newspaper at Charles Sturt University, Bathurst, NSW, Australia.

———. 1999. "Paradigmatic Shifts in Marketing: Ontology, Epistemology, and Methodology." In *The Current State of Business Disciplines*, ed. S.B Dahiya. Rohtak, India: Spellbound.

Tidwell, P.M. et al. 1996. *Consumer Behavior in Australia and New Zealand.* Sydney, NSW: McGraw-Hill.

Zouev, A., ed. 1999. *Generation in Jeopardy: Children in Central and Eastern Europe and the Former Soviet Union.* Armonk, NY: M.E. Sharpe.

10

Entrepreneurial Behavior in the Academic Environment

A Case Study of the Lviv Institute of Management

*Sharon V. Thach, Serhiy Gvozdiov,
and Galen Hull*

Unlike the Central European and Baltic countries, Ukraine had not agitated, organized, or planned for independence. However, the introduction of perestroika did result in the start of very small, limited private concerns in Ukraine. Among the surprising cooperatives that emerged were two business schools, one in Kyiv and one in Lviv, both begun before independence. Business schools would seem unlikely organizations at the start of perestroika, but there they were. This chapter focuses on the Lviv Institute of Management (LIM), an entrepreneurial venture that began with very limited resources in an environment not particularly conducive to such initiatives and has not only survived, but grown through innovation, skillful deployment of small initial resources to gain access to new resources, and successful leveraging of the resources acquired.

Quite apart from the importance of Ukrainian business schools in the transformation of the economy, from the perspective of a resource-based view of organizational structure and functioning, this higher education enterprise provides an interesting extended case in the uses, importance, and mechanisms by which new ventures can grow and develop their resources and then deploy them effectively while accommodating changing external environments. The intangible assets acquired, characterized by the tacitness, complexity, and specificity that make imitation difficult (Fahy and Smithee 1999) have allowed LIM to become a high quality, successful competitor despite limited financial and environmental resources. Consequently, this case history is structured around LIM's acquisition, development, and use of resources. It should also be noted that the entrepreneurship of this institute extends to its defined mission and ability to attract and mold students into that vision. That mission includes modeling the behavior taught: imaginative and flexible responses to environmental conditions emphasizing quality, despite the temptation to pursue immediate market payoffs. Along with lower than average tuition rates, there is a deliberate effort to keep classes small and personal in order to adapt basic materials to the particular industry or learning needs of the students.

External Environment in Central and Eastern Europe at Founding

At independence, Ukrainians had to rely primarily upon themselves for educational reform and modernization. During the early 1990s, the U.S. government began to provide development assistance to the Newly Independent States (NIS) in the region. The U.S. Agency for International Development's Management Training and Economics Education Project (USAID MTEEP) provided funding for partnering ten U.S. universities with universities in nine Central and East European (CEE) countries: Albania, Bulgaria, Czech Republic, Hungary, Latvia, Lithuania, Poland, Romania, and the Slovak Republic (Datex 1997).

By the end of 1997, the first graduates of the more mature programs gained access to the marketplace, utilizing their skills and knowledge to improve the operations for their firms. There were seven master of business administration (MBA) programs operating in five countries (Albania, Hungary, Latvia, Poland, and the Slovak Republic) with just over 1,000 students enrolled. Some 207 students had received their MBA degrees, and another 200 were expected to complete the degree by the spring of 1998. Even though few of the programs had attained official recognition, MBA graduates were finding success in the job market, large foreign firms, and the myriad of start-ups seeping up out of the informal sector (Hull 1999).

Management Education in Ukraine

The approach to assistance in Russia and Ukraine would be quite different for U.S. agencies as well as for Tacis. Official aid from the United States was *not* geared toward major institutional partnerships and university rebuilding. Support from European sources was mixed—some institutional support, some for training of trainers, some short courses (Tacis 1996). However, just as the knowledge of market economies and standards of communication and operation within them were new, so was the whole idea of grants and proposals. One of the most useful initial aid efforts in overcoming both challenges was the Peace Corps. In the case of LIM, Peace Corps volunteers were instrumental in developing networks and materials, and providing information on business education, obtaining grant funds, and ensuring that they addressed the most pressing resource needs. LIM was able to get grants from the Eurasia Foundation for case study writing and for extension of the library as well as from the Renaissance Foundation to cover part of the costs for internships of MBA students from LIM in the United States. The USAID grants paid for development of a Technology Promotion Center, enabling LIM to be the first Business School in Ukraine to launch an Internet-based distance learning MBA.

After independence, Ukraine passed the "Law of Ukraine on Education" (June 4, 1991), officially permitting the operation of nonstate educational institutions. In 1992, an accreditation system for higher education was devised, requiring a large number of documents, permits, inspections, and examinations plus multiple fees. LIM has attained the highest accreditation level allotted to private schools. Determination, financial resources, and creativity are necessary for any private institute to gain official standing.

The first two management education institutes in Ukraine were founded before independence and without formal assistance. They were both market ventures, not revised departments within an existing state institution. The first, International Management Institute (IMI) in Kyiv, resulted from a partnership with IMI Switzerland, while the second, LIM, was an entirely indigenous enterprise deriving early support through a network of professors and professionals from the Ukrainian diaspora. As there was no official way in which to gain state approval, these schools were operating in a gray area, but also providing the first opportunities for managers and potential business owners to learn skills appropriate to a market-based economy. Even now, there are only five MBA programs being offered in Ukraine out of the 129 nonstate educational institutions: four in Kyiv, and one in Lviv. A number of the state universities have developed business courses and programs, but only at the undergraduate level.

Development of all these programs has been slow for several reasons: lack of familiarity with the MBA among both potential students and employers, the new concept of paying for advanced education, and economic difficulties of the transition. Not only was the MBA concept virtually unknown, the cheery promises and often outright lies about each new reform in Soviet times had conditioned the population to disbelieve in new remedies and programs until they proved themselves. The heavy losses of capital at independence combined with high inflation defeated many new ventures and slowed formation of others. Money for tuition and the market for new training shrank.

Until the late 1990s, only the two original business schools offered viable MBA programs. Then four new ones, some with outside funding, opened in Kyiv and Dnepropetrovsk (now already defunct). Kyiv Business School (founded in 2000) worked with Kassel International Management School, and the International Institute of Business (2001) awarded a certificate in business administration from the University of New Brunswick. The other two, the School of Business and Management (1998) and Kyiv-Mohyla Business School (2001) are officially unaffiliated, although Mohyla received significant start-up funds from multinationals based in Kyiv and has an alliance with the Dnepropetrovsk Privatbank. These programs are officially for-profit ventures, and several are aggressively seeking European or American investors by promising profitability. Tuition at the Kyiv schools is significantly higher than LIM's, reflecting both the greater wealth and corporate presence in Kyiv and the profit-making goals of their founders. Tuition ranges from $6,000 to $9,000 per program as compared with $3,800 at LIM.

At the Beginning: Intellectual Resources Only

The original LIM founders were young members of the Lviv State University faculty, trained in the production engineering style of the former Soviet system and later joined by former government officials with *komsomol* training, the only management training available in Soviet times. These younger economists were largely self-taught in Western economics and business, using the few available materials (with glasnost, foreign books, materials, and contacts were easier to obtain than was formerly the case, but were still very limited) and visits with foreign scholars to gain sufficient understanding to begin operations; the professors began teaching in a basement wing of their former university.

The only resources available at the start were limited funds raised from a few backers, and a belief that expatriate Ukrainian communities would find ways to assist them. After independence, it was possible to tap the Ukrainian communities in North America and Europe for help, so in 1991 an International Supervisory Council was established and a computer laboratory installed.

The first model for the nascent MBA program was that of Wayne State University in Detroit, Michigan, home to a large concentration of the diaspora. Wayne State and the Ukrainian business community in Detroit provided training for the LIM professors, housing, access to the American business community, and assistance in translation and interpretation. They also created internships for the first groups of MBA students, housing and feeding them as well. They came to Ukraine to teach, bringing books and new teaching methods. The key resource acquisition facilities were the ability of the Ukrainian faculty to learn while working, the early introduction to Western businesses and internships, and low costs. The overseas Ukrainians were important sources of capital and access. During and after a first university partnership, the multiyear involvement with Wayne State, LIM was able to create alliances with other institutions that provided teaching, faculty training, and institutional credentials to the student population in the Lviv region.

In cooperation with Temple University, LIM established the Technology Promotion Center through an "Institutional Partnership" supported by the U.S. Information Agency and initiated by some in the diaspora community. Short-term cooperation with some other schools, such as Kansas University, was also useful in extending the geography of cooperation and helped to continue preparation of Ukrainian trainers.

European programs were more business oriented. For example, a Tacis grant supported the development of consulting skills in the local faculty. Eventually extending beyond the institute, nonacademic organizations formed to support small business development. These early alliances with international schools made it possible to adapt programs in business education from Europe and North America to the Ukrainian environment.

Early Expansion

With a solid, accepted MBA program in place and a faculty able to assume greater responsibility for teaching, LIM looked to expand. The institute moved into several floors of an office building not far from the city center. As the first MBA class graduated in 1992, LIM also began offering short-term courses, started a Business Support Center with funding from the Center for International Private Enterprise, and joined the European Foundation for Management Development.

The MBA program now offered two options: a full-time program and an evening part-time program. The early graduates proved to be the best advertising and support for the program, recruiting new students and hiring other graduates. Following the model of many North American programs, LIM formed an alumni association that reinforced the networking aspects, making an LIM degree more valuable and, at the same time, provided the opportunity for additional training and selection of some graduates to become faculty members themselves.

LIM has found that faculty members themselves are in demand by other organizations who seek multilingual, business-astute personnel who can work effectively in the increasingly international economy of Ukraine. Most of these organizations can offer far higher salaries and perks. Multinationals, Ukrainian companies, and consulting companies vie with the institute so the costs of training have not always worked to the institute's advantage. Thus, while LIM has created a small, stable cadre of faculty, it also has had to continue developing faculty and relying on outside partners to continue to offer high quality courses. Faculty training was partially addressed by several outside organizations. One such effective vehicle is the Central and East European Management Development Association, a private initiative bringing faculty together to exchange materials, training, and methods, and to address common problems. Another helpful resource is the USAID-funded Consortium for the Enhancement of Ukrainian Management Education (CEUME) project coordinated by the University of Minnesota. A number of LIM faculty members have attended CEUME workshops on case development and have published in texts developed for Ukraine. Other LIM members have taught faculty in the summer workshop programs and facilitated conferences on teaching methods. While these programs have been available to all institutions in Ukraine, LIM placed particular emphasis on them, supported faculty involvement, and became an academic leader, eventually resulting in the Lviv Initiative for interorganizational cooperation. The visible achievements of the participating LIM faculty have solidified its reputation in Ukraine, highly important given the centrifugal pull of Kyiv in education and foreign investment.

As LIM created and attracted sufficient faculty with high-level qualifications and training, it was able to expand its program. While the MBA program continued to be successful, it was clear that institutional sustainability and impact on Ukraine would require expansion at the undergraduate level. In 1998, LIM inaugurated a bachelor of business administration (BBA) program, in line with the recommendations in the review of business programming needs in Ukraine conducted by McConnell and Prendergast for USAID in 1997. Undergraduate students could get a degree in either marketing or management, but could also obtain solid training in finance, accounting, information systems, and English as well. In the short period that this program has been in effect, student enrollment has steadily increased (with 27 students at the start, to more than 300 bachelors' students currently enrolled at LIM), internal traditions and organizations have developed, and the outlook for continued expansion is good on the demand side. One external event that has helped the program is the introduction of tuition for some students in the state university system along with "unofficial" fees for teaching in many of the state programs in high demand areas such as economics and business. The superior conditions, teaching, and honesty of the LIM program are now even more attractive. Along with the undergraduate program, LIM expanded early, with significant help from Peace Corps volunteers, Tacis partners (Mons University and Valenciennes University), and USAID, into management consulting and small business development, training classes, and certificate programs.

During this time, LIM began to host foreign students, bringing students from Ivey Business School, University of Western Ontario to Lviv for coursework and study in the Lviv region. Thus, what began as an alliance to learn case method teaching and gain access to Western-style education for faculty became a lasting partnership with benefits to both participants.

Unlike many others, however, they did not expect a single partner to advance the organization nor did they seek duplicate efforts from each partner. Rather, each new alliance focused on some specific benefits, and the partners were chosen with an eye on LIM goals rather than a general "get whatever kind of help you can" approach. Also, although appreciative of the efforts of outside institutions, LIM used its own resources in the later initiatives in order to be a partner in these alliances, allowing them to shape the direction of the partnerships and the type of participation. This is in contrast to many of the institutions in the NIS area, where, as the USAID and Tacis reports concluded, fearful of losing grants and support, institutions often accepted programs and assistance that were not particularly relevant to the institutions' developing mission.

In particular, LIM was determined to obtain teaching methods training for its own faculty, particularly in the areas of case analysis and simulations. These more interactive learning situations were a very definite departure from traditional university teaching in Ukraine. Thus, the program for bringing European and North American academics into LIM to offer either full courses or some classes served a dual purpose: faculty observed and participated in learning methodologies they could adapt and apply themselves, while students exposed to the latest Western materials and techniques were able to assure potential employers that they held degrees very equivalent to those gained at Western institutions. Both purposes enhanced the institutional prestige of LIM and yielded higher enrollments of high quality students. Linkages with faculty in the partnering schools also gave faculty access to journals, research materials, and ancillary teaching materials (overheads, CDs, and manuals).

The other faculty priority was gaining access to advanced academic degrees. Although most would complete their doctorates in Ukraine universities, the partnership and grant arrangements allowed many to study for semesters or in intensive courses at Western universities and to develop dissertations in appropriate areas. These dissertations have often dealt with some of the most pressing issues, especially small business, equipping the faculty with skills useful for LIM consulting and outreach efforts.

Finally, LIM focused on student language capabilities in English and other European languages. Coincident with the BBA program was the founding of an English Department, and all students were required to take a full course throughout their studies within the MBA program while a substantial number of the faculty developed facility in English.

New Initiatives

The assessment of the Ukraine economic and education situation undertaken in 1997 was the basis for LIM's new strategic plan adopted in 1998. The BBA, the master's in marketing, and the distance MBA programs were major components of this plan. Preparation for the distance program included working with the Open University of the United Kingdom in a mentoring situation. With these new initiatives planned, LIM is determined to find assistance in developing, promoting, and expanding these programs.

One major development under the new strategic plan was the purchase of land and the building of dedicated facility for LIM. A corporate-type edifice with offices, classrooms, café, auditorium, library, and computer laboratories are in the first building of a planned campus. More than the attraction of studying in a clean, warm, and well-planned building, the permanence of the investment is a statement of intent to potential students, employers, and donors. Funds for the building were raised in Ukraine, the expatriate community, and a $100,000 grant from the International Renaissance Foundation, the balance being paid by tuition. The new facility was opened officially during the tenth anniversary festivities in 2001. Representatives of the various alliances and partnerships from the first decade came to Lviv to join in the commemoration, itself a reaffirmation of the original determination as well as a celebration of the very real achievements.

The new competitive environment requires LIM to continue innovating. The distance MBA has competition only from Kyiv Business School, and only Kyiv-Mohyla is offering a specialist masters, both begun after LIM's introduction of the concepts in Ukraine. A recent LIM internal study examined the country market in two ways: geographical coverage of programs and industry-specific growth. Compiling data from recruiting agencies, they concluded that current and near future demand for sales/marketing specialists, retail managers, and production/supply chain personnel are greatest.

Despite major manufacturing operations and improving consumer markets, there is little penetration of business programs in East Ukraine outside of state university programs. None offers a graduate degree comparable to an MBA, so LIM is looking for American partners to expand its distance program, perhaps even offering a joint MBA degree with an American university. With sufficient enrollment, intensive, onsite sessions could be offered in eastern Ukraine rather than Lviv. The results of the initial distance effort are encouraging as the quality of the enrollees is excellent, with most employed by international firms and agencies. If the word of mouth regarding the program is as high as it is for the Lviv in-person programs, the distance option should be a good one. First-mover advantage is important here in order to gain sponsored enrollments from multinationals. This would permit higher fees that would subsidize new program development.

LIM is actively looking for an accrediting body that would fit the Ukrainian situation. American standards, which put a lot of emphasis on infrastructure, are not yet feasible. Some of the European programs insist on lengthy internships that are not workable in a situation where most enrollees are already employed. Alternatively, another European accreditation program requires high enrollments of nonnative students. Until English is a thorough standard for teaching, such outside enrollments are likely to remain small. A Russian language program might possibly enlarge the market, but only Kyiv as a location is likely to provide sufficient non-Ukrainian enrollments to pursue this option. Hence, either a suitable outside accrediting body must be located, or the offering of a joint program with an already accredited institution is important to continue validating the high quality of the LIM program to potential students and donors.

LIM has also begun a youth initiative. Somewhat like an intensive Junior Achievement program, the plan is to encourage entrepreneurship, instill an appreciation of the demands and benefits of a market economy, and develop a feeder system for the LIM undergraduate program.

The new focus for LIM lies in two areas: increased emphasis on consulting as an institutional operation and the generation of applied research. The consulting operation has two major objectives: providing faculty the chance to keep abreast of industry problems and needs, and also generating funds both for LIM institutionally and as a method for supplementing faculty salaries. The research function is needed given the difficulty of getting information on many aspects of the economic environment. Information could be sold or subscribed to by companies. The income would support the operation.

The first research initiative resulted in two reports. One is the previously mentioned survey of educational needs by geography and industrial sector. The second is an impact study of the effects of LIM on the Lviv region. This research was the result of institutional capacity developed over the past ten years. Individual faculty research is also increasing. Dissertation-related research is now being generated on Ukraine-related topics with a solid theoretical foundation. Partnerships are producing joint publications in Western research journals, and survey research is under way that has both application uses and potential publication prospects.

New courses have been introduced. LIM has identified areas where local demand appears high and has adapted partner courses with local content added and will continue to refine them. The continuing difficulty in obtaining books, journals, and other reference works, characteristic of all business schools in Ukraine, is still a limiting factor for faculty in developing courses as well for students in more specialized fields. This is mitigated by membership in the Consortium of European Research Libraries and the ability to use the online libraries of partner institutions as well as the ongoing effort to build a library (currently the largest and most current in Ukraine business schools), all resources added through alliances with foreign universities and foundations.

Perhaps the best indication of how effectively LIM has used its resources lies in the activities it undertakes with its partners. In addition to hosting students from a major Canadian university as students in Ukraine, LIM faculty are also lecturing and teaching full courses in the American schools. From limited knowledge and virtually no other resources than willingness to work at a risky proposition, LIM has grown into an institution with the confidence to interact institutionally and individually as equals with its Western counterparts. Although still without an endowment and dependent on tuition and outreach activities to meet expenses, the school has an excellent physical plant, current equipment, a library, and a trained, effective faculty.

The problems LIM now faces will require additional capacity building and strengthening of current initiatives. Growing competition from other Ukrainian schools, the entrance of European schools with distance education programs, the need to acquire expensive books, simulations, and software, developing a student base beyond the Lviv region, and enhanced outreach activities are the contemporary issues. Given the past history of LIM's entrepreneurial ability to find support for creating internal resources, they may become a formidable force in their region.

Management Capacities for Private Sector Development: Partnership Among Lviv Institute of Management, Tennessee State University, and Lincoln University

The following account of one of its recent partnerships shows how LIM determined ways to use the partnership to more effectively leverage the obtained resources beyond the original intent of the partnership. LIM initially sought assistance in two areas: course development and business outreach. In searching for one partner, they found two.

The 1997 strategic planning operation identified private sector involvement as a key growth area for LIM. Accordingly, LIM was looking for assistance. LIM agreed to enter into a partnership with Tennessee State University (TSU) for the submission of a proposed USAID grant, and TSU proposed adding Lincoln University as a partner institution. In October 2000, a two-year USAID partnership grant entitled Developing Business Management Capacities for Private Sector Development was awarded.

The goal of the partnership was to enhance management-training capabilities in each of the three participating institutions, while promoting private sector relations between western Ukraine and the United States. The partnership initially had two activities:

1. Arranging faculty exchanges among the partner institutions to develop curriculum reform and collaborative research in the area of business development.
2. Promoting private sector relations between western Ukraine and the United States by facilitating visits of Ukrainian business persons to the United States.

Over the lifetime of the partnership there were twenty-three faculty and staff exchanges, seven from TSU and five from Lincoln University to Ukraine, and eleven from LIM to the United States. Exchanges of U.S. faculty to Ukraine consisted of offering intensive courses in marketing and management, working with LIM faculty in adapting materials and concepts to create new courses for LIM, and discussing methods and curriculum design. U.S. faculty also met with Ukrainian business people expanding their knowledge of economies in transition. Exchanges of Ukrainian faculty to the United States involved observation of business school management, industry contacts, course lectures and case discussions, and collaborative research.

In the first exchange, two TSU College of Business faculty members participated in the second Annual International Conference of CEUME in addition to regular exchange activities. LIM had arranged attendance at the conference to enable the U.S. faculty to learn about the challenges of management education in Ukraine, meet administrators and faculty, and share knowledge about developing accreditation systems.

With knowledge gained from this first onsite visit, the partnership delegation visit from LIM to Nashville resulted in detailed discussions of mutual needs within the grant framework. The executive director of LIM and the director of international relations were joined by a delegation from Lincoln University, and all participated in TSU's Windows onto the World public lecture series. The Ukrainian delegation then visited Lincoln University.

Subsequently, a TSU marketing professor presented a course on e-commerce to undergraduates in the LIM bachelor of business administration program, and the course design, notes, and material were left for LIM faculty use. Then an LIM professor of marketing and the dean of the undergraduate management program traveled to Nashville for study and observation in marketing and program administration and intensive visits with advertising executives. The visit resulted in collaboration between TSU and LIM faculty in developing materials in advertising and advertising firm management for use in advisement to Lviv firms. An additional research effort on comparative business ethics also issued from the visit.

In June 2001, TSU and Lincoln faculty traveled to Ukraine to attend LIM's tenth anniversary, which also coincided with the official opening of the institute's new facilities. Later, faculty from Lincoln and TSU conducted a course in operations management and supply chain at LIM, an area of intense business interest in Ukraine. Then TSU hosted a group of four LIM MBA alumni who met with local firms in gas production and distribution, construction, hotel and restaurant management, and breweries.

The second major objective of the partnership was a business exchange involving Ukrainian business owners and managers traveling to the United States to observe U.S. firms in their respective industries, making contacts that might enhance their own firm's productivity. Two groups, consisting of two and five Ukrainian executives, respectively, spent several weeks in Missouri and Tennessee where they visited businesses in each state. The first Ukrainian business owners and managers of printing and travel firms were hosted by companies in their line of business. A second group of five executives from firms engaged in the production and distribution of cheese as well as manufacturing and marketing of other food products visited the United States.

Following these first courses and the business interns, in March 2002, the director of academic programs at LIM traveled to Nashville and Jefferson City to participate with his counterparts in planning for the balance of partnership activities, modifying plans based on the experience gained in the first year. One outcome was a significant partnership activity, not initially anticipated. LIM requested that its U.S. partners host Ukrainian MBA student interns, many of whom were also senior managers in their respective firms, on short-term visits. These visits became a regular part of partnership activity and have continued beyond the period of grant funding.

Another unanticipated result of the linkage has been faculty exchanges outside the grant. An LIM faculty member enjoyed a sabbatical with Lincoln University; another, who had served as interpreter to visiting U.S. faculty, was also invited to visit Lincoln University at the latter's expense. A TSU professor of marketing was awarded a Fulbright fellowship that enabled her to spend six weeks at the Lviv Institute of Management, teaching, consulting, and helping with faculty development. LIM provided accommodation and living expenses during this period, a demonstration of its ability to assume partnering responsibilities.

Collaboration between TSU and LIM marketing faculty members resulted in two research products: a paper accepted for publication in a leading American scholarly journal, and data on business advisory assistance organizations in western Ukraine, which will be used for both advisory assistance at LIM and additional publications. LIM faculty came to express a keen interest in continuing collaborative research efforts beyond the life of the grant. LIM had not, heretofore, been able to focus sufficiently on research, owing to the demands of the teaching and training programs.

Although the grant proposal made only a brief reference to undertaking collaborative research, this element of the partnership was to take on considerable importance. TSU's Office of Business and Economic Research (OBER) was commissioned to conduct an impact survey of the university on the Nashville metropolitan area. At LIM's request, the OBER director conducted a weeklong seminar on impact research methods for LIM faculty and staff, sharing both the methodology and results of his own survey with LIM in order to encourage them to carry out a similar study of LIM

The shared cost portion of the original grant included providing housing for visitors in homes. There were two positive results of this. First, the faculty at all three institutions got to know each other very well, both professionally and personally. These closer ties allowed for more open discussions of needs, wants, and adjustments as well as cultural insight useful in teaching and research. Additionally, the greater than anticipated savings from these stays (and careful airfare management) provided for a six-month no-cost grant extension resulting in two previously unanticipated activities. The primary purpose for requesting the extension was organizing a conference on Management Development and Business Education in Ukraine. LIM put together a conference agenda with this as the theme, held in the Hetman Hotel, Lviv in March 2003. The conference brought together some 100 participants from academic institutions, government agencies, and the Ukrainian private sector, as well as representatives from the two U.S. partner universities. Presenters, including two successful entrepreneurs, grappled with issues confronting private sector development in Ukraine.

At the annual North American Small Business International Trade Educators meeting in San Antonio, Texas, April 2003, there was a formal presentation on the business manager exchange. Both these activities enhanced LIM's quality position in Ukraine.

This reflects the ability of LIM to respond quickly to opportunities, direct relationships to accomplish strategic goals, and be an equal partner in these undertakings. From this relationship, LIM was able to obtain new courses in desired areas, continue to provide teachers from Western schools to its students, obtain resources for business leaders, and begin operating wholly new programs in research and conferences. Although LIM brought very limited funds into the partnership, they were major participants through in-kind contributions obtained from LIM faculty and staff, former students, and supporters in the Lviv business community. Faculty from LIM were able to clearly define book and research needs, determine their own contributions, and establish working relationships beyond the parameters originally spelled out in the grants. The opportunities for internships by both students and business professionals, needed for Ukraine development, and to maintain LIM's competitive position were important results of the alliance. Finally, LIM has been able to create ongoing ties, perhaps with new funding, for expansion of its distance education programs.

Appendixes

Accreditation and Degree Granting in Ukraine

All educational institutions must have a license, which is granted by the Ministry of Education after approval of the application packet. This does not give the right to confer degrees—that is a second stage attestation. An institution's activities and capacity are inspected before attestation is approved. There are four levels of accreditation. Although universities, academies, and institutes are all eligible for third- or fourth-level accreditation, no private institution has yet been given a fourth-level accreditation. LIM has received third level.

MBA Placements in Ukraine

From an LIM 2001 study (internal document):

- Only two programs offering an MBA in Ukraine have operated sufficiently long to examine the placement of MBA graduates: Lviv Institute of Management and International Management Institute, Kyiv.
- Number of Graduates: IMI—954, Lviv—254.

160

Appendix 10.1 **Number of Students in Academic Programs**

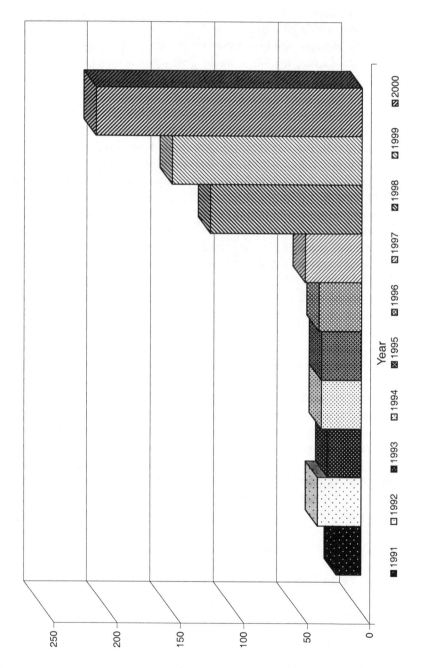

161

Appendix 10.2   **Number of Students in Education Programs**

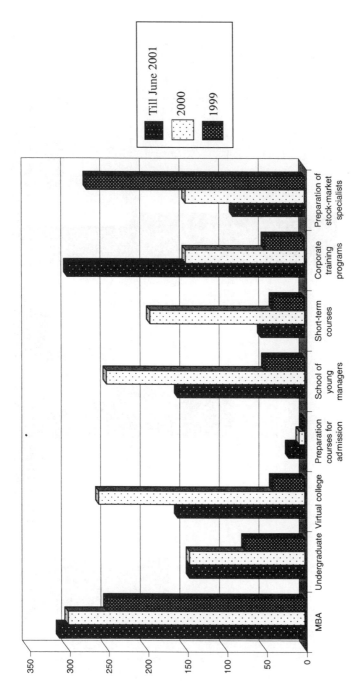

162

Appendix 10.3 **Student Geography**

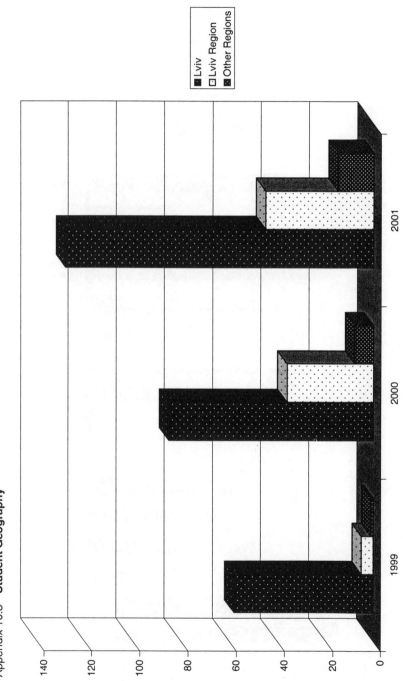

- More LIM graduates work directly in trade and manufacturing as compared to IMI, where graduates are more likely to work for banks and government. LIM alumni are also more like to own companies and work as senior managers, while IMI graduates are slightly more likely to be functional specialists.

Excerpts from the Impact Study: Lviv Institute of Management, Spring 2003 '

Proportional samples of BBA, MBA, and alumni students were questioned. There was near convergence in the three groups in agreement that the LIM program was high quality, aligned with business needs, a program with excellent job market demand, and of good value. Most also would give priority to an LIM graduate in hiring for their own staff. Very few received tuition assistance.

References

Datex (USAID contractor to evaluate MTEEP). 1997. Semi-Annual Formative Monitoring & Evaluation Report. (July 1–December 31). Submitted to the Office of Democracy, Governance and Social Reform, Human Resources Development Social Reform Division, Bureau for Europe and the Newly Independent States, USAID, Washington, DC.

Fahy, J., and A. Smithee. 1999. "Strategic Marketing and the Resource Based View of the Firm." *Academy of Marketing Science Review* 10.

Hull, G.S. 1999. *Small Businesses Trickling Up in Central and Eastern Europe.* New York: Garland.

Kyiv Business School. 2003. MBA in Ukraine.

Lviv Institute of Management. 1999. *Report on Management Education and Training in Ukraine.* Internal document.

McConnell, D., and W. Pendergast. 1997. "Assessment of Ukrainian Business Management Institutions." USAID.

Ministry of Education and Science of Ukraine, Ukrainian Association of Management Development and Business Education, Lviv Commercial Academy, and Lviv Institute of Management. 2003. Third All-Ukrainian Scientific-Practical Conference entitled Entrepreneurship and Management: Ukrainian Reality and Development Prospects, Lviv, Ukraine, March 21–23.

Office of International Business Programs, Tennessee State University. 2002. Institutional Partnerships Program Final Report. *Developing Business Management Capacities for Private Sector Development in Lviv, Ukraine.* Submitted to Association Liaison Office. September 30.

Tacis ETF. 1996. Evaluation of Activities in the Field of Management Training in the NIS.

11

The Internationalization of Business Education in Lithuania

The Vilnius University Master Program in International Business

Vytautas Pranulis and Audra I. Mockaitis

Lithuania is on the crossroads to permanent integration into the European Union (EU) and international markets. Growth in the country's economy and standard of living are influenced a great deal by the expansion of Lithuania's international business ties, the growth in quality and in volume of foreign capital enterprises, and the creation of international business networks. With the backdrop of a relatively high unemployment rate, companies working in Lithuania are faced with a lack of highly skilled specialists, who are able to communicate effectively with foreign partners and create and maintain international ties. The need to develop such employees points to the importance of master programs in international business that are tailored to meet the needs of the local and international markets. This chapter presents a new master program in international business at Vilnius University and discusses some of its strengths and weaknesses. The results of a study of university students are briefly presented and related to the aims and goals of the program.

Background

It is commonly known that graduate business education programs were developed in the United States at the beginning of the past century (Chaudhry 2003). European graduate programs were slower to develop, while such programs in

East European countries began to emerge only after the fall of the Soviet Union. Educational reforms in these countries have been ongoing since the 1990s with the aim of moving from a Soviet-type education system to models based on Western educational systems. More and more higher education institutions in these countries are now offering master of business administration (MBA) degrees. However, only in recent years have the universities in the Central and East European (CEE) countries begun to better tailor their programs to market demands and base their curricula on the interests of employers and the future managerial workforce. Yet the quality of curricula is still being assessed, and results will most likely be apparent only after comparing the qualifications and skills of graduates from these countries within the context of the EU.

The levels of education in the CEE countries are comparatively high. However, although quantitatively levels of education in these countries are similar to Organization for Economic Cooperation and Development countries, it is yet unknown whether the type and quality of higher education offered in these countries meet the expectations of business firms, especially those of foreign-owned firms, and whether they will be able to compete and attract students from the EU.

The traditional Lithuanian system is similar to those of other CEE countries and differs from those of Western Europe, and especially the United States. Traditionally, university education was based on a five-year degree program. Contrary to degree programs in the United States, which are based on more general knowledge, the curricula of universities in the former Soviet Union were based on a specialization already taken at the undergraduate level. The Soviet management system was based on the development of technical skills and knowledge and was far more scientific than Western management. Upon completion of university education, managers received appointments to positions in enterprises throughout the country.

Since the 1990s, all universities in Lithuania have changed their focus from management as an exact science to management, corresponding to Western conceptions. Exchanges between faculty and collaborations on programs with West European institutions have been increasing steadily over the years and have resulted in various types of programs, ranging from those based on Scandinavian-type management education to those relying heavily on U.S. management principles. Currently programs are including more and more of the "soft" skills required for management as well as courses contributing to their increasing internationalization. The programs attract more and more youth each year, which has also increased the number of private management schools, part-time education, and colleges, previously nonexistent under the former system. In fact, according to McNulty (1992), the number of management education programs per manager in Eastern Europe is by far greater than that in any Western country, including the United States. However, the question remains as to what types of programs are needed and are indeed the most effective. It is apparent that modules and programs directly taken from Western and especially American-style management cannot be directly applied (McNulty 1992) and that programs must be tailored to the current needs of the market and the specific demands and interests of future managers (Mintzberg and Gosling 2002).

Assessing Graduate Programs in Business

Much of the current debate in the literature about the quality of graduate business programs is focused on their comparison as well as their relevance to the changing needs of the business environment. It has been argued (Friga, Bettis, and Sullivan 2003) that business education will be the most affected of any other branch of education by changing market forces. A recent study by Chaudry (2003) of companies in six world regions, with the exception of the United States, for example, concluded that MBAs worldwide are not fully meeting the expectations of businesses. It is interesting to note that the results of this study point to the relatively enduring emphasis on technical knowledge in MBA programs, as opposed to communication and interpersonal, or more "soft" skills. A study of Fortune 1000 companies (Neelankavil 1994) found a similar emphasis on technical skills, with the least satisfaction by companies given to soft skills. Rynes and colleagues (2003) point to a number of additional surveys of executives who note poor attitudes, behaviors, and social skills of graduates as their main negative traits. Mintzberg and Gosling (2002) also call for a new structure of management education, in which emphasis is shifted from the functions of marketing, finance, human resources, and strategy to interpersonal aspects in order to truly develop students' managerial skills. However, business students generally view these aspects as far less important than functional ones (Rynes et al. 2003).

The management programs in Lithuania, however, are based mostly on functional aspects and less on interpersonal aspects. However, most business students in Lithuania may already have the necessary interpersonal skills needed to effectively work in an international environment. In a study conducted in 2003 of seventy-five undergraduate students in the Faculty of Economics at Vilnius University, 89 percent of students indicated that they spoke one or more foreign languages, and 19 percent spoke three or more (Mockaitis 2003).

Nonetheless, the management programs in Lithuania, Latvia, and Estonia are considered to be among the best programs of all the countries of the former Soviet Union, according to some American experts (McNulty 1992). The results of Chaudry (2003) support this claim; of all the regions included in the study, the East European one stands out in terms of correspondence between MBA education and company needs and satisfaction with hired graduates. Kwok, Arpan, and Folks (1994) also concluded that European business programs are more internationalized than their counterparts in the United States. This evidence gives some hope as to the ability of East European MBAs to compete in the international labor market and perhaps even outperform their counterparts from MBA programs in the United States in international jobs, where interpersonal and language skills are not emphasized to the same extent, and where many programs are only beginning to internationalize (Friga, Bettis, and Sullivan 2003; Kwok, Arpan, and Folks 1994).

In a global study of international business programs, Kwok, Arpan, and Folks (1994) distinguished the following criteria as among the most important in evaluating the quality of curricula: the inclusion of international business in university strategic plans and missions, the level of international business education sought, the functional areas internationalized, the level of faculty knowledge and international experience, and the extent of exchange programs and internships offered to students. In the following sections, the Master Program in International Business at the Vilnius University Faculty of Economics is presented in detail. Some of its most important strengths and weaknesses are discussed in the final section of the chapter. Although it is still too early to state where this new program stands in relation to long-existing programs in the West and to other CEE university programs, it is hoped that this presentation will at least generate interest and spark discussion as to the quality of the newly emerging business programs in the region.

Case Study: The Master Program in International Business at Vilnius University

The Vilnius University Master Program in International Business was developed jointly with Aalborg University, Denmark. According to the Master Program in International Business guidelines, this program is geared toward the development of students' knowledge and skills, which will allow them to reveal, analyze, and independently solve the various problems and issues of international business and develop the qualifications necessary for working in international firms and institutions.

Program Objective and Structure

Main Program Objectives

The main objective of the program is to provide studies encompassing understanding, goal seeking, and the development of knowledge and skills within a dynamic international business environment.

The program distinguishes the following goals:

- To provide students with knowledge about the changing international and global environment.
- To provide the theoretical knowledge and practical skills needed for analyzing and understanding the macro- and microenvironments of international business.
- To improve students' knowledge and practical skills of business expansion and problem solving in a competitive international business environment.
- To develop students' abilities for setting international strategic management goals, choosing among alternatives and implementing strategy on a theoretical and practical level.
- To foster a sense of social and moral responsibility and understanding regarding the expansion of international business.
- To provide relatively flexible opportunities for study, through distance learning and other modern technologies and didactic methods.

Many of the above-mentioned program goals are already being implemented by means of distance education, where students in groups of four to five complete practical international business research projects. The program goals are currently being modified and adjusted to the main program objectives, with the aim of obtaining a better balance between theoretical studies and practical problem-solving skills. More time and attention will be given to the analysis of practical problems, while lecture hours will be reduced. More of the program aspects will also be transferred to distance education and independent study.

Program Structure, Content, and Methods

The duration of the Master Program in International Business is two years. Students, who have completed eighty credit hours of study (one credit hour is equal to forty classroom hours) and completed and defended a final thesis are granted a Master's Diploma in International Business. During the course of the program, students are required to complete twenty-six credit hours of compulsory subjects and twelve credits of elective courses. Fifteen credits are granted for a required research project, three credits for practical work, and fifteen credits for the final thesis. The research project is centered on semester projects, the purpose of which is to assist students in preparing their final thesis and to develop research skills.

The program structure (the inclusion of required and elective subjects and research projects) is based on the following principles: (1) required courses include courses that necessarily provide general international business knowledge; (2) the combination of elective and required courses during a given semester guarantees consistent and systemic acquisition of knowledge; and (3) the balance between theoretical courses and research projects allows students to develop their skills to independently recognize international business problems and seek analytical solutions to these problems (see Tables 11.1–11.3).

Bearing in mind similar master's programs in international business at universities abroad, it was decided that the following courses are essential for developing a fundamental understanding of international business: (1) regional economic and microanalysis models and theories (Regional Economics, Microeconomic Analysis, European Union Labor and Social Policy); (2) understanding and assessing the international business environment (International Marketing Research, Comparative Accounting, Seminar: The Lithuanian Business Environment); and (3) economics and politics of international business (International Business Finance, International Trade Policy, Total Quality Management).

The courses included in the different blocks of the program (required and elective) in each semester are logically interrelated and complement one another. The first semester course block includes the following required courses: Microeconomic Analysis, Regional Economics, and Comparative Accounting. Microeconomic Analysis covers such topics as optimal conditions, utility, cost and profit functions, their characteristics and application. This course complements the Regional Economics course, which provides students with knowledge about the world economy, regional and national problems, the internationalization of production and capital, and the relationships between economics and politics. Comparative Accounting provides students with insight into accounting models and their development in different countries and regions, the internationalization, harmonization, and standardization of accounting principles. Four elective courses are offered in the first semester, of which students must choose two, according to their interests: International Marketing, International Private Law, International Business, and the Internationalization of the Firm, Business, Research Strategy. During this semester students are already expected to develop their research problem, assess its empirical and theoretical relevance, and begin delving into its theoretical aspects.

The second semester required courses are: International Marketing Research, International Business Finance and European Union Labor, and Social Policy. Having obtained knowledge about regional economics, macroeconomics, and comparative accounting, during the second semester students obtain different country policy and international business finance information and knowl-

Table 11.1

Composition of Required Courses for Semesters I–III

Course code	Title	Classroom hours (credits) by semester				Instructor name and title
		I	II	III	Total	
EMIA7116	Microeconomic Analysis	32 (3)			32 (3)	Lecturer Dr. J. Rasimavičius
EREK7116	Regional Economics	32 (4)			32 (4)	Assoc. Prof. R. Gaižutis
ELYG7116	Comparative Accounting	32 (4)			32 (4)	Assoc. Prof. D. Poškaite
ESDS7116	EU Labor and Social Policy		32 (3)		32 (3)	Prof. J. Lazutka
ETMT7116	International Marketing Research		32 (4)		32 (4)	Prof. V. Pranulis
ETVF7116	International Business Finance		32 (4)		32 (4)	Assoc.Prof. A. Paškevičius
ESRM7116	Strategic Marketing			32 (4)	32 (4)	Lecturer Dr. A. Gaižutis
EVKV7116	Total Quality Management			32 (3)	32 (3)	Lecturer Dr. R. Adomaitiene
ETPP7166	International Trade Policy			32 (4)	32 (4)	Assoc. Prof. A. Miškinis
					288 (33)	

edge about the specifics of marketing research in different countries and cultures. International Business Finance covers such topics as international financial activity, financial management goals, market imperfections and international business success indicators, international money markets, exchange rates, interest, and other topics. The goal of International Marketing Research is to develop sufficient knowledge and skills to conduct marketing research in different cultures and countries. This course analyzes primary and secondary·information collection methods, equivalence issues, data analysis and expert evaluations, and decision making. Five elective courses are offered in this semester: Intercultural Comparative Management, Business Information Systems, International Human Resources Management, Export Promotion, and Twentieth Century Economic Theory.

The required courses for the third semester are: International Trade Policy, Strategic Marketing, and Total Quality Management. International Trade Policy follows economic analysis, and Strategic Marketing logically follows the International Marketing courses, and the emphasis moves from practical problem and situation analysis to the strategy formation level. In this semester students are familiarized with total quality management theory and practice. Knowledge about marketing strategy and quality management is necessary in dealing with problems of competition in international markets. Seven elective courses are offered, of which students must select two: Business Ethics, Money Market Derivatives, International Transport and Logistics, Product Standardization and Certification, Sales Management, Sources of International Commercial Information, and Applied Econometrics. The increased number of elective courses during the third semester provides students with greater freedom to choose courses according to their own interests.

During the fourth semester, the program emphasis shifts to an analysis of the business environment and practical studies. The coursework is comprised of a required seminar—the Lithuanian Business Environment—and research work. Because the studies conclude with the defense of student theses, the final semester is devoted toward mostly thesis completion.

According to the Lithuanian Law on Higher Education (Article 42, Paragraph 5), master's level programs are intended to prepare students for independent work in the sciences or arts, which requires more advanced academic knowledge and skills. The guidelines for the consecutive studies program provide general master studies requirements, which guarantee the attainment of this goal. The Master Program in International Business, in line with the Guidelines for Consecutive Studies (Article 29), is based on knowledge and skills acquired during the first level of university studies. Most of the program courses have bachelor level prerequisite courses. If students do not have the required background, lecturers may provide additional literature to

Table 11.2

Composition of Elective Courses for Semesters I–III

Course code	Title	Classroom hours (credits) by semester				Instructor name and title
		I	II	III	Total	
EVST7126	Business Strategy Research	32 (2)			32 (2)	Assoc. Prof. M. Kucinskiene
ETAV7126	International Business and the Internationalization of the Firm	32 (2)			32 (2)	Assoc. Prof. V. Tamaševičius
TPRT7126	International Private Law	32 (2)			32 (2)	Assoc. Prof. D. Foigt
ETAM7126	International Marketing	32 (2)			32 (2)	Assoc. Prof. R. Balniene
EETV7126	Twentieth Century Economic Theory		32 (2)		32 (2)	Dr. E. Ulvidiene
EVIS7126	Business Information Systems		32 (2)		32 (2)	Assoc. Prof. Z. Brazaitis
ETLV7126	Intercultural Comparative Management		32 (2)		32 (2)	Assoc. Prof. D. Diskiene
EZVA7126	International Human Resources Management		32 (2)		32 (2)	Assoc. Prof. R. Česyniene
EESK7126	Export Promotion		32 (2)		32 (2)	G. Jatuliaviciene
ETVL7126	International Transport and Logistics			32 (2)	32 (2)	Assoc. Prof. R. Minalga
EVET7126	Business Ethics			32 (2)	32 (2)	Assoc. Prof. D. Diskiene
EPRI7126	Money Market Derivatives			32 (2)	32 (2)	Assoc. Prof. R. Kropiene
EPSS7126	Product Standardization and Certification			32 (2)	32 (2)	Lecturer Dr. D. Serafinas
ETSK7126	Sources of International Commercial Information			32 (2)	32 (2)	J. Šiaučiūniene
ETEK7126	Applied Econometrics			32 (2)	32 (2)	V. Kvedaras
EPAV7126	Sales Management			32 (2)	32 (2)	Assoc. Prof. S. Urbonavičius
					512 (32)	

Table 11.3

Composition of Research for Semesters I–IV

		Classroom hours (credits) by semester				
Course code	Title	I	II	III	IV	Total
EMTD7116	Research Project	(5)				(5)
EMTD7216	Research Project		(5)			(5)
EMTD7316	Research Project			(5)		(5)
EVAL7116	Seminar: The Lithuanian Business Environment				32 (2)	
EMTP7116	Practical Research				(3)	(3)
EMBD7116	Final Thesis				(15)	(15)
						32 (35)

guarantee effective studies. Some of the course materials in the International Business Program are available on the WebCT distance learning Web site. If students desire, they may use these materials anywhere they have access to the Internet.

As required by Article 30 of the Guidelines for Consecutive Studies, the Master Program consists of eighty total credits, of which forty-seven credits are obtained from theoretical studies (no fewer than twenty-five credits are required), and thirty-three credits are obtained from research projects and the required master's thesis, including three credit hours for practical research work (40% of the program is required, i.e., thirty-two credits).

The International Business Program also adheres to the requirement in Article 6 that no less than 30 percent of second-tier studies be comprised of independent student work, as well as Article 7, which requires that the number of courses during any given semester be no more than seven, and no fewer than two credits may be given per course; course evaluations are based on examinations, assessment of individual student work, or pass/fail grades. Article 9 requires that every program of study conclude with final examinations and/or a final thesis (project) defense.

Implementation of Studies—Teaching, Learning, and Evaluation

The balance between theoretical and research work guarantees not only that students gain knowledge and analytical thinking skills, but also that they acquire the skills needed to conduct independent research and solve real-life problems. The research project is conducted throughout the entire span of studies and is an integral part of the learning process. Two types of research are included in the program. First, students conduct semester projects on different disciplines. Students from different theoretical disciplines form groups of four to five students, which, based on the course materials, develop specific business problem recognition, analysis, and problem-solving skills. The project concludes with a presentation and defense. Sometimes the projects are presented to the specific businesses, whose problems students have analyzed. Each presentation is challenged by a faculty member, audience members, and another student group that has been assigned to do so. Second, each student independently works on his or her master's thesis beginning from the first semester. During the course of preparation, the student identifies a business problem, based on theoretical and other knowledge obtained during the studies. The final thesis is coordinated through consultations with faculty members, supervision of student work, and discussion. In this way, the student integrates practical and theoretical problem identification aspects and reveals his or her creative problem analysis and solution skills in his or her chosen area.

The Master Program in International Business studies is oriented toward the recognition and solution of international business problems and the implementation of business decisions. The studies are intended to augment the knowledge students have acquired during their bachelor studies, relating it to international business management problems, the search for advanced theory, its analysis and interpretation, and connection between theory and empirical practical problems. Through reliance on theory and practice, students search for original solutions to business problems.

Student work is organized according to requirements in each individual course syllabus, which includes information about deadlines and evaluation procedures. An example of the International Marketing Research course syllabus is provided at the end of this chapter. Students participate in two types of research activities:

1. The final research project, which is spread over four semesters.
2. Semester projects, completed in groups of four to five students. Many of the semester projects are based on case studies of local and international companies.

Admissions and Student Graduates

The International Business Program has been head by the Department of Marketing since 2001. Since then, 58 students have graduated from the program. Each year 25 students are admitted to the International Business Program, however, not all students complete the program. In 2001, the program received 111 applications, and 19 students finished the program. In 2002 the number of applications was 61, with 19 graduates, and in 2003, 20 students completed their degrees.

Faculty

According to Article 31 of the Guidelines for Consecutive Studies, no less than 10 percent of master's level courses must be taught by professors of corresponding academic disciplines. Other courses are taught by faculty who specialize in their disciplines. The program adheres to these guidelines. Ten percent of courses are taught by professors and the remainder by faculty with advanced degrees, with the exception of two courses that are taught by faculty without advanced degrees.

Discussion: The Strengths and Weaknesses of the Program

In summarizing the Master Program in International Business structure, content, and study methods, it may be asserted that the program attains its main goal—to produce qualified, creative, and independently thinking international business graduates. A survey of graduates conducted in the spring of 2003 revealed that overall, the students have a positive view of the program. However, most of the students feel that too little time is allotted for practical work and that the choice of courses offered, which are necessary for their chosen profession, is too small. The Economic Faculty partners positively evaluated the program, however, the question was raised whether the Comparative Accounting course is necessary and whether it should be replaced with additional courses in strategic planning and information sciences. A survey of Lithuanian part-time bachelor-degree students revealed that the international business major would be their primary choice in their future MBA studies.

It may be asserted that the program satisfies the main criteria outlined by Kwok, Arpan, and Folks (1994). First, the program mission, aims, and goals are directly linked to international business and place ample emphasis on the program's internationalization. It is expected that graduates of the program have not only fundamental knowledge but also specialized knowledge in certain subjects, which may be utilized in their future international careers. The program also strove to create a balance between the functional aspects of business and soft skills, as evidenced by the inclusion of intercultural human resources and comparative management courses. Second, the level of faculty expertise is rather high, as virtually all members have advanced degrees in their fields. Third, students are encouraged to combine theoretical and practical work in the form of case studies, group projects, and final theses, which may provide further international experiential opportunities. The survey of future students and program graduates also indicates a high level of satisfaction with the program.

However, the program is still in its initial stages, and the university still has little experience in internationalizing its degree programs. Some additional areas of improvement regarding the program structure and study methods may be noted. First, as indicated in the first sections of this chapter, study programs must reflect the needs and satisfy the expectations of business. There is a need to strengthen the International Business Program structure by developing closer ties to international businesses in order to better improve students' business skills. Currently, the program does not have experience or traditions of cooperation between academia and the business environment. Students and faculty usually choose their thesis topics on their own, and their communication with businesses depends largely on their own initiative. For this reason, their chosen topics may be of little relevance to business firms and do not receive enough attention and support during the data collection and analysis stages, presentation of results, and their practical application. The Department of Marketing has begun to compile a database of student research projects and requests by businesses for research. The database will be made available on the Internet. Business leaders will also be invited to serve as consultants for student projects.

Second, students in this and other master programs often request newer and more flexible technologies and methods. For this reason the Department of Marketing is currently developing and organizing distance studies opportunities, at the same time guaranteeing cooperation between faculty and students. Distance learning allows access to more teaching materials, and students may access it at more convenient times. The International Marketing Research course materials are already available through the WebCT system, which students willingly use.

Third, bearing in mind the internal and external changes in the Lithuanian economy, after only a few years, it is already time to modify the Master Program in International Business, along with all the other business studies programs offered by the university, and provide students with more opportunity to choose their programs of study and majors according to their future careers. Thus, a new Master Program in Business is being developed that will allow students to choose an additional major in their third semester. Three majors will be offered—Marketing, International Business, and Operations Management. Whether these programs will close the gap between Lithuania and the EU in education and business and be competitive in the European academic market remains to be seen.

References

Ammermueller, A.; H. Heijke; and L. Woessmann. 2003. "Schooling Quality in Eastern Europe: Educational Production During Transition." IZA Discussion Paper No. 746. Bonn, Germany: Institute for the Study of Labor.

Chaudhry, A. 2003. "The International Finance Corporations's MBA Survey: How Developing Country Firms Rate Local Business School Training." World Bank Policy Research Working Paper 3182 (December).

Friga, P.N.; R.A. Bettis; and R.S. Sullivan. 2003. "Changes in Graduate Management Education and New Business School Strategies for the 21st Century." *Academy of Management Learning & Education* 2, no. 3: 233–50.

Kwok, C.; J. Arpan; and W. Folks. 1994. "A Global Survey of International Business Education in the 1990s." *Journal of International Business Studies* 25, no. 3: 605–24.

Law on Education of the Republic of Lithuania. Available at www.smm.lt (accessed December 8, 2004).

McNulty, N.G. 1992. "Management Education in Eastern Europe: 'Fore and After.'" *Academy of Management Executive* 6, no. 4: 78–87.

Mintzberg, H., and J. Gosling. 2002. "Educating Managers Beyond Borders." *Academy of Management Learning & Education* 1, no. 1: 64–76.

Mockaitis, A.I. 2003. "The Implications of Cultural Differences for Mobility in the Baltic Sea Region: Challenges and Opportunities." Paper presented at the BaltSeaNet International PhD conference The Challenge of Mobility in the Baltic Sea Region, Gdansk, Poland, October 23–26.

Neelankavil, J. 1994. "Corporate America's Quest for an Ideal MBA." *Journal of Management Development* 13, no. 5: 38–52.

Rynes, S.L.; C.Q. Trank; A.M. Lawson; and R. Ilies. 2003. "Behavioral Coursework in Business Education: Growing Evidence of a Legitimacy Crisis." *Academy of Management Learning & Education* 2, no. 3: 269–83.

Vilnius University (n.d.). The Vilnius University Statute. Available at www.vu.lt/menu/welc01/Dokumentai/dokumentai.htm.

12

Reforming Accounting Education in Armenia

Robert W. McGee

Armenia is a small country in the Caucasus. It is bordered by Georgia to the north, Iran to the south, Azerbaijan to the east, and Turkey to the west (Hewsen 2001). It is in Asia geographically, although most Armenians insist that they are European. Its population is between 3 million and 3.5 million, although it is impossible to say how many Armenians actually live in Armenia at any given time because so many of them emigrate for short or long periods to work in other countries.

Many Armenians would prefer to work outside the country, either temporarily or permanently, because of the perception that there is no future for them in Armenia. Although they would prefer to work in Western Europe, the United States, or Australia, it is difficult for them to obtain visas and working papers for these countries, so countries like Russia and Ukraine are really their fallback choices. One attraction that the U.S. Agency for International Development (USAID) accounting reform program offered was the possibility to obtain a credential that would make them marketable in more than 100 countries, which we shall discuss in more detail below. Many of the younger students saw the programs offered by USAID as a one-way ticket out of the country, which greatly increased demand for the programs.

When the Soviet Union broke up, Armenia declared its independence (Libaridian 1991), but it retained the Russian administrative system, including its system of accounting. The Russian accounting system was, and still is, highly centralized. The various Soviet republics got their chart of accounts from Moscow, and they had to stick to it. What the Soviets called accounting, accountants who live in market economies would call bookkeeping. In fact, there was not even a word in the Armenian language for accountant in the Western sense of the term, a fact that sometimes caused translation problems.

There was no analysis of balance sheet or income statement ratios because they did not have any balance sheets or income statements. Mostly they had journal entries and some kind of statement that looked quite similar to a funds statement. Cost accounting was nonexistent, which made it impossible to calculate costs or determine whether they were making a profit or loss. As a result, there was a massive misallocation of resources. In fact, at least one economist predicted as far back as the 1920s and 1930s that their lack of a cost accounting system would eventually lead to the demise of their system (Mises 1981, 1990; Kirzner 2001). Thus, there was a need to adopt an accounting and financial reporting system that would allow the former Soviet republics to participate and compete in the market economy after the collapse of the Soviet Union.

The USAID, the World Bank, European Union-Tacis (EU-Tacis), and other organizations have established programs to assist economies in transition to make the necessary changes to their accounting systems. Some accounting reform programs started shortly after the fall of the Berlin Wall in 1989. After the Soviet Union collapsed, additional accounting reform programs were undertaken in various East European countries and several former Soviet republics. Armenia was one such republic that received USAID assistance. This chapter summarizes the phase of that program that aimed at upgrading accounting education to international standards.

One of the factors that attracts foreign investment is financial transparency. Investors have to know what they are investing in, and that requires financial statements that are based on some kind of recognized accounting principles. There are various ways that a country can gain the confidence of foreign investors. It can adopt International Accounting Standards (IAS) in that such standards are accepted in dozens of countries. It can adopt the system used in the United States, which is highly regarded throughout the world, but is not used in nearly as many countries as is International Accounting Standards. Or it can adopt some other system that has a high recognition factor.

Adopting some kind of recognized accounting standards is only the first step. If companies start using some such standard and there are other impediments to investment, such as the lack of a rule of law, corruption, or too many regulations, investors will bypass the country and invest where the investment climate is more to their liking.

Although Armenia has adopted IAS, it is still not an extremely attractive place to invest (McGee 1999), although it is getting better. The *1999 Index of Economic Freedom* ranked it 106 out of 161 countries (Johnson, Holmes, and Kirkpatrick 1998), which means there were 105 countries that provided a better investment climate than Armenia. Its rank has improved markedly in recent years (perhaps because of accounting reform and the resulting transparency in financial reporting). The *2002 Index of Economic Freedom* ranks it 45 out of 161 countries, which places it in a tie with France and Poland (O'Driscoll, Holmes, and O'Grady 2001). It is possible to purchase an investment guide to Armenia (International Business Publications 2002), which is an encouraging sign, since it indicates there is now a market for such information.

The Impetus for Change

After the dissolution of the Soviet Union, the various Soviet republics retained their old Soviet accounting system, which consisted almost entirely of the chart of accounts that Russia had been using for the past seventy years. That system worked well enough for a centrally planned economy, at least as far as record keeping was concerned. However, the old Soviet system was not adequate for the other functions that a good accounting system must perform. Accounting should be used not only for record keeping but also for decision making, and the old Soviet system was not up to the task. Thus, there was an impetus for change. However, having an impetus for change is not always enough to actually make a change.

It is a general rule of any bureaucracy that the best way to do something is precisely the way it is presently being done. There is tremendous inertia against making change, especially when the system is not driven by the profit motive (Friedman and Friedman 1984). Somehow, that inertia had to be overcome. In the case of accounting in former centrally planned economies, there are actually two inertias that must be overcome: the change to a new, market-oriented accounting system and a change in the education provided to future and existing accountants.

The Finance Ministry realized that Armenia would have to adopt some sort of modern, market-oriented accounting system. It briefly considered the French system, mostly because Armenia had historic ties with France, but adopted IAS and International Standards on Auditing (ISA) because of the belief that these standards were more internationally recognized. The USAID accounting reform project helped the Finance Ministry adopt IAS and ISA, not only by paying for and supervising the translation of these documents into the Armenian language, but also by providing technical assistance and answering questions as they developed.

Adopting IAS and ISA triggered an instantaneous demand for a change in accounting education throughout the whole country, both in the universities and institutes and in the training of existing practitioners. When the new rules were adopted and made mandatory, they were adopted into law just a few months before accountants had to start using them. However, practically none of the practicing accountants and auditors in Armenia knew anything about IAS or ISA. Courses in these subjects were not part of the university curriculum, and, until they were translated into Armenian, the standards were not available to the local accounting population. Armenian accountants and students were not even able to get a Russian translation of the standards because the people working on the Russian translation in Moscow had not yet completed their work. Thus, there was immediate and strong demand to learn the new rules that they would have to use and limited opportunities for learning what they needed to know. In economic terms, one might say that the demand curve for accounting education had shifted swiftly and sharply to the right.

As is true whenever the demand curve shifts sharply to the right while supply remains constant (almost nonexistent in this case), the price of the product or service goes up. This fact created another problem because Armenian accountants and students were not able to pay the market price for the materials and training they needed. This problem was solved by having USAID subsidize accounting education throughout the country.

Accounting Education Under the Soviet System

Universities in the old Soviet system did not offer a degree in accounting. Accounting education consisted of a course or two that students took as part of their economics study. One course consisted basically of learning the chart of accounts and learning how to make journal entries. Another course consisted of some kind of auditing (Enthoven et al. 1998), although it is difficult for a Westerner to imagine what might be included in such a course since there were no financial statements to audit. Footnotes and other disclosures did not exist in the old Soviet system.

Accounting education in Armenia was modeled on the Soviet system. The only innovation was that some of the textbooks had been translated into Armenian. Russian texts were used for some courses as well. After the USAID Accounting Reform Project came to Armenia, some minor changes were made to the Armenian chart of accounts, but most of the Soviet chart of accounts remained intact.

When one of the USAID consultants suggested to the Finance Ministry that the Soviet chart of accounts be scrapped and that each company be allowed to make its own chart of accounts; the Finance Ministry official at first thought that the USAID consultant was joking. To him, it was inconceivable that the Soviet chart of accounts could be replaced. When it was explained to him that American companies are completely free to make their own chart of accounts, and that companies in many other countries also have this freedom, he could not understand how it could be possible to make your own chart of accounts and still comply with International Accounting Standards. So the matter was dropped, and USAID decided to assist Armenia in converting to a market oriented accounting system within the parameters that were feasible, which meant that the old Soviet chart of accounts would only be tweaked, not scrapped.

The USAID Approach to Accounting Education Reform

USAID's approach to accounting education reform was as comprehensive as possible, given the constraints that existed in the present system, including the inertia that had to somehow be overcome. There were also some cost constraints that had to be faced.

There were a number of different audiences or target markets that had to be educated. The immediate need was to educate existing accountants and auditors, since they would be the ones who had to work with and implement the new rules within a matter of months. This group consisted of both public accountants and auditors and also enterprise accountants. Tax inspectors also had to be educated at some point, since they would have to understand the new rules when they visited companies to perform their audits. Or at least that was USAID's opinion when it initiated accounting training.

As an adjunct to the accounting education phase of the USAID project, there was also a need to upgrade certification requirements to meet international standards. Another large part of the resources that USAID had available had to be devoted to the training of future accountants and auditors. That meant that at least some of the universities and institutes in Armenia had to adopt a completely new accounting curriculum.

When USAID agrees to go into a country to reform its accounting, economic, or legal system, it generally deals with people at the top—the prime minister, the finance minister, the justice ministry, and so on. The agreement that is hammered out is hammered out at the highest levels of government. But implementation is done by the people who work at the third tier. In the case of the USAID Accounting Reform Project in Armenia, the individual at the Finance Ministry who was in charge of seeing that the reforms were successful reported to the assistant finance minister. In other words, he was a third-tier employee of the Finance Ministry. No one consulted with him before the agreement was finalized. He had no input into the process until after the deal was made. Luckily for the project, and for Armenia in general, he fully supported the reform effort, and the agreement that was entered into did not have any major flaws. However, such is not always the case.

Oftentimes, when USAID or some other government agency makes a deal with a particular government to reform something in the target country, the fact that people on the third level are not consulted can lead to major problems, especially if the people on tier one do not know what is going on below them, which is often the case if they are political appointees. Another reason why some reform projects fail is because the people who have to implement the reforms have something to lose if the reform is successful. Luckily, that was not the case here, but it has been the case in other reform projects in other countries.

The University Curriculum

There was general agreement that the accounting curriculum at the university level had to be drastically changed if future accountants and auditors were to be competently trained in market-oriented accounting. The question was how shall the reform be accomplished and where should the reform start? There were a number of different approaches that were considered in the early planning phase of the project, before the deal was finalized between USAID and the Finance Ministry. The present curriculum could be replaced with one that is modeled on the American system, with about ten accounting courses plus some other business courses in economics, management, and the like. Another option was to implement a curriculum that followed international accounting standards. A third option was to adopt a syllabus that paralleled the one used for the Canadian Certified General Accountant (CGA) designation.

One might think that the American model would have been chosen, since USAID is an American organization, part of the U.S. State Department. But this was not the case. It was thought that Armenian accountants would benefit more if they learned international accounting standards and rules, since most of the countries they would be dealing with had adopted at least some of the international accounting rules. Whether the Canadian system should be adopted was debated briefly because the Canadian system was adopted by some former Soviet republics in Central Asia, but the international approach was deemed to be the best in this case, mostly because its curriculum was more generally recognized on a worldwide basis.

One positive aspect of the international approach was that the course materials were readily available, although not in the local language. The Association of Chartered Certified Accountants (ACCA) is a British organization that provides certification testing at three different levels for accountants on a worldwide basis. At the time the accounting reform program started in Armenia, ACCA certification was recognized in 150 countries. That number has since increased to 160. With such widespread acceptability, it was easy to sell the program to the university administrators, especially after the Finance Ministry told them they had to accept the changes being suggested by USAID.

Another decision had to be made with respect to which universities and institutes should be approached first with the revised curriculum because not all institutions that offered accounting programs could be approached at the same time. The private consulting firm that won the USAID Accounting Reform contract had only one expatriate assigned for reforming the university curriculum, so decisions had to be made about how the curriculum reform would spread throughout the country.

The USAID Accounting Reform Project was headquartered in Yerevan, the capital of Armenia, and there were several institutions that offered accounting training, so the initial decision was made to start by contacting the largest institutions in Yerevan, which also happened to be the largest institutions in the country. One institution was generally considered to be number one, because most of the country's finance ministers had graduated from there, so that was the first institution targeted for the new program.

Once the word got out that the premier institution for accounting education in Armenia was going to replace its existing curriculum with the help of USAID, there was no need to contact the other institutions. They contacted USAID and asked for assistance in reforming their accounting curriculums as well. Their eagerness to adopt the new curriculum was not so much because they were concerned for the quality of the education their students were receiving, but because of the perception that if they did not also adopt the new curriculum, they would not have any accounting students in a few years. Their decision was mostly, or perhaps completely, based on competitive forces. The fact that the transformation could be made at absolutely no cost to them did not hurt either, since USAID was subsidizing the whole program.

The new curriculum consisted of adopting the ACCA syllabus in total. That curriculum consisted of fourteen courses, most of which were in accounting but some of which were other business-related courses. It was thought that adopting the ACCA syllabus would kill two birds with one stone, since not only would the accounting curriculum meet international standards, but also the students would be well on their way toward passing the national certification exams, which would also be based on the ACCA syllabus. Those students who were fluent in English would also have the opportunity to take the ACCA exams, which were offered only in English, so some segment of the student population would qualify for a certification that was internationally recognized. More information on the new certification requirements is given below.

Once the decision to adopt the ACCA syllabus was made, the choice of which texts to translate had to be decided. Several publishing companies publish texts to prepare students for the ACCA exams. The two choices given the most consideration were Foulkes Lynch and BPP Publishing, both British companies. Foulkes Lynch was chosen because it was the official supplier of texts for ACCA and because the individual who made the decision thought that the Foulkes Lynch books were marginally better in quality than the BPP texts. Interestingly enough, that same person chose to use the BPP books for the USAID Accounting Reform Project in Bosnia shortly thereafter.

The texts published by both companies are quite similar in terms of layout and content. The texts are designed to prepare students for the ACCA exams and cover the ACCA syllabus completely. It might also be mentioned that the ACCA syllabus complies with International Federation of Accountants and United Nations Conference on Trade and Development guidelines. There are two texts for each exam. One book consists of textual materials with plenty of examples. The other book, somewhat smaller, consists of prior examination questions and answers. Those who are familiar with the Gleim and Wiley books that are used to prepare American students for the certified public accountant (CPA), certified management accountant (CMA), and other professional certification exams would find much in common with these texts, although there are practically no multiple choice questions.

After the texts were chosen, the next step was to determine which language they should be translated into, since many of the students were not sufficiently fluent in English to use the English-language versions, and even if they were fluent enough, some of their professors were not. One might think that such a decision would be easy, since the program was being implemented in Armenia, where Armenian is spoken. However, Armenian was not the language chosen, which caused a bit of a problem.

Russian was selected because the Armenians were also fluent in Russian and because USAID did not want to pay to have the texts translated into more than one language. There were other USAID accounting reform projects going on in several other countries where Russian was one of the languages spoken, and USAID wanted to use the books in several of these other former Soviet republics. It did not want to have to translate them into Georgian, Azeri, Kazakh, and so on, and it felt that there was no need to do so. This decision upset some of the Armenians in both the Finance Ministry and universities as well as in the local accounting association, but they did not complain too loudly because the books they were getting were practically free. Besides, they did not have the resources to do their own translations into Armenian even after they had the Russian version to refer to.

The next step was to assemble a translation team to do the translations. That task might not seem difficult. One might just go to the local yellow pages of the telephone directory or call the local Berlitz school for names. If that failed, surely there were people in the local universities who could do the job. Unfortunately, that approach did not work. The people needed for the task had to be fluent in both English and Russian and also be familiar with accounting terminology. It was impossible to find individuals who met all of those qualifications. Not even the university professors were familiar with the accounting terminology. Furthermore, the Russian language did not even have terms for some of the concepts that had to be translated.

The solution was found by trial and error. Positions for translators were advertised in all the obvious places, translators were interviewed, and those who passed the first hurdle were given a short assignment, which they were paid to translate no matter how bad the final product was. If they did a good job, they were given more and longer assignments. Those who did not do a good job were not called in for further assignments. After a few months, the best individuals were identified and given more permanent offers of employment. There was a core staff that worked full time on company premises. They were supplemented by a cadre of part-timers who completed the work whenever and wherever they could.

The core staff consisted of physicists, geologists, English literature majors, and a few people who had an economics background. Since they were unfamiliar with the terminology, they asked one of the expatriates, who was also a certified public accountant, to explain what the term meant. Then the translators had discussions among themselves to decide how they would translate this term that had no Russian equivalent.

There were some coordination problems, especially in the early stages, since each translator seemed to use different words to express the same thought. This created problems for the editor, who had to go through each translation meticulously and tried to conform the different vocabularies and styles to be more uniform. In the early stages, it took the editor as much time to edit the work as it would have taken for him to translate the material from scratch. A partial solution was found by creating a glossary of terms, which expanded on a daily basis at first. This glossary was distributed to both the full-time and part-time staff. As new terms were added, new versions were distributed.

The same trial-and-error method that was used to select the full-time translators was used to select the part-timers. But in the case of the part-timers, another complication set in. If there were too many part-timers turning in materials, the editor was not able to coordinate the submissions. He had his own work to do in addition to coordinating and merging the translations that the part-timers were doing, and if the project had more than about six part-timers submitting manuscripts, the system broke down. The solution, which was arrived at only after several breakdowns occurred, was to cut back on the number of part-timers by retaining only the best ones.

There was another problem that developed with the translation portion of the project. Although the texts were (nearly) all translated into Russian, some materials, such as the International Accounting Standards and International Standards on Auditing, had to be translated into Armenian because those documents were to be used by the Finance Ministry and practicing accountants and had to go through Parliament. Also, there was a certain nationalist sentiment that had to be reckoned with. USAID could get away with translating textbooks into Russian, but not documents that would be enacted into law.

So another group of translators had to be found who could translate from English into Armenian. One might think that the same group of translators who were translating books into Russian could be used for this task, but this was not the case. Although they were all fluent in Armenian as well as Russian, some of them were not sufficiently fluent to translate technical accounting materials into Armenian (for which there were no terms in any event).

During the Soviet era, Armenia had two different school systems. Some schools taught primarily in Armenian and also taught enough Russian so that the students could be fluent in Russian as well. Other schools taught mostly in Russian, and taught enough Armenian so that the students could function in that language, too. The Russian schools were considered to be the better choice to send children to, since the language needed for advancement within the system was Russian. As a result, many Armenians, although fluent in the Armenian language, were better in Russian.

Fortunately, the project was eventually able to find individuals who could translate the standards into Armenian to the satisfaction of the Finance Ministry. One of the translators, the one who translated most of the International Standards on Auditing, was also an auditor. He was later retained to teach the auditing course, the text for which was in Russian.

As the translations for the first-year texts were nearing completion, some decisions had to be made about how to introduce the new courses into the system. Although the universities had agreed to accept and implement the new syllabus, none of the professors were qualified to teach the courses. There was no such thing as cost accounting in the old Soviet system, and there was not much financial accounting either. Even the professors who had been educated in Moscow did not get any exposure to Western style accounting. Something had to be done to bring at least a few of the professors up to speed.

Two remedies were implemented. The first stage consisted of giving a pilot course in financial accounting to professors and practicing accountants. This course was held in the training facility of the Armenian Association of Accountants and Auditors. The fees for practicing accountants were subsidized because they could not afford the course otherwise. Tuition of $100 was charged, which is a lot of money in a country where $80 a month can support a family with two children. Professors could take this initial course for free.

The only person who could teach this initial course was the American CPA who was working with the USAID contractor firm, but he could not speak Armenian. So an interpreter was hired to assist. He lectured in English. The interpreter translated into Armenian. The textbooks the students used were in Russian. So the translator had to know both the Russian and Armenian terms. Using an interpreter slowed everything down by 50 percent, but there was no alternative.

At the end of the course, participants were given a written examination. Those who had the highest scores were offered jobs as part-time instructors. Luckily, some of the professors who took the course also received some of the highest grades. This pilot course, which also served as a train-the-trainer course, had to be given in an accelerated format because practically all of Armenia wanted to take these new courses, and trainers were desperately needed to conduct the courses.

After some trainers had been selected to teach the first course, a second course on management accounting was offered. The same process was used for that course. The American CPA did not have to teach the auditing course, which came later in the sequence, because the Armenian auditor who translated the International Standards on Auditing into Armenian was able to teach that course. However, a problem developed as soon as he stepped into the classroom. A large percentage of the class did not want him to be their instructor. There was a widespread perception that the foreigner—the American CPA—would do a better job. But the American did not want to teach the course and was not available in any event because he had to coordinate a large chunk of the accounting reform project in addition to teaching multiple sections of the lower level courses.

The Armenian auditor was a good choice for several reasons. For one thing, he knew all the terms in both Russian and Armenian. He was one of the few people in the whole country who had read the International Standards on Auditing in any language, insofar as the ISA had not yet been published and distributed to the Armenian auditing community. And because he could speak Armenian, there would be no need for an interpreter, which would speed up the presentation by 100 percent. When all his advantages were explained to the class, and when they were told that they had no alternative, they grudgingly accepted their plight. However, that class had a high absentee rate because many of the students decided to study on their own at home.

The second phase of preparing professors to teach the courses consisted of sending some of the better English-speaking students to the United States for a year to earn a master's degree in accounting. Most of the applicants who applied for this opportunity had taken one or two of the courses offered by USAID, but a few applicants were new to the program. Forty-three people applied for the five openings. The five people who were chosen were the cream of the crop. They were selected by USAID to prevent any politics or nepotism from entering the process. Several universities were considered. The University of Texas at Dallas was selected, partly because of its reputation for international accounting and partly because it had experience with foreign students.

The program was a success. All five students completed the program, and all five returned to Armenia, although one of the five later returned to the University of Texas to work on a second master's degree, this time in information systems.

Concluding Comments

The USAID Accounting Reform Project in Armenia had some unique features, but the basic model has been used in every country where USAID has an accounting reform project. Accounting education is a big part of an accounting reform program, but a comprehensive accounting reform program includes other activities as well, such as helping a country to adopt IAS and ISA, which was not discussed in the present chapter. Another task of most USAID accounting reform programs includes forming a national accounting association or strengthening an existing association. That aspect of the reform project in Armenia also was not discussed. Upgrading the certification requirements of the target country includes many aspects that were not included in the present chapter. Space also does not permit a discussion of the continuing education programs that were instituted at the Association of Accountants and Auditors of Armenia or the training programs for enterprise accountants that trained hundreds of Armenian accountants. There were also programs to convert enterprise accounting systems, which would warrant a chapter of its own. There are some interesting synergies and problems that take place when all phases of an accounting reform program are started at the same time rather than undertaken sequentially, but space does not permit a discussion of these synergies and problems.

USAID now has several accounting reform programs that are either completed or nearing completion. Some other programs are just starting or have a long way to go before completion. They all have some common elements but also some differences. Although USAID is far up the learning curve, accounting reform projects do not lend themselves to a cookie-cutter approach. Each must be customized to the needs, conditions, and circumstances of the target country. While the education segment of the USAID Armenian accounting reform program was successful, using an identical approach in another country might not prove to be so successful because the facts, situation, and the culture may be different.

References

Enthoven, A.J.H.; Y.V. Sokolov; S.M. Bychkova; V.V. Kovalev; and M.V. Semenova. 1998. *Accounting, Auditing and Taxation in the Russian Federation.* The IMA Foundation for Applied Research and the Center for International Accounting, University of Texas at Dallas.

Friedman, M., and R. Friedman. 1984. *The Tyranny of the Status Quo.* New York: Harcourt Brace.

Hewsen, R.H. 2001 *Armenia: A Historical Atlas.* Chicago: University of Chicago Press.

International Business Publications. 2002. *Armenia Investment & Business Guide.* Washington, DC.

Johnson, B.T.; K.R. Holmes; and M. Kirkpatrick. 1998. *1999 Index of Economic Freedom.* Washington, DC: Heritage Foundation and New York: *Wall Street Journal.*

Kirzner, I.M. 2001. *Ludwig von Mises: The Man and His Economics.* Wilmington, DE: Intercollegiate Studies Institute.

Libaridian, G.J., ed. 1991. *Armenia at the Crossroads: Democracy and Nationhood in the Post-Soviet Era.* Watertown, MA: Blue Crane Books.

McGee, R.W. 1999. "The Investment Climate in Armenia: Some Legal, Economic and Ethical Issues." *Journal of Accounting, Ethics & Public Policy* 2, no. 2: 310–17.

Mises, L. von. 1981. *Socialism: An Economic and Sociological Analysis.* Indianapolis, IN: Liberty Fund, Inc.

———. 1990. *Economic Calculation in the Socialist Commonwealth.* Auburn, AL: Ludwig von Mises Institute.

O'Driscoll, G.P. Jr.; K.R. Holmes; and M.A. O'Grady. 2001. *2002 Index of Economic Freedom.* Washington, DC: Heritage Foundation and New York: *Wall Street Journal.*

13

Educating Professors in a Transition Economy

A Case Study of Bosnia and Herzegovina

Robert W. McGee

The United States Agency for International Development (USAID) and various other governmental and nongovernmental organizations have been expending resources in developing countries for decades to improve the infrastructure of their economies. In recent years, various projects have aimed at reforming the accounting and financial reporting systems of several countries, most notably in Central and Eastern Europe (Kemp and Alexander 1996; Cheney 1990; Rolfe and Doupnik 1995; Jermakowicz and Rinke 1996; Adams and McMillan 1997) and the former Soviet Union (Ichizli and Zacchea 2000), including Russia (Cornish 1999), Uzbekistan (Crallan 1997) and Armenia (McGee 1999b), but also in African countries such as Madagascar (Berry and Holzer 1993). Other countries, including China, have been attempting to reform their accounting and financial reporting system without direct foreign aid or assistance (Tang 2000; Chen, Jubb, and Tran 1997). In some countries, including Bahrain, corporations adopt International Accounting Standards (IAS) even when their government does not force them to do so (Al-Basteki 1995).

Several different strategies have been employed as part of an overall economic development plan (Larson and Kenny 1996; Wallace 1993). Sometimes the accounting reform is aimed at adopting IAS throughout the whole economy. At other times, reform projects concentrate on a single sector such as banking (Ramcharran 2000; Prindl 1992; Rudnick 1994). Part of the reform effort for the larger accounting reform projects often also involves implementing IAS after they have been adopted, certifying accountants and auditors

(Petrov 1999; McGee 1999a, 1999c), supporting the development of accounting associations (ICAR, 2000; Burnham 2000; Ruf 1999; Anonymous 1999; Scopes 1999), and reforming the accounting curriculum of the target country's universities by upgrading it to international standards.

Not much has been written about how international agencies assist in upgrading accounting education in developing or transition economies, although Enthoven and colleagues (1998) devote a few pages in their book to the present state of accounting education in Russia. The International Federation of Accountants (IFAC 2000) has also published a summary of case studies on accounting educational assistance in developing economies.

When agency assistance is given, two of the more popular models are the Association of Chartered Certified Accountants (ACCA) model and the certified investment management analyst model (Anonymous 2001). International exchanges of students and/or professors are also used to aid in the upgrading (Coyle and Platonov 1998; Anonymous 1994). While such training helps to upgrade the profession, the long-term goal of assisting in the training of accountants should include the installation of an appreciation for lifelong learning (Needles et al. 2001).

One problem these projects always face is the educational preparation and experience of the professors who will be expected to teach the new curriculum. Most of them are inadequately prepared. They are not familiar with International Accounting Standards, perhaps because the standards have not yet been translated into their language. They are unfamiliar with Western accounting rules and techniques, in part because textbooks are not available in their language. These problems can partially be overcome by translating the necessary materials and making them available to students and professors. But more than translation is needed. The education of the country's professors must be enhanced by exposing them to the material they will be expected to teach and supplementing that exposure with lectures that give them the opportunity to ask questions. This chapter presents an example of how that problem can be addressed, using the USAID Accounting Reform Project in Bosnia and Herzegovina as a case study.

Overview

One of the USAID Private Sector Accounting Reform Project tasks in Bosnia and Herzegovina (BiH) is curriculum reform. In April 2001, all eight universities in BiH signed a Memorandum of Agreement to adopt the accounting curriculum reform proposals made by USAID. The universities agreed to implement USAID's suggestions over four years, starting with the fall 2001 semester. They agreed to implement the ACCA fourteen-course syllabus.

USAID has used this syllabus in other accounting reform projects, including in Armenia and Georgia and several African countries. This syllabus was chosen because it complies with the United Nations Conference on Trade and Development and IFAC education guidelines. Furthermore, the ACCA program is well known and accepted. ACCA exams are given in the English language in 160 countries, making it the only truly international accounting certification. The first four of these courses were to be given during the 2001–2 academic year. Two of the four courses are on nonaccounting subjects. The other two courses are financial accounting and managerial accounting.

Why Train Professors?

Why train professors at all? After all, they have already received graduate training, some of them to PhD level. The materials they will be using in their classes are being translated into their language. So why should resources be expended to teach them accounting?

On none of the eight faculties from which candidates were being considered for training had anyone previously been exposed to much of the material contained in the first ACCA financial and managerial accounting courses. Some financial and managerial texts were available in the local language, but these texts are based on U.S. accounting (Generally Accepted Accounting Principles; GAAP), and they needed texts that were based on International Accounting Standards. USAID needed to train professors over the summer so they could start teaching the new courses in the fall.

Why Train Them in America?

It would have been cheaper to train the professors at some Bosnian location. But that would not have given them the full American experience. USAID wanted them to experience the teaching methods that are used in American universities. It wanted them to see an American university and meet American professors. It wanted to show them what university life is like in America. USAID also wanted them to visit various American institutions so they could see what accounting in America is all about.

How Were They Chosen?

USAID needed to train professors who would teach financial and managerial accounting, so the first requirement was that they had taught one or both of these courses in the past and were scheduled to teach one or both of these courses during the 2001–2 academic year.

The second requirement involved where they taught. USAID wanted to send at least one professor from each of the eight universities to America. It was not able to do that because two of the universities did not nominate anyone. So it sent professors from six of the eight universities. Here is the breakdown:

University of Sarajevo	4
University of Srpska Sarajevo (Pale)	1
University of Banja Luka	2
University of Brcko	1
University of Mostar (East)	1
University of Tuzla	1
University of Mostar (West)	0
University of Bihac	0

Another issue, at least initially, was ethnicity. Some of the Serbians wanted 49 percent of the professors to be Serbian because the Dayton Peace Accord gave the Serbians 49 percent of the land in Bosnia. Serbs comprise much less than 49 percent of the country's population, but the negotiators in Dayton offered the Serbs 49 percent of the Bosnian territory because that was the percentage they figured they needed to get the Serbs to sign the peace agreement (Daalder 2000). Now that percentage has become etched in the minds of the Serbs whenever they are negotiating with the other two ethnic groups in BiH for resources.

This issue became less important as the process moved forward. In addition, it was difficult to determine who was what. For example, one of the professors USAID sent from the University of Sarajevo was born in Croatia, but his father was Slovenian and his mother was Serbian.

The professors were chosen by a committee consisting of representatives from World Learning, USAID, and International Business and Technical Consultants, Inc. (IBTCI), the private contractor that was awarded the accounting reform project in BiH.

Duration of Training

The professors flew from Sarajevo to Newark, New Jersey, on July 7, 2001. The first class started July 9. The last class was August 9, after which there was an awards ceremony. They flew to Atlanta, Georgia, on August 10 to attend the Annual Meeting of the American Accounting Association and returned to Bosnia on August 16, so the total experience was about six weeks.

Classes were held for four hours a day, from 9 a.m. to 1 p.m., Monday through Friday. The first two weeks were spent studying financial accounting. The last three weeks were spent studying managerial accounting. About two chapters were covered each day.

Not all the professors could speak English, so an interpreter was used. The interpreter was originally from Split, Croatia. He had taught at the University of Sarajevo for twenty years, until about 1991, when he left the country, going first to England, and then to the United States. He is presently a professor of English at Grand Valley State University in Michigan. He has worked on other World Learning and USAID projects. He was one of the interpreters the U.S. State Department used at the Dayton Peace Accord.

Location of the Training

The training took place at Seton Hall University in South Orange, New Jersey. Seton Hall is in a nice suburban community. It is a college town that is within easy commuting range of New York City. The professors stayed in the dorm. USAID chose Seton Hall because the expatriate in charge of curriculum reform for the contracting firm that won the USAID contract taught there. USAID was pressed for time because the decision to send professors to America was made just a few months before they boarded the plane, and it did not have the luxury of shopping around for a university.

The Texts

The text chosen for the financial accounting course was *Financial Accounting: A Global Approach* (Gray and Needles 1999). This text was chosen because it incorporated IAS rather than American GAAP. It was translated into Serbian by a group of translators in Banja Luka, the capital of Republika Srpska, which is in the northern part of Bosnia.

The text chosen for managerial accounting was *Cost Accounting: A Managerial Emphasis*, 10th ed. (Horngren, Foster, and Datar 2000). It was translated into Bosnian, using the Latinic alphabet, by a group of translators in Sarajevo. This text was one of several under consideration. The project chose the text by Horngren and colleagues because one of the senior professors at the largest university in Bosnia had studied under Horngren at Stanford during the 1960s, and he strongly urged the project to choose the Horngren book for translation. It seemed like a reasonable selection, since it covered the material needed for an entry-level managerial accounting course and also included enough advanced material that it could be used for several advanced courses as well. Moreover, at least one professor was already familiar with the material, which gave the Horngren book an edge over the other books being considered.

A word needs to be said about the languages of Bosnia and Herzegovina. Before the wars—there were two of them, the first when Slovenia and Croatia seceded from Yugoslavia in 1991 and the second when Bosnia and Herzegovina seceded in 1992–95—the main language of Yugoslavia was Serbo-Croatian. These languages—Serbian and Croatian—are basically the same except that Serbian uses the Cyrillic alphabet and Croatian uses the Latin alphabet, which they call the Latinic alphabet. After the war, as part of the Dayton Peace Accord, Bosnia had three official languages and two alphabets. Serbian was spoken mostly in the Republika Srpska and used the Cyrillic alphabet. Croatian was spoken mostly in Herzegovina and used the Latinic alphabet. And Bosnian was spoken in the Muslim part of Bosnia. According to Bosnian law, both the Latinic and Cyrillic alphabets can be used for the Bosnian language.

Before the wars of secession, students in Yugoslavia learned both alphabets equally. One week they would use textbooks that were in Cyrillic, and the next week they would use books that were in Latinic. That approach might seem like a relative waste of resources, since they needed twice as many books, but using that approach prevented triggering what would have been major ethnic conflicts, so the added expenditure for books was a good investment in keeping the peace among the three ethnic groups.

This fact is mentioned because language plays an important part in the BiH accounting reform project. USAID had to make sure that the translation process remained nonpolitical. It was not cost effective to translate every text into all three languages, so the decision was made to alternate translations between the Latinic and Cyrillic alphabets. That is why the financial accounting book was translated into Serbian, and the Horngren cost book was translated into Bosnian using the Latinic alphabet.

The Croatians could not be accommodated by this decision, but by choosing to translate the Horngren book using the Latinic alphabet, the Croatians were placated, since Croatian also uses the Latinic alphabet and since the Bosnian and Croatian languages are almost identical except for a few words and some pronunciation differences. It should also be pointed out that two of the texts that will be used in the more advanced courses have already been translated into Croatian by a publishing company in Zagreb, Croatia, so the Croatians' turn is coming.

The financial and managerial accounting texts USAID chose to use in the universities had not been fully translated by the time training in America started. They had been mostly translated but not edited, so they were in rough form. That was both good and bad. It was bad because the quality of the texts the class had to use was rather poor at that stage. But the class was able to salvage something positive from it. The professors all acted as editors, making comments and corrections about the content and terminology. The professors had a tremendous incentive to do a good job in editing the books since they would have to use the books in their classes in a few months. These corrections and comments were given to the editors upon the professors' return to America, so the editors had some good feedback. However, it is not recommended that this approach be adopted as a regular policy. It would have been better to have had texts that were in final form.

Another problem both the professors and the translators of the texts faced was terminology. Some of the terms used in the texts, especially in the Horngren text, did not have any local language equivalent. The trainer had to explain what some of the terms meant, which provided a good learning experience, but which also slowed down the pace of the class. The translators finally resolved this terminology problem by providing a glossary that explained the various terms.

The trainer also spent a few hours going through the annual report for the Coca-Cola Company. For those who did not know English, they had to rely mostly on the interpreter, because the Coca-Cola annual report was not translated into the local language. However, they were all able to see how the financial statements were structured, even if they did not understand most of the words.

Many of the professors had never seen the annual report of a Western company before, so showing them how such a report was structured was a learning experience for them. Most of the discussion centered on footnote disclosures, which was a new topic for them. The trainer spent a few minutes going over each footnote, explaining what disclosures companies had to make and why. The Coca-Cola disclosures included more topics than what IAS covered, so even the professors who were somewhat familiar with IAS were exposed to some new material.

The Coca-Cola presentation was given after the discussion of stocks and bonds, so by the time the professors saw the Coca-Cola annual report, they had already been exposed to much of the material that was in the financial accounting course. The back of the Gray and Needles financial accounting book included the fully translated annual report of a major international company that used IAS, so by the time the class reached the end of the book, they were prepared to go into more detail. This annual report was translated into Serbian so the whole class was able to follow the discussion.

Choosing the Coca-Cola annual report was an excellent choice for other reasons as well. The professors could relate to the company because Coca-Cola was a popular drink in BiH. But this choice proved to be good for another reason as well. The chief executive officer (CEO) of Coca-Cola was one of the speakers at the annual meeting of the American Accounting Association in Atlanta, which the group attended after the training in New Jersey. The CEO spent most of his time talking about the financial situation at Coca-Cola, including some of the items that were discussed in class. The professors who could not speak English gathered around the interpreter, who translated the CEO's comments as he made them. Part of the CEO's presentation included multicolored PowerPoint graphics and spreadsheets.

The Classroom Experience

The classroom experience brought the professors together for twenty hours per week. Some of the professors knew each other well or at least casually before the classes started, but a great deal of bonding went on during the sessions, which was apparent both in and out of the classroom. Although not part of the original USAID training plan, this bonding was viewed in very positive terms by USAID. A few years before (1991–95), the three ethnic groups—Muslim Bosniaks, Roman Catholic Croats, and Orthodox Christian Serbs—had been killing each other (Burg and Shoup 1999; Zimmerman 1999; Silber and Little 1997; Rieff 1995). Before the trip to America, some concern was expressed about having them stay in the dorms together and attend classes in the same classroom. Such concerns quickly evaporated as the classes began.

The classroom used for the sessions was one of the most advanced rooms in the university. It had all the latest gadgets as well as plenty of board space, something that is lacking in most Bosnian classrooms. The furniture was new, and each professor had more than adequate room to spread out books, and so on. This aspect of the training is mentioned only because Bosnian students usually sit in small, cramped rooms with old desks or tables.

During the course of the five-week training, the trainer noticed that there were large gaps in the professors' knowledge. While they were quite knowledgeable about basic concepts like debits and credits, some terminology was new to them. Terminological problems were complicated by the fact that their language did not have equivalent terms for some of the things that were being discussed in the book or in class. These problems were overcome by group discussion. Usually at least one of the professors was familiar with the concept being discussed and was able to explain it to the others in the group.

In the financial accounting book, the chapters on stocks and bonds presented special problems because these things do not yet exist in Bosnia. The USAID privatization project is introducing these things, but at the time the class was given, all they knew about was vouchers, which was the method used to privatize corporations in Bosnia. One professor asked what the difference was between a stock and a bond, which gave the trainer the opportunity to launch into a broad discussion of the various aspects of each method of financing and the pros and cons of each.

The book by Horngren and colleagues, *Cost Accounting*, also presented some problems for the class. Aside from terminology problems, some of the professors were not familiar with a number of concepts. One professor asked why there were so many variants and suggested that perhaps two or three would be sufficient.

Another aspect of the training that was especially beneficial to the professors was all the examples that the trainer presented in class. Texts in Eastern Europe and the former Soviet Union generally do not have many examples. It is a standing joke within the expatriate accounting community that the only numbers you will see in an East European accounting book are the page numbers. While this is not quite true, it is also not too much of an exaggeration. Most East European and Soviet accounting texts concentrate on the chart of accounts, which is handed down from Moscow in the case of the former Soviet Union.

The professors were amused to find that the Gray and Needles text did not devote more than about five lines to the chart of accounts. Some of them were not aware that American companies are completely free to make their own chart of accounts. One of them asked how reliable the financial statements could be if all companies used a different chart of accounts. The trainer explained that the rules and journal entries always led to the same endpoint and that the chart of accounts a company had was just the path to that destination. It was not certain that all of the professors were convinced, however, as there were some puzzled looks in the audience after this explanation was given.

Case studies were also new for some of them. The end of each chapter contained numerous examples and some case studies, which the professors found quite helpful. Some of the solutions to these exercises, problems, and case studies were translated so that the professors could see what the solutions looked like. The project translated some of these solutions so that the professors would be able to use them in their classes upon their return to Bosnia.

The chapter on cash flow statements drew some lively responses. Bosnia now requires cash flow statements, so the professors had some knowledge in this area. However, the method the trainer used to construct the statement, using T accounts, was new to them. They were familiar with T accounts but had never seen them used to construct a cash flow statement before.

Both the direct and indirect methods were discussed, which presented a slightly touchy political situation. The country of Bosnia and Herzegovina consists of two separate political entities. The Federation of Bosnia and Herzegovina (FBiH) consists mostly of Muslim Bosniaks and Roman Catholic Croats, while the Republic of Srpska consists mostly of Serbs. The two entities combined to form the country of Bosnia and Herzegovina. They each have their own way of adopting International Accounting Standards.

The IAS allows both the direct and indirect method of accounting for cash flow statements. But the RS allows only the direct method and the FBiH allows only the indirect method. The reason for adopting the different approaches is because the people in charge of accounting standards in one of the entities did not want to have the same accounting rule for cash flow statements that the other entity adopted. Their decision to have different treatments of cash flow statements was purely political. It had absolutely nothing to do with good accounting. So the trainer had to present both approaches without visibly favoring one approach over the other.

Each professor also received a detailed syllabus for each book, complete with suggested homework and class exercises, the idea being that they would use the USAID-prepared syllabi when they returned to their universities. When the professors saw these syllabi, some of them asked the business school dean if she could provide the syllabi Seton Hall University uses for all of its accounting courses. The dean was happy to comply with their request. Each professor also received a copy of the undergraduate and graduate Seton Hall University catalog, which they wanted so that they could read the course descriptions and see what the requirements were for American bachelor's and master's degrees.

Some of the professors asked about the requirements for the various certification exams, so the trainer gave a short lecture on the education and experience requirements for the certified public accountant (CPA) exam and the topics that are covered on the CPA exam. He also discussed some of the other certification exams that some accountants and auditors take in America. These questions arose because the trainer, who had a background in CPA exam preparation, kept mentioning exam techniques that would help gain points or save time on the CPA exam. He also discussed the study techniques he used to pass the CPA exam.

Examinations in some East European and former Soviet countries often have an oral component. In fact, some exams are 100 percent oral. It surprised some of the professors that the CPA exam did not have any oral component and that the exam was given under strictly supervised conditions. Some professors requested sample copies of the exams given by Seton Hall University professors. The Seton Hall professors were glad to comply with this request.

Other Activities

The professors did not just go to class then return to their rooms. They had a number of other activities, both planned and spontaneous. The first few days they were on campus, the trainer made it a point to introduce them to the various eating places in town. They seemed to prefer the Mexican restaurant and the Irish pub, which had music on Thursday and Sunday evenings. For lunch they almost always chose the faculty dining room because it was convenient, and the food was good and also in expensive. They had an expense allowance of $34 per day, and lunch was only $5, which left plenty for other things.

The dean invited the group for a barbecue at her house. The director of the Institute for International Business invited them to dinner at one of his favorite restaurants in South Orange. The trainer also showed them how to take the train to Manhattan and gave them a one-day tour. They subsequently made other trips to Manhattan, where they visited the World Trade Center, New York Stock Exchange, Chinatown and Little Italy, Greenwich Village, Rockefeller Center, St. Patrick's Cathedral, the Metropolitan Museum of Art, and other locales. The trip to the New York Stock Exchange was especially interesting. They were amazed that an average of $40 billion of securities is traded there every day.

Some of the professors spent a great deal of time in the library. They needed to do research for their PhDs, which they had not yet completed, and the trainer introduced them to the librarian who speaks Croatian. They learned how to use the databases and were able to print out many of the materials, which they took back home with them.

USAID sponsored field trips to the American Institute of Certified Public Accountants (AICPA) and the IFAC, both in Manhattan, and the Institute of Management Accountants (IMA) in Montvale, New Jersey. While on these field trips, the professors met with representatives of these organizations, who made presentations outlining what their organization did. Most of the professors had heard of the IFAC, but several of them had never heard of the AICPA or IMA, or if they had, they only had a vague idea of what these organizations did. Some of the senior professors in the group were also officers of their local accounting associations, and it was hoped that they would bring back some of the ideas they encountered during their trip to America. Another part of the USAID Accounting Reform Project in Bosnia involved forming local accounting organizations that are modeled after the AICPA and the various state accounting organizations, so exposing them to the largest accounting association in the world (AICPA) was thought to be a good idea. Business cards were exchanged, and it was hoped that contact between the U.S. accounting organizations and the Bosnian professors would continue after they returned home.

The group had planned to make a trip to visit the accounting department of a large American corporation in Manhattan, but it turned out that the corporation (Verizon) preferred to send one of its representatives to visit the group at the university instead. The Verizon representative discussed a number of accounting policies, procedures, and events that the professors found fascinating. The presentation was scheduled for sixty to ninety minutes, but lasted three and a half hours because the professors were so responsive to what the Verizon representative had to say. It boggled their minds that a company could have 265,000 employees. Bosnia is a small country. Not even their army has 265,000 people.

The group also made some non-USAID-sponsored field trips. In addition to several New York City trips, they rented a van and went to Atlantic City and Washington, DC. The Atlantic City trip was a day trip. They went and returned the same day. For the Washington, DC trip, they stayed overnight. The trainer's daughter and her husband live in Frederick, Maryland, so the group stopped there on Friday night. Their house was not large enough to accommodate all the professors, so the two female professors stayed in their spare bedroom and the males stayed in a few motel rooms down the road. Interestingly, the professors' choice of roommate was not based on ethnicity, a fact that was important, since it showed that the animosity among the ethnic groups that was exacerbated during the several wars that occurred between 1991 and 1995 did not present an insurmountable barrier. The bonding that had taken place during the first few weeks of the training overcame this potential problem.

On Saturday they went to Washington and walked around. The Croatian English professor who acted as interpreter was familiar with the city, so he helped show them around. He also did some of the van driving (the trainer did the rest). Sunday they had a barbecue at the house and returned to New Jersey. They stopped in Philadelphia at a yuppie café close to the Liberty Bell on the way to DC and on the way back. The professors insisted that they stop there on the way back. They also insisted on playing country music on the radio.

There was an awards ceremony at the conclusion of the five-week training program where the professors received certificates from the Seton Hall business school. The Seton Hall librarian of Croatian descent and the university's main Russian professor organized the event. The Russian professor has a reputation for being a bake-aholic, and she lived up to her reputation. Much of the food was prepared by the Russian professor and some of her friends. Several East European dishes were served. The Seton Hall public relations department was able to generate some press coverage, but the main news event of the day was the record-breaking heat. They were able to schedule a news conference on one of the local cable television stations.

Atlanta American Accounting Association Meeting

The American Accounting Association has its annual meeting the third week of August each year. In 2001 it was held in Atlanta. USAID scheduled training so that it would end a few days before the American Accounting Association (AAA) meeting. The professors flew to Atlanta the day before the meeting started. They spent the remainder of the day meeting other professors, mostly from the United States, but from a variety of other countries as well. During the meeting they attended a number of presentations, some with a translator and some without. There was also an official AAA-sponsored tour of the Atlanta Zoo. Some of them also went to the Coca-Cola Museum, which was a fifteen-minute walk from the hotel.

They were quite impressed with the Atlanta Marriott Marquis, which served as the headquarters of the meeting. From the lobby one could look up to the roof, forty-seven floors above. Most of the elevators were partially glass, so one could look out at the various floors while going up or down. It was visually tantalizing, except for one of the professors who had trouble with heights. However, the hotel also had internal elevators with no glass, so it was possible to go up and down without being traumatized by the spectacular view. The same professor who hesitated to use the glass elevators at the Marriott Marquis also hesitated to take the elevator to the observation deck of the World Trade Center. Luckily, he garnered the courage to go to the top, as he will not have another opportunity to make that particular trip.

Attendance at the AAA annual meeting gave the professors an opportunity to sample some of the hundreds of paper presentations that academics from all over the United States and abroad were giving at the various sessions. The professors also had the opportunity to meet and network with other professors. It was the first time that some of the professors had ever observed the kind of presentation that is common in such meetings. One of the professors remarked to the trainer that he had never seen papers critiqued and criticized before. He mentioned that in Bosnia, people just present their papers and no one makes any comments, formal or otherwise. He thought it was a refreshing experience to see papers critiqued. It was a new methodology for him.

There were dozens of booths at the meeting, where various publishers were giving away books in the hope that the professors would adopt a few hundred copies for their classes. It is a normal marketing practice of publishers at such meetings. They were told to take an empty suitcase with them to America. The professors collected free texts aggressively. Some of them decided to take the books to the Atlanta post office and have them shipped back to Bosnia by M-Bag, which costs just $1 a pound. On the evaluation forms that USAID gave the professors at the end of the trip, most of them mentioned the Atlanta experience as the best part of the trip, mostly because of the impression they got from seeing thousands of accounting professors from all over the world.

International Business and Technical Consultants, Inc., the private contractor that was awarded the USAID contract, sponsored an open house on the second evening of the meeting. It was poorly attended, mostly because there were so many competing parties going on. However, the open house was not a total loss. The professors got to meet and chat with Charles Horngren and Belverd Needles, two of the authors of the books they used for their training. The senior Bosnian professor who studied under Horngren at Stanford during the 1960s got to see Horngren again after more than thirty years. Horngren gave a short talk describing how he came to write his classic cost accounting book. He had approached Prentice Hall with the idea of writing a financial accounting book, but the Prentice Hall editor told him that what they really needed was a book on cost accounting.

What Would Be Done Differently

IBTCI probably will not sponsor another open house because it was not cost effective in Atlanta. There were just too many other groups sponsoring open houses and other events.

The textbook translations were not in good shape for the summer training. USAID learned from that experience and started translating the texts for the second-year classes much sooner.

For the summer 2002 training, USAID is going to make the professors promise to teach in the continuing professional education programs that the local Bosnian accounting associations offer for professional certification as a condition of going to America. In 2001 it did not do so. USAID is going to start offering continuing professional education courses in the Republika Srpska, one of the entities within Bosnia, in the near future, and only three of the four Serbian professors that USAID trained have agreed to take part. USAID would like all of the professors it trains to be available to teach continuing professional education courses in the future, since the number of qualified individuals in Bosnia is quite low.

Concluding Comments

The training program turned out to be successful. The major goals were accomplished. The professors were exposed for sixty hours to the material they would be teaching, under the guidance of a trainer who had more than thirty years of practice and teaching experience. The textbooks, although not in final form, were usable, and the suggestions the professors made for editing enhanced the value of the books. By the end of the trip, all ten professors were strong supporters of the curriculum reform, and they returned to their universities in a position to help make the curriculum reform a success. The model developed at Seton Hall University will be used for the next three or four years as part of the Bosnian Accounting Reform Program and may also be adopted by some of the other USAID accounting reform projects, and perhaps by some World Bank accounting reform projects as well. The World Bank accounting reform project in Kosovo is looking at the model, and the USAID accounting reform projects in five Central Asian republics will have a close look at it as their reform projects evolve to the point where they are in a position to send professors to America for training.

References

Adams, C.A., and K.M. McMillan. 1997. "Internationalizing Financial Reporting in a Newly Emerging Market Economy: The Polish Example." *Advances in International Accounting* 10: 139–64.

Al-Basteki, H. 1995. "The Voluntary Adoption of International Accounting Standards by Bahraini Corporations." *Advances in International Accounting* 8: 47–64.

Anonymous. 1994. "Tanya Bondarenko Seeks American Education." *Baylor Business Review* 12, no. 1 (Spring): 12–14.

———. 1999. "Setting Up Shop in the Former Soviet Union." *Association Management* 51, no. 4 (April): 105.

———. 2001. "Accountants in Russia Gain International Skills." *Financial Management* (London) 44 (April).

Berry, M., and P. Holzer. 1993. "Restructuring the Accounting Function in the Third World: Madagascar's Approach." *Research in Third World Accounting* 2: 225–44.

Burg, S.L., and P.S. Shoup. 1999. *The War in Bosnia-Herzegovina: Ethnic Conflict and International Intervention.* Armonk, NY: M.E. Sharpe.

Burnham, L. 2000. "SRO Development Recommendations." *International Center for Accounting Reform (ICAR) Newsletter* (December).

Chen, Y.; P. Jubb; and A. Tran. 1997. "Problems of Accounting Reform in the People's Republic of China." *International Journal of Accounting* 32, no. 2: 139–53.

Cheney, G.A. 1990. "Western Accounting Arrives in Eastern Europe." *Journal of Accountancy* (September): 40–43.

Cornish, K. 1999. "Taking IASs to Russia." *Accountancy* 124 (July): 54–55.

Coyle, W.H., and V.V. Platonov. 1998. "Insights Gained from International Exchange and Educational Initiatives Between Universities: The Challenges of Analyzing Russian Financial Statements." *Issues in Accounting Education* 13, no. 1 (February): 223–33.

Crallan, J. 1997. "Accounting in the CIS." *Management Accounting* 34 (January).

Daalder, I.H. 2000. *Getting to Dayton: The Making of America's Bosnia Policy.* Washington, DC: Brookings Institution Press.

Enthoven, A.J.H.; Y.V. Sokolov; S.M. Bychkova; V.V. Kovalev; and M.V. Semenova. 1998. *Accounting, Auditing and Taxation in the Russian Federation.* Dallas: IMA Foundation for Applied Research and the Center for International Accounting, University of Texas.

Gray, S.J., and B.E. Needles, Jr. 1999. *Financial Accounting: A Global Approach.* Boston and New York: Houghton Mifflin.

Horngren, C.T.; G. Foster; and S.M. Datar. 2000. *Cost Accounting: A Managerial Emphasis,* 10th ed. Upper Saddle River, NJ: Prentice Hall.

Ichizli, S., and N. Zacchea. 2000. "Accounting Reform in the Former Soviet Republics: An Essential Ingredient for Economic Independence." *Government Accountants Journal* 49, no. 2 (Summer): 46–53.

International Center for Accounting Reform (ICAR). 2000. *Accountants and/or Independent Auditors SRO Framework.* Moscow.

International Federation of Accountants (IFAC). 2000. "Assistance Projects in Accountancy Education and Development: A Study Based on the Experiences of IFAC Member Bodies." New York: International Federation of Accountants. (Study paper, February.)

Jermakowicz, E., and D. Rinke. 1996. "The New Accounting Standards in the Czech Republic, Hungary, and Poland vis-à-vis International Accounting Standards and European Union Directives." *Journal of International Accounting Auditing & Taxation* 5, no. 1 (July): 73–88.

Kemp, P., and D. Alexander. 1996. "Accountancy and Financial Infrastructure in Central and Eastern European Countries." *European Business Journal* 8, no. 4: 14–21.

Larson, R.K., and S.Y. Kenny. 1996. "Accounting Standard-Setting Strategies and Theories of Economic Development: Implications for the Adoption of International Accounting Standards." *Advances in International Accounting* 9: 1–20.

McGee, R.W. 1999a. "International Certification of Accountants in the CIS: A Case Study of Armenia." *Journal of Accounting, Ethics & Public Policy* 2, no. 1 (Winter): 70–75.

———. 1999b. "The Problem of Implementing International Accounting Standards: A Case Study of Armenia." *Journal of Accounting, Ethics & Public Policy* 2, no. 1 (Winter): 38–41.

———. 1999c. "Certification of Accountants and Auditors in the CIS: A Case Study of Armenia." *Journal of Accounting, Ethics & Public Policy* 2, no. 2 (Spring): 338–53.

Needles, B.E., Jr.; K. Cascini; T. Krylova; and M. Moustafa. 2001. "Strategy for Implementation of IFAC International Education Guideline No. 9: 'Prequalification Education, Tests of Professional Competence and Practical Experience of Professional Accountants.'" *Journal of International Financial Management & Accounting* 12, no. 3: 317–53.

Petrov, A. 1999. "We Should Have One Profession." *International Center for Accounting Reform (ICAR) Newsletter* (September).

Prindl, A. 1992. "Building a Banking System from Scratch—Advice for the Emerging Market Economies." *Banking World* 10, no. 3 (March): 18–20.

Ramcharran, H. 2000. "The Need for International Accounting Harmonization: An Examination and Comparison of the Practices of Russian Banks." *American Business Review* 18, no. 1 (January): 1–8.

Rieff, D. 1995. *Slaughterhouse: Bosnia and the Failure of the West.* New York: Simon and Schuster.

Rolfe, R.J., and T.S. Doupnik. 1995. "Accounting Revolution in East Central Europe." *Advances in International Accounting* 8: 223–46.
Rudnick, D. 1994. "First Sort Out the Banks." *Euromoney* 299 (March): 157–163.
Ruf, A. 1999. "CIS Audit Working Group and Prerequisites for Setting Up the 'Eurasia' Regional Federation of Accountants and Auditors." *International Center for Accounting Reform (ICAR) Newsletter* (September).
Scopes, G.M. 1999. "Mission Practically Impossible." *Association Management* 51, no. 8 (August): 50–56.
Silber, L., and A. Little. 1997. *Yugoslavia: Death of a Nation.* New York: Penguin Books.
Tang, Y. 2000. "Bumpy Road Leading to Internationalization: A Review of Accounting Development in China." *Accounting Horizons* 14, no. 1 (March): 93–102.
Wallace, R.S.O. 1993. "Development of Accounting Standards for Developing and Newly Industrialized Countries." *Research in Third World Accounting* 2: 121–65.
Zimmerman, W. 1999. *Origins of a Catastrophe.* New York: Random House.

14

Is Albania Ready for a Business School Model?

Diagnosis and Prospects

Vera Ivanaj, Silvester Ivanaj, and Palok Kolnikaj

As other countries in the Western Balkans, Albania is seeking solutions simultaneously to multiple problems flowing from the destructive impacts of the Balkan wars of the 1990s, the economic regression of the past fifty years under the communist regime, and the brutal transition to a market economy (Pani 2003).

Starting in 1992, Albania realized that large-scale efforts were needed to launch the creation of new programs in business and management training, and initiated this process through international institutions and a number of countries (Sang 2000). Professors have increased their involvement through participation in numerous faculty development and training programs offered by these countries. The Albanian economic landscape has also been transformed, and, in the wake of this transformation, a new wave of small entrepreneurs has emerged, and they are keenly aware of their training needs. At the same time, students who have graduated from bachelor's and master's programs in business administration are playing a more important role in the Albanian economy's transition toward a real market-based system. Albanian society is also progressively evolving toward a more modern form of management.

This chapter presents the evolution of business higher education in Albania from the 1990s on and its response to the twin challenges of economic transition and meeting new European Union and world educational standards (Nicolescu 2003). We focus on an analysis of ongoing and future changes in business and management education in the context of a nascent market economy and a general ongoing reform of higher education (Nicolescu 2003).

Albania's business education system must first deal with the inertia and conformism of the communist era and the ensuing transition period (Ahmeti 2003). These changes must be ambitious, so that higher business education can play its part in the country's economic development. This role is both critical and complex, given the numerous problem areas it must address simultaneously: the specific Albanian political, economic, and policy-making contexts, the difficulties of ensuring long-term stability, integration into a globalizing economy, and meeting European Union benchmarks in the pursuit of higher educational system reforms.

For a better understanding of the root problems of Albanian business higher education, of the radical changes under way, and of future prospects for economic developments, we begin with an overview of Albania and its economy.

Albania and Its Economy

Albania is situated on the eastern shore of the Adriatic Sea, with Montenegro and Kosovo to the north, Macedonia to the east, and Greece to the south. It has a population of about 3,100,000 inhabitants, made up of roughly 70 percent Muslim and some 30 percent Orthodox and Catholic. Its area covers 28,750 square kilometers. The official language is Albanian. Albania may be divided into two major regions: a mountainous highland region constituting 70 percent of the land area, and a western coastal lowland region that contains nearly all of the country's agricultural lands and is the most densely populated part of the country.

Albania has inherited from the past a low level of economic performance and slow pace of development. Albania's economy is considered a transition economy that is transforming from a centralized communist system to a market-type economy. The transformation of the economic and social systems that took place at the beginning of the 1990s has generated a radical shift in economic structure. Before the 1990s, the economic structure was based almost totally on real estate transactions. At the beginning of the 1990s, the Albanian economy initiated a process of liberalization and privatization. During this transition phase the economy registered considerable progress. Gross domestic product (GDP) increased from year to year. According to official data from Instat (Albanian Statistical Institute), in 2003 GDP increased by roughly 6 percent, as compared with 4.7 percent for 2002. Per capita GDP is roughly US$1,600. Public finance has shown some strengthening, which has led to a decrease in fiscal deficits. In 2003, the budget deficit reached a level of 5.6 percent, while budget revenues went up to 26 percent of GDP. The prices of goods stabilized, with inflation lowering to 3.3 percent for 2003. The level of unemployment is around 15 percent and the main source of employment continues to be the private agricultural sector with around 57 percent (in 2002) of total employment; the public sector and the nonagricultural private sector employ 20 percent and 23 percent, respectively.

The actual development of the economy in Albania is planned in an official document, "National Strategy on the Economic and Social Development," in which the long-term strategic targets for the economic and social development of the country are defined. The concept and the implementation of this strategy are strongly related to the process of negotiation of the Association-Stabilization Agreement between Albania and the European Union, the goal of which is to open the road toward Albania's integration into the European Union. After the 1990s the Albanian economy registered a "boom" in the creation of private enterprises. In 2001, the total number of active enterprises in Albania was around 64,000, of which about 60,000 are Albanian enterprises, some 2,000 are joint ventures, and roughly 1,500 are foreign enterprises (Cepani 2002). The majority of these enterprises may be considered small and medium enterprises. Less than 1 percent of these enterprises have more than 100 employees, 48 percent have a turnover of around US$50,000, and only 38 percent of the enterprises reach the level of US$125,000 in turnover (Cepani 2002). Albania's most dynamic sector of the economy is its private sector, which contributes more than 70 percent of GDP. The small and medium enterprises, in such sectors as construction, manufacturing, services, trade, and transport are creating considerable employment potential: The number of new jobs is estimated at around 215,000 (Cepani 2002). These enterprises, according to a 2002 survey, are aware that they will require continuous training and acquisition of management skills and credentials (Cepani 2002). The majority of these enterprises declare that they exercise permanent quality control, in spite of the fact that Albanian products are not yet competitive with imported ones. Cepani notes "Quality remains the Achilles' heel, which fails to provide a needed competitive advantage to SMEs [small and medium enterprises], even when compared with the large companies operating within the country . . . [and] still 94% of the SMEs acknowledge these constraints to becoming competitive" (2002: 1).

Besides the achievements noted during the transition period, the Albanian economy continues to experience problems that slow the pace of growth and promote a black market, a gray economy, corruption, organized crime, and outmigration of intellectual capital, among others (Pani 2003; Papapanagos and Sanfey 2001; Kule et al. 1999).

The System of Higher Education in Albania

As in many other countries of Eastern Europe, the organization of higher education in Albania was based on the Soviet model "which had its roots in traditional 19th-century Prussian methods and systems" (Norbert 1996: 73). The reforms initiated during the transition period have led to the restructuring of its legal bases: all the public higher education institutions in Albania are now based on Law No. 8461, dated January 25, 1999. On the basis of this law, all higher education institutions have revised their statutes and regulations to comply. An important point of the new law is that it allows the creation of private higher education institutions.

The institutions of public higher education include eight universities, two academies, and one advanced school. All universities and academies offer the bachelor's degree. Since 1998, a system of distance learning as well as departments of distance learning have been created near some of the universities. The main educational activity of this system is concentrated on postgraduate qualification in the economic and social science areas. Some universities offer nonuniversity diplomas. Private higher education is in its infancy. There are at this stage only two private higher institutions: New York University of Tirana in the area of business and the Higher School Luarasi in the area of jurisprudence.

Higher education programs in Albania are still undergoing restructuring in the wake of Albania's commitment to the European Union's Bologna Declaration. Degree-seeking structures are of the two-tier variety, despite an undergraduate studies cycle of four to six years' duration. This current cycle "is considered to be a Bachelor's Degree or equivalent level and leads up to the Doctor Degree through a Master" (Totomanova 2000).

In conformity with the Bologna Declaration, to be implemented in 2005–6, university education in Albania will be organized according to the "3 + 2 system," which means that the three first years will lead to the bachelor's degree, and the next two years will lead to a master of science degree.

Regarding the system of admission to the public universities, quotas are set by the Ministry of Education and Science, according to the principle of *numerus clausus* (a national preset number of admissions). The necessary criteria for admission are a diploma and the results of admission tests. The semester is the basic unit of the academic year, which is composed of two semesters. The basic elements of evaluation are examinations.

Registration is considered effective after the payment of a tuition fee. These fees are unified for all the public universities, different for each year of education, and determined by the Ministry of Education and Science in line with the country's general economic level. The cost to students is relatively low. The universities have the right to use 90 percent of the income generated by tuition fees. Regarding student scholarships, the Student Grant System is applied in all the institutions of higher education. These scholarships are allocated on the basis of agreed criteria. This system is used as a planning tool by Albanian students who study at home or abroad, and also by foreign students coming to Albania under bilateral agreements. All higher education diplomas as well as the curricular contents are recognized by the state according to law. The National Agency of Accreditation was established in 1999 to guarantee program quality and curricular integration. According to Ministry of Education and Science data, 47,669 students were registered in public universities during academic year 2003–4: 36,244 part-time and 11,425 full-time students. A total of 5,229 students graduated in academic year 2002–3. The new admission quota for 2004–5 for part-time students is to be set at 13,086 students. The academic and administrative staffs in public higher education are evaluated from year to year. Referring to data of the Ministry of Education and Science, during school year 2002–3, the composition of the academic staff was as follows: faculty—1,750, external staff—1,932, and administrative staff—315. Regarding the qualification level of the teaching staff, employees with doctoral degrees in science and technical fields constitute the minority, 33 percent of staff, including those with the rank of full professor, 10 percent, those with the rank of associate professor 12.3 percent, and at the assistant professor level, 10.5 percent. Around 67 percent of professors do not have science or technical degrees.

Higher Education in Business and Management

Undergraduate and graduate business education is generally provided by the faculties of economics of public universities. According to the Albanian Ministry of Education and Science, there was a total of 2,158 new students for studies in business administration during academic year 2004–5. Tirana is the main university, with its Faculty of Economics accounting for some 750 new students. The regional universities accept fewer students, whose numbers fluctuate between 150 and 300. The proposed branches in these universities are business administration, financial accounting, marketing, tourism, and agribusiness. Business administration and financial accounting enroll the majority of students, with 71 percent of the total number of admissions. Not unlike East European countries (Galen 2000; Slantcheva 2000; Svejnar 2000), Albania has recently allowed the creation of private institutions of higher learning in the business field. One noteworthy example is New York University of Tirana (NYUT). This university was created in 1992 and received its charter from the Ministry of Education and Science in 2004.

Graduate programs in business and management are four years in duration. The diploma obtained at the end of these studies approximates the level of a bachelor's degree, which permits students to continue with postgraduate courses at the master's and PhD levels.

Business education in Albania is also supplemented through numerous programs of practical training for managers, entrepreneurs, and government officials and also for the educational staff of universities. This continuing education is offered in the framework of international assistance projects supported by the European Union (EU), the United Nations Development Programme (UNDP), the Soros Foundation, the United States Agency for International Development (USAID), and other donors. Some institutional innovations are direct descendants of these training programs, for example, the business assistance centers located at the Universities of Korca, Shkodra, and Vlora, or the technology management center at the Polytechnic University of Tirana financed by USAID and the Network on Teacher Training Education in Europe (NTEE). Offering training programs of great interest to local business communities, these centers occasionally extend their activities into the area of scientific research in management, marketing, labor economics analysis, and feasibility studies for new ventures (Sang 2000).

Reforming the Educational System: Achievements and Roadblocks

Restructuring the higher education system during the transition period has produced major changes in business education. These changes are extensive and have affected almost all facets of the educational experience: curriculum, pedagogical methods, admission and evaluation of students, faculty development, relationships with enterprises, facilities, quality control, international cooperation, and research activity. Change often engenders new problems, which are, in many cases, similar to the problems faced by most transitioning economies (Qano et al. 2000). But specific factors make the Albanian case particularly challenging.

Change in Curriculum

Present-day Albanian university structures, in which higher education in business takes place, have imported their education models from the former Soviet system. Past programs were oriented toward economics with an emphasis on macroeconomic subjects such as macroeconomics, the theory of economic thought, and capitalist and socialist economies. Marxist-Leninist theory and authentic socialist ideology were obligatory topics as were historical and dialectical materialism, history of the Labor Party of Albania, and political economy. Emphasis was unfailingly placed on physical education and military science. Professional subjects were oriented toward planning and managing in a centralized socialist economy. Only mathematics and statistics can be said to have approached international educational standards. The duration of studies ranged from four to five years and the diplomas were principally of the bachelor's degree level.

Recent political and economic changes in Albania have yielded a fairly thorough reform of the business curriculum. This reform is geared toward harmonization and normalization of educational content, improvements in the way knowledge is transmitted, enhancement of documentation, and attainment of minimal standards of student performance. The ongoing changes have forthrightly espoused West European and American approaches.

To gain a better grasp of the business curriculum reforms, we analyze the content for the bachelor's degree in business administration at the University of Tirana, based on the university's annual report (University of Tirana 2002). The program has three cycles, is four years in duration and organized over eight semesters. The first cycle, the common body of knowledge for all business subfields, extends over two academic years. The second cycle, foundations of business administration, covers one full academic year and includes introductory courses for all functional modules. The third cycle, covering one academic year, consists of the selection of a specialty. The proposed specialties are management, public administration, marketing, and tourism. Analysis of the first cycle's content demonstrates the following changes: the abolition of ideologized subjects and the introduction of the philosophical foundations of market economy management. The only subjects carried over from the old programs are mathematics, computer science, and foreign languages. In the second cycle are laid the techniques of market economy management with topics heretofore nonexistent such as process operations, organizational behavior, strategic management, and human resources management, to cite but a few. The third cycle, very similar to West European and American programs, deepens management and leads to a specialization. In general, the educational process is carried out according to the European model: lectures, seminars, and exercises. A noteworthy change is the use of the European Credit Transfer System (ECTS), which permits easy transfer of overseas credits and vice versa.

One of the most important developments is the development of the master's level that had not previously existed. In this regard, the common master of business administration (MBA) program is offered by the Faculty of Economics at the University of Tirana in partnership with the College of Business Administration at the University of Nebraska, Lincoln. This MBA is designed for part-time students and is similar to the Nebraska MBA. It is made up of twelve subjects, six core courses, five interdisciplinary subjects, and one cross-cutting theme. The program can be completed within two years. The selection criteria include proficiencies in English, applied mathematics, and computer literacy; an undergraduate academic record; recommendation letters; and interviews with the faculty. There are about thirty students, most of whom have full-time jobs (Cepani 2002).

Achievements in the area of curricular reforms are considerable in intent and scope, but much remains to be done. Taking into consideration the fact that the Albanian economy is principally one of small entrepreneurs and the further fact that this sector has experienced rapid growth, university education in entrepreneurship is a priority. Entrepreneurship courses are gradually being introduced. The number of lectures has increased and their content has improved, showcasing the fundamental knowledge needed to create new enterprises. The problem is that these reforms in entrepreneurship and management of the small and medium enterprise have not so far become an option for those seeking degrees.

Teaching Methods

Educational experience follows the traditional model inherited from the past: lectures, seminars, and exercises. Lectures occupy the major part of the educational process. Lecturing is rather traditional and often rigid: The professor gives information and the students learn by rote. Student participation in active learning and debates is lacking. Real case studies, group work, and written work are in the early development stages (Cepani 2002; Pani 2003). Modern education technologies are introduced with difficulty. Educational equipment such as computers, video projectors, educational software, among others, is in short supply (Cepani 2002; Pani 2003). These methodological and material obstacles slow the pace of reform.

Exam System

Reforms undertaken thus far have led to changes in the evaluation of student knowledge acquisition. Assessment efforts now take into account not only written exam results but also student participation and contributions during seminars, practical exercises, projects, written homework, oral presentations, and laboratory work. Despite all these changes, exam results still play the central role in final grade determination. Exam taking is the same as in the past: oral, written, or both at the same time. Oral exams continue to be the golden standard and are administered according to the old system: preparation of an exam topic that is selected randomly. Student preparation time is long when compared to West European countries, about six weeks. Paradoxically, oral and written expression skills are not equally developed (Sang 2000). While enterprise-based practices are increasingly valued they do not yet matter in evaluating students' work and determining grades. Student participation in extracurricular activities such as business clubs is very limited. Furthermore, the introduction of games and business simulations remains an exception. Meeting the requirements for the degree takes two forms: examinations or the successful defense of a thesis. The principle for the latter option is similar to the international practice of supporting mini theses. Students have the right to choose between the exam and the thesis routes. In the majority of cases, students choose the exam.

Faculty

As a result of international faculty and educational exchange agreements, faculty development and state-of-the-art knowledge have improved significantly in comparison with the communist era. A great number of professors are taking advantage of this process of continuous improvement by participating in international faculty development programs at home and abroad. These programs are often undertaken through international projects such as ACE, Phare, Tempus, and the like. For example, in the case of the faculty of the Department of Farms and Agribusiness Administration at the Agriculture University of Tirana, an average of fourteen months is devoted to faculty training and qualification, both at home and abroad, for individual professors (AUT 2001).

The exchange experience of Albanian professors has considerably improved the quality of teaching. International exchanges and faculty development can have perceived negative impacts related to fear on the part of some Albanian professors of losing autonomy, identity, and the capacity to manage their own professional development. These reactions have also been observed in other transition economies (Norbert 1996; Tucker 2000).

The level of qualification of business professors often follows the general low level of higher education qualification. Hagelund notes that "the insufficient training of the teachers, professionally and pedagogically, is the greatest problem facing higher education in Albania today" (2001: 16). Compared with the average level of qualification in public higher education, the average level of qualification of the business school professors is better, with 52 percent possessing at least a degree approximating the PhD level, which, in practice, means 18 percent better than the average level in public higher education at large. This percentage is still far from the norms of the Western and American universities. Lower levels of qualification are observed in the regional universities (Pani 2003), particularly in Vlora and Elbasan.

As do public university lecturers in Central and Eastern Europe (Norbert 1996), Albanian lecturers face financial difficulties. Wages are low, at roughly

US$300 to US$500 per month, as compared with the average Albanian standard of living (Pani 2003). This phenomenon has caused outmigration and movement toward other professions that are better remunerated. In many cases, lecturers also have second and third professions (e.g., as interpreters, consultants for international organizations, in private undertakings, etc.). This practice, also observed in East European countries (Norbert 1996), reduces the time that a lecturer can dedicate to research and educational activities.

A positive element that may contribute to raising educational quality is a teacher evaluation system. With some noteworthy exceptions (e.g., the Department of Farms and Agribusiness Administration at the Agriculture University of Tirana), these practices are not system wide.

An important indicator is intensity of research output. In recent years, thanks to relationships with foreign universities and donations received, research publications have increased significantly. Research output in the business programs still suffer from lack of international exposure, owing in part to the low level of foreign language proficiency of faculty (Husi 2002). A further and related concern is the minuscule number of Albanian students pursuing doctoral studies and the lack of support for such undertakings. The University of Tirana (OECD 2002) is the only institution where the degree of Doctor of Economics is granted by the Faculty of Economics. Many of the more promising graduate students leave the country to pursue a PhD in the area of business and often do not return to Albania, further deepening the brain drain and negatively affecting the supply of quality teachers and researchers.

Educational Facilities

The available facilities for business education in Albania are old and date from the communist era. Equipment is antiquated and does not meet basic international standards. The majority of universities have not recovered from the physical plant damage caused by the vandalism attendant on the crisis of 1997 (Qano et al. 2000; Sang 2000). The fire in the buildings of the Faculty of Economics at the Agriculture University of Tirana and its library is one of the most flagrant examples of wanton acts of destruction. With rising assistance from international organizations, business educational institutions have improved their infrastructure in many regards: new buildings and equipment (a noteworthy example is the Faculty of Economics at the Agriculture University of Tirana), construction of new lecture halls, computer rooms, and actual computer equipment. The Organization for Economic Cooperation and Development (OECD 2002) has noted the evident lack of funds and its deleterious impacts on higher education in all professional fields. Library resources are woefully insufficient, and public budgets for this purpose are limited. Library resources and access have come principally from international donors such as the Soros Foundation, UNDP, EU, the U.S. Information Agency, USAID, and so forth (Pani 2003; Sang 2000).

International Cooperation

International collaboration with foreign universities, particularly in Western Europe and the United States, supplemented by international institutions, has played an essential role as catalyst in implementing the reform process. This collaboration has opened the road to internationalization of business education and has produced lasting results in all aspects of the educational chain. All universities have established close relations with a range of foreign universities and are involved in implementing international assistance projects. Another positive step is enhanced collaboration with the universities of neighboring countries such as Macedonia, Kosovo, and Turkey and the ensuing mutual recognition of diplomas. Still, an overall lack of coordination prevails among various universities as they undertake to establish links with the international community. Much duplication and replication is often evidenced and a long-term strategic integrative vision is not readily forthcoming in building on past efforts.

A Development Perspective

Just as it is in all transitioning economies, the demand for business education is evident in Albania. Partly pent-up and partly growing because of liberalization, privatization, and globalization and rising expectations, this demand is not being met (Qano et al. 2000). Further highlighting this growing demand are the need for university-trained managers in response to a rapid rate of urbanization associated with a shift toward white-collar occupations, a change in student preference for social and economic sciences and especially for business as fields of study, the need to retrain older executives in the tools of market economy management, and, not to be underestimated, the requirements of international enterprises and organizations that began moving into Albania in the 1990s.

Deepening the Educational Reform Process

To deepen the change process already initiated, some propositions provide guidelines.

Taking into account the specifics of the Albanian economy and its labor market in the formulation of future higher educational development strategies. According to West European studies (Paul and Murdoch 2000; Schomburg

2000; Moscati and Rostan 2000; Arnesen 2000; Kellerman and Sagmeister 2000; Woodley and Brennan 2000) and based on the principles of neocorrespondence theory (Saunders and Machell 2000; Nicolescu 2003), the restructuring of business education must track the needs of enterprises and the employment prospects for future managers. These studies highlight the need for today's firms to hire managers with broad, generic, and flexible skills, who are motivated to work hard and capable of working in a group (Nicolescu 2003: 78). A study on the subject (Cepani 2002) shows that the needs of business firms in Albania are clearer in these areas: management of industrial operations, textiles, agribusiness, handicrafts, mineral processing, and particularly in entrepreneurship and enterprise creation. Applied and responsive research must become a permanent part of the legitimate, rewarded activity of faculty. Responding to firms' needs should result in curricular and programmatic reforms, and, while not solely guiding the process, it should be organically linked. Public higher education in business should also play a key role in business incubation. In this connection, the university should play a salient role in establishing sustainable relationships between state institutions, business management centers, and nonprofit international institutions. Finally, another important element in building long-term strategies for business education is the continuous survey of qualitative and quantitative indicators on the employment of new graduates: firms willing to hire, skills and abilities required, employment techniques, time needed to find a job, wages, and so forth. These indicators have to be published and communicated to political decision makers, organizations, students, and researchers alike.

Integrating Albanian culture into the selection and implementation of the best models of reference. The future system of higher education in management and business should be sustainable, independent, responsible, and specific. The unique features of Albanian education and its economy must be more carefully considered in order to select and adapt available European and North American models to the cultural, institutional, and social features of Albanian economy and society. The experience of other European countries in transition (Norbert 1996) has shown that the exact replication of foreign models can compromise the process of business educational reform and slow the implementation phase. Perhaps unexplored ground in this field are models of business schools in transition economies in Southeastern Europe and emerging countries because they come close to Albanian specificities in terms of commonality of historical, political, ideological, and social features. Teaching programs should include courses that compare and contrast Albanian and European culture.

Integrating the faculty in a systematic, open, and flexible process of research and pedagogic qualification leading to theoretical and practical teaching applications. It is important to consider research as a significant part of professors' activities and to find the right qualitative and quantitative criteria to assess it and its impacts. Professors' level of involvement in research ought to be used as a criterion for the management of a university career. A closer look should be given to a system of incentives for young students who have the ability and desire to become professors. Professors should improve teaching and research skills by increasing their mastery of foreign languages, thereby enhancing access to international scholarship as well as teaching methods, case studies, and simulation material. Web-based distance learning via the Internet is a further avenue toward facilitating the reform process.

These directions for reform require funding to improve infrastructure and raise wage levels for faculty. Much discussion today focuses on ways and means to promote the financial autonomy of universities in Albania.

Private Education Initiatives

Private education as a tool for developing management education in Albania is still in its infancy. The recent birth of the first private institution in business and management education at once makes us wonder about its future in Albania and its ability to meet market demands and students' financial capacity to defray private sector educational costs.

The role of the Albanian government remains critical but actions indicate that the government intends to maintain the status quo rather than to implement radical changes. It is surprising to outsiders that the fall of the communist regime in Albania and the transition to a trade regime without government intervention did not lead in short order to the decentralization of higher education. This is contrary to what happened in many countries of Central and Eastern Europe. Much as in Belarus and Slovakia (Tucker 2000), however, the state continues to control most aspects of the higher education system, considering it too important a governmental function to privatize large segments of it. Reforms in higher education in business management in Albania have, paradoxically, legitimized the state's role and strengthened its position, somewhat at the expense of momentum in private initiatives. The commitment of the Albanian government to adopt the bachelor/master system and to apply the Bologna Declaration in the academic year 2005–6 is a concrete example of sound decision making and reform whose implementation and impact bear watching.

It is not unlikely that the current educational system has a vested interest in maintaining the quasimonopoly currently enjoyed by the state (Tucker 2000). Promotion, employment, elections to representative academic bodies, and the control of fee income distribution and funds flowing from foreign projects are thus likely to remain in traditional hands. Competition is not likely to be a system driver under this set of assumptions.

Decisions to create new institutions or new jobs in universities as well as the attribution of funds are seemingly based on political interests rather than on the real needs of the Albanian economy. This phenomenon has been observed in other ex-socialist countries with similar political cultures (Norbert 1996; Voros and Schermerhorn 1993).

As highlighted by Norbert (1996) many people who retain power over critical resources and who have no motivation to change or to learn new business concepts still remain. These behaviors are well known and have been studied both in theory and in practice. They are tightly related to the egregious lack of resources and their allocation and distribution (Pettigrew 1973). Low economic activity and low family income in Albania are two constraining factors that will brake the expansion of private higher education.

Small company size, limited capital, low yearly investment capability, lack of a system for funding business education, such as might be found in France, can reduce the supply of students (employed or unemployed) able to undertake private studies. The higher spending that the public system requires does limit private sector growth. In borrowing successful strategies from management schools in Western Europe or North America, there are two major avenues to explore: establishing focused and specialized programs not offered in the public education system and evolving "niche" strategies aimed at specific categories of potential students.

Private schools are more apt to build partnerships with foreign universities and knowledge networks that offer their students a window on the world, access to state of the art training, and a greater range of job opportunities. Such schools may be the generator and guarantor of needed reforms that have thus far stalled. As mentioned by Madhavan and Fogel, "a fundamental premise for working in Central and Eastern Europe is that transferring a business education program to a reforming economy involves more than just teaching its managers a specific set of skills. This transfer also requires a cultural and philosophical infrastructure that supports modern management practice" (1992: 4).

Conclusions and Future Trends

Higher education in business and management and the overall higher education system in Albania are in a state of flux: structural changes are in motion as the Albanian economy becomes integrated, willy-nilly, into a regional and global economic system, free of ideology and placing a premium on innovation and adaptability. Albania, the Land of the Eagles, cannot be shielded anymore from the pressures of its external environment. A road map and a harbinger of future changes are contained in Albania's commitment to the EU's Bologna Declaration. In some public universities the aim thus far has been the restructuring of curricula along the following lines (Bohn et al.

2001): modularization of curriculums, introduction of bachelor and master degrees, the introduction of ECTS, sounder organization of degree awarding, and the transfer of credits. While it is too soon to assess the impact of these "early stage" reforms, there can be little doubt that business higher education institutions will need to work within the existing overall higher education system. It will take time and focus. Overcoming resistance will require a proper mix of internal and external incentives.

References

Agriculture University of Tirana (AUT). 2001. "Faculty of Agriculture Report." Evaluation of Farm and Agribusiness Department. Tirana, Albania.

Ahmeti, A. 2003. "Public Health Management and Policy Education and Training: Albania." Paper presented at the eleventh NISPAcee Annual Conference, Enhancing the Capacities to Govern: Challenges Facing the CEE Countries. Bucharest, Romania, April 10–12.

Albanian Business Information Center Portal. Available at www.albic.net (accessed December 9, 2004).

Arnesen, C. 2000. "Higher Education and Graduate Employment in Norway." *European Journal of Education* 35, no. 2: 221–28.

Bohn, A.; G. Kreykenbohm; M. Moser; and A. Pomikalko. 2001. "Modularization and Introduction of Master's Degrees: Preliminary Experiences and Recommendations." Report based on experience from the program Modularization. Joint project for the Introduction of Bachelor and Master Degrees in Agricultural Sciences, University of Applied Sciences, Neubranderburg.

Cepani, A. 2002. "The Contribution of Universities in Developing Entrepreneurial Potential of the SME Sector in Albania." International Symposium on Learning Management and Technology Development in the Information and Internet Age, University of Bologna, November.

Galen S.H. 2000. "U.S. MBA and Management Training Programs in Central and Eastern Europe." *Journal of Technology Transfer* 25: 319–27.

Hagelund, B. 2001. "Higher Education in Albania." Unpublished paper. University of Copenhagen, faculty of Social Sciences, Copenhagen, Denmark.

Husi, G. 2002. "Country Profile—Albania." In *Europe at Schools in South Eastern Europe—Country Profiles,* ed. R. Biermann, 9–23. Center for European Immigration Studies.

Kellerman, P., and G. Sagmeister. 2000. "Higher Education and Graduate Employment in Austria." *European Journal of Education* 35, no. 2: 157–64.

Krbec, D. 2002. "Shaping New Paradigms in Higher Education Development: Dilemmas for Transitional Countries." Paper presented at the IS2002 Informing Science and IT Education Conference, Cork, Ireland, June 19–21.

Kule, D.; A. Mançellari; H. Papapanagos: S. Qirici; and P. Sanfey. 1999. "The Cause and Consequences of Albanian Emigration During Transition: Evidence from Microdata." Paper presented at a workshop at University of Tirana, July 1999, and at the International Economics and Finance Society, Brunel University, November 1999.

Madhavan, R., and D.S. Fogel. 1992. "In Support of Reform: Western Business Education in Central and Eastern Europe." Paper presented at the Symposium on Business Education in Eastern Europe. *Review of Business*, March 22.

Moscati, R., and M. Rostan. 2000. "Higher Education and Graduate Employment in Italy." *European Journal of Education* 35, no. 2: 189–200.

Nicolescu, L. 2003. "Higher Education in Romania: Evolution and Views from the Business Community." *Tertiary Education and Management* 9: 77–95.

Norbert, F.E. 1996. "Management Education in Post-Socialist Hungary: Observations on Obstacles to Reforms." *Journal of Management Education* 20, no. 1.

Organization for Economic Cooperation and Development (OECD). 2002. *Thematic Review of National Policies for Education—Albania: Stability Pact for South Eastern Europe*. Report of Task Force on Education, Center for Cooperation with Nonmembers, Directorate for Education, Employment, Labor and Social Affairs, Education Committee, Paris.

Pani, P. 2003. "The Albanian System of Higher Education—Current Status and Perspectives." *Center for European Integration Studies*, Special Edition: Education Reform and Its Political Repercussions 3, no. 3: 5–8

Papapanagos, P. and P. Sanfee. 2001. "Intention to Emigrate in Transition Countries: Case of Albania." *Journal of Population Economics* 14: 491–504.

Paul, J.J., and J. Murdoch. 2000. "Higher Education and Graduate Employment in France." *European Journal of Education* 35, no. 2: 179–87.

Pettigrew, A.M. 1973. *The Politics of Organizational Decision-making*. London: Tavistock.

Qano, V.; S. Wright; G. Wagne; and P. Aerts. 2000. "Working Groups Reports: Albania." Presented at the Seminar on Strategies of Educational Reform in South-East Europe, Bled, Slovenia, June 8–10. *Proceedings of Seminar*: 85–88.

Sang, M.L. 2000. "Restructuring Albanian Business Education Infrastructure." Second International Conference on Transition and Enterprise Restructuring in Eastern Europe, Hillerød, Denmark, August 17-19.

Saunders, M. and J. Machell. 2000. "Understanding emerging trends in higher education curricula and work connections." *Higher Education Policy, The Quarterly Journal of the International Association of Universities* 13, no. 3: 287-302

Schomburg, H. 2000. "Higher Education and Graduate Employment in Germany." *European Journal of Education* 35, no. 2: 189–200.

Slantcheva, S. 2000. "The Challenges to Vertical Degree Differentiation Within Bulgarian Universities: The Problematic Introduction of the Three-level System of Higher Education." *Tertiary Education and Management* 6: 209–25.

Svejnar, J. 2000. "Economics Ph.D. Education in Central and Eastern Europe." *Comparative Economic Studies* 42, no. 2: 37–50.

Totomanova, A. 2000. "Comparative Study of Higher Education Systems in the SEE Countries." South East European Educational cooperation network portal: www.see-educoop.net (accessed December 9, 2004).

Tucker, A. 2000. "Feature: Higher Education on Trial." *East European Constitutional Review* (Summer): 88–89.

University of Tirana. 2002. "Faculty of Economics Annual Report." Tirana, Albania.

Voros, J. and J. Schermerhorn. 1993. "Institutional Roles in Higher Education for Business and Management in Hungary." *Management Education and Development* 24: 70–82.

Woodley, A., and J. Brennan. 2000. "Higher Education and Graduate Employment in the United Kingdom." *European Journal of Education* 35, no. 2: 139–249.

Part IV

Latin America

15

Toward the Internationalization of Business Education in Latin America

Jaime Ortiz

The governing body of the higher business education system in Latin America calls for innovative educational programs that could serve the business student cohort of the twenty first century. Essentially, the governing body of the higher business education system is made up of four types of institutions: an assortment of reputable business colleges established under very traditional public universities, relatively new private ones, professional institutes, and advanced technical training centers. Policy making at those levels is the responsibility of a Board of Directors supervised by the Ministries of Education. Such boards govern member institutions and grant university officials broad discretion to establish their institutions' policies and manage their campuses. Along those lines, business deans have acknowledged the need to increase the academic stature of their colleges in light of current globalization challenges (Scott 2000). In turn, they are striving to encourage internationalization as a way to improve students' understanding of the world and emerge as truly international academic institutions.

Institutions of higher business education in Latin America are seeking further support to accomplish their mission. They have managed to survive despite currently adverse funding conditions and shifting ideological priorities. Therefore, business education has been subject to more stringent reviews in terms of intended merit or historical support. Nowadays it is being developed in a context that more closely resembles the structure and interests of their own institutions as well as those of the students (Finney 1997).

Thus, business education has had to adjust curricula to better meet the demands faced from different constituencies.

The globalization phenomenon requires Latin American business students to adequately function in a more interdependent and integrated economy. Shifting social, legal, economic, political, and technological (SLEPT) conditions pose a different set of challenges to business colleges in Latin America. Their response to satisfy the demand from business students should be framed in a context in which students emerge better prepared to cope with the forces that govern today's world economy. This chapter underscores a conceptual approach to allow business students in Latin America to acquire a true international business culture. A combination of a distinctive business curriculum, corporate internships, and study abroad programs should allow them to become more effective, problem-solving individuals.

The Role of Business Colleges

Business colleges are the primary bodies responsible for providing skills across functional disciplines. They have department-wide responsibility for establishing and coordinating academic activities for students as well as faculty. Accepting some degree of generalization, the mission of business colleges can be stated as *consistently creating and delivering the most relevant business and economics teaching, research, and consulting programs for the strategic profit and not-for-profit industries in their service area.* At the international level, they assist undergraduate and graduate students seeking corporate overseas internships under the auspices of an agreement with a foreign institution. Business colleges also encourage faculty to develop new courses and to enhance existing ones. In particular, they may assist those interested in obtaining overseas professional assignments consistent with the priorities established by their departments, as well as awarding credits for teaching courses under an agreement with an affiliated foreign institution.

One way to internationalize the business curriculum among Latin American business colleges is to encourage an increasing number of business students to travel overseas. This implies letting them participate in corporate overseas internships and study abroad programs. It can also mean developing visiting scholar programs in which business faculty spend time overseas on teaching or research assignments. Foreign faculty may come to the hosting institution as well. Much can be learned from this "foreign" experience by both the visiting and the hosting party. Finally, as the international reputation of the college grows, it becomes a desirable location for eminent business executives and policy makers to visit and lecture. At this stage, a critical function of a business college is to serve as a link across its departments in consolidating ties with international partners.

Over time, business colleges need to increase their funding for hiring additional faculty with proven international expertise. Deans committed to the international scene need to place a higher priority on their colleges and encourage expansion into new areas. A good complementary activity is a relationship with a foreign business school through a joint research center. This particular relationship is appropriate as it offers a foreign language of choice for the majority of students. Another corresponding option is an overseas study center. Overseas study centers, particularly those that are part of a business program, can accommodate faculty language and geographic preferences. Full utilization of permanent overseas study centers can generate a steady source of revenue. However, the discretionary nature of these categories can be debated because a fundamental activity of a business college is preparing students to meet the challenges posed by the globalization phenomenon.

In practice, Summers (2002) suggests that developing business programs in institutions of higher learning requires fostering more globally oriented campuses, with an emphasis on putting students first and getting them overseas. One option is to treat each business college the same as an independently funded initiative, with a base budget large enough to properly fund its mission as agreed to by its many constituencies throughout the college. A second option is simply to allocate the necessary funds to effectively meet the obligations created by its mandate. Under Latin America's current economic climate, both options appear difficult to achieve.

The Globalization Framework

The process of globalization is generally understood as the flow of expertise, information, resources, and technology leading to the integration of economies and societies around the world. As such, it involves activities undertaken by people and organizations in more than one country or region. Main drivers that explain the globalization process include technological advances in communication and information processing along with lower trade and investment barriers that, in turn, translate into increased competition (Sullivan 1999). Undoubtedly, the concept of globalization helps to explain a gradual homogenization of cultures, ethics, and exchange practices. Businesses seem to be among the most visible activities of how a changing international environment transforms the appreciation of diversity.

The SLEPT conditions in Latin American countries offer as many similarities as divergences influencing the practice of business. These conditions,

Figure 15.1   **Business Environment**

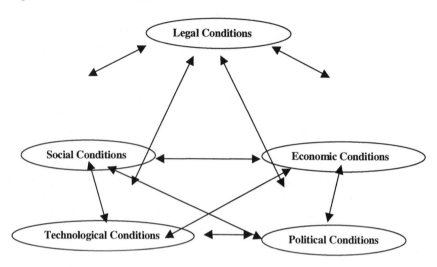

by themselves, impose acute restrictions on responsiveness and adaptation of firms to local individual markets. As shown in Figure 15.1, each one of the SLEPT conditions is highly dependent on the others and hence mutually reinforcing within the business environment. Therefore, one of the greatest challenges business colleges face is to provide a true international education to their business students. In this context, it is not surprising that international education is at the center of many political agendas. Learning about another culture increases tolerance and leads to further appreciation and understanding among nations (Woolf 2002).

In the present context of globalization, a business curriculum, particularly at the undergraduate level, must accurately capture the main elements of each SLEPT condition. Failure to identify those elements will distort the intended purpose of educating successful individuals and business managers. The idea is that business faculty can reach across and beyond the SLEPT conditions in a way that both similarities and divergences can be understood by acknowledging the world's diversity. In view of this, a cost-effective way of achieving a global understanding would be offering on-site opportunities to improve the perception of the business environment.

Business education in Latin America is becoming a complex endeavor. As such, it is closely linked to the challenges imposed by an increasingly interdependent world. Such an interrelation compels academic deans and business faculty to stress the SLEPT conditions. In Pohan's (1996) view, quality services rendered to business students should come from faculty knowledgeable about the different dimensions offered by the countries or geographical areas in question. Students enhance their business education vision when each one of the SLEPT conditions is incorporated in their curriculum. It has widely been recognized that personal and professional cross-cultural knowledge obtained by having an immersion experience overseas far outweighs the monetary costs involved (Cobbin and Lee 2002).

Business education should prevent Latin American students from becoming ethnocentric individuals, reluctant to open their minds to individuals from other continents. Faculty teaching courses with an international flavor have a responsibility to provide educational opportunities to eliminate ethnocentrism. However, Cushner and Mahon (2002) assert that most faculty lack a significant, long-term, intercultural experience abroad that can be translated into significant contributions in terms of language proficiency, global competency, and intercultural sensitivity. In some instances, they simply choose to ignore the need for students to function in an international business setting. Latin American countries are a case in point. According to the Institute of International Education (2003), less than 190 Latin American scholars came to the United States during academic year 2001–3 to specialize in business and management.

Social Conditions

Understanding the dynamics of multiculturalism discourages business students from using stereotypes and enhances their professional skills. Study abroad programs provide students with the opportunity to make worldwide distinctions in cultural differences throughout in situ experiences. There are a variety of attitude changes such as increased commitment to international understanding. Lambert (1989) notes that experiences overseas provide students with an empathetic appreciation of the variety of perspectives that govern people's behavior throughout the world. Such a skill is critical to developing effective cross-cultural understanding and maintaining good communication. As for faculty, they tend to be more effective motivators after enriching their personal and professional experience with several assignments abroad.

Knowledge and professional experience are indeed necessary, but not sufficient prerequisites for Latin American managers to successfully compete in the corporate world. According to the Koe Corporation, proficiency in the English language is a must among Latin American business managers (Meller and Rappoport 2003). Exposure to English within a unique cultural situation is just as important as learning and mastering the language itself. Ultimately, it allows for greater depth in language training and the social understanding necessary for undertaking change. The current trend among Latin American firms is to hire bilingual individuals who effectively understand protocols, convincingly communicate ideas, and empathetically relate to their business counterparts. Therefore, language classes, especially English, should be attuned to those parts of the world where Latin American countries and local businesses maintain regional geographic interests.

Religion and education are also critical elements within the social aspect. Both have to be tackled in the context of cultural diversity and treated in terms of their inclusiveness rather than their exclusiveness. There is a tendency to persistently see something wrong with other countries instead of just pinpointing their business culture as unique to the people of that country. Sharp business models and snazzy technologies are indeed necessary, but they will prove useless if they do not take into account the fact that goods and services that are popular in one country may not prove to be such hits in others.

Legal Conditions

The legal framework sets the boundaries of international business in terms of contracts, investments, and corporate laws. National, regional, multilateral, and international laws are constantly invoked to settle disputes ranging from labor practices to intellectual property rights or from marketing regulations to foreign direct investment. A stable and coherent legal system provides transparency to foreign investors eager to engage in strategic alliances with local entrepreneurs. In cases when conciliation cannot be reached based either on arbitration or consensual agreement among the parties involved, business litigation becomes unavoidable. Corruption, in its many forms, still prevails in Latin America despite numerous denials and oversights.

Awareness of blackmail and bribery as a nonacceptable but, nonetheless, common business practice requires the careful attention of Latin American business students. Illegal offering, giving, soliciting, or receiving of something of value negatively influences business decisions and distorts resource allocations from a social viewpoint. Notwithstanding, the legal conditions in Latin American economies tend to be more convoluted and bureaucratic than those observed in developed nations. In the former group of countries, a relatively fragile institutional structure imposes an unnecessary burden on their economies discouraging attempts to foster economic relationships. Hence, regular contacts with the legal community become compulsory to ensure full compliance with the processes by which laws and regulations are enacted and enforced in each country.

Economic Conditions

Globalization, propelled by an increased flow of international trade and capital, seems widely accepted despite sporadic critics. Some criticism of this ongoing transformation of the world economy is related to whether or not emerging economies and developing countries have raised their living standards. The United Nations (1999) notes that both poverty and income concentration have increased between and within emerging economies as a result of globalization. In contrast, the World Bank (2001) goes on to say that well-functioning economies, fully integrated into world markets, offer chances for trade expansion and technology diffusion that allow them to provide safety nets for the poor. Therefore, exploring the operational aspects of local and global competition and their impact on poverty alleviation and income redistribution becomes critical to understanding the rationale of certain macroeconomic policies and development programs. As a result, sound fiscal and monetary policies along with strong financial systems constitute the means by which Latin American economies achieve sustained rates of economic growth.

Market-oriented policies adopted by several Latin American countries have increased opportunities for doing business in those nations. In particular, market deregulation, privatization of state-owned enterprises, and incentives to foreign investment have all triggered firms' expansion to take advantage of the cost and quality differences of production factors. Besides, conducting cross-border production, investment, and trade activities involves foreign currency exchange that is highly dependent on changing economic conditions both locally and abroad. Consequently, there are a number of elements to be taught to business students for a better appreciation of the globalization process from an economic viewpoint. Along these lines, Aninat (2002) holds the view that necessary elements should include, at a minimum, structural reforms and adjustment policies along with stability of international financial markets.

Political Conditions

Political forces influence all aspects of the business environment in a way that may adversely affect the long-run profitability of specific firms (Ortiz 2001). Business managers across Latin America perform under governments identified with varied political ideologies. They are concerned with the stability of these governments and with whether economic decisions are centralized or decentralized. Government systems in Latin America have ranged from democracies to totalitarian regimes. Each implies a completely different set of benefits, costs, and risks at the time of doing business. Collective goals are overemphasized with respect to individual goals when the needs of society are seen as more important than individual ones. Regardless of the extent of those government ideologies, political upheavals, repression, violence, terrorism, strikes, or cabinet changes, all create an atmosphere of risk and instability. Government decisions taken in highly political environments may even trigger the risk of nationalization. This occurs when governments allow the transfer of private, foreign-owned assets with (expropriation) or without (confiscation) any form of compensation.

Decision-making processes depend heavily on the degree of involvement of society and its constituencies. It seems acceptable nowadays for Latin American citizens to enjoy a minimum of constitutional guarantees regardless of the assortment of political doctrines available. These include, at a minimum, a free media, decentralized political power, freedom of expression and organization, and regular and transparent democratic elections. Political extremism based on religious principles, tribal interests, and military uprisings often give rise to various forms of dictatorship. Political ideologies and economic systems are interrelated to such a high degree that both provide their own philosophical interpretation regarding ownership of production factors and the extent to which market forces and competition answer the main economic questions regarding production and consumption of goods and services.

Technological Conditions

Technical change is regarded as the main determinant of long-term economic growth. Although expensive and risky, research and development are instrumental for any industry to survive in a competitive global market. In its many forms, technical change encompasses new techniques, processes, and managerial practices to solve specific manufacturing problems. A market economy provides more ingredients for successful innovation than any other economic system. The incentives offered by the market induce a cadre of entrepreneurs to seek communication and information technology solutions for profitable business activities. Capitalizing on the learning effects and seeking economies of scale help firms to boost productivity, achieve efficiency gains, decrease production costs, and widen product differentiation options that, ultimately, will allow them to maximize their profits.

However, and without exception, Latin American economies lag well behind their developed counterparts in terms of expenditures on research and development as a proportion of gross domestic product. It then becomes crucial for Latin American business students to understand the importance of technical progress and how it translates into different processes and operational tasks. Innovation is forcefully a continuous development process that takes some time to occur and differs from one industry to another. Besides, it may not automatically lead to the creation of competitive advantages. However, generation and adaptation of new technologies do help to counteract the pervasive effects of diminishing returns and obsolescence. Future business managers must take an increasing interest in the way technological events occur and in their impact on different Latin American countries, as well as the role of governments in shaping a culture of innovation. Successful business managers are those open to innovation, capable of selecting those technologies that will contribute most to productivity increases. Meller and Rappoport (2003) point out that Latin American countries fall well behind developed nations not only in terms of quantity but, more worrisome, in terms of the quality of their professionals.

Strengthening the International Business Curriculum

This section suggests a standard business curriculum for business colleges in Latin America at the undergraduate level after following the U.S. model of business education, presented elsewhere in Ortiz (2004). It redesigns a new undergraduate business curriculum to enhance students' competency to function in the business environments previously identified by the business schools. In this regard, promising geographical areas in which to attain knowledge and/or immersion experience include North America, Western Europe, and Asia. The Middle East and Sub-Saharan Africa may follow suit if, and only if, overall conditions in those areas improve quite dramatically. Business colleges should realize the need to strengthen their curriculum and make it more appealing to the current needs of their undergraduate student body.

The curriculum presented below allows for specific subjects that could be transferred to a business track in order to enhance its already supposedly "global features." Following the template steps for analyzing curriculum development suggested by Cobbin and Lee (2002), the array of course offerings is aimed at undergraduate degree-seeking students in their last year of studies. Syllabi must subsequently be designed to ensure full coverage of an enriched set of subjects needed to conceptualize the main business strategies. Competent business faculty should succeed in instilling confidence in students to enable them to grasp the dynamics of competing in the global marketplace.

Despite its attractiveness and appeal, internationalizing the business curriculum may be an inherently rough and difficult endeavor to be undertaken by many business colleges. However, they should depose self-centered stances

Table 15.1

Proposed Courses in the Business Track

Business core (6 courses)	Business electives (2 courses)
International Business	Cross-cultural Human Relations and Negotiations
Global Strategy and Policy	International Finance
Marketing Strategy	International Marketing
Advanced Managerial Finance	International Relations
Global Supply Chain Management	International Accounting and Taxation
Managing Micro and Small Enterprises	

General electives (1 course)	Economics electives (1 course)
Trade and Investment Law	Economic Growth and Development
Advanced Quantitative Methods	International Economics

Foreign language (2 courses)
English
German
French
Japanese

in order to accept their ultimate goal of transferring managerial skills to students who are able to cope successfully with the magnitude of the SLEPT changes taking place throughout the world. Finally, the implicit assumption continues that each course is worth three credits and that the students have completed all of their lower division and/or general education courses. Table 15.1 indicates the range of possible courses that might be offered in a business track to achieve the required level of knowledge.

First Step: Recognition and Commitment

The first step in initiating a change in an existing business curriculum in Latin America is acknowledgment by the business colleges of the need to nurture their international dimension. Adherence to the importance of widening a global perspective through an internationalized curriculum comes from the vision held by the business school, and, ultimately, by the university. Willingness to recognize the benefits of incorporating the global perspective in the curriculum is identified as the primary step to strengthening the business discipline. Exposure to an international context is likely to be enhanced through curriculum initiatives that complement student placements in different business settings. Identification of subjects and issues with a strong international flavor as well as those more closely influenced by local factors will allow for mutually reinforcing synergies.

In a recent international seminar held in Santiago de Chile, both academic administrators and policy makers agreed that the current higher education system in Latin America constrains the chances that its graduates will be able to successfully compete with their equals from developed countries. Their ability to compete is hindered by lengthy and expensive programs that are barely connected with the current needs of a dynamic international labor market (Expansiva 2003). Relatively long and specialized academic programs, delays of almost two years in obtaining degrees, and a severe disconnect between learning topics and skills required by the business sector compel business colleges to reassess and modify their curricula.

Therefore, the business curriculum needs to be broader and more flexible through a streamlined combination of general, basic, and advanced courses in order to better tailor business education to future employers' needs. An option for Latin American countries is to shorten the completion of their programs leading to the *Ingeniero Comercial* or *Licenciado* degree by bringing them more in line with the American model. Well-prepared students coming out of high school would be able to attain the required capabilities to successfully perform in their functional business area after just four years. Within this framework, students would obtain intermediate academic degrees equivalent to a U.S. bachelor's degree. Subsequently, if they choose, they could proceed to specialized graduate work leading to a master's or doctoral degree. At the same time, Latin American universities should implement a credit system that is both compatible and homogenous across institutions of higher learning to ease the process of transferring course work.

Second Step: Issue Selection

The second step in strengthening a business curriculum throughout Latin America involves gathering information about the issues that should be incorporated into each one of the courses being offered. A solid business track requires an assortment of specific disciplines that many times differs from more conventional approaches to offer stand-alone business subjects. A truly "internationalized" business curriculum must provide students with the knowledge and skills to successfully improve their decision-making process to efficiently allocate resources on a worldwide basis. Conversely, a general and flexible business curriculum would add international issues that could be implemented regardless of the regional educational market of interest. It would, in turn, foster awareness among Latin American students of the global business environment and let them grasp a basic understanding of the business field. In contrast, graduate level programs would be more suitable to increase knowledge and provide expertise in one or more of the several functional fields relevant to the business dimension.

In the past three decades, the neoliberal model has been adopted by Latin America with different intensities across countries (Biglaiser 2002). These changes have brought into being a small select group of private universities specialized in business administration to meet the rising demand for graduate students, and business courses are being offered to students with strict adherence to the prevailing neoclassical framework of resource allocation. Future managers hold managerial positions in both the public and private sectors, perform in a context of market-oriented economic policies, and are, ultimately, assessed according to those very same criteria. Hence, it is deemed important to introduce a business curriculum that allows for immediate training and immersion in the benefits, costs, and risks of functioning in open markets and fierce competition. Along these lines, Biglaiser (2002) goes on to say that the interaction with professors in formal and informal settings helps to develop a cohort of students more attuned to the importance of free-trade policies and private ownership.

A contrasting approach can be found among the critics of the neoliberal model being implemented throughout Latin America (Valdés 1995). Recognizing the importance for students to excel in a rigorous set of courses, it becomes imperative to ensure that such a business curriculum is designed taking into account the specific and complex needs of Latin American countries. A random extraction of courses and contents taken almost verbatim from each major business school in the United States or Europe will prove wrong, out of context, and unrelated to the limited SLEPT conditions of Latin America. Consequently, each subject must pragmatically align sound business competencies and techniques with their applicability to the Latin American reality. Business students need to achieve a minimum level of professional maturity to understand their role in the resource allocation process within a context plagued by poverty and income inequality. Hence, from a government perspective, the ultimate tacit responsibility of business students would be to help make a contribution to the economic development of their countries.

Third Step: Implementation

The final crucial step in redesigning a business curriculum is to develop a specific planning and coordinating approach to manage its implementation. Such an undertaking requires the business colleges to serve as a catalyst in allowing the students to acquire skills that they can use in their jobs. It can also seek the comparative strength of the faculty members and the surrounding environment in which the university is situated (AIB 1999). This includes exposure to training in business topics and language training in the areas that the business colleges have selected as the top regional focus of business programs. As noted by Buckley (2002), specialized, multidisciplinary, undergraduate business degree programs are arguably a good method for developing expertise, particularly those that require regional competencies. However, overseas experience through corporate internships and study abroad programs should also be, if not compulsory, at least required within an international business curriculum. Field trips and partnering with multinational corporations greatly help students to compete more effectively in the global economy.

Quality assurance has to be seen as the foundation for empowering institutions of higher learning in Latin America. A comprehensive set of long-term policies must set up and exert overall quality standards in business education. This would be particularly important at the time of exposing students to the wider context of internationalization, establishing a national undergraduate and graduate accreditation system, and strengthening the institutional capacity for self-regulatory and self-assessment processes. Accordingly, business colleges would define the mechanisms that will facilitate student transfers, implement actions that will strengthen their institutions, and establish the necessary foundations for a coherent financial aid policy for business students. A competitive fund with each institution of higher business education would encourage its business college to improve the academic services to students. Resources would be channeled to strengthening business programs and providing equipment and infrastructure. Specific initiatives submitted for consideration would conform to the mission and strategic objectives of each business college. Eligible projects would be those addressing scholarships for study abroad, corporate internships, and visiting faculty and scholars.

Concluding Remarks

It becomes imperative for business colleges in Latin America to provide sound educational packages to ensure that their students will successfully cope with current globalization and technology trends. The internationalization process at colleges of business begins as soon as the colleges recognize the need to immerse themselves in today's global economy and commit themselves to a set of "best international practices." Unveiling business education overseas requires a much tighter network of cooperation that crosses academic disciplines and transcends institutional boundaries. Worldwide collaboration is enticed only when long-term partnerships among agencies, consortia, and organizations are present. Business colleges eager to meet the challenges imposed by a fast-changing society must begin by incorporating the international dimension into their study programs. Given their multidisciplinary nature, business faculties seem keener to deal with international issues than other academic constituencies.

Corporate overseas internships and study abroad programs tend to be seen as substitutes to academic education in campus classrooms. In reality, they are complementary means to offer a rounded education by allowing participating students to gain business exposure. Overseas interaction with fellow business students and seasoned international managers helps them to acquire a sense of awareness that will enhance their global competency. The role of business colleges extends beyond setting up exchange agreements with foreign institutions. It also serves as a liaison between business colleges and specific international opportunities for business majors. Therefore, business colleges require adequate and timely financial support to promote and fund undergraduate student participation. In addition, business colleges should pay attention to issues such as course comparability, credit transferring, and length of academic programs.

The integration of social, legal, economic, political, and technological issues within business disciplines is a must for policy purposes and curriculum design at institutions of higher learning in Latin America. Business colleges and their faculties should embark on the modernization of teaching methods and curriculum in light of the globalization phenomenon. It seems overly ambitious to recommend a "template" of core courses to prepare students for doing business in a global context that can be applied to all Latin American institutions of higher learning. Common sense suggests, however, the need to determine a minimum number of subjects and topics for undergraduate business students to adequately prepare them for shifting social, legal, economic, political, and technological scenarios. This would entail curriculum identification, course selection, content adjustment, and program implementation.

References

Academy of International Business (AIB). 1999. Internationalizing the Business School: A Global Survey of Institutions of Higher Learning.

Aninat, E. 2002. "Surmounting the Challenges of Globalization." *Finance & Development* (March). Washington, DC: International Monetary Fund.

Biglaiser, G. 2002. "The Internationalization of Chicago's Economics in Latin America." *Economic Development and Cultural Change* 50, no. 2: 269–86.

Buckley, P. 2002. "Is the International Business Research Agenda Running Out of Steam?" *Journal of International Business Studies* 33, no. 2: 365–73.

Cobbin, P., and R. Lee. 2002. "A Micro-level Approach to Internationalizing the Accounting Curriculum." *Journal of Studies in International Education* 6, no. 1: 59–77.

Currie, J. 1999. "Globalization Practices and the Professorate in Anglo-Pacific and North American Universities." *Comparative Education Review* 42, no. 1: 15–30.

Cushner, K. and J. Mahon. (2002). "Overseas Student Teaching: Affecting Personal, Professional, and Global Consequences in an Age of Globalization." *Journal of International Education* 6, no. 1: 44–78.

Expansiva, Inc. 2003. El Mercurio online. Available at http://diario.elmercurio.com/ 2005/05/06-portada/index.htm. Accessed September 29.

Finney, J.E. 1997. State Structures for the Governance of Higher Education: Florida Case Study Summary.

Institute of International Education. 2003. "Report on International Educational Exchange." New York.

Lamet, M.S., ed. 2000. *Abroad by Design*. Washington, DC: NAFSA Association of International Educators.

MECESUP. 1997. "The Improvement of Quality and Equity in Higher Education." Minister of Education, Chile.

Meller, P., and D. Rappoport. 2003. "Educational Skills Among Working Professionals." Report presented at the World Class Seminar, Santiago, Chile.

Ortiz, J. 2001. "Business Strategy Under a Simultaneous Policy-making Setting." *Portuguese Management Review* 3: 26–31.

———. 2004. "International Business Education in a Global Environment: A Conceptual Approach." *International Education Journal* 5, no. 2: 255–65.

Pohan, C. 1996. "Preservice Teachers' Beliefs About Diversity: Uncovering Factors Leading to Multicultural Responsiveness." *Equity and Excellence in Education* 29, no. 3: 62–69.

Scott, P. 2000. "Globalization and Higher Education: Challenges for the 21st Century." *Journal of Studies in International Education* 6, no. 1: 59–77.

Sullivan, J. 1999. *Exploring International Business Environments*. Boston, MA: Pearson Custom Publishing.

Summers, L. 2002. *Business Week,* February 18.

United Nations. 1999. *Human Development Report.* New York.

Valdés, J.G. 1995. *Pinochet's Economists: The Chicago School in Chile.* Cambridge: Cambridge University Press.

Woolf, M. 2002. "Harmony and Dissonance in International Education: The Limits of Globalization." *Journal of Studies in International Education* 6, no. 1: 5–15.

World Bank. 2001. "Globalization, Growth, and Poverty." Policy Research Report. Washington, DC.

16

University Entrepreneurship Education in Argentina

A Decade of Analysis

Sergio Postigo and Maria Fernanda Tamborini

The relationship between education and business creation has been studied in the international literature from different perspectives and approaches (Clark, Davis, and Harnish 1984; Lafuente and Salas 1989; Robinson and Sexton 1994; Upton, Sexton, and Moore 1995; Kolvereid and Moen 1997; Delmar and Davidsson 2000; Charney and Libecap 2000; Cowling and Taylor 2001; Levie, Brown, and Steele 2001; Lüthje and Franke 2002). Likewise, many authors mention the extraordinary increase in the quantity and quality of entrepreneurship programs in the past twenty-five years, as well as the foundation of research centers, conferences, and publications in this area responding to university initiatives and the increasing demand for these types of courses (Fayolle 1998; Kolvereid and Moen 1997; Vesper and Gartner 1997).

Entrepreneurship research in Latin American countries is limited. In addition, there is a low level of systematic information (Kantis et al. 2002), which is even more acute in the area of entrepreneurship education. However, a recent study by Varela (1997) concerning entrepreneurship education in this region points out that many different factors explain its underdevelopment. Among them, he stresses that Latin American culture does not promote the entrepreneurial spirit or entrepreneurial attitudes. Meanwhile, given the difficult circumstances these countries have to face, he argues that new ways of promoting social and economic development have to be found. He emphasizes the need for significant changes in the education system in Latin America with the aim of producing the transformation in culture and values necessary to stimulate entrepreneurial spirit.

But the academic programs of most universities of the region have a tendency to focus the education of their students toward a professional career as employees and they rarely consider the opportunity of developing competencies that will allow alumni to start their own businesses.

The case of Argentina is not an exception. Argentine society neither promotes nor values an entrepreneurial career. The educational system does not generate skills or competencies for entrepreneurs. Graduates lack entrepreneurial attitude, given that both the education they receive and their social expectations are oriented toward working and being promoted within large corporations. Nevertheless, throughout the past decade, this trend has begun to change. Several universities, both public and private, have started introducing entrepreneurship courses and business-plan contests. It is worth mentioning that the course offerings are not homogeneous in terms of target, objectives, depth, or professors' backgrounds.

As in other countries, Latin America, in general, and Argentina, in particular, show a strong commitment to the development of entrepreneurial skills of students and alumni (Braidot 2001; Postigo and Tamborini 2002; Ussman and Postigo 2000). Therefore, studies that demonstrate the evolution of entrepreneurship education and analyze the reasons contributing to its evolution are relevant to understanding the phenomenon and developing active plans to promote its initiatives.

Literature Review

Entrepreneurship education started to develop almost twenty-five years ago. During the past decade, clear signs have appeared showing the importance of this young field of research.

With reference to the analysis of the evolution of entrepreneurship education at the university level, Vesper (1974) provides background information demonstrating that entrepreneurship education was to become one of the areas that would develop relevant knowledge in years to come. In fact, the literature developed in the past decade has increased in quantity and quality. Several studies describe this phenomenon in detail with respect to different countries. A review and analysis of all these studies allow us to distinguish at least four lines of research.

The first is related to the impact of entrepreneurship education at the university level on the economy (Clark, Davis, and Harnish 1984; Price and Monroe 1993; Charney and Libecap 2000; among others).

The second line of research focuses on the analysis of pedagogic instruments and methodologies used to teach entrepreneurship (Gartnet and Vesper 1994; Mitchell and Chesteen 1995; Plaschka and Welsch 1990; Sexton and Upton-Upton 1987; Solomon, Weaver, and Fernald 1994; Van Clouse 1990; Laukannen 2000; among others).

The third line of research compiles the research related to state-of-the-art entrepreneurship education (McMullan, Long, and Wilson 1985; Gorman, Hanlon, and King 1997; Block and Stumpf 1992; Vesper and Gartner 1997; among others).

Finally, the fourth line of research reports practical experiences at different educational levels (McMullan, Long, and Wilson 1985; Zeithaml and Rice 1987; Vesper and McMullan 1988; Robinson and Haynes 1991; Kate 1994; Fleming 1996; Williams and Turnbull 1997; Levie, 1999; Obrecht 1999; Tackey, Perryman, and Connor 1999; Louksm, Menzies, and Gasse 2000; Mason 2000; Solomon, Duffy, and Tarabishy 2002; among others).

Given the characteristics of this research, the topics related to the fourth line most coincide with the theoretical framework. Because no background of similar research has been conducted in Argentina, it is necessary to describe some definitions and concepts used in this study. The concept of entrepreneurship courses used in this study is defined as a series of classes focused on entrepreneurship, new venture management, or starting a new business. That is, the courses concentrate on new rather than existing business activity.

Entrepreneurship education can be divided into two different areas, according to the distinction made by Laukannen (2000).

Education about entrepreneurship develops, constructs, and studies the theories referring to entrepreneurs, the creation of firms, contributions to economic development, the entrepreneurial process, and small and mid-sized firms. It addresses both graduate and undergraduate students, masters, PhDs, policy makers, and researchers—in other words, everyone interested in entrepreneurship as a social phenomenon.

Education for entrepreneurship addresses current and potential entrepreneurs. The objective is to develop and stimulate the entrepreneurial process, providing all the necessary tools for the start-up of a new venture both inside and outside existing organizations. According to Mason's (2000) definition, entrpreneurial education serves to develop the skills and attributes necessary to start a new venture as well as identify the needs of the new entity.

There is a fundamental difference between the above definitions. The first definition is based on the construction and transfer of knowledge about the field, while the second one focuses on the learning experience and the development of competencies, skills, aptitudes, and values (Ussman and Postigo 2000). Therefore, the teaching methods used in each of these areas differ.

Finally, to group and analyze the program types and contents of the courses given in the Argentinean university system, the typology of entrepreneurship development programs defined by Interman (1992) were used.

Data and Methods

For this research, all of the approximately seventy academic units of the Argentinean university system were analyzed. Only those that had courses, programs, centers, or academic units focused on teaching entrepreneurship at both the undergraduate and graduate levels were selected.

A detailed questionnaire was developed specifically for this purpose. The instruments of data and information collection were of two kinds: (1) self-conducted surveys to program directors, and (2) in-depth interviews with key informants and founders of each of the university units.

The procedure used to determine the sample started with a detailed inventory of all the educational institutions in the country. Then, the academic units that had ongoing programs or an area of research in entrepreneurship were identified. Finally, personal contact was established with each program director.

The variables collected included: (1) information about the type of activities developed (i.e., courses, seminars, business plan competitions, etc.); (2) number of courses taught; (3) mandatory status and scope of course content; (4) academic year in which they were taught; (5) average class size; (6) types of courses (entrepreneurship orientation and awareness programs, new enterprise creation programs, small business development, training for trainers, and others); (7) teaching methods used; (8) entrepreneurs' participation; (9) position within the institutional structure; and (10) staff composition. Interviewees were also questioned about the main obstacles to developing entrepreneurship education as well as the factors that promote it.

Results

Throughout the study, it was confirmed that Argentinean universities did not have academic units dedicated to teaching and developing entrepreneurial skills before 1996. The results of this study clearly mark 1996 as a key date for Argentina's inclusion of topics of entrepreneurship in the educational system. In this year, only 4 percent of all universities had programs somehow related to entrepreneurship. Nevertheless, at the beginning of 2003, that percentage had increased to 31 percent, which reflected an increase of three to twenty-one universities with initiatives in this area. This growth shows an important change in the trend of the university educational system in Argentina and an increasing interest of the academic community in the phenomenon of business creation.

Interestingly, unlike other cases such as Canada and the United Kingdom, in Argentina the beginning of these programs was not promoted by government policies. In Argentina, the phenomenon was born of a mix of cultural and socioeconomic factors (marked by immigration roots and high levels of population alphabetization). Among the most relevant factors were the growing unemployment rate and a five-year-old stagnant economy that increased the demand for entrepreneurship education. There is a positive attitude toward entrepreneurship, particularly among students. At the same time, senior students get their degrees but have unfavorable chances of obtaining jobs suited to their skills and requirements. Thus, they are forced to consider independent projects that will give them opportunities to develop professional careers. In addition, big firms, for their part, are increasingly recognizing the value of including individuals with entrepreneurial profiles on their staffs. Most agree that universities have a responsibility to respond to social needs, and therefore cannot ignore the importance of entrepreneurial education and the strengthening of an entrepreneurial culture in society.

Those interested in this field have collaborated to accelerate the development of this phenomenon. This comes as no surprise given that those same academics were the ones with the initiative needed to introduce the subject in their respective institutions; at least this seems to be the case for most Argentine universities.

Level of Provision of Entrepreneurship Education

This section presents the different types and course levels developed by all universities in Argentina (around seventy counting both public and private). Because it does not include postgraduate or graduate degrees in entrepreneurship, the range from postgraduate through undergraduate courses (class series, core courses, modules, or electives) focuses mainly on other subjects, occasional seminars, or nothing at all.

- Only 7 percent of the postgraduate programs developed by Argentinean universities have one course of entrepreneurship in the program. All of the courses (100%) are focused on the development of a business plan.
- Twenty-one percent of the universities have distinct courses (i.e., a series of classes such as a module, core course, or elective) in entrepreneurship. About 75 percent of these offer a course whose primary aim is to prepare students *for entrepreneurship*, as opposed to teaching *about entrepreneurs* and their role in economic development.
- Sixteen percent of the universities have entrepreneurship only within other courses that focus on other subjects.

- Twenty-nine percent of the universities report occasional seminars in entrepreneurship. This tends to be seen as a supplement rather than as a replacement for courses in the subject.
- Fifty-seven percent of the universities do not have any action plan in the area of entrepreneurship education.
- Finally, of all the universities, only 9 percent have formal lines of research in the area of entrepreneurship.

Other activities related to the educational system are annual contests organized by slightly more than 35 percent of the universities in which almost 1,000 participants develop and present business plans.

Geographic Distribution of Entrepreneurship Education

Analysis of the geographic distribution of entrepreneurship education reveals that 85 percent of the available courses are concentrated in the country's capital and principal province, Buenos Aires, where almost a third of the total population of the country resides. However, many other cities are making considerable efforts that have resulted in important achievements in this subject.

Undergraduate Course Characteristics

This is the segment that, compared to the graduate course, shows major growth and consolidation in the area of entrepreneurship education. Almost 21 percent of the universities offer entrepreneurship courses in the last years of the graduate coursework. It is interesting to note that only one of those universities has reliable experience in developing mandatory entrepreneurship courses during the first years of the career.

As has been the experience in other countries, the main providers of entrepreneurship courses are the universities with management and economics orientations followed by very few with engineering orientation and only some isolated cases of universities that teach architecture, veterinary medicine, and biotechnology.

The number of students attending the courses is very uneven, ranging from ten students to eighty or more. Therefore, it can be established that there are an average of thirty-five students per course at the undergraduate level and twenty-five per course at the graduate level.

In line with the teaching methodology in business administration and under the influence of Harvard Business School, education in entrepreneurship has traditionally focused on the case study (McIntyre and Roche 1999). This trend continues in Argentina.

The main topic of all these courses is the development of a business plan (in 95% of the analyzed cases). Subjects related to general information about entrepreneurship and its process are taught in 8 percent of the courses. Fifty percent of the courses provide information related to small and medium-sized companies. Only 10 percent develop theoretical units around the origin and background of entrepreneurship. This general overview confirms some of the observations presented previously about the trend to design programs focused on teaching "for entrepreneurship" instead of "about entrepreneurship."

With respect to the profile and background of the professors of entrepreneurship courses, a high percentage have university education (95%), half have real life experience in business creation, and only 10 percent have specialized training in the area of entrepreneurship. The percentage of entrepreneurs, all at senior level, who have no academic background but participate in courses is 5 percent. Of all the courses, 20 percent invite foreign professors to participate in the courses, and they participate for an average of two weeks.

Teaching Methodology

During this research seventeen different pedagogic methods were used: reading, lectures, guest speakers, testimonial videos, tutorship in companies, development of business plans, simulations, case development, business visits, role play, work with entrepreneurs, thesis, workshops, consulting work, research, entrepreneur associations, and analysis of case studies. Of all these, it is interesting to point out that those most frequently used (in 93% of the cases) were lectures, guest speakers, work performed with entrepreneurs, and development of business plans. On the other hand, the least used methods were case development and testimonial videos.

It is important to emphasize that only 60 percent of the interviewees use reading material as a teaching method in their courses and almost 70 percent require students to develop a field case study. Finally, only 24 percent registered visits to companies and 42 percent used case studies as a teaching tool.

As mentioned above and according to international experience, the presence of the entrepreneur in classes is very relevant given that one of the main objectives is to provide experience to the class in creating a company. Even though class participation is low, it is interesting to see the different types of participation that entrepreneurs experience within the courses in Argentinean universities. Almost 30 percent of the entrepreneurs participate in classes, sharing their experiences with the students orally; 25 percent participate as part of a programmed activity previously coordinated by the professor; and in 22 percent of the cases the entrepreneurs act as counselors on business projects together with the students. Finally, in 23 percent of the cases they participated in the development of local cases or as potential investment projects.

Information About the Academic Unit Developing the Program

Among all the universities investigated, it was not possible to observe a common denominator related to the institutional independence of these academic units or programs. As will be seen later, fundraising activities to sustain the academic unit are among the most pressing goals of all the programs (only one academic unit receives financial support from an entrepreneur in the form of a donation).

The team leader is usually a professor with full-time dedication to the project. To this can be added a team of professors (no more than two or three) and a team of assistant instructors (no more than six).

The network with the business community, entrepreneurs, alumni, and organizations linked to entrepreneurship is stronger in the academic units that demonstrate more "academic production," advanced pedagogic models, or start-up businesses that are successfully implemented by students. In this group only four universities out of the total sample were found.

Obstacles and Factors of Future Development

Throughout this study, it is possible to observe explosive growth in the area of entrepreneurship as well as the process to include this subject in universities and curricula in Argentina. However, there are obstacles blocking the development of entrepreneurship, among which five are clearly important.

• Strong resistance to the formal educational system and established academic programs by authorities in the area of education. There are no governmental educational policies that support the development of entrepreneurship education. This is demonstrated by the simple fact that there has been no formal study, such as the present one, conducted by universities that teach entrepreneurship. This leads to the conclusion that for the time being, topics of entrepreneurship are not part of the working agenda of policy makers in the area of education.

• A clear dissociation between the interests of the academic authorities of universities and the students' needs. The universities do not consider "being an entrepreneur" a legitimate career option. In all cases the interviewees reported that student acceptance of entrepreneurship courses was higher than perceived by the authorities, even in the top-rated universities in this subject.

• A traditional culture of university teaching based on the development of professionals to offer labor instead of demanding labor. Traditionally, the university system was focused on developing "good and efficient employees" instead of prominent independent business people, without developing the subject of entrepreneurship. As a result, change will be more difficult if only one course focuses on the development of entrepreneurial capacities instead of distributing knowledge throughout all the courses of the career.

• The lack of funding and professors specialized in the area. The same phenomenon can be found in the American university system where departments that are opened each year generate a demand for specialized professors that cannot be met by the existing supply.

• The limited match of the university supply to the needs of the labor market. Unemployment is an international phenomenon; currently no company has the capacity to generate the absorption of the available labor as it did a decade ago. In this context, to be an entrepreneur is a legitimate career alternative for young professionals, and not noting this need, the universities continue to provide traditional programs.

In spite of the barriers mentioned above, it is important to note a group of factors that are helping and will continue to help development of this area in the university context. Among the five most important points revealed in this study are:

• The incipient but permanent production of academic research in this area. For Latin America this is a recent phenomenon, but, fortunately, an increasing number of researchers and academics are interested in the evolution of entrepreneurship at the regional level. This generates the interest of international organizations that finance this type of research, and the results help generate a favorable environment for developing entrepreneurship in the educational field.

• The strong partnership of institutions related to the area. During the current research, it was very interesting to observe the high degree of partnership existing among all the institutions related to entrepreneurship. Very close to the universities, foundations and business associations are supporting the growth of this area. Members of the academic group are well known among themselves, and their network contacts have many common areas of activities focused on promoting entrepreneurship education even among competing universities.

• The progress and impact that entrepreneurship has on economies in the international context. This increases interest in research of this phenomenon and constitutes a fundamental factor at the moment of defining the research areas. In this sense, the results of these studies contribute to the process of developing these initiatives.

• Increased interest from university students and the public in general about business creation. This contributes to the development of programs specialized in entrepreneurship.
• Finally, the rupture of the traditional labor system and the particular economic crisis of the country. This causes us to focus on new teaching methods that allow the generation of a great number of businesses with rapid growth and that can contribute to the development of a new leadership model of entrepreneurs with a sense of social responsibility.

Conclusion

As demonstrated in other research on this topic (Fleming 1996; Williams and Turnbull 1997; Levie 1999; Louksm, Menzies, and Gasse 2000; Solomon, Weaver, and Fernald 2002; Obretch 1999; Finkle and Deeds 2001), the results of this study show the growing awareness and favorable development of university education in entrepreneurship. However, in the case of Argentina, other reasons have motivated it, such as unemployment rates, economic crisis, and changes in the labor market, which have played key roles in this trend.

Around 33 percent of public institutions and 25 percent of private ones are engaged in some kind of entrepreneurial program but they are still geographically concentrated. The major obstacles are the rigid curriculum, program funding, and the lack of professors with specialization in the field. An unusual characteristic of this case is that the emergence of entrepreneurship at the university level does not answer to governmental policy.

There is no doubt about the potential progress and future development of this discipline at every level in Argentina. However, there is a need to face issues such as institutional academic legitimacy, the chair's funding, training for specialists, and local case development applied to the teaching environment. According to this, in Argentina and in Latin America, it is necessary to develop more research around entrepreneurship education.

References

Block, Z., and S. Stumpf. 1992. "Entrepreneurship Education Research: Experience and Challenge." In *The State of the Art of Entrepreneurship*, ed. D.L. Sexton and J. Kasarda. Boston, MA: PWS-Kent.
Braidot, N. 2001. "Educación para la Empresarialidad en el contexto universitario argentino: ¿Opción o necesidad?" Universidad Argentina de la Empresa (mimeo).
Charney, A., and G. Libecap. 2000. "Impact of Entrepreneurship Education." *Insights: A Kauffman Research Series*. Kauffman Center for Entrepreneurship Leadership.
Clark, B.; C. Davis; and V. Harnish. 1984. "Do Courses in Entrepreneurship Aid in New Venture Creation?" *Journal of Small Business Management* 4 (April): 26–31.

Cowling, M., and M. Taylor. 2001. "Entrepreneurial Women and Men: Two Different Species?" *Small Business Economics* 16, no. 3: 167–75.

Delmar, F., and P. Davidsson. 2000. "Where Do They Come From? Prevalence and Characteristics of Nascent Entrepreneurs." *Entrepreneurship and Regional Development* 12, no. 1: 1–23.

Fayolle, A. 1998. "Teaching of Entrepreneurship: Outcomes from an Innovative Experience." Paper presented at the Internationalizing Entrepreneurship Education and Training Conference, IntEnt98, Oestrich-Winkel, Germany.

Fleming, P. 1996. "Entrepreneurship Education in Ireland: A Longitudinal Study." *Academy of Entrepreneurship Journal* 2, no. 1: 95–119.

Finkle, T., and D. Deeds. 2001. "Trends in the Market for Entrepreneurship Faculty, 1989–1998." *Journal of Business Venturing* 16: 613–30.

Gartnet, William B., and Karl H. Vesper. 1994. "Experiment in Entrepreneurship Education: Successes and Failures." *Journal of Business Venturing* 9: 179–187.

Gorman, G.; D. Hanlon; and W. King. 1997. "Some Research Perspectives on Entrepreneurship Education, Enterprise Education, and Education for Small Business Management: A Ten Year Literature Review." *International Small Business* 15, no. 3 (April/June): 56–77.

Interman, International Management Development Network in Cooperation with the United Nations Development Programme (UNDP) and the International Labour Organization (ILO). 1992. *Networking for Entrepreneurship Development*. Geneva: International Labour Organization.

Kantis, H.; S. Postigo; J. Federico; and M.F. Tamborini. 2002. "The Emergence of University Graduates Entrepreneurs: What Makes the Difference? Empirical Evidence from Research in Argentina." Paper presented at the RENT XVI Conference, Barcelona, Spain.

Kate, J.A. 1994. "Growth of Endowments, Chairs and Programs in Entrepreneurship on the College Campus." In *The Art and Science on Entrepreneurship Education*, vol. 1, ed. Frank Hoy, Thomas G. Monroy and Jay Reichert. Cleveland: Baldwin-Wallace College.

Kolvereid, L., and O. Moen. 1997. "Entrepreneurship Among Business Graduates: Does a Major in Entrepreneurship Make a Difference?" *Journal of European Industrial Training* 21, nos. 4–5: 154–57.

Lafuente, A., and V. Salas. 1989. "Types of Entrepreneurs and Firms: The Case of New Spanish Firms." *Strategic Management Journal* 10: 17–30.

Laukannen, M. 2000. "Exploring Alternative Approaches in High-level Entrepreneurship Education: Creating Micro Mechanisms for Endogenous Regional Growth." *Journal of Entrepreneurship and Regional Development* 12: 25–47.

Levie, J.; W. Brown; and L. Steele. 2001. "How Entrepreneurial Are Strathclyde Alumni?" Paper presented at the conference International Entrepreneurship: Researching New Frontiers, Strathclyde University.

Levie, J. 1999. "Entrepreneurship Education in Higher Education in England." London Business School.

Louksm, K.; T. Menzies; and Y. Gasse. 2000. "The Evolution of Canadian University Entrepreneurship Education Curriculum over Two Decades." Paper presented at the conference Internationalizing Entrepreneurship Education and Training, Tampere, Finland.

Lüthje, C., and N. Franke. 2002. "Fostering Entrepreneurship Through University Education and Training: Lessons from Massachusetts Institute of Technology."

Paper presented at the second Annual Conference of the European Academy of Management, Sweden.

Mason, C. 2000. "Teaching Entrepreneurship to Undergraduates: Lessons from Leading Centers of Entrepreneurship Education." University of Southampton. Department of Geography.

McIntyre, J.R., and M. Roche. 1999. "University Education for Entrepreneurs in the United States: A Critical and Retrospective Analysis of Trends in the 1990s." Study Commissioned by the Japanese Ministry of Education. Georgia Institute of Technology, Atlanta.

McMullan, W.; W.A.Long; and A. Wilson. 1985. "MBA Concentration on Entrepreneurship." *Journal of Small Business and Entrepreneurship* 3, no. 1: 18–22.

Mitchell, R.K., and S.A. Chesteen. 1995. "Enhancing Entrepreneurial Expertise: Experiential Pedagogy and the New Venture Expert Script." *Simulation and Gaming* 26, no. 3: 288–306.

Obrecht, J. 1999. "Entrepreneurship Education and Training in France: A New Challenge to the Universities." Université Robert Schuman, Strasbourg, France.

Plaschka, G.R., and H.P. Welsch. 1990. "Emerging Structures in Entrepreneurship Education: Curricula Designs and Strategies." *Entrepreneurship Theory and Practice* 14, no. 3: 55–71.

Postigo, S., and M.F. Tamborini. 2002. "Entrepreneurship Education in Argentina: The Case of University of San Andrés." Paper presented at the Conference Internationalizing Entrepreneurship Education and Training, Malaysia.

———. 2003. "Entrepreneurship Education in Argentina: Lessons from the Experience of University of San Andrés." Paper presented at the Annual National Conference of the United States Association for Small Business and Entrepreneurship, Hilton Head, South Carolina.

Price, C., and S. Monroe. 1993. "Educational Training for Woman and Minority Entrepreneurs Positively Impacts Venture Growth and Economics Development." Paper presented at the conference Frontiers of Entrepreneurship Research, Babson College, Babson Park, MA.

Robinson, P., and E. Sexton. 1994. "The Effect of Education and Experience on Self-employment Success." *Journal of Business Venturing* 9, no. 2: 141–57.

Robinson, P., and M. Haynes. 1991. "Entrepreneurship Education in America's Major Universities." *Entrepreneurship Theory and Practice* 15, no. 3: 41–52.

Sexton, D.L., and N. Upton-Upton. 1987. "Evaluation of Innovative Approach to Teaching Entrepreneurship." *Journal of Small Business Management* 25, no. 1: 35–43.

Solomon, G.; S. Duffy; and A. Tarabishy. 2002. "The State of Entrepreneurship Education in the United States: A Nationwide Survey and Analysis." *International Journal of Entrepreneurship Education* 1, no. 1: 1–22.

Solomon, G.T.; K.M. Weaver; and L.W. Fernald, Jr. 1994. "Pedagogical Methods of Teaching Entrepreneurship: An Historical Perspective." *Gaming and Simulation* 25, no. 3: 338–52.

Tackey, N.; S. Perryman; and H. Connor. 1999. "Graduated Business Start-ups." Institute for Employment Studies, Brighton, UK.

Upton, N.; D. Sexton; and C. Moore. 1995: "Have We Made a Difference? An Examination of Career Activity of Entrepreneurship Majors Since 1981." Paper presented at the conference on Entrepreneurship Research, Babson College, Babson Park, MA.

Ussman, A., and S. Postigo. 2000. "O Papel da universidade no fomento da funçao empresarial." *Anais universitarios. Ciencias Sociais e Humanas.* 1990–2000 Yearbook Special Issue: 219–33.

Van Clouse, G.H. 1990. "A Controlled Experiment Relating Entrepreneurial Education to Students' Start-up Decisions." *Journal of Small Business Management* 28, no. 2: 45–53.

Varela, R. 1997. "Entrepreneurial Education in Latin America." Center for Entrepreneurship Development.

Vesper, K. 1974. "Entrepreneurship Education 1974." Society for Entrepreneurship and Application. Milwaukee, WI.

Vesper, K., and W. Gartner. 1997. "Measuring Progress in Entrepreneurship Education." *Journal of Business Venturing* 12, no. 5: 403–21.

Vesper, K., and W. McMullan. 1988. "Entrepreneurship: Today Courses, Tomorrow Degrees?" *Entrepreneurship Theory and Practice* 13, no. 1: 7–13.

Williams, S., and A. Turnbull. 1997. "First Moves into Entrepreneurship Teaching in Scottish Universities: A Consortium Approach." Robert Gordon University, Aberdeen, Scotland.

Zeithaml, C., and G. Rice. 1987. "Entrepreneurship/Small Business Education in American Universities." *Journal of Small Business Management* 25, no. 1: 44–50.

17

Undergraduate Students as a Source of Potential Entrepreneurs

A Comparative Study Between Italy and Argentina

Sergio Postigo, Donato Iacobucci,
and Maria Fernanda Tamborini

Business creation and the encouragement of an entrepreneurial culture have become fundamental topics for politicians, economists, and academics in all countries. This interest is based on the existing evidence that new businesses contribute to job creation, political and social stability, innovation, and economic development (Schumpeter 1934; OECD, 1998; Wennekers and Thurik 1999; Audretsch and Thurik 2001; Reynolds et al. 2000, 2002). Different samples, including countries of the Organization for Economic Cooperation and Development (OECD), over different time periods have attained consistent results; increases in entrepreneurial activity tend to result in subsequently higher growth rates and in a reduction of unemployment (Audretsch and Thurik 2001). For the purposes of this chapter, entrepreneurship is viewed as the identification and creation of new economic opportunities combined with decision-making on the location and the resources to be used in the activity (Wennekers and Thurik 1999).

Nowadays, innovation and knowledge are the main sources of economic growth; therefore, education is one of the key variables for the emergence of new ventures and their development prospects (Kantis et al. 2002). The relationship between education and entrepreneurship has been examined at length in different studies. Some of these studies have found a positive relationship between the level of education of individuals and their probability of becoming entrepreneurs (Rees and Shah 1986; Gill 1988; Lafuente and Salas 1989; Robinson and Sexton 1994; Karcher 1998; Delmar and Davidsson 2000; Cowling and Taylor 2001). Baumol (1968, 1993) considers entrepreneurs as people who identify new ideas in motion while Bygrave (1997) defines an entrepreneur as someone who perceives an opportunity and creates an organization to exploit it. Another group of works studies different types of entrepreneurs, such as those who are technology based and have a relatively high level of education (Litvak and Maule 1976; Colombo and Delmastro 2001). There are also several surveys designed to evaluate the impact of entrepreneurship courses and the characteristics of the businesses founded by graduate entrepreneurs (Clark, Davis, and Harnish 1984; Upton, Sexton, and Moore 1995; Kolvereid and Moen 1997; Tackey, Perryman, and Connor 1999; Charney and Libecap 2000; Levie, Brown, and Steele 2001; Lüthje and Franke 2002).

The increasing interest in the relationship between entrepreneurs' education, their businesses, and their prospects of success is evidence of the growing importance of graduates and undergraduates as a source of potential entrepreneurs, especially to encourage the emergence of knowledge and technology-based firms. Veciana (2002) states that education will be increasingly needed for the creation of new ventures and emphasizes that empirical evidence shows a positive relationship between formal education and venture success. He also explains that the failure rate for new firms created by individuals with low levels of education is almost 80 percent, while the failure rate for businesses created by graduates is well under 20 percent.

Authors such as Kourilsky (1995) state that the economic growth of countries will hinge on the ability to create new jobs through entrepreneurship. Effective initiatives in entrepreneurship education will be increasingly critical for expanding the flow of potential entrepreneurs from the educational system. According to Laukkanen (2000), the introduction of entrepreneurial education at undergraduate levels can be understood as a strategic response of universities and business schools.

In this context, many universities have recognized the significance of this phenomenon and have included in their curriculum contents and initiatives oriented to promote entrepreneurship as a legitimate career option. Several authors have analyzed the extraordinary increase in the number and importance of entrepreneurship programs over the past twenty-five years (Vesper and Gartner 1997; Kolvereid and Moen 1997; Fayolle 1998; Finkle and Deeds 2001; Lüthje and Franke 2002). The work of Vesper and Gartner (1997) established that the number of universities with entrepreneurship courses grew from 16 in 1970 to 400 in 1995. Furthermore, in recent years, some governments have been developing programs and initiatives oriented toward promoting entrepreneurship potential through universities. Examples of such schemes are the German EXIST program, the Business Birth Rate Strategy in Scotland, and Brasil Emprende, IG in Italy, among others.

Business creation by university graduates is particularly crucial in emerging countries like Argentina because the industrial structure is based on traditional firms with relatively low technological content. Such firms do not play a significant role as "incubators" for dynamic new entrepreneurs (Kantis et al. 2002). A recent study of business creation in Latin America has shown that 50 percent of the most dynamic firms are created by university graduates (Kantis, Ishida, and Komori 2002). Therefore, there is a need for significant change in the education system in order to produce a change in the culture and values necessary to stimulate entrepreneurship (Postigo and Tamborini 2002, 2003).

Traditionally, the Argentinean educational system did not promote the necessary skills to develop entrepreneurs. Students were not brought up with an entrepreneurial attitude because education and social aspiration were mainly oriented toward working in large corporations. However, in the past decade, this trend has started to reverse, revealing changes in the university education system. One sign is the increased interest in entrepreneurship within the educational system and society in general. Moreover, in the context of high unemployment, individuals and institutions consider encouraging entrepreneurship as a vital answer to job creation.

Unemployment started to grow in the past decade. In 1990, it was approximately 8.6 percent, in 1993, 9.9 percent, and it reached 18.4 percent two years later. In 2002, it reached 21.5 percent, with 18.6 percent of underemployment (INDEC 2002). Adding to the unemployment issue, the gross domestic product has been declining since 1999. Available information indicates that it decreased 3.4 percent in 1999, approximately 1 percent in 2000, 4.4 percent in 2001, and 11.2 percent in 2002 (IMF 2002).

Over the past ten years or so, we have noted a progressive increase in courses, chairs, incubators, and other activities oriented toward promoting entrepreneurship. Today, around 33 percent of the public institutions and 25 percent of the private ones are engaged in some kind of activity concerning this subject, but the initiatives are still geographically concentrated. The major obstacles are rigid curricula, a lack of funding, and difficulty in finding professors specialized in this field. The characteristic of the Argentinean case is that the emergence of entrepreneurship programs within universities is not a response to a specific government policy.

Although the general economic conditions of Italy are quite different from those of Argentina, the country faces similar problems concerning entrepreneurship. According to a number of surveys, Italy has one of the highest firm birthrates in European countries (Reynolds et al. 2000). The majority of new firms are founded by former employees, most of whom have a technical background. These new entrepreneurs typically show good skills in managing the production process, but a low level of formal education and little ability in other key management functions (like marketing or finance).

The lack of managerial competence in small and medium-sized enterprises (SMEs) is partly compensated by their belonging to industrial districts. These districts are concentrated mostly in traditional sectors (e.g., textiles and clothing, footwear, furniture, ceramics). As the majority of new firms develop from existing ones, they usually belong to the same sector of activity. In this regard, there is growing concern in Italy that firms in these sectors will experience increasing competitive pressure from emerging countries.

It is therefore acknowledged that to improve the development prospects of SMEs, it is necessary to stimulate the creation of new firms in other sectors of activity, mainly the ones associated with new technology. In this case, entrepreneurs spinning off from universities are expected to play a greater role than entrepreneurs spinning off from existing companies.

Despite acknowledging the potential impact of graduate entrepreneurs, very little has been done in Italy to promote entrepreneurial education within universities. Compared with the United States and other European countries, entrepreneurial education in Italy is still in its infancy; at the moment there are no specific curricula in entrepreneurship and just a few courses in some of the main universities. Given this situation, there is large scope in Italy for introducing entrepreneurial courses into the university curricula.

The main aim of this study is to analyze the opinions and attitudes of undergraduate students about entrepreneurship. Specifically, the chapter aims at analyzing the influence of different contexts—developed and developing countries—in the attitudes toward entrepreneurship (whether and why students consider it desirable to create their own business), the influence of social background, perceptions about the impact of the social and economic environment on business creation (positive or negative factors), and the image that students have about entrepreneurs.

Two groups of students were analyzed, one made up of students from San Andrés University (Argentina) and the other from Università Politecnica delle Marche (Italy).

Literature Review

The Role of Universities in Promoting Entrepreneurship

The creation of business is a complex process. Within the large number of variables that can be considered, three conditions are required for the creation of a new venture: the existence of entrepreneurs, an entrepreneurial culture, and an adequate environment. Education has a fundamental role in the first two conditions. The university has to promote entrepreneurial activities in partnership with its students and the business community with the purpose of encouraging self-employment as a career path as well as giving young people the competencies, skills, and knowledge base required for the creation of a new venture.

Students are all potential entrepreneurs who need a university environment to foster their growth and development. The university fulfills its role to society and its students by providing a rich entrepreneurial learning experience (Ussman and Postigo 2000). Labor market structures are currently changing; finishing college is no longer a guarantee against unemployment. Currently, youths have to face the uncertainties and complexities of the labor market. Therefore, universities can help diminish unemployment by developing entrepreneurs.

In summary, entrepreneurship education can be a way to: (a) legitimize entrepreneurship and develop an entrepreneurial culture with the purpose of fostering economic growth, (b) develop and stimulate entrepreneurial skills, and (c) prepare students for a dynamic labor market.

Culture and Institutions

Culture is defined by Hofstede (1980, 2001) as a set of shared values, beliefs, and expected behaviors. This means an entrepreneurial culture is a society with a high production of entrepreneurs and a high degree of acceptance of entrepreneurial individuals. The cultural aspect is important, especially because some cultures produce more entrepreneurs than others. Authors such as Mueller and Thomas (2000) reveal a relationship among values, beliefs, and behaviors and point out that those differences in culture may influence individual decisions as to whether to be an entrepreneur.

The institutions are another relevant factor. They are made up of formal (laws and regulations) and informal (behavioral rules) limitations. The institutions, according to North, are "the humanly devised constraints that structure human interaction" (1994: 360). The family, education, and political and economic systems are institutions that define the incentive structure as a whole for a society.

Finally, as part of the culture, a key factor is the social legitimization of the business career. According to Wilken (1979), the degree of approval or disapproval of business activity will influence its emergence and characteristics, being favored by those environments in which entrepreneurs enjoy greater legitimacy. Nevertheless, this does not imply that the norms and values are sufficient to cause or to inhibit the rise of this phenomenon, but its influence should be considered and integrated into the context of other non-economic factors.

Role Models

Minniti and Bygrave (1999) explain that, as occurs with other human decisions, the individual choice to become an entrepreneur is determined by a set of information available to the individual. Such individuals, or "economic agents," are heterogeneous and have different information, thus different perceptions about the uncertainty and cost associated with becoming an entrepreneur. Randomly, each individual is endowed with an initial set of characteristics (biological and sociological). Those characteristics, as well as social circumstances such as prospect of employment and education, determine the relative tendency of a person toward entrepreneurship. Moreover, role models play a fundamental part in the determination of entrepreneurial choices. Role models can emerge from family, friends, society, and networks.

The reasoning is as follows: those persons that have more possibilities and opportunities to observe entrepreneurs directly are more likely to become entrepreneurs, given that awareness increases and the opportunity costs of business activity decrease This is a consequence of two main factors—the first is related to networking that tends to decrease the transaction costs. The second, the existence of role models, increases the probability that new entrepreneurs will appear. When an individual does not have an entrepreneurial role model in his or her family, the university, via courses and teaching methods, can promote an entrepreneurial culture.

Motivation

Gibb and Ritchie (1982) make a distinction between three critical aspects of entrepreneurship: the acquisition of motivation, influences on the process of deciding to become an entrepreneur, and the identification and validation of the business idea. The acquisition of motivation is the result of influences throughout one's life (social background, family, education, career, etc.).

Shapero (1984) presents a model indicating that the following conditions are necessary for the creation of a business: displacement, disposition to act, credibility, and availability of resources. Displacement refers to the idea that each business is an act initiated from some class of displacement or change in the life path of the individual. It is dependent on a prior situation of stability and precipitates the action. The factors that cause these changes in situation can be positive (i.e., the need to achieve) or negative (i.e., unemployment).

The disposition to act depends on certain personal characteristics of the entrepreneur, the existence of role models, and of a positive environment.

In summary, these are, in general terms, the influences and relevance of universities, role models, motivations, culture, and institutions on the perception of and attitude toward new business creation.

Data and Methodology

Data were collected through a direct survey conducted between March and May 2003 on a sample of students from Universidad de San Andrés (Argentina) and from the Università Politecnica delle Marche (Italy). Students from different orientations, levels of education, gender, and age were surveyed. The Argentine sample is made up of 100 students from the Faculty of Business and Economics. The students come mainly from the province of Buenos Aires, where more than 30 percent of the country's total population lives. It is the most prosperous region with a great amount of industrial activity. Most students surveyed from Argentina were younger than age twenty-two and there was a slight prevalence of males over females.

The Italian sample is made up of 162 students from the Faculty of Engineering. Male students dominate the sample because it is still mainly males rather than females who pursue engineering courses in Italy. Students come mainly from the Marche region (of which Ancona is the capital). The Marche region is a small, highly industrialized region in central Italy that, following World War II, experienced an intensive process of industrialization, mostly based on small firms concentrated in "traditional" industrial districts.

Besides differences in the courses they pursued, age, and sex, another important difference between the Argentine and the Italian sample is the social background of students. In the Argentine sample there is a prevalence of students whose parents are entrepreneurs, professionals, or executives, while in the Italian sample there is a prevalence of students whose parents are office or manual workers. The Italian distribution of parents' occupation is similar to the average for the population while the Argentine sample is biased toward the higher income classes.

The questionnaire used for the survey was organized into three sections. The first section collected general information about the student: age, sex, courses pursued, work experience, parents' occupation, and so on. The second section was dedicated to analyzing the career prospects of students with a specific interest in their intention of becoming entrepreneurs (i.e., starting up their own firm). In this section, questions were also asked about their image of entrepreneurs and the possible reasons for and obstacles to becoming entrepreneurs.

The third section was intended to collect information on how students perceive the general environment with regard to facilitating or hindering entrepreneurship. Data analysis is based on descriptive statistics and on mean comparisons between subgroups of students. We were specifically interested in analyzing the role of some demographic variables in attitudes toward entrepreneurship and in studying the differences between Argentine and Italian students.

Results

The discussion of results is organized into three parts: (1) career aspirations and propensity to start up a firm; (2) image of entrepreneurs and reasons for starting (or not starting) an entrepreneurial career; and (3) environmental factors that facilitate or hinder entrepreneurship.

Career Aspiration and Propensity to Start Up a Firm

Argentine and Italian students showed both similarities and differences when asked about their prospective careers. Both groups were similar with regard to the possibility of becoming employees, in large as well as small firms, or in the civil service. One-third wanted to enter a large firm, while only a small percentage considered entering the public sector or a small firm (the higher percentage of Italian students who considered entering a small firm can be explained by the large presence of SMEs in the Marche region). Students from both countries also agreed on the fact that firms no longer guarantee lifelong employment and that one should be prepared to work for more than one firm.

Differences between the Italian and the Argentine students center around three aspects: (a) the intention to pursue a master's degree after graduation; (b) the propensity to work abroad for a period (true for 85% of Argentines and only 55% of Italians); and (c) the propensity to start up a firm.

The low percentage of Italian students that intended to enter a master's program after graduation is explained by two factors, the first being that until last year, master's degrees were not offered by Italian universities. The second factor involves the high prospect of engineering students getting a job soon after graduation. The latter aspect probably also explains the lower percentage of Italian students interested in working abroad. On the other hand, the majority of the Argentine students wanted to work abroad for a period. This is because the high unemployment rate reduces the probability of finding initial employment. Indeed, the answer to this question was more dependent on the country than on the social background of students. But students

Table 17.1

Students Declaring the Statement Is True (percentage values)

	Argentina	Italy
Start up a firm soon after graduation	13.3	3.1
Start up a firm in a few years	34.3	3.8
Start up a firm after a few years	43.4	16.9
Start up a firm if opportunity arises	63.6	31.6

from high-income families (entrepreneurs, executives, and professionals) showed, in both countries, a higher propensity to work abroad for a period of time.

The Argentine students showed a remarkably higher propensity to start up a firm than Italian students (see Table 17.1). The difference was particularly significant in the case of creating a new firm some years after graduation or if the opportunity arises. It seems that Argentine students are more eager to enter an entrepreneurial career (although as a later prospect) and more ready to take this opportunity.

There are two possible reasons for this result. One is that the high unemployment rate in Argentina reduced the opportunity costs of self-employment. Second, because Universidad de San Andrés has an academic program oriented toward promotion of entrepreneurship, students were more interested in taking the opportunities entrepreneurship provides.

The high propensity of Argentine students to create their own firms also emerges from the answer to whether they have ever taken into consideration the idea of starting up a firm. While in both samples almost half of the students have only vaguely thought about the matter, 32 percent of Argentine students declare they have "serious" intentions to do so, as compared to 8 percent of Italian students. Among the Italian students, one-third have never thought about this possibility (see Table 17.2).

The propensity to start up a firm shows a clear relationship with the social background of students. The percentage who are seriously thinking of creating a new firm or who already have a plan for this is significantly higher for students whose parents are entrepreneurs or executives compared with students whose parents are manual or office workers. Indeed if we control for the social background of students' (parents' occupation), much of the country difference disappears. Unfortunately, this control can be done only for students whose parents are entrepreneurs or executives because we have just a few Argentine students whose parents' occupation is manual or office work.

Overall family background seems to play a more important role in the

Table 17.2

People Who Have Considered the Idea of Creating a New Firm
(percentage values)

	Country		
	Argentina	Italy	Total Weighted Average
No, never	8.0	29.2	20.6
Yes, a little	45.0	53.7	50.2
Yes, seriously	32.0	8.2	17.8
Yes, I plan to create my own firm	15.0	8.8	11.4
Total	100	100	100

entrepreneurial attitude of students than general cultural variables associated with the country. At the same time, it is interesting to note that even after controlling for social background, Argentine students show a slightly higher propensity to start up their own firm than their Italian counterparts.

Image of Entrepreneurs and Reasons for Becoming Entrepreneurs

The question regarding the image of entrepreneurs revealed similarities and differences between Italian and Argentine students.

Overall, the image of the personal attributes of entrepreneurs was similar in the two countries: students agreed that entrepreneurs are skillful individuals (they are dynamic, able to tolerate risk, have good entrepreneurial vision, etc.) who have a low sense of social justice and honesty. Students seem to think of entrepreneurs as clever people who use their skills and abilities in ways that are not always or completely socially acceptable. This homogeneity is remarkable given that the majority of Argentine students have entrepreneurs as parents while the majority of Italian students have employees as parents.

With regard to the differences between Argentine and Italian students, two points are worth mentioning. The first concerns the social and economic role of entrepreneurs: A larger percentage of Italian students, compared to Argentine students, thinks that entrepreneurs create jobs and contribute to the country's economic development. Perhaps this difference can be attributed to the different economic conditions in Argentina and Italy at the present.

A higher percentage of Italian students agreed on the fact that entrepreneurs earn a lot of money (see Table 17.3). This seems to contrast with their poor attitude regarding the start up of an entrepreneurial career compared

Table 17.3

Reasons for Creating One's Own Firm (percentage of students indicating the reasons as important or very important)

	Argentina		Italy*	
	%	Rank	%	Rank
To put own ideas into practice	86	1	71.6	1
Personal independence	80	2	66.0	2
To create something of one's own	76	3	64.8	3
To be at the head of an organization	57	4	34.6	6
Economic independence	47	5	34.7	7
To earn more than an employee	39	6	55.6	4
To accumulate a personal fortune	33	7	38.9	5
Difficulty in getting a satisfying job	32	8	24.7	10
Not satisfied with current job	25	9	14.8	12
To get a salary that corresponds to abilities	22	10	34.0	8
Social status	20	11	29.6	9
Family tradition	15	12	7.4	13
To invest family assets	15	13	15.4	11
Other	11	14	3.7	14

*Answers were limited to five items.

with Argentine students. This paradox is only apparent because earning money does not represent the main reason for becoming an entrepreneur. Indeed, both Argentine and Italian students indicate noneconomic reasons as the most important for starting up their own firms. It is significant that the first three reasons rank in the same order in both countries and are all related to personal rather than economic attainment.

At the same time, it is also worth noting that the Italian students placed more importance on economic reasons than Argentine students. With respect to the difficulties of starting up their own firms, the differences between Argentine and Italian students are more evident. Among the first five difficulties, they agree on three items: the perception of too much risk, the lack of initial funding, and the presence of too much competition.

After these, the Italian students indicate the fear of being unsuccessful and fiscal pressure while Argentine students express doubts about their entrepreneurial abilities and bad prospects after retirement. The differences involving the importance of fiscal pressure or the prospects after retirement may be attributable to differences in the institutional situations in the two countries. The other two items are interconnected to a certain extent, as the fear of being unsuccessful is linked to a lack of confidence in personal capabilities.

Obstacles to and Incentives for Starting Up a New Firm

In both countries, the majority of students thought it was more difficult to create a firm now than it was in the past. The percentage is higher for Italian students. Even in this case, the difference depends on the lower percentage of Italian students coming from entrepreneurial families. Indeed, if we consider only the students whose parents are entrepreneurs, the difference between the two countries disappears. It is worth noting that even in this case, two-thirds of students think that creating a firm at present is more difficult than it was in the past.

Except with respect to excessive competition, the obstacles perceived by students to the start-up of new firms are very different in the two countries. Argentine students point out general economic factors such as globalization, the presence of uncertainty, and difficulties in penetrating markets (market concentration and market saturation). Italian students point out more specific factors such as fiscal pressures, difficulty in raising adequate funding for start-up, competition from large firms, and bureaucracy. These differences can be clearly explained by differences in the general economic conditions in the two countries.

The lack of education was not considered one of the main obstacles for entrepreneurial activity by either country. This seems consistent with the image of entrepreneurs as people with special personal attributes, but without specific education and training.

Conclusions

This is a preliminary study of the factors influencing the way undergraduate students perceive the phenomenon of entrepreneurship and their attitudes toward starting up an entrepreneurial career. It is also intended to assess how country differences influence these perceptions and attitudes.

The social background of students (specifically, parents' occupation) plays a crucial role in the attitude of students toward becoming entrepreneurs while country specificity has little impact.

On the contrary, social background has less impact on the image of entrepreneurs. This image shows remarkable similarities in both countries: entrepreneurs are seen as people with specific personal attributes who use their skills and abilities in ways that are not always or completely socially acceptable (e.g., demonstrating a lack of honesty or sense of social justice). The different country environments influence the image of the economic role of entrepreneurs in creating jobs and fostering economic development, a role that is more recognized by Italian than Argentine students.

Remarkable similarities between the two groups of students are also found in the reasons for creating their own firms. Both groups stress personal attainment—such as putting their own ideas into practice, personal independence, creating something of one's own—rather than economic reasons (earning or accumulating money). The latter reasons are considered more commonly by a larger percentage of Italian students than Argentine students.

The perceived obstacles to starting up their own firms are also similar: Both Argentine and Italian students emphasize the risk associated with new venture creation combined with the lack of initial funding. Among the main obstacles they also consider the fear of being unsuccessful (Italian students) and doubts about their entrepreneurial skills (Argentine students). Overall, in both countries students emphasize reasons related to their personal status or to the characteristics of the ventures they are going to set up rather than variables related to the general environment (only in the case of Italian students is fiscal pressure indicated as an important obstacle).

More than two-thirds of students believe that it is more difficult to create a firm at present than in the past. The result is highly dependent on the social background of students and not on the country. Students coming from entrepreneurial, professional, and executive families seem more confident about the possibility of setting up their own firms than do students coming from other social backgrounds. On this point, it is interesting to note that two-thirds of the students perceived the present situation as more difficult than the past situation.

The major differences between the two countries emerge with reference to the obstacles to entrepreneurial activity in general. Argentine students point out general economic factors—such as the effect of globalization and the presence of uncertainty—while Italian students point out more specific factors —such as fiscal pressures, the difficulty of raising adequate funding at start-up, and competition from large firms.

Overall the results of the study show that there are more similarities than differences between Argentine and Italian students in their perceptions of entrepreneurship and in their attitude toward starting up their own firms. The differences concerning these aspects can be attributed mainly to the students' social background—specifically to their parents' occupation—rather than to the country. This has two important consequences.

The similarities between the two countries allow the design and experimentation of similar university programs for entrepreneurship development. The second, and most important, consequence is that the problems and attitudes shown by students with regard to their prospective careers as entrepreneurs seem to provide a large scope for entrepreneurship programs and several interesting indications regarding the aims and contents of these programs. The importance of the influence of family background on the propensity to enter an entrepreneurial career strongly supports the importance of university courses designed not only to develop specific entrepreneurial skills but also to give students the opportunity to gain a general knowledge of the phenomenon and to directly interact with entrepreneurs by identifying role models.

With regard to entrepreneurial skills, courses on entrepreneurship should address the following topics: improvement of personal capabilities and confidence in managing the risks associated with the start-up of new ventures; information about the possibilities and instruments for raising external funds for new ventures; development of a business plan with specific regard to the evaluation and control of entrepreneurial risks; sociocultural aspects of entrepreneurship and the forces encouraging or inhibiting it.

The study has several limitations that give space for further development both at the theoretical and empirical levels. At the empirical level, the main limitation concerns the number of students in the sample and the lack of variability of some of their demographic aspects. In order to overcome this limitation, we intend to enlarge the sample to include a larger typology of students in terms of university curricula, social background, and countries. At the theoretical level, more is needed to identify the several factors (demographic, cultural, personal, etc.) influencing the perceptions of and attitudes toward entrepreneurship and the mechanisms through which they operate.

References

Audretsch, D.B., and R. Thurik. 2001. "Linking Entrepreneurship to Economic Growth." Science Technology, and Industry (STI) working papers. Paris: Organization for Economic Cooperation and Development.
Baumol, W.J. 1968. "Entrepreneurship in Economic Theory." *American Economic Review* 58, no. 2: 64–71.
———. 1993. "Formal Entrepreneurship Theory in Economics: Existence and Bounds." *Journal of Business Venturing* 8, no. 3: 197–210.
Bygrave, W.D. 1997. *The Portable MBA in Entrepreneurship*, 2d ed. New York: Wiley.
Charney, A., and G. Libecap. 2000. "Impact of Entrepreneurship Education." *Insights: A Kauffman Research Series.* Kauffman Center for Entrepreneurial Leadership.
Clark, B.; C. Davis; and V. Harnish. 1984. "Do Courses in Entrepreneurship Aid in New Venture Creation?" *Journal of Small Business Management* 22, no. 2: 26–31.
Colombo, M., and M. Delmastro. 2001. "Technology-based Entrepreneurs: Does the Internet Make a Difference?" *Small Business Economics* 16, no. 3: 177–90.
Cowling, M., and M. Taylor. 2001. "Entrepreneurial Women and Men: Two Different Species?" *Small Business Economics* 16, no. 3: 167–75.
Delmar, F., and P. Davidsson. 2000. "Where Do They Come From? Prevalence and Characteristics of Nascent Entrepreneurs." *Entrepreneurship and Regional Development* 12, no. 1: 1–23.

Fayolle, A. 1998. "Teaching of Entrepreneurship: Outcomes from an Innovative Experience." Paper presented at the conference Internationalizing Entrepreneurship Education and Training, IntEnt98, Oestrich-Winkel, Germany.

Finkle, T., and D. Deeds. 2001. "Trends in the Market for Entrepreneurship Faculty, 1989–1998." *Journal of Business Venturing* 16, no. 6: 613–30.

Gibb, A., and J. Ritchie. 1982. "Understanding the Process of Starting Small Business." *European Small Business Journal* 1, no. 1 (September).

Gill, A. 1988. "Choice of Employment Status and the Wages of Employees and the Self-employed: Some Further Evidence." *Journal of Applied Econometrics* 3: 229–34.

Hofstede, G. 1980. *Culture's Consequences: International Differences in Work Related Values.* Beverly Hills, CA: Sage.

———. 2001. *Culture's Consequences: Comparing Values, Behaviors, Institutions and Organizations Across Nations,* 2d ed. Thousand Oaks, CA: Sage.

International Monetary Fund (IMF). 2002. Available at www.imf.org/external/pubs/B/WEO/2002/02.

Instituto Nacional de Estadísticas y Censos (INDEC). 2002. www.indec.gov.ar (accessed December 10, 2004).

Kantis, H.; M. Ishida ; and M. Komori. 2002. *Empresarialidad en Economías Emergentes: Creación y Desarrollo de Nuevas Empresas en América Latina y el Este de Asia.* Banco Interamericano de Desarrollo, Departamento de Desarrollo Sostenible, División de Micro, Pequeñas y Medianas Empresas.

Kantis, H.; S. Postigo; J. Federico; and M.F. Tamborini. 2002. "The Emergence of University Graduates Entrepreneurs: What Makes the Difference? Empirical Evidence from Research in Argentina." Paper presented at the RENT XVI Conference, Barcelona, Spain.

Karcher, B. 1998. "Does Gender Really Matter? The Influences of Gender and Qualifications on Self-employment and Their Implications for Entrepreneurship Education." Paper presented at the Internationalizing Entrepreneurship Education and Training Conference, IntEnt98, Oestrich-Winkel, Germany.

Kolvereid, L., and O. Moen. 1997. "Entrepreneurship Among Business Graduates: Does a Major in Entrepreneurship Make a Difference?" *Journal of European Industrial Training* 21, nos. 4–5: 154–57.

Kourilsky, M.L. 1995. "Entrepreneurship Education: Opportunity in Search of Curriculum." *Business Education Forum* (October).

Lafuente, A., and V. Salas. 1989. "Types of Entrepreneurs and Firms: The Case of New Spanish Firms." *Strategic Management Journal* 10: 17–30.

Laukkanen, M. 2000. "Exploring Alternative Approaches in High-level Education: Creating Micro Mechanisms for Endogenous Regional Growth." *Journal of Entrepreneurship and Regional Development* 12: 25–47.

Levie, J.; W. Brown; and L. Steele. 2001. "How Entrepreneurial Are Strathclyde Alumni?" Paper presented at the International Entrepreneurship: Researching New Frontiers Conference, University of Strathclyde, UK.

Litvak, I., and C. Maule. 1976. "Comparative Technical Entrepreneurship: Some Perspectives." *Journal of International Business Studies* 7, no. 1: 31–38.

Lüthje, C., and N. Franke. 2002. "Fostering Entrepreneurship Through University Education and Training: Lessons from Massachusetts Institute of Technology." Paper presented at the second annual Conference of the European Academy of Management, Sweden.

Minniti, M., and W.D. Bygrave. 1999. "The Microfoundations of Entrepreneurship." *Entrepreneurship: Theory and Practice* 23, no. 4: 41–52.

Mueller, S.L., and A.S. Thomas. 2000. "Culture and Entrepreneurial Potential: A Nine Country Study of Locus of Control and Innovativeness." *Journal of Business Venturing* 16: 51–75.

North, D.C. 1994. "Economic Performance Through Time." *American Economic Review* 84, no. 3: 359–68.

Organization for Economic Cooperation and Development (OECD). 1998. *Fostering Entrepreneurship, the OECD Jobs Strategy.* Paris

Postigo, S., and M.F. Tamborini. 2002. "Entrepreneurship Education in Argentina: The Case of University of San Andrés." Paper presented at the conference Internationalizing Entrepreneurship Education and Training, Malaysia.

———. 2003. "Entrepreneurship Education in Argentina: Lessons from the Experience of University of San Andrés." Paper presented at the Annual National Conference of the United States Association for Small Business and Entrepreneurship, Hilton Head, South Carolina.

Rees H., and A. Shah. 1986. "An Empirical Analysis of Self-employment in the UK." *Journal of Applied Econometrics* 1: 95–108.

Reynolds, P.D.; H. Michael; S.M. Camp; and E. Autio. 2000. *Global Entrepreneurship Monitor. 2000 Executive Report.* Babson College, Babson Park, MA.

Reynolds, P.D.; W.D. Bygrave; E. Autio; L. Cox; and M. Hay. 2002. *Global Entrepreneurship Monitor: 2002 Executive Report.* Babson College, London Business School, and Ewing Marion Kauffman Foundation.

Robinson, P., and W. Sexton. 1994. "The Effect of Education and Experience Self-employment Success." *Journal of Business Venturing* 9, no. 2: 141–57.

Schumpeter, J.A. 1934. *The Theory of Economic Development.* Cambridge, MA: Harvard University Press.

Shapero, A. 1984. "The Entrepreneurial Event." In *The Environment for Entrepreneurship*, ed. C.A. Kent. Lexington, MA: Lexington Press.

Tackey, N.; S. Perryman; and H. Connor. 1999. *Graduated Business Start-ups.* Institute for Employment Studies, UK.

Upton, N.; D. Sexton; and C. Moore. 1995. "Have We Made a Difference? An Examination of Career Activity of Entrepreneurship Majors Since 1981." Paper presented at the Entrepreneurship Research Conference, Babson College, Babson Park, MA.

Ussman, A., and S. Postigo. 2000. "O Papel da universidade no fomento da funçao empresarial." *Anais universitarios. Ciencias Sociais e Humanas.* 1990–2000 Yearbook Special Issue: 219–33.

Veciana, J. 2002. "Comentarios sobre los resultados de la investigación comparada sobre la empresarialidad entre América Latina y el Este de Asia." In *Entrepreneurship in Emerging Economies: The Creation and Development of New Firms in Latin America and East Asia*, ed. H. Kantis, M. Ishida, and M. Komori. Inter-American Development Bank, Department of Sustainable Development, Micro, Small and Medium Business Division.

Vesper, K., and W. Gartner. 1997. "Measuring Progress in Entrepreneurship Education." *Journal of Business Venturing* 12, no. 5: 403–21.

Wennekers, A.R.M., and A.R. Thurik. 1999. "Linking Entrepreneurship and Economic Growth." *Small Business Economics* 13: 27–55.

Wilken, P. 1979. *Entrepreneurship: A Comparative and Historical Study.* Norwood, NJ: Ablex.

18

Business Education in Chile

A Case Study for Successful Transition to Market Economy in Developing Countries

Maria-Teresa Lepeley

Late Twentieth Century: Landmark of Economic Transformation in Developing Countries

The last part of the twentieth century was a landmark for economic transformation in developing countries around the world. By then, the inward-looking import substitution development strategy, which had prevailed for over a century, showed clear signs of exhaustion, leading economies to stagnation and people to starvation in many countries on different continents. Hence in the early 1970s, developing countries in Asia and Latin America started to drift apart from centralized economies and experimented with market systems to improve growth and welfare.

Economic history shows that in order to solve endemic social problems, the governments of developing nations made efforts to substitute the traditionally high degree of central intervention in the national economy with increasing economic freedom and individual responsibility toward market systems in these regions. Two decades later, in 1991, the countries of Eastern Europe joined the market movement when they broke away from the Soviet Union. Although many countries selected the market system as the national development strategy, the inducing factors of economic transformation, as well as the outcome, were different.

In Asia, for instance, Singapore, Taiwan, and Hong Kong—the Three Asian Tigers—became successful examples of a market model in the "new global economy," largely because Japan played a determinant role, leading, supporting, and expediting their economic transformation.

In contrast, developing countries on the American continent lacked the guidance, support and stimulus of a similar leader. It took the United States twenty years to activate a free trade agreement with Canada and Mexico, the North American Free Trade Agreement (1993), and thirty years to initiate a free trade agreement with Chile (2004).

The economic transition to a market system on the American continent has been uneven and often erratic because the nations of Latin America had highly centralized economies and the countries lacked the education, discipline, responsibility, and ethics necessary to build a sustainable and healthy market system beyond political interests. Attempts to achieve economic transformation in Latin America were subject to trial and error and strong political powers and influences so very few countries were successful in the economic transition. At the beginning of the twenty-first century, most countries in the region of Latin America were still trying to control political unrest and social adversity, and they retained a high degree of economic centralization that hinders markets and deters economic stability in the age of globalization.

Chile: A Successful Transition to a Market Economy on the American Continent

In 1973, Chile, a developing country in the southern cone of the American continent, initiated one of the deepest transformations in economic history, and, associated with deep economic change and decentralization, so did business education as a discipline of study.

Chile was the first country in Latin America to undertake deep economic transformation. Before the transformation, Chile was one of many countries in the region affected by a highly volatile economy, recurrent hyperinflation, and high unemployment. Now Chile is the most stable economy in Latin America, and has one of the most open economies and progressive market systems in the world.

The 2002–3 Report of the Global Entrepreneurial Monitor (Enrione 2002–3) shows that among the thirty-seven developed and developing countries that participated in this study, Chile has the highest proportion of entrepreneurs in the population. It took Chile a decade to accomplish the transition from a highly controlled economy to a market system (from 1974 to 1984). The successful outcome, the result of deep and rigorous national economic restructuring, privatization, and liberalization policies, has been broadly documented in economic and business literature in the United States and around the world.

This chapter reveals factors that have received less attention in the literature although they have had an important impact on the consolidation of the market economy in Chile. These factors are: (1) the elements that contributed to the development of the entrepreneurial spirit among the Chilean people, (2) the discipline of a government with a vision for change and the mission to substitute a controlled economy with a high-performance market system, and (3) the liberalization reform of higher education, which was essential to expand business education as a necessary condition to meet the demands of a fast-growing private sector in a developing country.

Special attention will be placed on the Higher Education Liberalization Reform of 1980 because it had a significant impact on successful economic transformation in Chile and may be replicated to consolidate a market system in other countries.

The economic transformation in Chile was strengthened by the synchronization between the economic development strategy and educational liberalization policy. The liberalization of higher education was a key factor that allowed the rapid expansion of business education necessary to facilitate the development of a skilled labor force.

This highly educated labor force was required to meet the demands of emerging industries in the private sector and it was paramount in a newly open economy confronting with surmounting international competition and the challenges of globalization.

Background of the Chilean Entrepreneurial Spirit

Geographically speaking, Chile is a long, narrow, and densely mountainous country on the west coast of South America. It has a highly diverse territory that extends over more than 3,000 miles and ranges from a dry desert, in the north, to the southern pole on a willowy pathway between the Pacific Ocean and the Andes Mountains.

Chile lies on the Pacific Ocean. The widest part of the country extends 200 miles in the north and it narrows down to less than 10 miles wide in the southern archipelago region. Only one-third of the territory is suitable for agriculture, and prominent geographic accidents define its international boundaries. Chile is bound on the east by Argentina and the Andes Mountains, which includes Mount Aconcagua, the third tallest mountain on earth. Northern Chile has the driest desert on the planet, the Atacama Desert, and borders Perú and Bolivia. Chile ends at the southern pole.

Chile was discovered by the Spanish conqueror Pedro de Valdivia in the sixteenth century. In demographic terms, the Chilean population is highly homogeneous compared with other Latin American countries, largely because the territory that would become Chile after the discovery was less hospitable than warmer and flatter lands allowing for easier harvesting of food and cattle.

History tells that the Chilean aborigines were notoriously brave, had a war-faring nature, and confronted the Spanish conquerors with fierceness. Many aborigines died in violent battles and those who survived largely mixed with the Spanish. The Chilean population has a significant component of Spanish ancestry, culture, and customs.

Chile obtained its independence from Spain on September 18, 1810, and since then freedom and education have been important concerns of its people. Chilean educational standards are recognized as among the most progressive in Latin America and the world. The literacy rate is 98.5 percent and women's participation in education has historically been high. Today women's enrollment in higher education is 46 percent of total student enrollment (UN 2000: 104).

In terms of the foundations and development of the Chilean stereotype, during the nineteenth and twentieth centuries large immigrations of people from European nations found refuge in Chile, as they did in Argentina and Uruguay, the other two southernmost countries of the American continent.

In addition to the Spanish, who arrived in Chile continuously for four centuries, the country became homeland to Germans, Italians, English, and Yugoslavs, among other European groups. Chilean governments welcomed the Europeans and facilitated their settlement because they contributed to foster growth and development. The hardworking newcomers relocated in inhabited territories, cultivated idle lands, developed large extensions of isolated forest, established new industries, increased trade with Europe, and developed the tourist industry, widely and wisely promoting the extraordinary variety and beauty of Chilean landscapes.

At that time most emerging nations on the American continent had urgent needs to speed development and they competed to attract the immigration of people with advanced skills and education.

The Europeans who migrated to Chile had abandoned their native countries to get away from the deteriorating conditions and the hardship of World Wars I and II, and they were seeking opportunities to improve their standard of living on the "new continent."

Europeans in Chile expanded commerce and trade with the "old continent," and created the roots of business growth and ethics, as well as the entrepreneurial spirit that has been a crucial element in the development and consolidation of the market economy in this nation.

From a Controlled System to Economic Freedom and a Market Economy that Worked

Chile, like most developing countries in the twentieth century, adopted import substitution as its development strategy because this strategy was sponsored by the most important international development agencies, such as the World Bank, the United Nations, the Inter-American Development Bank, and the Organization of American States. But, over time, import substitution exacerbated the power of governments with central control, and reinforced closed economies with a high degree of protectionism and command over national sources of production.

In the decade of the 1960s Chile had reached a population close to 10 million. Income per capita was low compared with other countries in Latin America. The country had a relatively small consumption market and therefore import substitution provided a haven for an enclave of protected industries that produce enough to meet national demands at high prices, *hurting Chilean consumers.*

Then, over 90 percent of Chilean exports were copper products. Imports were limited and subject to high tariffs, quotas, and other restrictions, making them prohibitive for most Chilean consumers.

In the late 1960s, a Christian Democratic government strengthened the centralization of power and national resources with widespread agrarian reform. Large portions of land were expropriated from the landowners and transferred to people who worked on farms, most of whom did not have the knowledge or access to loans and the financial means necessary to increase the production of cattle, farm, and diary products, which was originally the justification for reform and property confiscation. As a result, farm products became scarcer and prices increased considerably, *hurting Chilean consumers.*

The nationalization trend generated growing distrust among Chilean landowners and mistrust of the population at large toward the government and the political elites.

Until the 1960s Chile had been an example of democracy in Latin America with a solid tradition of respect for law and order. This characteristic was clearly expressed in extensive voting to elect public officials, but later in that decade drastic changes in economic order and political unrest rapidly eroded national confidence.

A Split Presidential Election

In 1970, Chile had a presidential election. There were three candidates who represented the major political tendencies. The electoral preferences of the population divided evenly among them. One of the candidates was politically independent, Jorge Alessandri, a former president of Chile and the son of another former president. He had the support of independent voters, economic liberals, and the political conservative party. Radomiro Tomic was the representative of the Christian Democrat Party, who, given the performance of the previous government, had lost the support of an important part of the Chilean electorate in a traditional Roman Catholic nation. The third candidate was Salvador Allende, a socialist senator, supported by socialist and communists, and this was his third attempt to win the Chilean presidency, after presidential elections in 1958 and 1964.

Because none of the candidates obtained a clear majority, the Chilean Parliament had to select the president from among those with relative majorities. A difficult deliberation of the parliament, which had a majority of Christian Democrats, gave the presidency to Salvador Allende, who had received a small number of votes over the runner-up, Jorge Alessandri.

Chileans were skeptical of politicians but initially they regarded Allende and his administration favorably, and were inclined to think that Allende would not drive Chile on a road to communism as in Cuba. But events showed otherwise. In a short period of time, the socialist government had increased controls and intensified the nationalization process and these actions hit hard on the tolerance of most Chileans.

During the second year of socialist administration, the government further restrained the freedom of the Chilean people by imposing tighter controls on the financial system, money exchange, and access to foreign currencies that were used for trade and international travel. Moreover, people could not travel freely in Chile due to shortages of gasoline and other essential products and services. In 1973 production in most industries was stagnant. Food became scarce and long lines of people appeared on the streets in front of food stores waiting to buy bread, cooking oil, and essential products. The production and supply of products and services deteriorated rapidly.

The Chilean "Brain Drain" and Women's Power to Protect Freedom

Chileans in large numbers started to leave a country where it was increasingly burdensome to live. Many relocated in the United States. Many were highly skilled individuals who pursued studies in colleges and universities. It was a case of "brain drain" in Chile.

By 1973, opposition to the socialist government had escalated. In retaliation national restrictions were increased. The Chilean economy was deeply constrained by widespread strikes in all productive sectors. Chileans were tired and clamored for change, but neither the parliament nor the judicial system had the power or capacity to negotiate a peaceful solution with a government that was consistently operating outside of the constitution.

Chilean women, housewives and mothers in particular, who had to stand in line to get food for their families, became deeply troubled by food shortages, disturbances in public life, and mounting government intrusion on individual freedom. Mothers were outraged because their children were leaving Chile in large numbers to relocate in other countries. This was unknown among Chilean families, where siblings by tradition live with their parents until they get married, or move to another city, but until now, seldom to another country.

Women became infuriated and they got organized, gathering daily and forming long lines in the streets of Santiago, the capital of Chile, and in all major cities. They "made noise" to call for public attention, hitting pots and pans with kitchen utensils in loud protest against the government. But the situation did not change, and actually got worse. So women reacted by barricading military headquarters in cities across the country. Initially they pleaded with the military for support and action, but in response to the lack of military action, they blockaded the path of military personnel calling them "cowards" and "chickens," and saying "you are the only force left to overthrow an abusive government apparatus."

The movement of the Chilean women contributed significantly to the fight for national freedom against oppressive governance.

The socialist government was overthrown by a combination of military forces on September 11, 1973. In the middle of the takeover battle, Allende made a plea by radio to the Chilean people. When he did not get the support he expected, he committed suicide (Yañez 2003).

A military junta, formed by four generals representing the four branches of the armed forces in Chile, took charge of the country government. Augusto Pinochet, an army general, became director of the military junta. In 1979 Pinochet was elected president of Chile in a national referendum. In 1989, the military government called another referendum where the Chilean people voted for the resignation of the president. Pinochet called for democratic elections and left the government in 1990. A Christian Democrat candidate was elected and a new period of Christian Democracy governance started in Chile. The three administrations that followed the military government were predominantly Christian Democrat but built a political alliance with center parties and moderate socialist political parties. To a large extent these administrations adhered to and have consolidated the market strategy established by the military administration.

Chile had a long democratic history and the Chilean army, a solid tradition of discipline, order, and organization. Therefore, although the military intervention was not a desirable outcome for the people, or the military, history demonstrated that the military government was a solution for Chile and the only option the country had to revive economic and political freedom. In 1973 Chile experienced a revolution, and confrontation was inevitable in an otherwise peaceful nation. There were casualties on both sides.

The Benefits and Constraints of a Successful Economic Transition in the Twentieth Century

For the first time in Chilean governance, during the military government, professional teams, instead of political interests, led the departments of state, and these teams conducted the economic transition to the new economy. These leaders significantly shared the value that the majority of Chileans assigned to national freedom and respect for national order. The government rapidly created the conditions to substitute for the centrally controlled economy with a free market system and a broadly open economy.

The new economic order was based on low government intervention in economic activity, a coherent monetary policy, opening the economy to trade with the world, decreased tariffs and quotas and increased international trade, extensive privatization of the industries nationalized by previous administrations, increased individual freedom and economic responsibility, significant promotion of entrepreneurial activity to expand the private sector to promote national and international investment, and the production of goods and services for national consumption and exports.

It must be emphasized that Chile undertook deep economic transformation and liberalization at a time when the world was polarized between the hegemonic powers of the United States and the Soviet Union and developing countries showed a strong tendency toward socialism to solve endemic development problems of unemployment and poverty. Consequently, economic liberalization in Chile was a monumental challenge for a small developing country, for the government and the Chilean people who valued political and economic freedom.

Chilean economic success was totally unexpected for a small country in Latin America that abruptly broke off from international socialism. Since then Chile has become a focal target of attack and resentment from the Soviet Union, Cuba, and their allies.

The Chilean "Brain Gain"

The Chilean transformation represented one of the purest examples of economic decentralization and became known as the "Chilean miracle" in the economic literature of the 1980s. To "achieve the miracle," but first to comply with the demand for economic freedom of the Chilean people, the military government seeks the advice of world-recognized free-market economists. Milton Friedman and Arnold Harberger, among others, contributed to the design of the new Chilean economy.

The changes adopted by the administration of the military government attracted many Chilean professionals and business people who had left the country during the socialist government, but now returned to work and contribute to the national transformation. A considerable number of them had obtained advanced degrees in prestigious universities in the United States and when they returned they worked in Chilean universities. These scholars and professionals with extensive experience in economics and business, made a significant contribution to the economic transformation and to the expansion and improvement of business education in Chile.

Graduates of the University of Chicago, Harvard University, Massachusetts Institute of Technology, and Stanford University, became the architects of the new economy and the creators of the "Chilean miracle." Graduates of the University of Chicago, who had a significant impact on the transition, were nicknamed "The Chicago Boys."

The success of the economic transformation in Chile was largely the result of a vigorous case of "brain gain."

The Opening of the Chilean Economy and Growth of Business Education

The monetary and economic policies that expedited economic transition in Chile have been extensively documented in the economic literature so I will concentrate on the policies that had a direct impact on the expansion of business education in Chile.

Growth of Nontraditional Exports

One of the most important contributions to the development of business education in Chile was the opening of the Chilean economy to world trade. To this end, in 1974 the government created Pro-Chile, a national agency that had the mission to promote Chilean exports around the world. Pro-Chile opened offices in fifty-six countries on every continent and the entity especially emphasized the support of small and medium-sized exporting companies. The companies that produced "nontraditional" export products received primary attention. International trade expanded rapidly.

But as is well known, the opening of the economy imposed great challenges and radical transformation in the industrial sector. Traditional industries suffered significant hardships during the transition. Some perished and new companies emerged. Corporations had to adapt to the new challenges of increasing international competition. Unemployment grew significantly during the period of adjustment.

Industries producing nontraditional exports boomed rapidly. Within a decade Chile was no longer a mono-exporter of copper, but had a highly diversified and sophisticated economy, which included the best-known "nontraditional" Chilean exports, such as wine, fruits, seafood, and wood products, among many others.

Between 1974 and 1989, copper exports decreased from 90 percent to 40 percent and new export products became important sources of national income.

Chile and Free Trade Agreements

Chile has made consistent efforts to further international integration consolidating trade agreements with Asia-Pacific (Asia-Pacific Economic Cooperation), Europe, Mexico, and Canada. It is an affiliate member of MERCOSUR. Chile was the first country in South America to establish a free trade agreement with the United States in January 2004.

Privatization in Chile

The privatization model implemented in Chile has been replicated in countries around the world. One of the best-known cases of privatization was the Chilean Pension System, which has been adopted by developed and developing countries.

When the national pension system was privatized in 1980, the Chilean workers who contributed to the national social security system had the option to remain in the public system or to establish retirement accounts in the emerging private system. Within a year, 94 percent of the Chilean workers had transferred their pension funds to individual capitalization accounts administered by an Association of Pension Funds in the private sector.

José Piñera, the secretary of labor who enacted the pension reform in 1980, and holds a PhD in economics from Harvard University, assessed that "the reform allowed 94 percent of the Chilean workers to become owners of the national capital."[1]

On the other side of the equation, the privatization of the retirement system had a positive impact on national investment, industrial development, and economic growth in Chile.

Other examples of privatizations in Chile include health care services (National Association of Pre-paid Health Plans), banking, utility industries such as electricity, telephone, and the national airline.

New industries emerged in Chile. The banking, financial, and technology sectors did remarkably well. In a short time, Chile attracted a considerable number of multinational corporations. And Chile, a traditional "importer of capital," turned into a "capital exporter nation" as Chileans became investors in other Latin American countries and the United States.

A Decade-long Transition to Economic Stability

The adjustment of economic transformation took one decade in Chile, from 1973 to 1983. By 1984 the Chilean economy was stabilized. Between 1985 and 1997 Chile had an average annual growth rate of greater than 7 percent. The poverty level decreased from 40 percent in 1970 to 23 percent in 1995. Chile became the country with the highest income per capita and the lowest rates of unemployment (4.5%) and inflation in Latin America. These were the statistics that underlined the "Chilean economic miracle."

The Liberalization Reform of Higher Education and Expansion of Business Education in Chile

Today business education is receiving considerable attention in developed and developing countries largely because employment in other sectors, including government agencies, is decreasing due to advancements in technology and labor restructuring imposed by the forces of globalization.

The expansion of market economies in developing countries in parallel with the opening and decreased protectionism in developed nations is significantly increasing work opportunities for individuals with business acumen. So universities around the world are evaluating this phenomenon and estimating future demand for this discipline and the programs offered.

A word of caution is necessary in relation to the analysis of the demand for business education. The assessment may be futile if business colleges or professors do not have a clear understanding of the impact of globalization and the dynamics that induce interaction and interdependence between developed countries and developing nations with emerging market economies. This aspect is important because until now developed countries have largely ignored the potential of business education as a "building block" for world peace and stability.

In Chile business education experienced significant growth in the 1980s and 1990s after a comprehensive reform to liberalize higher education. This reform facilitated the rapid expansion of business education and it was a critical element in speeding up the transition to a market economy (Lepeley 1987).

The reform was necessary to meet the emerging demands of an opening economy in the twentieth century because the traditional higher education system had two centuries of existence without adjustments or actualizations to new conditions. Chile was the pioneer country in Latin America in establishing a well-grounded higher education system that closely follows the European model of structure and instruction.

Until 1980 the original Chilean higher education system consisted of only eight large public universities that had a main campus in Santiago, and regional campuses distributed in cities across the country. There was also a large private Catholic university.

The system had only these large universities as options for higher education and they were highly centralized. Tuition was free for all students but access to higher education was highly restricted to students with high grades and to those who obtained high scores on a standardized national admission test, the Academic Aptitude Test (PAA), equivalent to the Scholastic Aptitude Test in the United States.

The reform of 1980 replaced the European model of structure and instruction with a similar U.S. model of higher education. The new system was decentralized, reached a necessary degree of diversification, and facilitated fast growth in enrolment.

The reform provided the conditions for the creation of new institutions, namely, professional institutes, equivalent to four-year colleges in the United States, and technical education centers, similar to two-year community colleges (Lepeley 1987).

Until the year of the reform the universities were tuition free but were highly selective and elitist institutions. After the reform, all students had to pay subject to a differential based on household income. Scholarships became available for the first time for the 25,000 students who obtained the highest scores on the national admission test, PAA, and applied to the universities.

Change in the system was necessary to increase equity and access, particularly for lower income students, a cohort that until the 1980s had been largely excluded from higher education in Chile (Lepeley 1987).

The higher education reform was implemented at a time when the transition to the market economy was advanced and international trade and business opportunities were abundant in Chile. Therefore, business rapidly became a preferred field of study.

Significant demand for business programs had an immediate effect on program innovation and quality, and institutions responded quickly to meet the emerging need (Lepeley 1987).

For the past quarter-century, business education has been a "growing business" in Chile. Until 1980 traditional universities offered only eight business programs based on a fix and traditional curriculum. In 2003 private and public universities alike were offering seventy business programs in different specializations.[2] Business programs are also offered in professional institutes and technical education centers, the other levels of higher education in Chile.

The rapid expansion of business education is consistent with the results of the 2002–3 Global Entrepreneurial Report, which identifies Chile as the country with the highest proportion of entrepreneurs among developed and developing countries.

The Chilean Master of Business Administration

Voris (1997) found that in contrast to universities in the United States, universities in Latin American countries have experienced slower development of business education because they have followed the European tradition emphasizing studies in the arts and sciences. His statement is accurate, except in the case of Chile after economic transformation and the higher education reform.

Erich Spencer, the director of the Executive Master of Business Administration (MBA) Program at the University of Chile School of Business said that in Latin America, no other country has achieved more progress in advancing MBA education than Chile.[3]

In effect, the Chilean MBA is a highly competitive world-class professional degree. A considerable number of MBA programs in Chile have evolved from prestigious MBA programs in the United States, where Chilean professors have obtained advanced degrees.

But there are other factors that increase the prestige of the Chilean MBA programs:

- Chile has thirty years of experience with a dynamic market economy that generates constant demand for business managers skilled at performing in a highly competitive international environment.[4]
- Business professors in Chile are subject to constant challenges to design and deliver MBA programs comparable to the best in the world.[5]
- To meet demands for quality business programs professors either work part time in corporations or collaborate closely with chief executive officers (CEOs) of international corporations (Lepeley and Spencer 1997).
- There is a significant degree of interaction between business programs and corporations.
- Chilean CEOs contribute to the improvement of MBAs, particularly those offered by their alma mater institutions.

All of these factors indicate that Chilean MBAs have bright prospects for the future and that the high demand will continue based on the following assumptions. The exchange rate differential between the Chilean peso and the U.S. dollar makes a business degree from a university in the United States very expensive for Chilean students and highly competitive for students from other countries in Latin America and around the world. Latin American students from South and Central America will increasingly attend Chilean universities.

Chile offers these students another benefit. Except for Brazil, all Latin American countries speak Spanish. But Spanish and Portuguese share the Latin origin, so Spanish facilitates communication and understanding for Brazilians.

But in general students from other counties around the world show an interest in studying for an MBA in Chile because they are attracted by Chile's successful transition to a market economy. Additionally, a country with a broadly open economy requires that MBA programs emphasize business internationalization, international development, and globalization, which provide a value-added component compared with other countries.

Matko Koljatic, dean of the School of Business Administration at the Catholic University of Chile in Santiago, predicts that enrollment in his school will double in the next five years (Spencer and Contreras 2002). This program obtained international accreditation from the Association to Advance Collegiate Schools of Business in 2001, and it is the only program in South America with this distinction.

As a professor of business in universities in the United States, Latin America, Europe, and the Middle East and professor to people from Africa who have attended our programs in the United States, I have had extensive opportunities to compare business education in different countries. In contrast with other countries, professors in Chile emphasize business internationalization, globalization, and the use of technology. Chilean professors are aware that business students need to be exposed from the beginning of their studies to the global issues that affect businesses and they need to develop skills to maximize the benefits and minimize the costs of the irreversible process of globalization.

Business professors in Chile transmit business confidence to students. They feel the responsibility to train world-class business managers. This is rarely the case in countries where business professors have not been exposed to such a drastic economic transformation. And it is also not the case in developing countries where the transition to a market system has not been as successful and as a result people are reluctant to trust and believe in business, entrepreneurship, or business opportunities.

Globalization, its causes and effects, benefits and costs, are important components of business education in Chilean MBA programs. But in the United

States, globalization is still a contentious proposition, which is absent in most business programs, if not in theory, notoriously in practice.

Globalization is a major challenge in today's business education because only direct exposure to international challenges can prepare business professors for effective teaching. Business professors in Chile have confronted intense international challenges for three decades. In comparison, a smaller proportion of business professors in the United States, or in other countries, have faced a similar experience.

Women and Business Education in Chile

Until the late 1970s the proportion of women studying business in Chile was less than 20 percent of total enrollment. Today it is over 50 percent.[6] This proportion is comparatively higher than in the United States.

Nonetheless, this statistics shows only "the tip of the iceberg" in terms of the real need for business education in developed or developing countries around the world. This is primarily because higher education still serves mainly young, traditional-age students, while the greatest need for business education is among older people, and particularly older women.

I became aware of the great need for business and entrepreneurial education among women when I was professor of business at the largest university in Chile, and later president of an entrepreneurial college in Chile. We developed and offered the country's first continuing education program in entrepreneurship for women. This program was designed as a certificate program in continuing education rather than an academic degree. This decision was based on the results of a survey we conducted to assess the needs of women for business education, where we found that although women had a need to increase business knowledge, most of them did not have the time, the interest, or the financial resources to pursue academic degrees.

Since 1997 the semester-long Certificate Program for Women in Entrepreneurship has helped Chilean women business owners, women with an interest in opening a business, or those wishing to have increased participation in a family business. The program provides business knowledge and the managerial skills necessary to allow women to advance careers and increase personal income.

I have taught entrepreneurial education to women in countries around the world and have observed a great demand for entrepreneurial education among older women that has not been met either in developed or developing countries.

In 2003, I conducted a pilot study for the World Bank to identify the educational needs of Chilean women entrepreneurs who were members of the business association for women FINAM (Finanzas Internacionales y Nacionales para la Mujer), an affiliate of the Women's World Bank in Chile. We found that the most pressing needs for business education among older women are business management, negotiation, and the use of technology to improve business performance (Lepeley 2003).

Women entrepreneurs have identified the following as the most important obstacles to advancing their businesses: difficulty in obtaining credit and a lack of the knowledge and skills required to deal effectively with government bureaucracies. Women around the world confront these same obstacles.

Conclusion

The successful transition to a market economy in Chile was significantly facilitated by the liberalization reform of higher education that allowed for the rapid expansion of business education. This was essential to developing a skilled labor force capable of meeting the labor demands of emerging industries in a growing private sector confronted with surmounting the challenges of globalization and international competition.

The experience of Chile provides clear evidence of the critical need to synchronize economic development strategy with education policies in countries in transition to market systems. Effective coordination with higher education is particularly important because this level not only provides the skilled labor necessary for development but also uses the largest proportion of the national resources and investments allocated to education.

Developed and developing nations need to strengthen the quality and relevance of business education through a focus on globalization. National policies and institutions need to place special attention on expanding educational opportunity and access for women to stimulate their participation in business and economic activity. Women's participation makes a significant contribution to economic growth and social development in developed and developing countries.

Globalization offers exceptional opportunities for business development in countries with market economies. But it is increasingly clear that these opportunities will go to people who receive relevant business education from professors with a deep understanding of globalization and the complex process of internationalization. People with skills to maximize the benefits and with innovative solutions to minimize the costs of globalization will be increasingly desirable among business graduates.

Quality and relevance in business education are necessary to empower people and develop a globally competitive workforce as a necessary condition to reach sustainable growth and progress in developing and developed countries.

Today, as never before, business education has the unique potential to become an instrument that will strengthen positive globalization for world peace. Needless to say, this is indeed a major challenge for business professors, but it is also a great responsibility and a meaningful opportunity to actually change and improve the world.

In memory of Claudio Milman: a good friend, classmate, and colleague, professor of international business at Rollins College, for his devotion to markets and economic freedom.

Notes

1. Personal discussions with José Piñera and his book *La Batalla de las Pensiones* (1995).
2. Interview with Juan Saavedra, dean, School of Business Administration, University of Concepcion, Chile, March 2003.
3. Interview with Erich Spencer, director of the MBA Program at the School of Economics and Business Administration, University of Chile, May 10, 2003.
4. Ibid.
5. Ibid.
6. Interview with Juan Saavedra, March 2003.

References

Enrione, A., ed. 2002–3. Global Entrepreneurship Monitor (GEM). Chile.
Lepeley, M.T. 1987. *The Impact of the Higher Education Reform on Economic Development in Chile*. Master's Thesis. University of Miami.
———. 2003. *Women in Entrepreneurship in Chile*. Chile: FINAM—Women's World Bank Chile. Mimeo (April).
Lepeley, M.T., and E. Spencer. 1997. "The Internationalization Process of Large Corporations in Chile. A Managerial Approach." School of Economics and Business Administration, University of Chile. Mimeo.
The M.B.A. Program Information Site. 2001. "The M.B.A.—An Introduction." Available at www.mbainfo.com/mbaintro.html (accessed December 10, 2004).
Piñera, José. 1995. *La Batalla de las Pensiones* (The Battle for Pension Reform), 6th ed. Santiago: Zig-Zag.
Spencer, E., and J. Contreras. 2002. "M.B.A. Education in Latin America: The Case of Chile." University of Chile. Mimeo.
United Nations (UN). 2000. *The World's Women. 2000 Trends and Statistics*.
Universidad de Chile-M.B.A. en Administracion-Caracteristicas (2001). Available at www.graduados.facea.uchile.cl/administ/02caract.htm.
University of Chile, Santiago de Chile—M.A.D.E. 2001. Available at http://fae/magisters/made/programa.htm.
Voris, William. 1997. "A Retrospective of International Business Education in the United States over the Past Fifty Years." *International Executive* 39, no. 2: 271–82.

Wikipedia: Chile/Economy. 2001. Available at www.wikipedia.com/wiki/Chile/ Economy (accessed December 10, 2004).

Yañez, Nelly. 2003. "Interview with President Allende's Physician, Dr. Patricio Guijón." *El Mercurio,* September 11.

Part V

Africa and Near East

19

Management Education in Developing Countries

What Can Business Schools Contribute?

Guy Pfeffermann

It is a truth universally accepted that development in developing countries starts with primary education. However, just as Jane Austen started *Pride and Prejudice* with these first six words in order to show later that simple truths often do not cover the whole picture, it is suggested that higher education in general, and business education in particular, do indeed have vital roles to play in bringing nations out of poverty.

This chapter will try to show how well-designed business education does in fact contribute not only to individual achievement but also to high societal aspirations—what is generally called "development." While this chapter is intended to apply to the whole of the developing world, it is particularly focused on Africa and is intended to have as practical a slant as possible, drawing on recent work done, initiatives launched, and research performed by the World Bank Group and other organizations. In order to answer what business schools may contribute, three questions shall be asked:

- First, what is the role of enterprise in reducing poverty?
- Second, how do business schools serve the needs of society?
- And third, how can business education be strengthened?

Enterprise and Poverty Alleviation in a Competitive World

The answer to the first question—what is the role of enterprise in reducing poverty?—may seem obvious to some and may puzzle others. It may seem obvious to those who are engaged in modern businesses, producing goods and services, or to business school faculty and staff. It may puzzle those who worry about pharmaceutical patents, genetically modified foods, and corporate scandals.

The starting point to answer this question is a fact: In this increasingly competitive world, there are fewer and fewer places to hide. This is true of firms. Inefficient firms, whether in the United States, in Europe, or in poorer countries, can no longer expect to survive; sooner rather than later, they will go under or be taken over by more efficient companies. This is the flip side of the same coin that is giving billions of consumers access to cheaper consumer goods. Certain people may not like it (although some of us are enjoying the less expensive goods being produced). Indeed most people do not like all of the consequences of competition, but this is the reality with which we must cope.

How do governments cope with this competitive world? In a nutshell, governments of rich countries are coping reasonably well, protecting those who might fall by the wayside. Citizens of most of these countries have fairly universal access to many social programs: health care, early retirement benefits, unemployment compensation, government retraining programs and so forth. This is not so in poor or even middle-income countries. These countries do not have sufficient resources to provide such generous protection. In these countries, many of the best qualified individuals are scrambling for scarce government jobs that give them and their families the prospect of a relatively safe existence instead of working in a private sector that is perceived to be much more fragile and much less prestigious than it is in richer countries. This leaves the vast majority of the world's population without adequate income, let alone a social safety net.

Paradoxically, for that reason, it is even more essential that firms in the poor countries be as efficient as possible because people depend on them even more than in the rich countries for their livelihoods and that of their families. Likewise, the development of social safety nets in these countries will be financed to a large extent by the taxes paid by growing businesses.

This raises a very basic question—every year millions of poor people manage to escape out of poverty. How do they do it? The answer lies in the mainsprings of development, which Nick Stern, the World Bank's chief economist, has cast into a framework consisting of two interlocking parts. One is what he calls the "investment climate," the institutional environment in which businesses operate. Where the investment climate is poor, where, for example, start-up businesses are being snuffed out by corrupt officials as they are in an alarming number of countries, or where inadequate infrastructure translates into very high costs, few people manage to escape the poverty trap

(Stern 2002). Yet businesses, large and small, are the main generators of jobs, incomes, taxes, and technological innovation. There is no economic and social development without dynamic firms. As expressed in a recent World Bank book, firms are the means through which knowledge becomes productive (Klein 2003).

The second part of the framework has to do with empowerment. This refers in a broad sense to health, education, civil liberties, political conditions, and so forth. Just as a favorable investment climate enables enterprises to grow, so favorable empowerment conditions enable individuals to find jobs, start small companies, and earn a better living. In short, enterprise and empowerment are mutually reinforcing. Together, they provide ways to escape poverty.

The World Bank has been conducting surveys of company executives in many countries (Schiffer and Weder 2001). These surveys show that small firms are especially vulnerable to poor business environments. Lack of financing, inflation, taxes and tax regulations, policy instability, street crime, and corruption top the list of institutional obstacles for small firms worldwide. Much also can be done to empower people, and this is especially true in Africa. Why do more Africans not become entrepreneurs in the manufacturing sector in Sub-Saharan Africa? And when they do choose to create firms, why do they not become important players? Recent World Bank research on the socioeconomic backgrounds of African entrepreneurs clearly shows that lack of business experience and education are *major* obstacles to African entrepreneurship. Other factors are important, too, such as lack of access to finance and lack of professional networks, but inadequate education stands out as the most important factor preventing the growth of African-owned firms.

In sum, education that meets the unmet demands of aspiring business people matters hugely to development.

Business Schools in Society

The lack of business training does not impede progress only in the manufacturing sector. Governments and aid organizations have worked for decades, trying to move African subsistence farmers into commercial agriculture. This involves the establishment of small general stores where farmers can sell their produce and can buy seeds, tools, and perhaps some fertilizer. All too often such efforts come to no avail because running even the most rudimentary store requires a modicum of business knowledge, of accounting, for example, and no one can be found who possesses such skills. Throughout the developing world, one runs into woeful shortages of competent managers. This is true in the private as well as in the public sector.

The question thus arises as to whether business schools are addressing these needs. Unfortunately, it is thus far the experience of the World Bank that the answer is far from a resounding, "Yes." To determine why this should be the case, it is instructive to look at the situation in the United States first. That is where business schools were invented and where more than 100,000 master's level business students graduate each year. A recent article in the *Bulletin of the Association of Commonwealth Universities* by Sarah Cripps points out "the critical role of business education in economic development [which] is evident from the fact that in the U.S., more jobs are created by M.B.A. [master of business administration] graduates than any other grouping in society" (Cripps 2002: 16). Yet a study by Jeffrey Pfeffer and Christina Fong (2002) of Stanford University, which has received a great deal of attention recently, notes that there has been little evaluation of the impact of business schools on their graduates or the profession of management. The authors argue that "what data there are suggest that business schools are not very effective: Neither possessing an M.B.A. degree nor grades earned in courses correlate with career success, results that question the effectiveness of schools in preparing their students. And, there is little evidence that business school research is influential on management practice, calling into question the professional relevance of management scholarship" (Pfeffer and Fong 2002: 78). This study has generated a wider debate over the value of business education, which will hopefully stimulate more research on these important issues. The evidence, for example, on whether the MBA degree leads to an increase in the earnings of graduates, compared to those who do not go to business school, is conflicting: Some studies have shown a positive correlation, while others have observed no economic gains from the degree. This is not to say that students do not benefit in other ways, most notably by becoming part of high-powered networks, but in terms of educational content and student learning, the research results are mixed.

Raskin (2002), in a *Business 2.0* article, notes that in a recently conducted survey of 1,500 graduates of 18 full-time MBA programs, the Association to Advance Collegiate Schools of Business found that students are not being taught what they need to know to succeed in business. In a nutshell, the survey suggested that many of the top-rated business schools have been caught up by competition for academic excellence at the expense of serving practical real-world business needs. In particular, business school curricula are often of little use in facing everyday problems in developing countries. According to Raskin this lack of real-world focus has resulted in a situation in which few professors have real experience in brand management, team building, or in negotiating business deals (Raskin 2002). He quotes James Bailey, an associate professor at George Washington University's business school as saying that faculty from social science disciplines such as economics and sociology are replacing real-world practitioners in classrooms. He adds that only Harvard and the University of Virginia's Darden, continue to use the case method (Raskin 2002). At the same time, practitioners are not always as skilled as trained faculty in explaining, "Why?" or providing the needed fundamental concepts to students trying to prepare themselves for careers in business.

Clearly, however, a balance between academic theory and practical training is necessary. Business schools have an important role to play in teaching the fundamentals of management education, which provide the basis for more specific training, lifelong learning, and career development. All of what business schools teach may not be directly applicable to an MBA graduate's day-to-day work. A business education should provide a graduate with an understanding of the fundamentals of the theory behind finance, accounting, marketing, and human resource management, for example. MBA students can build on their understanding of the basic tools of management with coursework specializing in particular areas and through internships, while MBA graduates can complement their business education with executive education programs and on-the-job training. Business schools, then, like other professional schools, must offer an education that provides the academic theory and fundamentals of management, as well as practical business skills and training.

Business schools in developing countries have made great strides in developing curricula that provide such education. In the past, only the most elite students had access to high-quality business education and most often had to leave their countries to attend programs in industrialized countries. Now, more students than ever before can attend business schools in their own countries and regions.

Yet, many of these schools still lack sufficient capacity to provide a management education that enables graduates to compete fully in a globalized world. A recent worldwide survey was carried out by the International Finance Corporation (IFC), the member of the World Bank family that deals directly with developing country companies (Chaudhry 2003). The survey asked business executives what they thought of their country's MBA graduates. Across all regions, 28 percent of respondents said that MBAs lacked sufficient work experience and practical knowledge. In Africa, 31 percent said that locally trained MBAs were inadequately prepared, a far higher proportion than in the other regions. Such responses suggest that developing-country business schools share some of the basic problems found in the more affluent countries.

Pressure for greater societal relevance is coming not only from employers but also from the students themselves. Indeed, there is strong demand for what is broadly defined as "social entrepreneurship." Social entrepreneurship consists, for example, in managing microcredit institutions and nongovernmental organizations (NGOs), or helping small businesses. In this regard, the IFC has taken such actions as sponsoring internships for MBA students from some of the world's most prestigious schools. These students spend the summer in small firms in developing and transition countries, working in teams with local business students. The first time this was attempted, ten internships ·were advertised, and the IFC received 780 applications. Even considering the very depressed labor market in the Organization for Economic Cooperation and Development (OECD) countries at the time (the first batch of interns was sent out in July 2003), this suggests enormous interest in social entrepreneurship on the part of students. Yet, in the words of a Wharton newsletter, "The limiting factor is faculty who cannot see these concerns as becoming important business issues" (Wharton School 2003).

Based on the above, there is no doubt in the minds of those at the IFC who are involved in business education that the potential contribution of business schools to society is substantial. For example, in the wake of Enron and other such disasters, the world is focusing on corporate governance. Business schools are ideally positioned to dispense knowledge about how boards of directors function and should be functioning, about the rights of minority shareholders, and other important aspects of corporate governance.

Another important contribution to society, which business schools are making, but in which they could have a much larger role, is entrepreneurial education geared to the needs of small and medium-sized enterprises (SMEs). Just as traditional banks increasingly realize that microcredit activities represent a lucrative market for them, business schools could expand their executive development courses for managers of SMEs. Such courses need to be user-friendly for the clients who are running small firms. Even small firms are usually willing to pay to acquire knowledge, if it is of value to them. Indeed, their willingness to pay is a required market test, without which such education programs could not be sustained long. Besides providing executive education, business schools can also help small and medium-sized enterprises link up with larger companies and become part of a dynamic value chain. Reaching out more to the small- and medium-firm market will generate some additional revenue for the schools and will provide a golden opportunity to begin to reshape curricula so as to make them more relevant to real-world local business problems. The University of Cape Town Center for Innovation and Entrepreneurship is a very promising starting point.

Another example is the IFC initiative designed to strengthen local NGO networks providing education and training to small business entrepreneurs. Recognizing that a small increase in productivity will have a significant economic impact with the sector that provides 75–95 percent of employment, they are providing support to increase the capacity and effectiveness of existing networks. One such program, developed by FUNDES and introduced with the Tec de Monterrey in Mexico, has trained professors and students with practical business diagnostic tools and methodologies that are applied with local entrepreneurs through six-month student internships. The program has generated benefits for all parties. The business owner gets relatively inexpensive interns backed by university professors and FUNDES-trained consultants; the student gets a feel for what an entrepreneur faces, probably experiencing the challenges of making a profit for the first time; and the university and FUNDES gain a potential future client for their business courses. The results after just three years are very positive. Not only have entrepreneurs requested more interns (1,500 to date), but they are willing to pay more for them. The reason for this is that instead of producing theoretical term papers, the interns have to roll up their sleeves and apply basic analytical tools to the most pressing problems identified by a standard business diagnostic. The program has now been successfully expanded to five other countries and seven universities in Latin America. The IFC began transferring the FUNDES programs to eight African countries last year.

Governments also have an important role to play in meeting local needs. Large firms send executives for business training, but few SMEs can afford this. Following the examples of New Zealand, and more recently the thirty-two signatory countries to the Bologna Declaration in Europe, governments are realizing the importance of frameworks that will accommodate "transferability of credits" for "certified" education and training. The European countries will share a common framework of degrees by 2010. In the case of business schools, such a system enables a manager completing an executive development course, for example, to earn credits toward a more formal qualification, which takes account of what has been learned. Portable credits enable staff of even small firms to identify and develop career paths. Such a system could transform the lives of people working in small firms, who are presently excluded from most lifelong learning opportunities. To take such a system a step further, governments, firms, business associations, and universities could work together to establish Industry Training Organizations. Such organizations may be able to reach out to the SME sector more effectively and provide more affordable and scalable support services for workforce training. In order for these examples to bear fruit, government must think of itself less as "a controller" and more as "an enabler" that can facilitate the development of lifelong learning systems supported by quality-based regulations and incentives.

Business education at the high-school level is also important. In the case mentioned above of a small rural general store, lots of farmers might have been able to improve their lives had a high-school graduate been available who knew how to keep books. Business schools can have a role in helping to train high-school business teachers. Even a small amount of training may help the smallest businesses. A German business professor experimented with one- and two-day training of African entrepreneurs running tiny businesses. This training focused on crucial elements of entrepreneurial orientation, on how to be proactive rather than reactive, and on elementary planning. A year after the courses took place, the businesses of those who had taken them were doing better than control groups.

Strengthening Capacity

The broad picture that emerges is one in which business schools can help to alleviate the acute shortages of competent managers in poor countries, but that they have a very long way to go. In Africa in particular, South Africa is fortunate in that it has several good business schools that can advance such efforts. Other African countries are far less well endowed in business education. The same is true to some degree in every developing country. Everywhere there is need for substantial capacity building so that schools can extend their reach and increase their impact on society. Such capacity building is, of course, a long-term proposition, but getting the process started is urgent.

Development of faculty and research capacity in developing-country business schools is especially important. A key finding of *Peril and Promise,* a recent report of the World Bank/United Nations Educational, Scientific and Cultural Organization (UNESCO) Task Force on Higher Education in Developing Countries, is the critical importance of striving to "increase the amount and quality of in-country research, thus allowing the developing world to select, absorb, and create new knowledge more efficiently and rapidly than it currently does" (World Bank 2000: 10). Enhancing the research capacity of developing country business schools will also enable them to better adapt their curricula to local circumstances and needs.

Part of the problem currently facing business education, especially at the graduate level, comes from the fact that international aid donors have moved away from supporting schools of business management during the past ten or fifteen years. Before then, for example, bilateral aid agencies and international foundations devoted substantial resources to establishing and nurturing developing country business schools. Several of Africa's best schools were created with such support. Outside Africa, Lahore University of Management Sciences in Pakistan and Integrating Competitiveness and the Environment in Central America are examples of successful bilateral assistance to institutions of business management that have enabled fruitful, and in fact essential, institutional partnerships with Harvard Business School as the provider of technical assistance. In recent years, however, the focus of donors shifted to basic education, to the neglect of support for higher education. Today, except to some extent in countries of the former Soviet Union, the international development community is paying amazingly little attention to business education. Yet unless more is done to train local managers, how are poor countries ever going to compete? The *Peril and Promise* report determined that education strategies in developing countries should not focus solely on primary education alone. If this is the case the societies will be dangerously unprepared to face the challenges of the future (World Bank 2000). It concluded that higher education is important to both the present and future of the developing world. Although higher education does not guarantee rapid economic development, sustained progress is impossible without it. This is certainly true in the realm of management education as in other areas. Fortunately, the G7 countries are beginning to hear the message. At their Evian meeting, capacity building *for the private sector* was included, for the first time, in the development agenda.

The World Bank had already begun to respond to this need. With governments of the developing countries, the World Bank Institute is working on business education on a number of fronts. For example, the African Virtual University offers courses in business administration.

At the IFC, the Health and Education Department has invested in a number of universities that offer business education, specifically in Peru, Turkey, and Argentina. As the relevance of business education becomes more clearly appreciated, the IFC is seeing increasing activity in this subsector and expects to be working with many more universities in other parts of the world.

The IFC has also started a venture that is specifically designed to address capacity building in the form of the Global Business School Network. This network embraces many of the world's top business schools, who signed on to the initiative. Faculty of these schools stand ready to partner with developing country schools and so provide capacity building.

Conclusion

In conclusion, while it is not disputed that investing in primary education is and should be a priority for developing countries—after all, Elizabeth Bennet and Darcy eventually got married, so there was some truth to what was universally accepted—but consideration should also be given to the broader developmental framework outlined at the beginning of this chapter. This is the framework that encompasses economic growth by considering the investment climate and empowerment. The main point this chapter has sought to make regarding this framework is that growth and empowerment are mutually reinforcing. Growth, and especially the growth of businesses, is the main source of new jobs, new purchasing power, and increased consumption. Without jobs and income, people are also without a voice, indeed often lacking the self-respect that comes with holding a job. Conversely, without sufficient investment in health and education, many persons will be unable to find or to hold a job. Empowerment understood in this sense is a prerequisite for widespread growth, just as growth is necessary in order to widen empowerment. Management education contributes to growth as well as empowerment. It is time for societies to pay more attention to the future of business education and how it can contribute more to local as well as global needs.

References

Chaudhry, A. 2003. "The International Finance Corporation's MBA Survey: How Developing Country Firms Rate Local Business School Training." Global Business School Network, International Finance Corporation. Policy Research Working Paper 3182. Washington DC: World Bank.

Cripps, S. 2002. "Business Schools and Development: An African Model." *Bulletin of the Association of Commonwealth Universities*, no. 150: 16–18.

Klein, M. 2003. "Ways Out of Poverty: Diffusing Best Practices and Creating Capabilities—Perspectives on Policies for Poverty Reduction." Policy Research Working Paper, WPS 2990. Washington, DC: World Bank.

Pfeffer, J., and C. Fong. 2002. "The End of Business Schools? Less Success Than Meets the Eye." *Academy of Management Learning and Education* 1, no. 1: 78–95. Available at www.aomonline.org/Publications/Articles/BSchools.asp (accessed December 10, 2004).

Raskin, A. 2002. "What's an MBA Worth?" Available at www.business2.com.

Schiffer, M., and B. Weder. 2001. "Firm Size and the Business Environment: Worldwide Survey of Results." Washington, DC: World Bank.

Stern, N. 2002. "A Strategy for Development." Washington, DC: World Bank.

Wharton School. 2003. "Knowledge@Wharton. The Triple Bottom Line: Student Activists Demand More from B-schools." *Public Policy and Management*. Available at www.net-impact.org/index.php?id=795 (accessed December 10, 2004).

World Bank/United Nations Educational, Scientific and Cultural Organization (UNESCO) Task Force on Higher Education and Society. 2000. "Higher Education in Developing Countries: Peril and Promise." Washington, DC.

20

Education, Management, and the World's Work

Leadership Traits of Educators in Undeveloped and Developing Countries, Focusing on Uganda in Sub-Saharan Africa

Romie F. Littrell and Peter Baguma

Richard America, discussing the issues and outcomes of the United Nations World Summit on Sustainable Development held in Johannesburg, South Africa, August and September 2003, comments, "In all their discussions, however, very little attention was paid to the issue that may be the most important to the development of African nations—modern advanced management education. Development of Africa by indigenous peoples has been slowed or prevented by poor or nonexistent management training; the public sector is often mismanaged; success in private enterprise is hindered by a lack of well-trained senior and middle managers capable of competently operating in modern business, government, and economic systems" (America 2003: 1). In this chapter we will discuss various aspects of management and leadership in Sub-Saharan Africa and Uganda, present the results of a research project investigating subordinates' preferences for explicit leader behavior there, and compare the results to those from other geocultural areas.

Management Education: Where to Start?

Management Education Starts in Primary School

A nation's universities do not matter if no one in a country is educated to a level at which they can benefit from continuing education. In some countries

in Sub-Saharan Africa, fewer than half of children ages six to eleven attend
school (Sperling 2001). Universal schooling would produce big gains in health
and income standards. Sperling states that each year of additional schooling
in poor countries can raise a child's future earning power by 10–20 percent
and that research (sic: unreferenced by Sperling) suggests that, with globalization and technological innovation, substantial education can raise wages
even more, even in developing countries. Other studies show that access to
education will be critical in determining whether new trade brings increased
opportunity or inequality in these nations. Elementary and postsecondary
education have been made universally available in Uganda in recent years,
though the "universal" aspect suffers from the same economic restrictions
observed in virtually all countries (personal comment, Peter Baguma).

Expanding access to quality education can also facilitate agreement on a
second divisive issue: fighting abusive child labor in developing countries.
Efforts to outlaw exploitation without a corresponding commitment to universal education often simply leads to children being moved from dangerous
factories to drug-running, brothels, or starvation. However, genuinely free
schooling, with no fees or high costs for uniforms, transport, and textbooks,
encourages impoverished families to rethink their decision to send their children out to work when education becomes an affordable alternative.

A common failure in the use of aid flowing from developed to undeveloped and developing countries is local diversion of funds to personal, private, or unintended uses, leading to a failure to maximize opportunities for
improvement and a subsequent reluctance to provide additional aid.

The chief providers of aid for education in developing and undeveloped
countries, the World Bank, the United Nations Educational, Scientific and
Cultural Organization, and the United Nations International Children's Emer-
gency Fund, need to work with other donors to develop an effective structure
for a global fund or global alliance for basic education. These parties need to
come to the table with a plan to ensure that education initiatives are a collaboration between rich and poor nations, designed to meet donors' concerns
that resources are used effectively and developing countries' concerns that
intervention will not override their sovereignty in educating their own people.

Such a framework can be built and survive only if built on trust. Donors
must see that their funds are being applied as intended, with minimal waste
and corruption, to ensure effectiveness and maximize participation from donors and education recipients.

In Sub-Saharan Africa, only 3 percent of individuals over the age of twenty
have a postschool educational qualification. Research by the World Bank
shows an 89 percent correlation between the levels of tertiary education in a
nation and important economic indicators such as gross domestic product

(GDP) per capita, or labor productivity per capita (Nevin 2003). Cost is often the reason. Nevin points out a project in South Africa, the South African free tertiary institution, Community and Individual Development Association (CIDA) University, which allows financially disabled students to obtain business degrees at no cost. The question of support arises. Formal tertiary education is expensive; to support such expenditures as free universities requires a government with money, and governments with money exist in countries where a high proportion of the populace have higher-education degrees.

Not unexpectedly, CIDA University was made possible by the private sector. Founding partners include Puregas, Monitor Company, and Investec Limited. CIDA's "platinum" level partners include Investec, First National Bank, Dimension Data, KPMG, MTN, and the Kellogg Foundation. The "gold" partners are African Bank and Corpcapital. Other companies providing support are Microsoft, McGraw-Hill publishers, and technology equipment suppliers Amalgamated Appliances. PricewaterhouseCoopers donated the accountancy degree.

Costs of tertiary education are generally very high in Africa, relative to per capita income. In South Africa, the average cost to the country to educate a university student per year is around R35,000 to R40,000 per annum, and over R100,000 for a degree. However, only 15 percent of students currently graduate with their degree or diploma, so the true cost of producing a graduate is between R700,000 and R1.3 million. Nonetheless, higher education is of critical importance for the long-term social stability, progress, and competitiveness of Africa in a global marketplace.

Defining Effective Management Education

For management and leadership development programs in a tertiary education institution, one must distinguish between the academic and nonacademic functions of a typical institution. In some countries, academic departments/ units do not display the same authority hierarchies that are typical of the administrative/managerial support systems.

The academic side of the enterprise is analogous to what organization theory calls "associations." Professional partnerships and clergy are other examples. Tenured academics, partners, and clergy may not be considered as employees of a university, partnership, or church, but as members. In academic circles, this is expressed in the phrase "community of scholars." Academic leadership is not described in line-management terms, but rather by such phrases as "first among equals." The vice chancellor may or may not be a chief executive, or the dean a general manager, or the academic head of the department a manager. The work of a senior lecturer or a professor in an academic department is essentially the same work—teaching, research, and professional service. In a university, for example, rank is typically achieved by peer revue based on the professional quality of the incumbent's teaching, research, and professional service. The same applies to achievement of tenure.

The administration of a higher education institution, on the other hand, is organized hierarchically, with clear levels of responsibility and accountability, line and staff functions whether in academic, financial, or physical plant administration. The registrar of an academic institution is not the "first among equals." The decision making in an institution's human resource or finance department should follow general for-profit business practices.

The Centre for Higher Education Transformation (CHET), in South Africa, has stated that in addition to generic challenges, higher education in South Africa is confronted with challenges that are the product of a particular history and context. These challenges are related to the systemic flaws in the system of higher education inherited by South Africa's democratic government.

- Higher education is fragmented, inefficient, and there is no policy or plan for the country;
- Student access is grossly skewed and unequal; major inequalities exist in staffing, most academic and administrative posts are held by whites, and women are underrepresented in senior academic and administrative posts;
- Delivery of quality undergraduate education remains a problem, success rates are low, and throughput and graduation rates are poor;
- Research output is uneven, and national and institutional governance structures are inadequate.

These are statements concerning the system in a country generally considered to be the most developed nation in Africa, and we can assume that they are pandemic.

The Harvard Business School Executive Education course, Leadership Best Practices, suggests some organizational process issues requiring the presence and action of a leader:

- Time of crisis;
- Organizational change;
- Organizational conflict;
- Leadership transitions.

The issues enumerated by CHET indicate a requirement for education programs for development of leaders in Africa. There are research findings concerning Africa reviewed above. A recent project discussed below has collected data from teachers in Uganda concerning desirable leader behaviors.

The Study of Leadership

Bennis and Nanus point out that "a business short on capital can borrow money, and one with a poor location can move. But a business short on leadership has little chance for survival" (1985: 20). Leadership has quite probably been a topic of study since the evolution of sentient creatures. It appears possible to make a case for an "evolutionary" emergence of leaders and leadership, for if a group requires a leader and one does not emerge, the group does not survive. From this point of view, the specific characteristics of a leader might be unimportant, so long as one emerges, perhaps a clue to a reason for the plethora of definitions of leaders and leadership.

In 1990, Bass identified some 3,000 studies of leadership in the academic literature. Other reviews (House, Wright, and Aditya 1997; Littrell 2002a) indicate many theories of leadership, each supported by a body of research, and each criticized by a body of research calling the theories into question.

Most definitions of leadership accept that to be a leader one must have followers. After this, they begin to diverge. Whatever a naive literature on leadership may give us to understand, leaders cannot choose their styles at will; what is feasible depends to a large extent on the cultural conditioning of one's subordinates (Hofstede 1980: 7).

In the Western functionalist paradigm, leadership is legitimized largely on the basis of performance. It is dependent also on the level of support received from subordinates, hence the current emphasis on teamwork, empowerment, employee satisfaction, and morale. The emphasis placed on the leader's central role in building organizational culture implies the necessity to cultivate employee commitment, involvement, and morale. A leader fails to do this at his or her peril, as followership is earned and subordinates are keenly aware of their formal and informal power to dethrone or, at the very least, unsettle leaders.

Blunt and Jones point out that "many theories of leadership have been developed in the last 50 years. Like most other theories of human behavior, however, ways of testing these theories and, hence, of establishing their scientific credentials have remained elusive. The result is that such theories can be assessed only in terms of the intuitive appeal of the explanations they offer, rather than by their ability to withstand repeated attempts to falsify predictions drawn from them following conventional norms of scientific testing (see for example, Blunt, 1991; Popper, 1959). Theories of leadership which have fallen from favor are therefore more likely to have been victims of changes in fashion in the broad field of management than of anything else" (Blunt and Jones 1997: 10).

Leadership vs. Management

In business and business education, we have the never-ending story of separating leadership and management. Review of the literature concerning management, management across cultures, leadership, and cross-cultural leadership seems to indicate that we cannot separate leadership and management. They are perhaps one continuum of behavior, or, more likely, a set of interrelated continua, all or some of which may or may not be necessary in evaluating effective leadership and management in a single culture or across cultures. A reasonable conclusion is that when a competent manager needs a leader to accomplish organizational objectives, he or she finds one. Similarly, when a competent leader needs a manager to accomplish organizational objectives, one is found. A frequently encountered thread in the study of leadership is the use of the concepts "visionary leader" and "administrative leader." The "administrative leader" appears to be a management position.

In 1988, U.S. business educator Peter F. Drucker pointed out that the fundamental task of management is to make people capable of joint performance by giving them common goals and values, the right structure, and the ongoing training and development needed to perform and respond to change. During this period, the largest single group in the U.S. workforce, more than one-third of the total workforce, was classified as managerial and professional. Drucker notes that it is management that enables the more than a million U.S. college graduates a year to be put into productive work. The application of management to manual work, in the form of training, was important for its impact on enterprise. It was leadership in management, not technological innovation that made Japan a great economic power.

In the United States, ownership of public companies has shifted to institutional trustees of employees, primarily through pension funds. In 1986, U.S. employees owned more than 40 percent of U.S. companies' equity capital. The big issue was how to make the interests of shareholders compatible with economic and social needs.

Similarly, according to Drucker, the critical question for developing countries is how to create an adequate managerial knowledge base quickly to promote economic development. The job of the leaders of education in developing countries is still how to create an education system that will develop an adequate managerial knowledge base quickly to promote economic development, and how to make the interests of education and business stakeholders compatible with economic and social needs.

Leadership in Africa

Ugwuegbu states "problems of leadership in African organizations are responsible for the underdevelopment of organizations in many African countries" (2001: 65). He also states that many of the problems are due to the heritage of colonial governments as well as due to the fragmented ethnic and religious societies in Africa (68–69). These ideas are also espoused by Sow's African personality and psychopathology model. Chisholm, in a qualitative analysis of interviews with managers in education in South Africa, found that leadership competence was associated with "masculinity, rationality, and whiteness" (2001: 387), and a further comment, "white, male, middle-class, and heterosexual" (389).

The Colonial Heritage

Bierschenk (2003) and Geschiere (1993) reviewed French and British rule in colonial Africa. Typical of their conclusions, Geschiere, in a study of colonial Cameroon, indicates a continuous tug-of-war between the imposition of the management practices of the colonial powers and the ethnic practices, opinions, attitudes, and beliefs of the local peoples. A not unexpected result of this tug-of-war is the formation of a hybrid culture accommodating sufficiently the needs of the members of the leadership and management cadre, proposed by Graen and Hui (1996) and Heimer and Vince (1998), and supported by Littrell (2003). In a case study of multiethnic work teams, Heimer and Vince (1998) found that at the initial stages of their formation, the teams seem to move in one of two directions: toward the setting up of a "safe hybrid culture" for highly heterogeneous teams, or toward a "dominant culture" in more moderately heterogeneous contexts. Sustainable learning and change within international teams is created out of a further stage of development, the "challenging hybrid culture," capitalizing upon the multicultural synergies. Depending upon the initiative and competence of the leader and manager players in hybrid colonial-leader–local-leader interactions, we expect to see hybrid cultures of various characteristics emerging. The lasting effect of these hybrid cultures is, of course, a function of the time in power of the colonial government, the kinds of programs and interactions between the colonial and local leaders, and the "strength" of a local culture in maintaining itself.

Ethnic Diversity and Managerial Effectiveness in South Africa

Ghosh (2001) and Thomas and Bendixen (2000) examined the influence of ethnic diversity on organizational culture and effectiveness in South Africa. Thomas and Bendixen interviewed 586 South African middle managers, all of whom had hiring and firing authority. They identified 14 demographic subgroups of managers to control for sex, color, race, and geographic region, and interviewed a minimum of 20 managers from each subgroup. Those subgroups included white, English-speaking males and females; white, Afrikaans-speaking males and females; Asian males and females; mixed-race males and females; black Xhosa-speaking males and females; black Zulu-speaking males and females; and black Sotho-speaking males and females.

The researchers measured dimensions of each manager's ethnic culture using well-established cultural values based on research by Geert Hofstede: power distance, individualism, masculinity, uncertainty avoidance, and long-term orientation. Thomas and Bendixen gathered data on each manager's management culture and effectiveness through interviews with their subordinates.

Despite the managers' identification with their ethnic group, there was a common national culture at the managerial level. The dimensions of that national culture, including a high degree of individualism and a low tolerance for hierarchical differences in power, resemble those found in the Netherlands, England, and the United States. The authors suggest these similarities may indicate the historical impact of Dutch, British, and American cultures on South Africa, as well as the prevalence of British and American systems of management.

However, the low scores on tolerance for hierarchical power distribution may also be a reflection of South Africa's present political and ideological scenario, which promotes the values of participation and democracy. As Thomas and Bendixen indicate, such a scenario is, perhaps, an outcome of the past oppression of many ethnic groups that has resulted in an intolerance of hierarchy and authoritarianism.

Thomas and Bendixen note that the high scores in individualism deviate from previous studies on national culture in South Africa and the generally collectivist nature of African culture. They offer two potential explanations for the discrepancy:

1. Organizational cultures, which are largely shaped by American or British systems of management, may have influenced the cultural values expressed by the managers in the study; or
2. The apparent contradiction can be reconciled by the special nature of African collectivism in which individuals act autonomously, but remain socially united, a concept that has been referred to as communalism. As a form of collectivism, communalism coexists with personal freedom or individualism.

The authors also found that neither ethnicity nor race significantly influenced management culture; similarly, management effectiveness was independent of both ethnicity and race. Together, these findings suggest that management culture and management effectiveness are not affected by either culture or race in South Africa.

The results indicate that, despite a tumultuous history that includes apartheid, the country's ethnic diversity does not harm its management productivity. They also suggest that education and experience are viable tools to enhance management culture and effectiveness, and may ultimately increase South Africa's level of global competitiveness. Clearly, these empirical findings reinforce a management philosophy that underscores the benefits of diversity in the workplace.

On the other hand, Roodt (1997: 16) found that the typical South African corporate environment reflects the following characteristics and identified fears of what is to come:

- A "them and us" culture, which delineates a predominantly white management minority from the general workforce, which is a predominantly black and unskilled majority;
- Affirmative action and its prospects as new criteria for jobs and promotion create a great deal of stress and a mixture of aspirations, peer group pressure, and fear for job security;
- Adverse labor relations with very strong union backing and the tendency towards conflict and violence;
- Ethnic and language diversity within the workplace, faction fighting, as well as the way in which people continued to stereotype one other;
- The existing privilege and discrimination practices based mainly on race and ethnicity despite changes in legislation;
- The wealth and poverty gap that exists between the "haves" and the "have-nots"; and
- Illiteracy that is rife between the greater portion of the labor force and the ever-increasing demands of technology and skills, rendering the majority of the Black population unemployable.

Some Other Cultural Dimensions in Africa

Smith, Peterson, and Schwartz (2002) found African cultures to depend upon superiors and rules for guidance and that these traits are associated with collectivism and cultural embeddedness, hierarchy, power distance, mastery, and masculinity. Most of the nations of Africa are especially high on these cultural dimensions. Their regression analysis indicates that power distance

and mastery provide the most concise estimate of the country-level corre-
lates of reliance on hierarchical sources for guidance.

Specific Characteristics of Leadership in Africa

According to Blunt and Jones (1997):
- In Sub-Saharan Africa, economic psychology is generally characterized by powerful connections between objects, humans, and the supernatu-
ral; the emphasis put on each of these elements and the interrelationships
among them can vary from one ethnic group or tribe to another (Blunt and
Jones 1992). Self-reliance and self-interest tend to take a back seat to ethnicity
and group loyalty (Dia 1994: 176).
- In Africa, individual achievements frequently are much less valued than
are interpersonal relations. The value of economic transactions lies as much,
if not more, in the ritual surrounding them and their capacity to reinforce
group ties as it does in their worth to the parties involved. Wealth is, first,
extended family or clan wealth, and, second, ethnic or tribal wealth; often it
can be acquired legitimately at the expense of the organization (Dia 1994).
In many circumstances, ceremony, ritual, interpersonal relations, reciproc-
ity, and the distribution of scant resources to clan and ethnic affiliates are
therefore natural responsibilities of leadership in Africa (Kolawole 1996;
Nzelibe 1986; Warren, Adedokun, and Omolaoye 1996).
- African societies tend to be egalitarian within age groups, but hierarchical or gerontocratic between age groups (Linquist and Adolph 1996). As a
result, leaders often behave, and are expected to behave, paternalistically
(Jones, Blunt, and Sharma 1995). Leaders bestow favor and expect and receive obeisance or deference. Consensus is highly valued and decision making within levels can therefore take a long time (see Cosway and Anankum
1996). Between levels (downward) observance of hierarchy means that consensus can be achieved relatively quickly (Blunt 1978, 1983; Dia 1994).
- African societies seem to have a great capacity also for tolerance and
forgiveness, which can explain the attempts at reconciliation with former
oppressors by African leaders like Jomo Kenyatta, Robert Mugabe, and Nelson
Mandela. Many observers have wondered at this capacity to forgive and for-
get. This image of the benign acceptance of past wrongs is epitomized by
Nelson Mandela who, after three decades of imprisonment comes out, becomes an architect of black/white reconciliation, then goes to beg white terrorists who are prepared to fast until death, "Please, please, don't kill
yourselves. Please eat." This man, who had just lost twenty-seven of the best
years of his life, goes to beg white terrorists not to fast until death. Where
else but in Africa will you find this sort of thing? (Mazrui 1994: 134).

• Considerable emphasis is placed on a leader's ability to honor his or her obligations to ethnic affiliates, without denying others to an extent that causes conflict to break out into the open (Nzelibe 1986). It is expected that the organization will not pull together because of ethnic and/or family-based cleavages.

• Followers appear to prefer a leader who is kindly, considerate, and understanding to one who is too dynamic and productive and, possibly, too demanding. Leaders are seen to possess genuine authority, but are expected by their subordinates to use it only sparingly and in a humane and considerate way.

The above statements are supported by an empirical study conducted in Botswana by Jones, Blunt, and Sharma (1995) in which public sector managers reported that they perceive effective leaders primarily as those who provide clear direction and targets, accompanied by a paternal and supportive management style. Other researchers, Brown (1989), Leonard (1987, 1988) and Montgomery (1986, 1987), point to the preoccupation of African leaders with stability and internal administrative order.

The findings are consistent with the definition of high power distance, which is a central feature of many African cultures. In a society where power is concentrated at the top, even quite senior managers will not be in positions where they can set the direction or pace of change. Those above them will decide these matters, and decisions to be implemented will be passed down. The leader's job then becomes one of operationalizing directions received from above, making them clear to subordinates and providing advice and support.

Such responses suggest that African managers are concerned overwhelmingly about the quality of their relationship with their boss, rather than, for example, with individual or organizational effectiveness. That is, internal interpersonal issues predominate over those associated with the organization's performance, its long-term strategies, its clients, and its external environment. The effective manager is perceived to consult subordinates, treat them considerately, promote their self-development, support and help them, and provide them with clear direction. In this view, good managers are people oriented rather than task oriented. The phrases used by several respondents in the Botswana research (Jones, Blunt, and Sharma 1995) to describe the ideal boss—"teacher" and "father figure"—illustrate nicely the relationship with the boss that seems to be valued.

The impression that emerges from the Botswana data is of an organizational culture where authority is exercised in a rather paternal way and where deference to authority figures is high. This type of hierarchical relationship involves also a degree of dependence on seniors by more junior individuals, and this is accepted as normal.

An Instrument to Measure Explicit Leadership Behavior: The Leader Behavior Description Questionnaire XII

The Leader Behavior Description Questionnaire (LBDQ) XII has been used in several countries to study leadership behavior. Littrell (2002b) compared the results of several studies employing the LBDQ XII. The results were obtained using a Likert-style scale with 1 indicating that the ideal leader should never exhibit the behavior, and 5 indicating that the leader should always exhibit the behavior, with the anchor points:

Always = 5   Often = 4   Occasionally = 3   Seldom = 2   Never = 1

The original development of the Leader Behavior Description Questionnaire at Ohio State University in the United States identified two major characteristic behaviors of leaders: task orientation and nurturance of the members of the group. Stogdill (1963) redesigned the instrument into twelve factors. The twelve LBDQ XII subscales represent a complex and varied pattern of explicit leadership behavior described as follows:

Factor 1.   Representation: measures to what degree the manager speaks as the representative of the group.

Factor 2.   Demand reconciliation: reflects how well the manager reconciles conflicting demands and reduces disorder in the system.

Factor 3.   Tolerance of uncertainty: depicts to what extent the manager is able to tolerate uncertainty and postponement without anxiety or getting upset.

Factor 4.   Persuasiveness: measures to what extent the manager uses persuasion and argument effectively; exhibits strong convictions.

Factor 5.   Initiation of structure: measures to what degree the manager clearly defines own role, and lets followers know what is expected.

Factor 6.   Tolerance of freedom: reflects to what extent the manager allows followers scope for initiative, decision, and action.

Factor 7.   Role assumption: measures to what degree the manager exercises actively the leadership role rather than surrendering leadership to others.

Factor 8.   Consideration: depicts to what extent the manager regards the comfort, well-being, status, and contributions of followers.

Factor 9.   Production emphasis: measures to what degree the manager applies pressure for productive output.

Factor 10.   Predictive accuracy: measures to what extent the manager exhibits foresight and ability to predict outcomes accurately.

Table 20.1

Average Scores for Factors, Uganda

Factor:	Mean scores	Standard deviation
1. Representation	3.95	0.78
5. Initiation of structure	3.86	0.72
11. Integration	3.81	0.89
9. Production emphasis	3.74	0.68
12. Superior orientation	3.73	0.65
4. Persuasiveness	3.63	0.70
7. Role assumption	3.57	0.56
2. Demand reconciliation	3.32	0.79
10. Predictive accuracy	3.31	0.85
8. Consideration	3.24	0.65
6. Tolerance of freedom	3.00	0.72
3. Tolerance of uncertainty	2.98	0.51
Average all factors	3.51	

Factor 11. Integration: reflects to what degree the manager maintains a closely knit organization; resolves intermember conflicts.

Factor 12. Superior orientation: measures to what extent the manager maintains cordial relations with superiors; has influence with them; is striving for higher status.

Initial cross-cultural use by Black and Porter (1991) and Selmer (1997) reported acceptable reliability and validity in cross-cultural use. "Cross-cultural" reliability and validity are difficult to define, as the instrument must measure both similarities and differences across cultures that are inherently different, each consisting of individuals that differ one from the other within the culture.

LBDQ XII Scores from Uganda

From Table 20.1, for educators in Uganda, factors with high average scores, indicating desirable leader behaviors, were found to be as follows.

More desirable behaviors for Uganda educators include:

Factor 1. Representation: the manager should speak as the representative of the group.

Factor 5. Initiation of structure: the manager should clearly define own role and let followers know what is expected. This finding is supported by the study in Botswana by Jones, Blunt, and Sharma

(1995), in which public sector managers reported that they perceive effective leaders primarily as those who provide clear direction and targets, accompanied by a paternal and supportive management style.

The findings are consistent with the definition of high power distance, which is a central feature of many African cultures. In a society where power is concentrated at the top, even quite senior managers will not be in positions where they can set the direction or pace of change. Those above them will decide these matters, and decisions to be implemented will be passed down. The leader's job then becomes one of operationalizing directions received from above, making them clear to subordinates and providing advice and support.

Factor 11. Integration: the manager should maintain a closely knit organization and resolve intermember conflicts, consistent with a parental management style, consistently reported in the literature review above as an important aspect of African organizational culture.

Factor 9. Production emphasis: the manager should apply pressure for productive output. This is an "anti-empowerment." High scores for this factor were also observed in Mainland Chinese samples. This is in contrast to the conclusions above from Blunt and Jones (1997), indicating that followers appear to prefer a leader who is kindly, considerate, and understanding to one who is too dynamic and productive, and, possibly, too demanding. Leaders are seen to possess genuine authority but are expected by their subordinates to use it only sparingly and in a humane and considerate way. A possible explanation is in support of a high power distance, hierarchical leadership system where "the manager manages and the workers work."

Factor 12. Superior orientation: the manager should maintain cordial relations with superiors, develop influence with them, and strive for higher status. This high score is predicted from Jones, Blunt, and Sharma (1995) in discussions above, suggesting that African managers are concerned overwhelmingly about the quality of their relationship with their boss, rather than, for example, with individual or organizational effectiveness.

Factor 4. Persuasiveness: measures to what extent the manager uses persuasion and argument effectively; exhibits strong convictions.

Factor 7. Role assumption: measures to what degree the manager exercises actively the leadership role rather than surrendering leadership to others.

These results are generally supported by the conclusions of Blunt and Jones (1997). The low average scores on demand reconciliation and consideration could be explained in terms of Frederick Herzberg's Two-Factor theory, where these factors fall into the hygiene category (Herzberg 1968). If these extrinsic factors are absent, they may cause demotivation, but are an ingrained aspect of the local culture and as such are expected, and their presence is perhaps not even noticed.

For educators in Uganda, factors with relatively low average scores, indicating less desirable leader behaviors, were found to be:

Factor 2.   Demand reconciliation: reflects how well the manager reconciles conflicting demands and reduces disorder to system.

Factor 10. Predictive accuracy: measures to what extent the manager exhibits foresight and ability to predict outcomes accurately.

Factor 8.   Consideration: depicts to what extent the manager regards the comfort, well-being, status and contributions of followers.

Factor 6.   Tolerance of freedom: reflects to what extent the manager allows followers scope for initiative, decision, and action.

Factor 3.   Tolerance of uncertainty: depicts to what extent the manager is able to tolerate uncertainty and postponement without anxiety or getting upset.

The sets of more and less desirable behaviors, such as the data of Smith, Peterson, and Schwartz (2002), indicate a preference for high power distance on the part of education leaders in Uganda. The less desirable behaviors indicate a lower requirement for "employee empowerment" behaviors and for behaviors indicating "Western" performance competence than generally found in "Western" samples.

Meta-Analysis of Previous LBDQ XII Studies

To place the Ugandan sample in the context of available data, samples are available from seven surveys and the original surveys by Stogdill, yielding fifteen identified groups.

1. Littrell and Valentin (Ro, in preparation), 40 randomly selected managers in Romania, collected in 2003;

2. Black and Porter 1991 (B&P US, B&P HK, HK-US B&P): 77 respondents from 200 randomly selected U.S. citizens who were managers working in Hong Kong, compared with 53 from 115 randomly selected executive education participants from a western U.S. university, and 39 Hong Kong Chinese managers.

3. Littrell 2002b (Table 20.2 columns "CN 1999 M" for managers and "CN 1999 S" for supervisors): 122 managers and supervisors in a complex of two hotels in central China.

4. Littrell 2003: columns "CN 2002 M" and "CN 1999 S."

5. Lucas and colleagues 1992 (Lucas U.S. M, Lucas US Sub): Of 300 questionnaires distributed to defense plant employees in the United States, 178 were returned: 35 from management and 143 from labor (technical workers).

6. Schneider and Littrell 2003 (GB and DE): United Kingdom: 36 respondents from 100 randomly selected managers; Germany: 46 respondents from 100 randomly selected managers.

7. Selmer 1997 (HK Sel): 240 managers self-identified as having worked for both Hong Kong expatriate managers in Hong Kong, from 2,396 graduates of the School of Business of Hong Kong Baptist University.

8. Stogdill 1963 (U.S. Stogdill): a large number (unknown) of men and women identified by the LBDQ XII project as leaders in the United States.

The data are as yet sparse; however, analysis indicates that the LBDQ XII does discriminate between cross-cultural samples and provides consistent geographic (regional and national) groupings.

The cluster analysis of the scores shown in Table 20.3 separate into groups that, for the most part, can be reasonably explained, with Mainland Chinese and Northern European clusters appearing, with diverse cultures such as Romania and Uganda failing to consistently cluster with other groups, and the United States yielding a mixed set of sample responses.

Uganda clusters with the Black and Porter samples from the United States and Hong Kong, with the proximity matrix indicating closer similarities to the two Hong Kong samples. But Uganda separates from that group in the next set of clusters and remains in an isolated cluster thereafter. And the clustering seems to be based upon the fact that these groups have generally lower average scores on all factors than the other samples.

One might speculate that the commonality of long-term British colonial rule might have led to the similarities between the Uganda educators' scores and the Black and Porter manager scores in Hong Kong; however, Selmer's (1997) sample of English-speaking Hong Kong Chinese managers clusters with the Mainland Chinese samples of hotel managers and supervisors. The Mainland China sample data were collected using a Chinese-character translation of the LBDQ XII.

Conclusions

From the literature reviewed and the research conducted and analyzed, assuming Uganda to be a reasonable surrogate for Sub-Saharan African coun-

Table 20.2

Mean LBDQ XII Factor Scores by Country

Samples / Factors	Cn 1999 M	Cn 2002 M	Cn 1999 S	Cn 2002 S	HK Sel	HK B&P	US B&P	US B&P In HK	US Lucas M	US Lucas Sub	US Stogdill	GB	De	Ro	Ug	Average all samples
1 Representation	4.5	4.5	4.5	4.5	4.3	3.7	3.9	4.17	4.1	4.1	4.1	4.1	4.3	4.4	3.95	4.21
2 Demand Reconciliation	4.4	4.2	4.4	4.3	4.4	3.4	3.9	3.4	4.2	4.1	4.1	4.2	4.5	4.5	3.32	4.09
3 Tolerance of Uncertainty	3.5	3.6	3.6	3.7	3.9	3.0	3.4	3.0	3.7	3.7	3.8	3.6	3.8	4.1	2.98	3.56
4 Persuasiveness	4.3	4.2	4.3	4.2	4.2	3.4	3.7	3.4	4.1	3.9	4.0	4.3	4.2	4.7	3.63	4.04
5 Initiation of Structure	4.3	4.4	4.4	4.4	4.4	3.7	3.7	3.7	4.1	4.1	3.8	4.4	4.1	3.5	3.86	4.06
6 Tolerance of Freedom	3.7	3.9	3.8	3.7	4.3	3.6	3.9	3.6	3.9	4.0	3.7	4	4.1	4.4	3.00	3.84
7 Role Assumption	4.1	3.9	3.9	3.8	4.1	3.6	4.0	3.6	4.2	4.2	4.2	4.2	4.1	4.3	3.57	3.98
8 Consideration	3.8	4.1	4.0	4.1	4.2	3.5	3.9	3.5	4.0	3.9	4	4	3.8	4.0	3.24	3.87
9 Production Emphasis	4.4	4.1	4.2	4.1	3.9	3.4	3.3	3.4	3.5	3.3	3.7	3.8	3.0	4.1	3.74	3.73
10 Predictive Accuracy	4.3	4.2	4.1	4.0	4.4	3.7	3.7	3.7	4.1	3.9	3.9	4.1	3.9	3.9	3.31	3.95
11 Integration	4.5	4.3	4.5	4.5	4.4	3.7	3.8	3.7	4.4	4.2	4.9	4.4	4.3	4.1	3.81	4.23
12 Superior Orientation	4.2	4.02	4.1	4.0	4.3	3.7	3.8	3.9	4.0	3.9	4.1	4.1	3.8	4.2	3.73	3.99
Average all factors	4.16	4.14	4.15	4.11	4.23	3.53	3.73	3.58	4.03	3.94	4.03	4.10	3.99	3.85	3.51	3.94

Table 20.3

Hierarchical Cluster Analysis: Table B Data

Case							Clusters						
	14	13	12	11	10	9	8	7	6	5	4	3	2
Cn 1999 M	1	1	1	1	1	1	1	1	1	1	1	1	1
Cn 2002 M	2	2	2	2	1	1	1	1	1	1	1	1	1
Cn 1999 S	3	2	2	2	1	1	1	1	1	1	1	1	1
Cn 2002 S	3	2	2	2	1	1	1	1	1	1	1	1	1
HK Sel	4	3	3	3	2	2	2	1	1	1	1	1	1
HK B&P	5	4	4	4	3	3	3	2	2	2	2	2	2
US B&P In HK	7	6	6	5	3	3	3	2	2	2	2	2	2
US B&P	6	5	5	4	4	4	4	3	3	3	3	2	2
US Lucas Mgr	8	7	7	6	5	5	5	4	4	4	1	1	1
US Lucas Sub	9	8	7	6	5	5	5	4	4	4	1	1	1
US Stogdill	10	9	8	7	6	6	6	5	5	4	1	1	1
GB	11	10	9	8	7	5	5	4	4	4	1	1	1
De	12	11	10	9	8	7	5	4	4	4	1	1	1
Ro	13	12	11	10	9	8	7	6	6	5	4	3	1
Ug	14	13	12	11	10	9	8	7	2	2	2	2	2

tries, perceptions of desirable leader behaviors in Africa appear to be similar, to some degree, to Hong Kong, the other country in the survey with a British colonial heritage. The hierarchical cluster analysis comparing samples from various geographic areas indicated similarity of the sample of Ugandan educators to Chinese managers and to expatriate managers working in Hong Kong, perhaps suggesting a postcolonial influence in leader behavior preferences. Uganda achieved independence from the United Kingdom in 1962. Hong Kong became the Hong Kong Special Administrative Region of China on July 1, 1997. However, these two British postcolonial cultures did not cluster with the U.K. sample, indicating the development of a hybrid management and leadership culture in colonial cultures.

The sets of more and less desirable behaviors indicate a preference for paternalism and high power distance in leaders on the part of education leaders in Uganda. The behaviors need to be directed toward facilitating interpersonal interactions in organizations, rather than focusing upon task-oriented behaviors. The less desirable behaviors indicate a lower requirement for "employee empowerment" behaviors and for behaviors indicating "Western" performance competence than generally found in "Western" samples.

References

America, R. 2003. *"Advancing Africa." BizEd 2*, no. 4: 28–33.
Bass, B.M. 1990. *Bass and Stogdill's Handbook of Leadership: Theory, Research and Managerial Applications*, 3d ed. New York: Free Press.
Bennis, W.G., and B. Nanus. 1985. *Leaders: The Strategy for Taking Charge.* New York: Harper and Row.
Bierschenk, T., ed. 2003. "Administration Etatique Et Societe Locale A Tanguieta (Nord du Benin). Une Analyse Politique Suite À des Interprétations des Événements de février 1996 À Tanguiéta." Arbeitspapiere (Working Papers). No. 20, Tilo Grätz, Institut Für Ethnologie und Afrikastudien, Department of Anthropology and African Studies. Johannes Gutenberg-Universität. www.uni-mainz.de/~ifeas/workingpapers/graetz2.pdf (accessed December 11, 2004).
Black, J.S., and L.W. Porter. 1991. "Managerial Behaviors and Job Performance: A Successful Manager in Los Angeles May Not Succeed in Hong Kong." *Journal of International Business Studies* 22, no. 1: 99–114.
Blunt, P. 1978. "Social and Organizational Structures in East Africa: A Case for Participation." *Journal of Modern African Studies* 16, no. 3: 433–49.
———. 1983. *Organizational Theory and Behaviour: An African Perspective.* London: Longman.
———. 1991. "Organizational Culture and Development." *International Journal of Human Resource Management* 2, no. 1: 55–71.
Blunt, P., and M.L. Jones. 1992. *Managing Organizations in Africa.* Berlin: Waiter de Gruyter.
———. 1997. "Exploring the Limits of Western Leadership Theory in East Asia and Africa." *Personnel Review* 26, no. 1: 6–23.

Brown, D. 1989. "Bureaucracy as an Issue in Third World Management: An African Case Study." *Public Administration and Development* 9: 369–80.

Centre for Higher Education Transformation (CHET) (South Africa). Undated. "A Framework for Creating Management Capacity and Culture of Leadership in Higher Education Institutions." Available at www.chet.org.za/oldsite/management/framework.html (accessed December 11, 2004).

Chisholm, L. 2001. "Gender and Leadership in South African Educational Administration." *Gender & Education* 13, no. 4: 387–99.

Cosway, N., and S.A. Anankum. 1996. "Traditional Leadership and Community Management in Northern Ghana." In *Indigenous Organizations and Development*, ed. P. Blunt and D.M. Warren, 88–96. London: Intermediate Technology Publications.

Dia, M. 1994. "Indigenous Management Practices: Lessons for Africa's Management in the '90s." In *Culture and Development in Africa*, ed. I. Serageldin and J. Taboroff, 165–91. Washington DC: World Bank.

Drucker, P.F. 1988. "Management and the World's Work." *Harvard Business Review* 16, no. 5: 65–76.

Geschiere, P. 1993. "Chiefs in Colonial Cameroon: Inventing Chieftancy French and British Style." *Africa* 63, no. 2: 151–75.

Ghosh, S. 2001. "Ethnic Diversity and Managerial Effectiveness in South Africa." *Academy of Management Executive* 15, no. 3: 136–37.

Graen, G., and C. Hui. 1996. "Managing Changes in Globalizing Business: How to Manage Cross-cultural Business Partners." *Journal of Organizational Change Management* 9, no. 2: 62–72.

Harvard Business School. "Leadership Best Practices." Available at www.exed.hbs.edu/programs/lbp/ (accessed December 10, 2004).

Heimer, C., and R. Vince. 1998. "Sustainable Learning and Change in International Teams: From Imperceptible Behaviour to Rigorous Practice." *Leadership and Organizational Development Journal* 19, no. 2: 83–88.

Herzberg, F. 1968. *Work and the Nature of Man.* London: Staples Press.

Hofstede, G. 1980. "Motivation, Leadership, and Organization: Do American Theories Apply Abroad?" *Organizational Dynamics* (Summer): 42–63.

House, R.J.; N. Wright; and R.N. Aditya. 1997. "Cross-cultural Research on Organizational Leadership: A Critical Analysis and a Proposed Theory." In *New Perspectives on International Industrial and Organizational Psychology*, ed. P.C. Earley and M. Erez. San Francisco, CA: Jossey-Bass.

Jones, M.L.; P. Blunt; and K. Sharma. 1995. *Managerial Behaviour, Organizational Functioning and Performance in an African Public Service Organization.* Stockholm: Sida.

Kolawole, G.O. 1996. "The Ogbomoso Parapo: A Case Study of an Indigenous Development Association in Nigeria." In *Indigenous Organizations and Development*, ed. P. Blunt and D.M. Warren, 50–55. London: Intermediate Technology Publications.

Leonard, D.K. 1987. "The Political Realities of African Management." *World Development* 15: 899–910.

———. 1988. "The Secrets of African Managerial Success." *IDS Bulletin* 19, no. 4: 35–41.

Linquist, B.J., and D. Adolph. 1996. "The Drum Speaks—Are We Listening? Experiences in Development with a Traditional Gabra Institution—the Yaa Galbo." In *Indigenous Organizations and Development*, ed. P. Blunt and D.M. Warren, 1–6. London: Intermediate Technology Publications.

Littrell, R.F. 2002a. "Desirable Leadership Behaviours of Multi-cultural Managers in China." *Journal of Management Development* 210, no. 1: 5–74.

———. 2002b. "Comparative Analysis of Management Styles: Desirable Leader Traits Across Cultures." *Proceedings Academy of International Business Southeast Asia and Australia Regional Conference.* July 18–20, Shanghai, China, Hong Kong Institute of Business Studies, Lingnan University, Tuen Mun, Hong Kong. Available at www.romielittrellpubs .homestead.com (accessed December 11, 2004).

———. 2003. "Corporate and National Cultures: Influence of the Cross-cultural Composition of the Management Team on Leadership Preferences in a Chinese Organization, a Longitudinal Study." Proceedings of the 2003 International Human Resources Management Conference, University of Limerick, Limerick, Ireland. Available at www.romielittrellpubs.homestead.com (accessed December 11, 2004).

Littrell, R.F., and L.N. Valentin. (In preparation.) "Explicit Descriptions of Preferred Leadership Behaviors, West to East in Northern Europe: England, Germany, and Romania." Contact: romielittrell@yahoo.com.

Lucas, P.R.; P.E. Messner; C.W. Ryan; and G.P. Sturm. 1992. "Preferred Leadership Style Differences: Perceptions of Defence Industry Labour and Management." *Leadership and Organization Development Journal* 13, no. 7: 19–23.

Mazrui, A.A. 1994. "Development in a Multi-cultural Context: Trends and Tensions." In *Culture and Development in Africa*, ed. I. Serageldin and J. Taboroff, 127–36. Washington, DC: World Bank.

Montgomery, J.D. 1986. "Levels of Managerial Leadership in Southern Africa." *Journal of Developing Areas* 21: 15–30.

———. 1987. "Probing Managerial Behaviour: Image and Reality in Southern Africa." *World Development* 15, no. 7: 911–29.

Nevin, Tom. 2003. "A Free University for Africa's Disadvantaged." *African Business*, January 1: 26–27.

Nzelibe, C.O. 1986. "The Evolution of African Management Thought." *International Studies of Management and Organization* 16, no. 2: 6–16.

Popper, K.R. 1959. *The Logic of Scientific Discovery.* London: Hutchinson.

Roodt, A. 1997. "In Search of a South African Corporate Culture." *Management Today* 13, no. 2: 14–16.

Schneider, J., and R.F. Littrell. 2003. "Leadership Preferences of German and English Managers." *Journal of Management Development* 22, no. 2: 130–48.

Selmer, J. 1997. "Differences in Leadership Behaviour Between Expatriate and Local Bosses as Perceived by Their Host Country National Subordinates." *Leadership and Organizational Development Journal* 18, no. 1: 13–22.

Smith, P.B.; M.F. Peterson; and S.H. Schwartz. 2002. "Cultural Values, Sources of Guidance, and Their Relevance to Managerial Behaviour." *Journal of Cross-Cultural Psychology* 33, no. 2: 188–208.

Sperling, G.B. 2001. "The Developing World's Quiet Crisis: The Group of Eight Should Spearhead a Global Initiative on the Provision of Universal Primary Education." *Financial Times*, July 17: 15.

Stogdill, R.M. 1963. *Manual for the Leader Behavior Description Questionnaire-Form XII.* Columbus: Ohio State University, Bureau of Business Research.

Thomas, A., and M. Bendixen. 2000. "Management Implications of Ethnicity in South Africa." *Journal of International Business Studies* 31: 507–19.

Ugwuegbu, D.C.E. 2001. *The Psychology of Management in African Organizations.* Westport, CT: Quorum Books (Greenwood).

Warren, D.M.; R. Adedokun; and A. Omolaoye. 1996. "Indigenous Organizations and Development: The Case of Ara, Nigeria." In *Indigenous Organizations and Development*, ed. P. Blunt and D.M. Warren, 43–49. London: Intermediate Technology Publications.

21

Research Capacity Building

A North–South Knowledge Transfer Project

Jan-Erik Jaensson and Lettice Rutashobya

This project was established in the context of the broad objective of capacity and competence building for a sustainable national development plan. Specifically, capacity building through research capability and competence strengthening geared toward the creation of scientific knowledge are of prime importance in the economic development of Tanzania. This project serves as an example of successful university cooperation between the north and south.

The broad objective of the capacity-building project is the creation and strengthening of faculty capacity in research and teaching through knowledge transfer from Umea School of Business and Economics in Sweden. The ultimate goal is to enable the faculty to contribute to the socioeconomic development and poverty alleviation that are currently on the country's development agenda.

Faculty research had to be sufficiently developed. Major constraints included:

- A shortage of academic staff with adequate exposure to research activities.
- A shortage, and often unavailability, of research funds.
- Opportunities for research training through PhD were rare.
- The faculty library was understocked and partly out of date. Lack of journals was a great hindrance to conducting research.
- A computer laboratory existed within the faculty, which was used for all faculty activities, but its facilities were grossly inadequate. There were only three personal computers for use by all of the faculty's academic staff and postgraduate students. Furthermore, the faculty offered courses on systems analysis and computers. About 200 students from

the Faculties of Commerce and Management, Arts and Social Sciences, and Education took these courses. They had no access to the computer laboratory because of the shortage of equipment.

Despite the above constraints, some faculty members and postgraduate students have been able to conduct research in the following broad areas: enterprise development, female entrepreneurship, technology transfer, small business financing, restructuring of Tanzanian enterprises, trade liberalization, marketing concepts, international business, cost sharing in the education and health sectors, and more.

At the beginning of the 1990s, the faculty witnessed dramatic changes in the business environment as well as in government. For the faculty to contribute effectively to the socioeconomic development of Tanzania, research, and academic and nonacademic programs had to be able to address the country's current and future socioeconomic needs. The faculty needed assistance in strengthening its capacity and competence to enable it to play a leading role in the provision of knowledge in business administration and management of resources in the country, especially considering the fact that for many years the University of Dar es Salaam was the only university in the country offering business and management studies.

Over the seventeen years of its existence, the Faculty of Commerce and Management (FCM) at the University of Dar es Salaam has been one of the least endowed university departments for lack of donor support.

Problems

Since its establishment, the FCM has largely depended on government funding to carry out its teaching and research activities. This funding has dwindled from year to year as a result of the country's poor economic performance. According to World Bank and United Nations Development Programme (UNDP) statistics, Tanzania has consistently been ranked among the five poorest countries in the world, with a gross national product (GNP) per capita averaging about US$100.

Coupled with infancy problems, the capacity of the faculty in research development had remained rather low. Broadly put, the faculty faced a number of challenges and problems, including the following:

- Research, and in particular basic research, was seriously constrained by a number of problems, including lack of research funds and lack of research facilities. Inadequate remuneration for academic staff members compelled them to spend disproportionately large amounts of time

on short-term contract-based research and consultancies. As a result, experience in basic research was low among the majority of staff.
- The number of people with PhD degrees was relatively small due to lack of scholarships.
- Access to relevant and up-to-date literature was limited due to financial constraints.
- The faculty faced a serious shortage of teaching and learning materials. The university had very limited resources for buying books. Almost all management books had to be imported. Access to international journals was also seriously constrained by shortages of funds. On the other hand, the availability of local materials was constrained by the faculty's limited research experience. The publication of faculty journals, business management reviews, and occasional paper series had been very irregular due to lack of funds.

Support for Research Collaboration and Research Training

During the dean's visit to Sweden in 1997, a good understanding of research collaboration and capacity building was reached between the Umea School of Business and Economics, Department of Business Administration (USBE) and FCM. Given the profiles of the two universities, a cooperative project started on equal terms on January 1, 1998, with financial support from the Swedish International Development Cooperation Agency department of research cooperation (hereafter called Sida).

The Department of Business Administration at Umea School of Business and Economics

Research activities were conducted in the following areas (which to some extent were the same as at FCM):

- Entrepreneurship and small business management
- Regional development and restructuring of Swedish business
- Organizational principles and practices
- Knowledge-intensive organizations
- Internationalization of Swedish firms
- Financial and managerial accounting
- Marketing
- Temporary organizations and project management

The department also engaged in a staff exchange program with the Business Studies Department at the University of Zimbabwe beginning in 1994, financed by Sida and to some extent the Swedish Institute. One staff member was supervised for his PhD examination in 1998. Two staff members from the University of Zimbabwe were also working on their PhD projects, supervised by professors at USBE. The project also included other types of capacity building in Zimbabwe, mainly investments in prerequisites for research, for example, in computers, a computer network, and some literature.

The experience from this capacity-building project was positive, and the model used worked well. The PhD candidates graduated in Zimbabwe, and the period in Umea was limited, in an attempt to avoid brain drain in the event that the PhD candidates stayed abroad for several years. Communication between supervisors in Umea and PhD candidates in Zimbabwe was mainly through e-mail when they were not in Sweden.

The above-described conditions suggest that there were good possibilities for cooperation and knowledge transfer between FCM and USBE.

The Knowledge Transfer Project

In view of the capacity-building needs of the FCM, Sida provided direct financial support for the following knowledge transfer activities during 1998–2000:

1. Research training through PhD. Financial support for PhD training of junior members of staff was urgently required. This training was undertaken through the sandwich mode (three months in Sweden at three different times). A very good understanding was reached with USBE regarding this activity. A suitable sandwich mode to benefit at least four PhD candidates during the project period was created. It was expected that this kind of activity would enhance research collaboration with USBE. It was also expected that through this activity, research agendas would emerge. The faculty had more than ten staff members who were ready to undertake PhD studies.

2. Research collaboration. Direct financial support was provided for collaborative research projects acceptable at both USBE and FCM, with the research collaboration initially revolving around a long-term research program on entrepreneurship and small business development.

This research agenda was aimed at examining the context and process of entrepreneurship in Tanzania. Comparative studies between Tanzania and other countries such as Sweden would be encouraged. The following research themes were to be investigated:

- Determinants of small and medium-sized enterprise (SME) performance
- Entrepreneurial capacities, attitudes, and intentions
- Enterprise development services

- Financing and management issues in SMEs
- The informal sector
- Ownership and organization of businesses
- Gender and entrepreneurship

Project Objectives

The project objectives were as follows:

1. to conduct research training through PhD under the sandwich mode and to establish a PhD program at FCM;
2. to strengthen faculty research capacity through collaboration with Swedish institutions;
3. to strengthen faculty research facilities to enhance research capacity;
4. to improve faculty publication output; and
5. to forge long-term collaboration with Swedish institutions.

Expected Outputs

- Improved and strengthened teaching and research capacity and capability in both quality and quantity
- An improved research infrastructure of the faculty
- Increased research and publication output of the faculty
- Long-term collaboration established with Swedish universities
- Improved working morale of FCM academic staff
- Improved postgraduate teaching and supervision

Activities

- PhD training
- Curriculum development for the PhD program
- Organized research methodology workshops
- Research carried out in areas specified in the Faculty Five-Year Strategic Plan
- Conferences organized to disseminate research findings
- Published proceedings, readers, and journals
- Collaborative research carried out with Swedish institutions
- Short-term visits to Sweden to conduct literature review and prepare training materials

- Staff exchange visits for sabbaticals, PhD supervision, planning meetings, and postdoctoral research
- Purchase of research facilities to strengthen research capacity

The Results of the First Three Years of Cooperation—Phase One (1998–2000)

The cooperative project was very successful, and knowledge transfer was effective. One reason for this is that a high level of trust was built between the two project coordinators, Lettice Rutashobya and Jan-Erik Jaensson.

Each PhD candidate spent three months per year over three years in Umea. Because of limited resources, only two new PhD candidates were enrolled each year, and at the transfer's peak, six PhD candidates were in Umea during one year.

The results of these first three years were:

- One PhD candidate completed his exam;
- One more was expected to complete her exam early in 2001;
- Five PhD candidates enrolled in the sandwich-training program (one left the program);
- Curricula were developed for three PhD courses;
- Three PhD courses were by USBE professors in Tanzania (in the next phase, staff from FCM will conduct the courses under the supervision of USBE professors);
- A regional PhD conference in which university researchers from five countries participated was held in Zanzibar in October 2000;
- Computers were purchased to facilitate research and communication;
- One international conference was held each year in the area of SMEs and entrepreneurship;
- Staff exchange visits took place;
- Research papers were published;
- Journals were published.

Because of a lack of funding, it was not possible to begin research cooperation between the professors during the first three years. For the same reason, supervisor training that was planned to be held during the first three years also did not take place.

At the Zanzibar conference, a regional cooperation idea was born. The concept of the existing knowledge transfer project is that USBE should be superfluous after six years. Many other universities have approached USBE with the ambition to establish cooperation similar to that between FCM and

USBE. The ideal project would instead use the existing competence in the region to develop research capacity with only marginal involvement of universities in the north—that is, rely on knowledge transfer within the region (south–south cooperation).

A great deal of knowledge was gained in the first phase, and used to make some improvements in planning of the next phase One idea was to train supervisors from FCM during workshops at USBE in Sweden to enhance the communication between supervisors at FCM and USBE. Another option was to open the possibility for PhD candidates from Tanzania to take a mid-exam in Sweden, a licentiate exam before they completed their studies with a dissertation.

The Results of the Second Three Years of Cooperation—Phase Two (2001–3)

The results of the second three years were:

- One PhD candidate completed her exam as expected;
- Three new PhD exams were expected in 2004;
- Three licentiate exams were administered at USBE;
- Four licentiate exams were expected in 2004;
- Seven PhD candidates enrolled in the sandwich-training program;
- Two PhD courses were conducted in Tanzania (two sessions of each);
- Thirteen PhDs were trained during three supervisor workshops at USBE;
- One international conference was held each year in the area of SMEs and entrepreneurship;
- Staff exchange visits were conducted;
- Research papers were published;
- Journals were published.

Transfer of Knowledge from a Theoretical Perspective

There are different schools of thought dealing with the transfer of knowledge. We will describe them briefly and present our views.

Theories of knowledge transfer are rather young, with the majority of articles having been written during the past decade. The importance of transferring knowledge is undisputable, and its areas range from transfer within a single organization that disseminates knowledge to worldwide transfer of knowledge between north and south as a result of globalization. However, most literature discusses the transfer of knowledge only *to* organizations and people of the developing countries, and not between north and south. This implies that people in the Western world have little to learn from people in developing countries!

Knowledge management has emerged as the theoretical concept of this transferal both within and between organizations. The main concept is that knowledge management will contribute to competitive advantage and growth in an organization or in a network of organizations (Garvin 1993).

Knowledge management in organizations deals with factors such as leadership, the value of enhancing learning among the members of an organization, technology to facilitate and speed up the process, cooperation and collaboration, trust, dissemination within teams and hierarchical levels, and reward systems (Goh 2002).

Knowledge transfer in transnational operations deals partly with other factors such as relationship strength, innovation, social space, strategies, actors, socioeconomic order, people transfer, culture, absorption, and transformation (Goh 2002).

Since the project described here is a transnational project between an institution in Sweden and one in Tanzania that deals with capacity building in Tanzania, we will focus mainly on the latter group of factors.

The most essential factors for this project may be classified in two different groups: individual (leadership, actors, trust and relationship strength) and organizational (strategies, socioeconomic order, culture, social space, people transfer, absorption, and transformation).

Individual Factors of Knowledge Transfer

Individual factors are leadership, actors, and trust and relationship strength, as mentioned above. Without these factors, no significant transfer of knowledge will take place between organizations. Leadership in both organizations is essential to starting a project and to maintaining the knowledge management process. The leadership of both organizations was convinced of this project's importance.

The different actors in this project from the beginning were members of a team of four professors at USBE (of which one was chairman of the department), a dedicated project leader, and the dean of the FCM. A very important outside actor was the financing organization, Sida; without its help the project would not have been possible. Now in the sixth year of the project, one professor has left the team at USBE due to a heavy workload, but two other professors have been engaged, mainly as supervisors of PhD students. The team at FCM has grown, with a new dean and a committee to handle the formalization of the project in the future.

A very high degree of trust has developed over six years, and nothing has happened during the course of the project to damage that level of trust. One example of complete trust is that, due to financial delays in the payment from Sida to FCM, USBE has several times paid expenses in advance for staff from FCM and later sent invoices to FCM. Once the amount was substantial: US$23,000. The payments from Sida were delayed because of a lack of economic reporting from the University of Dar es Salaam and its faculties. The level of trust is also high between "the project" and the staff at Sida, which has been very supportive in discussing ideas for developing and improving the project. The project has also shown very good results, which itself contributes to the level of trust on the part of the staff at Sida. This project is one of the most successful capacity-building projects ever undertaken by the department of research cooperation at Sida.

Strong relationships have developed both because of formal activities within the project and through social activities that have strengthened personal relations. Examples of such social activities are dinners at restaurants and at homes of various persons, visits to animal farms and safaris, exchanges of personal experiences, and shopping. A network of thirty-two persons from both sides has taken part in one or more of these social activities, and all are in one way or another still linked to the project.

Organizational Factors of Knowledge Transfer

The organizational factors include strategies, socioeconomic order, culture, social space, people transfer, absorption, and transformation, as mentioned above. On the part of Tanzania, the overall goal was to build capacity in research, with the ultimate goal of contributing to the development of society. The FCM's strategy was to develop faculty through formal links with universities in Europe and the United States. When Dean Rutashobya contacted Sida, it was in an attempt to create such a link with a Swedish institution. The faculty has other projects together with universities in Europe and the United States, but these are not as well developed as the collaboration with USBE.

For USBE, the goal was to engage more in activities and formal links with other universities besides those in Europe and the United States. The USBE strategy was to create links to universities in Africa. This was part of USBE's strategic plan of internationalization and thus the inquiry from FCM through Sida was in line with that strategy.

The socioeconomic order refers to the outcomes of political and social processes that deal with knowledge transfer. Since the organizations on both sides from the beginning were positive about this project, very few "internal" problems have occurred. From the start, not many persons had full knowledge of the project, which was good for the sake of developing the project. With too many actors, projects can be put on hold for political reasons. As the project developed and experience was gained, it was made more public on both sides. Because the project is a success story, it has been well received by the public. It has also received some publicity in Swedish media.

Culture was a difficult factor when the activities and measurable indicators of the project were first formulated. One team from USBE visited FCM in Tanzania for one week in 1997 to formulate the project action plan, which was to be submitted for final approval. Several times during these discussions, misinterpretations occurred. However, we were fortunate to have one Tanzanian faculty member on the FCM task force who had taken his PhD in Sweden and spoke Swedish. He worked as a mediator and explained to both sides how the other system worked and what their statements meant. This significantly speeded up the proposal process for the project.

Some authors argue that there is a need for social space created by actors within the knowledge transfer system. In the social space, knowledge transfer occurs and knowledge "mingles" between the actors, causing learning to take place. It is also considered to be an arena where power holders meet and conflict, and consensus and resistance are played out (Geppert and Clark 2003). Several social spaces have been created in the project. One arena is the PhD courses given by USBE professors in Tanzania. Another consists of frequent meetings at the leadership level in the supervisors workshop conducted in Sweden, and informal meetings between various staff members both in Sweden and in Tanzania.

People transfer is also important because those with experience in a different environmental setting bring the knowledge back home (Bender and Fish 2000). In the project it has been essential that people transfer in both directions. For the PhD students, it has, of course, been a requirement of their enrollment in this joint project that they spend three months in Sweden three times to be supervised by Swedish professors. During that time they have the opportunity to experience another academic environment. This is also a form of knowledge transfer that is brought back to Tanzania. For the professors at USBE, the period of time in Tanzania has been limited to between one and five weeks. However, during repeat visits, knowledge transfer has taken place, both about the academic system and about their colleagues' working environment.

The transfer of knowledge requires transmission, absorption, and transformation (Davenport and Prusak 1998). This is seen as communication, and communication requires both a sender and a receiver to work. People create knowledge, and in this context it makes sense to mention this prerequisite. Obviously, different actors have participated in the project, and, occasion-

Figure 21.1   **Knowledge Hierarchy**

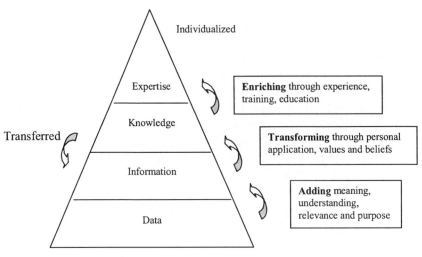

Source: Bender and Fish (2000, 126).

ally, miscommunication has occurred. For example, when the Swedish licentiate exam was explained. The format and requirements of the Swedish licentiate exam were in some respects unfamiliar.

There are different models in the literature describing knowledge transfer. One interesting model is presented by Bender and Fish (2000), who argue that there is a difference between knowledge and expertise. Knowledge builds on information that is obtained and transformed by the specific individual's other experiences. This knowledge differs from one individual to another because of an individual's interpretations of information. Expertise is special, in-depth knowledge, and this knowledge can contribute to the creation of new knowledge by an expert. This expertise is built individually over a long time, and it will remain within the individual. Figure 21.1 depicts this model of knowledge hierarchy according to Bender and Fish (2000).

In our knowledge transfer project, we will not stop with the examination of PhDs, which, from the perspective of the model in Figure 21.1, can be seen as teaching knowledge about how to do research and write a dissertation. Because we have received financing from Sida for a third phase (2004–7), we will also continue with postdoctoral training, which can be seen as educating experts, in order to improve knowledge transfer in both directions. The postdoctoral training will be done through short research projects consisting of a research team of one senior researcher from USBE, one senior researcher from FCM, and one newly examined PhD from FCM. These additional activities represent an improvement that leads to a very high degree of knowledge transfer in this north–south cooperation project.

The expected outcomes of the entire ten-year cooperation project are:

- Ten PhD examinations in Dar es Salaam;
- Fourteen licentiate examinations in Umea;
- Thirteen PhD supervisors trained at workshops in Umea;
- Eight postdoctoral projects conducted;
- Twenty-five conference papers presented;
- Ten journal articles published or accepted for publication;
- Equipment purchased to enhance research;
- Ten conferences held in the area of SMEs and entrepreneurship in Tanzania;
- One case writing seminar held at FCM to facilitate the dissemination of research results to the bachelor and master students;
- One project management course held;
- Regional cooperation established for south–south cooperation in the future.

Sida has financed the project with a total amount of US$2.6 million (US$1 = SEK7.4) for the whole ten-year period.

Conclusions

To undertake a knowledge transfer project between two institutions is not an easy task. If they are institutions from different continents and different cultures, it is even more difficult. However, to create understanding between both parties from academic institutions may be easier than a business relationship because the demands and expected outcomes of academic organizations are rather similar worldwide.

At the beginning of this project, nobody could have anticipated all of the driving forces and hindrances because of little previous experience in the area of social sciences. Sida had some experience but with mixed results. Most of the cooperative projects in which they had participated had not yielded output of this kind. There were some guidelines to follow for project administration, but not many guidelines for knowledge transfer in projects. This meant that no method of knowledge transfer was present at the beginning of the project other than the sandwich model. The present project has gained much experience, which Sida now uses for a new cooperative effort in the area of statistics, where the project coordinator in Sweden acts as a mentor.

The driving forces of this project proved to be very strong, and willingness to create output was high. There was an understanding of the importance of output for the continuation of the project, and people in the network were strongly motivated to perform well.

Obstacles have been few, and those that have occurred often involved uncontrollable environmental factors, for example, money disbursement.

The factors most critical to this project's success were the well-functioning leadership team, which managed to create a high level of trust among its members. This also affected all other persons involved in the network. Social activities became an arena for getting to know each other, which in turn strengthened relationships in the network even more. These activities led to substantial knowledge about the different cultures of each country.

This project is now looked upon by the University of Dar es Salaam and Sida as a role model for knowledge transfer in the area of academic institutions.

Acknowledgment

We are very grateful for the support provided by Sida, and thank all the staff for their positive and encouraging attitude.

References

Bender, S., and A. Fish. 2000. "The Transfer of Knowledge and the Retention of Expertise: The Continuing Need for Global Assignments." *Journal of Knowledge Management* 4, no. 2: 125–37.

Davenport, T.H., and L. Prusak. 1998. *Working Knowledge: How Organizations Manage What They Know.* Boston, MA: Harvard Business School Press.

Garvin, D. 1993. "Building Learning Organizations." *Harvard Business Review* (July/August): 78–91.

Geppert, M., and E. Clark. 2003. "Knowledge and Learning in Transnational Ventures: An Actor-centered Approach." *Management Decision* 41, no. 5: 433–42.

Goh, S.C. 2002. "Managing Effective Knowledge Transfer: An Integrative Framework and Some Practice Implications." *Journal of Knowledge Management* 6, no. 1: 23–30.

22

Reengineering Business Education

A Case Study of the "Modular Curriculum" of Sakarya University

Rana Ozen Kutanis and Serkan Bayraktaroglu

This chapter concerns educational curricula design and is set within the context of a national policy agenda to drive forward a knowledge-based economy and an enterprise society. The study was conducted with all the academic staff members of the Business School of Sakarya University as well as final year undergraduate and master of business administration (MBA) students. Empirical research was planned to analyze the perceptions of the academic staff and the students regarding the new upcoming program.

The aim of this chapter is to argue that university business schools are about to undergo a period of radical transformation as a result of pressure created by developments in external forces and changes in the economic environment favoring the evolution of knowledge work. In particular, the chapter assesses the ability of business schools to transform as they come to terms with these environmental changes.

The Need for Change

Unemployment is a growing global problem that besets industrialized countries, developing countries, and countries in economic transition alike. Virtually any country in the world is struggling to cope with the limitations of wage labor and the public sector and is turning, either by plan or out of sheer necessity, to the informal sector and self-employment to help address the unemployment problem. The position of business schools has been highlighted as being particularly problematic, primarily because business schools find themselves at the interface of the business and academic worlds. They therefore have to cope with the changing external environment earlier than other, more sheltered faculties of the university. The concept of this chapter is based on the "best practices" of the British universities in promoting business schools to update their curricula according to external factors. The British system recommends that higher educational institutions consider how entrepreneurship can be encouraged using innovative program design and specialist postgraduate programs.

In parallel with the necessity to compete in a global market, the government has a lifelong learning agenda that recognizes the need for individuals to engage throughout their lives in a personal process of learning and retraining. A recent trend in business education is to use the higher education sector to increase enterprise and entrepreneurship. The aim of this initiative is to increase the commercialization of science and technology from high quality university research and to promote enterprise and entrepreneurship in business schools. As part of a wider audit of enterprise within the curriculum, it has considered how academics themselves define enterprise, and thus how their conceptualizations of enterprise influence and shape the curriculum, and how enterprise may be embedded within the university.

The Context of Reengineering

Today, the economy is constantly changing, and trends in business education must change with it. Therefore, the structure of business education has undergone numerous changes and improvements during the past few years, and it is critical that developing countries such as Turkey note these changes in order to establish themselves in the world business arena as competent and reliable partners. To be such a partner, a country needs skilled managers in all areas of business and administration, especially in an environment of globalization where so many businesses must be part of the world economy. A major criticism of contemporary business education centers is the failure to help business students achieve sufficient educational breadth, particularly with regard to the external environment of business, and there is an excellent opportunity to address this deficiency. By developing curricular projects linked to community needs, faculty can further their students' technical skills while helping them simultaneously to develop greater interpersonal, intercultural, and ethical sensitivity.

The managers and entrepreneurs of the future should be professionally educated and equipped with sufficient tools to cope with increasing global competition. Contemporary business education should therefore take into account the changing environments of domestic and international markets.

Method of Research

This research has been conducted in the light of Yin's (1993) case study research. The representativeness of the department's innovative ideas and practices gave birth to the idea of presenting the case in the form of a "case study." Case study research requires a systematic investigation of one or more organizations, often with data collected over a period of time, with the aim of analysis of both the context and processes of the case under investigation. "Case study is not a methodological choice, but a choice of object to be studied" (Stake 1994: 236), and it is also a research strategy that "should not be confused with qualitative research" (Yin 1994: 14). The data collection methods used in our case study research have been observation, interviews, and questionnaires. Our case study is a single and detailed one, presenting a complete description of a phenomenon within its context (Yin 1993: 5).

Case study research has a vital role within the research framework, and it bears some similarities to qualitative research in general. The selection of cases is very important for the reliability, accuracy, and originality of the qualitative research.

Organization of the Case Study

Sakarya University, founded in 1992, is one of Turkey's newest universities. However, in a short time, the university has transformed and radically changed its educational practices, attitude and procedures. Parallel to its pioneering role in distance education practices in Turkey, the university has started to produce high quality publications both in the national and international academic platforms. The Faculty of Economics and Administrative Sciences is one of the leading faculties of the university in terms of conducting scientific research projects and producing scholarly publications. The Department of Business Administration, which has a promising profile of dynamic academics, is the most productive department of the faculty. Most of the academics have completed their PhDs abroad, generally in the United Kingdom and the United States or in high-level universities in Turkey.

Next year, Sakarya Business School will be launching what we call a "modular system" to enhance the quality and employability of business education graduates. This system includes placement programs in the third and final year, as well as a strategy of close relationships with industry. The modules are categorized under the main headings of human resource management, manufacturing, marketing, finance, and accounting. This is a very similar approach to that of British universities, such as Warwick Business School, in terms of business education. In this way, it is expected that students will plan their career paths earlier as this will increase specialization, and, hence, the chance of finding a job suitable to their educational background.

The emphasis of the undergraduate business program of our department is to train and educate students to be business-literate people who can adapt to increasingly keen global competition. The curriculum includes basic courses in business and social sciences as well as courses related to numerical methods and computer programming. In addition, the program provides an opportunity to select one of three specialization areas: production management and marketing, accounting and finance, or management and organization. The objective is to prepare students for professional life as specialists or researchers in both public and private sectors. Finally, we believe that this program prepares our graduates to be ready for the advances made in their field during the twenty-first century.

Students may specialize in areas such as marketing, operations management, human resource management, production, marketing, finance, or accounting, and they may choose modules that lead to professional career options.

The course aims to provide students with:

1. A firm core of knowledge of the basic disciplines that are fundamental to the study of management;
2. Experience of in-depth study in a series of management-related functional areas;
3. The requisite knowledge base for a potential manager and skills in the application of that knowledge to the analysis and solution of management problems;
4. Preparation for a career in an increasingly dynamic and international business environment and/or for further study of management at a higher level.

Creating a Suitable Environment for Entrepreneurship

In the case of Sakarya University, entrepreneurship is seen as a creative and dynamic process characterized by learning, an experience orientation, and interaction with the environment. Entrepreneurship as a process is something that concerns the human being as a whole. According to the present concept, entrepreneurship is divided into internal, self-initiated, and external entrepreneurship. Universities and other educational institutions should create in the student a capacity for the independent practice of a vocation. The foundations for these attitudes, readiness, and skills should be created in a comprehensive school environment. Quite a number of values, attitudes, fantasies, and prejudices are associated with entrepreneurship. Through entrepreneurship education and training, it may be possible to eliminate unnecessary stereotypic viewpoints. In this, teachers and teacher training are in a key position because they convey to students what they know about entrepreneurship as well as the attitudes they hold toward it. The surrounding culture and society make a contribution of their own in this regard. Today, the demands of working life call for internal entrepreneurship (so-called intrapreneurship) in the worker. By this term we refer to a collective entrepreneurship-oriented attitude within the organization. One of its features, for example, is teamwork, as well as initiative, creativity, risk-taking ability, and a sense of responsibility in the individual.

Entrepreneurship can be considered to be the individual's own development story, in which case the issue is spontaneous entrepreneurship. This is seen in the entrepreneurial thinking and behavior of the individual, for example, in learning, in interaction with others, and in the workplace community. Implicit in the exhaustive definition of entrepreneurship is the comprehensive development of the human being as a survivor in changing conditions. The entrepreneur—external, internal, or self-reliant—is forever learning something new, and has the ability to face failures as potential learning situations. According to this view, the different forms of entrepreneurship are interrelated and in a constant state of dialogue with each other.

Entrepreneurship Education and Training

What we mean by entrepreneurship education and training of entrepreneurs is the development of the individual's models of enterprise-oriented thinking and behavior, as well as increasing his knowledge of the different forms of entrepreneurship. All three forms of entrepreneurship, external, internal, and self-initiated, are currently seen as important properties, with entrepreneurship education and training considered a necessary process. It is essential to equip the students with learning abilities that allow them to manage in their own lives, especially, on the labor market. In the United States, the revolution into entrepreneurship during the past few decades has been considered more profound a change than was the industrial revolution.

We may well ask, for what kind of world—of the past, the present, or of the future—are we preparing the students? Global markets, changes in organizations, the advent of teamwork in workplace communities, as well as the emphasis on entrepreneurship, require changes in the skills and attributes of workers. Entrepreneurship education, training, and coaching do not aim merely at the establishment of new companies. It must be seen in a wider perspective, in which the goal is to make entrepreneurship a part of the student's life. In this way, both new companies and workplace communities already in existence will reach a higher qualitative level. Knowledge and skills can grow old, but positive values and attitudes do not easily grow old or become forgotten. The spirit of entrepreneurship can therefore be adopted in all professions and occupations.

The objective, at this point, is to educate individuals to act in the spirit of entrepreneurship in all walks of life. One important activity of Sakarya University's entrepreneurship education, training, and coaching program is the development work and cooperation directed at the existing companies in the region. In practice, this will take place within all fields of education as theses, as a variety of commercial development projects of companies, as enterprise-oriented learning cases, and as applied research activities in the universities. Interaction with companies and other organizations in the world of work must be continuously extended, developed, and concentrated to ensure that the learning process of as many students as possible takes place in a real enterprise context, allowing students to participate in the enterprise's own innovations, this being one of the most important development challenges of our university.

The Department of Business Administration is committed to providing all of its students with an understanding of the global environment. Especially important is the ongoing development of an International Business concentration that will provide students with the knowledge and experience to make them competitive in the market. The process is a dynamic one. It is the responsibility of the faculty and the administration to stay current in order to keep the curriculum up to date and to look for additional ways to provide the resources necessary to support the program.

New Insights for University–Industry Cooperation

In his classic study of the competitive advantage of nation states, M.E. Porter's analysis of Britain concluded that attention to the education and training system was the most pressing issue facing policy makers and an area in which "current policies provide the least comfort." Without a broader pool of well-trained employees, the competitive advantage of companies is being constrained. A key part of Porter's solution to the lack of investment in human resource development was that firms should forge a much closer working relationship with education providers. According to Porter, "companies will benefit by working closely with local universities in developing curricula, sponsoring research and in recruiting graduates" (1990: 721).

Results show that there is an increasing trend in university–industry collaboration over the past decade (Caloghirou, Vonortas, and Tsakanikas 2000). Universities are involved in large and longer-term consortia. Significant participation from peripheral regions is identified along with the emergence of a small group of universities with involvement in a large number of cooperation initiatives.

Universities both provide the qualified workforce and participate in the accumulation of scientific knowledge and technology that industry demands, along with their primary function of education. Today, there is intensive cooperation between university and industry in industrialized countries such as England and Germany. However, in such countries as Turkey, where research and development efforts are far from adequate and transfer of technology is preferred rather than design, the ways to realize such cooperation are being investigated with emerging intensive global competition. For this reason, both the universities' and industrialists' ideas, the problems encountered in this process, and some proposed solutions are analyzed in this study.

The socioeconomic impact of the higher-education sector on the economy includes three areas: (1) fundamental and applied research activities of universities contribute to the stock of knowledge in the economy; (2) universities provide highly trained human resources; and (3) the sector supplies ideas and inventions through technology transfer.

To analyze socioeconomic impact, economists are obliged to dissociate variables, and the most commonly known work focuses on the impact of academic knowledge creation on samples of firms. Analyses point to increased probability of innovation, profitability, and growth among firms that form linkages with universities, but, to locate and assimilate knowledge, expertise, and technology, such firms must already have in-house technical capabilities.

Studies of fast-growing, high-technology regions have shown that even if universities are not a direct causal factor, they are certainly catalysts for effective regional economic development. Successful innovation-based regional growth depends on a number of conditions that facilitate university–industry and firm-to-firm communications and collaboration, including:

- a regional knowledge-base, founded on a mix of universities, colleges, and research laboratories;
- clusters of large and small high-technology firms;
- proactive support groups and organizations, such as networks, intermediary organizations, and business service units, working jointly with the regional government;
- adequate local communication and transportation infrastructure that permit access to international, national, and local sites;
- a physical closeness between the relevant institutions; and
- complementary federal, provincial, and local policies supportive of university–industry links based on research and development and training.

Unfortunately, there appear to be very few recent analytical studies on the impact of Turkish regional organizations on university–industry cooperation and local economic development. It is hoped that by reengineering business education and also presenting the "best practices" of university–industry cooperation, regional development initiatives will be faster and more efficient.

References

Caloghirou, Y.; N.S. Vonortas; and A. Tsakanikas. 2000. "University–Industry Cooperation in Research and Development." *Proceedings of Organizational Issues in University Technology Transfer*. Krannert School of Management, Purdue University, Indianapolis, IN, June 9–11.

Porter, M.E. 1990. *The Competitive Advantage of Nations*. London: Macmillan.

Stake, R. 1994. "Case Studies." In *Handbook of Qualitative Research*, ed. N. Denzin and Y. Lincoln, 236–47. Newbury Park, CA: Sage.

Yin, R.K. 1993. *Applications of Case Study Research*. Newbury Park, CA: Sage.

———. 1994. *Case Study Research: Design and Methods*, 2d ed. Newbury Park, CA: Sage.

Additional Reading

Alasaarela, E. et al. 2002. *Higher Education as a Pathway to Entrepreneurship: Benchmarking Report*. Central Ostrobothnia Polytechnic, Finland.

Bailey, E.K. 1995. "An Academic Model of Excellence for International Business Education." *Management Development* 14, no. 5: 50–60.

Betz, F. 1994. *Strategic Technology Management*. New York: McGraw-Hill.

Carland, J.C.; J.W. Carland; and R. Higgs. 1997. "Innovative Education in an Integrated Business Core Curriculum: An Experiential Learning Paradigm." Working paper, Western Carolina University College of Business.

Davis, J., and K.T. Mehta. 1997. "Reengineering a School of Business of the Future: A Mission/Vision Model for Higher Education in Transformational Times." *SAM Advanced Management Journal* 62, no. 2: 8–15.

Garvin, D.A. 1995. "Leveraging Processes for Strategic Advantage." *Harvard Business Review* (September–October): 77–90.

Hammer, M., and J. Champy. 1993. *Reengineering the Corporation: A Manifesto for Business Revolution*. New York: Harper Business.

Ishida, H. 1997. "MBA Education in Japan." *Journal of Management Development* 6, no. 3: 185–96.

Joseph, M., and B. Joseph. 1997. "Service Quality in Education: A Student Perspective." *Quality Assurance in Education* 5, no. 1: 15–21.

Keithly, D., and T. Redman. 1997. "University–Industry Partnerships in Management Development: A Case Study of a 'World-Class' Company." *Journal of Management Development* 16, no. 3: 154–66.

Lantos, G.P. 1994. "Faculty Internships: A Means to Bridge the Academician-Practitioner Gap." *Journal of Product and Brand Management* 3, no. 4: 15–30.

Lasonen, J.L. 1999. "Lifelong Learning and Training: A Bridge to the Future Entrepreneurship and Self-employment Training." In *Technical and Vocational Education Second International Congress on Technical and Vocational Education* (April): 26–30.

Levie, J. 1999. *Entrepreneurship Education in Higher Education in England: A Survey.* London: London Business School.

Porter, J. 1993. "Business Reengineering in Higher Education: Promise and Reality." *Cause/Effect*: 48–53.

Prince, C. 1999. "Transforming the University Business School for the 21st Century." *Strategic Change* 8: 459–71.

Schlesinger, P. 1996. "Teaching and Evaluation in an Integrated Curriculum." *Journal of Management Education* 20, no. 4: 479–99.

Selen, W. 2001. "Learning in the New Business School Setting: A Collaborative Model." *Learning Organization* 8, no. 3: 106–13.

Tomovic, M. 2001. "University–Industry Cooperation in Curriculum Development and Delivery." Paper presented at the International Conference on Engineering Education, Oslo, Norway, August 6–10.

Walker, W.B., and E.L. Black. 2000. "Reengineering the Undergraduate Business Core Curriculum: Aligning Business Schools with Business for Improved Performance." *Business Process Management Journal* 6, no. 3: 194–213.

23

Open vs. Closed Minds

Lessons in Management Education from the International Leadership Development Academy in Ghana

Earl N. Caldwell II and Vanessa Gail Perry

Knowledge of cultural differences is key to global management education. It has been well documented that cultural values differ significantly between populations and that respective management styles are also likely to differ (Banai and Katsounotos 1993; Terpstra and David 1985). In addition, these differences have crucial implications for future working relationships between managers from the United States and Africa. One important cultural difference is dogmatism, which refers to the resistance to change of belief systems—that is, a group of ideas and beliefs organized into a closed system (Fiechtner and Krayer 1987). It represents the degree to which an individual's mind-set (belief-disbelief system) is open or closed. The purpose of this research is to inform the development of an entrepreneurship curriculum in Ghana that effectively takes into account the role of dogmatism, self-esteem, and locus of control, which are basic beliefs that people hold with respect to their interaction with others and the world around them.

Research Context

The International Leadership Development Academy (ILDA) is a summer program that contributes to the ongoing process of building tomorrow's leaders through leadership training, education, work experience, community development, and cultural understanding. In particular, the purpose of the ILDA is to foster entrepreneurship and business development in Africa by facilitating partnerships between African and American students. The ILDA and the Pan African Student Summit (Summit) are sister organizations. The Summit is an annual International African student conference hosted in Africa. The Summit not only provides a mechanism for foreign students to be introduced to Africa and African students, but a vehicle for African students to meet fellow African students from different countries.

The Summit and ILDA use traditional business pedagogical models such as case studies, cross-cultural experiences, an exchange program, research and scholarship, and entrepreneurship to create a vehicle for practical learning, historical and cultural enrichment, and leadership building. This multilayered approach brings together students, the academy, business, community organizations, and the public sector. Our goal is to design an educational approach that will help students develop leadership, critical thinking, and analytical skills that are appropriate across cultural contexts.

The ILDA is a four- to eight-week intensive summer study abroad program. The program is coordinated by an African educator who has extensive experience in directing and managing international students in summer programs in Africa. It includes lectures from African and American scholars, as well as those from the diaspora. There are presentations from government officials, business leaders, and community activists. Students engage in exercises inside and outside the classroom environment. The curriculum also includes individual and group projects. During this session students have the option of doing one, a combination, or all of the following: scholarly research that results in a publishable paper; work on a community development project or with a nongovernmental agency; or internship with a local business or governmental agency. Components of the ILDA are detailed in the Appendix.

Ghana

According to the *CIA World Factbook*, Ghana, which is located in West Africa, has a population of 20,244,154 as of July 2002, with an annual growth rate of 1.7 percent. Demographic statistics show that 66 percent of Ghanaians live in rural areas. There are five major ethnic groups in Ghana. English is the official language, although many Ghanaians speak local dialects. Sixty-three percent of Ghanaians are Christian, with Muslims and traditional religious adherents accounting for 16 percent and 21 percent, respectively. The private informal sector is the highest employer, accounting for 81 percent of the working population, while the government employs around 9 percent.

About 50 percent of the workforce is employed in the agriculture/forestry sector. Trading and manufacturing account for an additional 14.5 percent and 10.8 percent of the workforce, respectively (United Nations Development Programme).

Dogmatism

Rokeach (1960) suggests that highly dogmatic individuals are less open to change, are characterized by closed belief systems, and focus on future time. A person who is highly dogmatic is uncomfortable with the unfamiliar and approaches it defensively. Conversely, low dogmatic individuals are more open to change, are characterized by open belief systems, and are more occupied with present events. In other words, they evaluate information on a more objective basis (Palmer and Kalin 1991).

To say that someone is dogmatic, or that his or her belief system is closed, is to say something about his or her beliefs and information processing (Rokeach 1960). Since highly dogmatic persons are less receptive to different, unfamiliar, or unexpected information, they are more likely to discount or change the information during processing. Because this information is perceived as different, highly dogmatic individuals are more likely to respond in a negative way toward the information (Fiechtner and Krayer 1987).

Self-Esteem

Self-esteem refers to individuals' feelings of general worth and self-confidence (Rosenberg 1965). Self-esteem is a crucial part of every person and is essential to living a happy and productive life. Psychologists believe that the most well-adjusted people have moderately high self-esteem. That is, these individuals tend to feel good about themselves, but are able to admit that they have flaws. On the other hand, people with low self-esteem tend to struggle through life (Janda 2001). Research has demonstrated that individuals low in self-esteem tend to respond to experiences in a balanced way. More specifically, positive events lead to positive psychological states and negative events lead to negative ones (Taylor and Brown 1988). By contrast, high self-esteem individuals tend to embrace positive events but disregard or offset the potentially debilitating effects of negative events, and this is associated with maintaining positive psychological states (Campbell 1990). Given that dogmatism focuses on a closed system of beliefs and is related to individuals' high status beliefs, we expect a relationship between dogmatism and self-esteem.

Individualism and Collectivism

Individualism and collectivism have been identified as orientations held with respect to a person's or group's relationship with others (Hofstede 1980). Individualism can be broadly characterized as the tendency to value the individual over the group and give priority to personal goals over group goals (Triandis 1989). Accordingly, individualism stresses individual initiative, a greater focus on the self, and emotional independence (Hofstede 1980). In addition, it emphasizes self-reliance and freedom of choice, individual rights over duties, and cost-benefit analyses in determining behavior (Bellah et al. 1985). In contrast, collectivism focuses on sharing duties and obligations (Hofstede 1980). More specifically, the collectivism construct emphasizes the goals of the group over personal goals, stresses conformity and in-group harmony, and defines the self in relation to the group (Triandis 1994).

When studied at the cultural level, individualism and collectivism are considered to represent opposite ends of one continuum, and cultures are often described as being either individualistic or collectivistic in their orientation (Triandis 1994). At the individual level, however, research suggests that individualism and collectivism represent separate dimensions (Triandis and Gelfand 1998). Both individualism and collectivism can exist within the same culture, and a person may possess both individualistic and collectivistic tendencies (Triandis 1994). However, different situations may cause a person to exhibit individualistic or collectivistic aspects of the self (Trafimow, Triandis, and Goto 1991). Given research showing that dogmatic individuals possess closed belief systems, we expect that dogmatism may be related to a focus on the self and individual self-reliance. Because the present study measured collectivism among respondents from two cultures, we expect to find an inverse relationship between dogmatism and collective orientation.

Locus of Control

One of the most researched constructs in the field of personality, locus of control is the measure of how much people rely on internal or external variables to determine their fate (Rotter 1990). Accordingly, the concept has been widely applied to various interpersonal (e.g., seeking information, taking political action) and intrapsychic (e.g., defensive externality, attribution) phenomena. Internal control can be described as the extent to which people depend on their own behavior or personal characteristics in determining their fate (Rotter 1989). They typically perceive themselves as having control over their future and believe that outcomes are related to the work they put into achieving them (Lefcourt 1991). On the other hand, external control is the degree to which a person thinks that outcomes are a function of chance, luck, or fate (Rotter 1989). In other words, people who believe that they are relatively powerless and have little influence over outcomes are said to have an external locus of control (externals).

Triandis (1989 has noted that this psychological construct of locus of control is equivalent to the cultural-level value orientation dimension of beliefs about human-nature interactions. This construct reflects the extent to which a cultural group believes that it is superior to nature, lives in harmony with nature, or is subjugated to nature. We propose that individuals from Ghana, due to the agrarian and collectivist characteristics of the local culture, are more likely to be externals. Further, this reliance on external forces may encourage more closed belief systems with a focus on future time.

Numerous studies have found a significant correlation between self-esteem and locus of control. In one example, Martin and Coley (1984) demonstrated a negative correlation between external locus of control and self-esteem. In other words, internals had significantly higher self-esteem than their external counterparts.

Analysis and Results

Forty-one entry questionnaires and twenty-eight exit questionnaires completed at the ILDA in Accra, Ghana, in June 2002 were used in the present study. Summit participants included students from seventeen colleges and universities in Ghana and in the United States. The purpose of these questionnaires was to gather data about characteristics of student participants and to collect participants' evaluations of aspects of the conference. The analysis reported here is based on forty-one entry questionnaires, twenty-three of which were completed by students from Ghana, representing 56 percent of the sample. In addition, nineteen of the participants, or 46 percent, were males.

Figure 23.1 presents the average scores on dogmatism, collectivism, self-esteem, and external locus of control for Ghanian and American students. Results of an analysis of variance of these variables show that Ghanian respondents scored higher on dogmatism, collectivism, and external locus-of-control measures than their American counterparts ($p < 0.10$). In addition, Ghanians reported having significantly lower self-esteem than Americans.

Table 23.1 includes descriptive statistics for all model variables, as well as a matrix of correlations between these variables. Higher values for dogmatism indicate more closed-mindedness, while lower values suggest more open-mindedness. Collectivism is represented by higher values on this mea-

Figure 23.1   **Individual Differences: United States vs. Ghana***

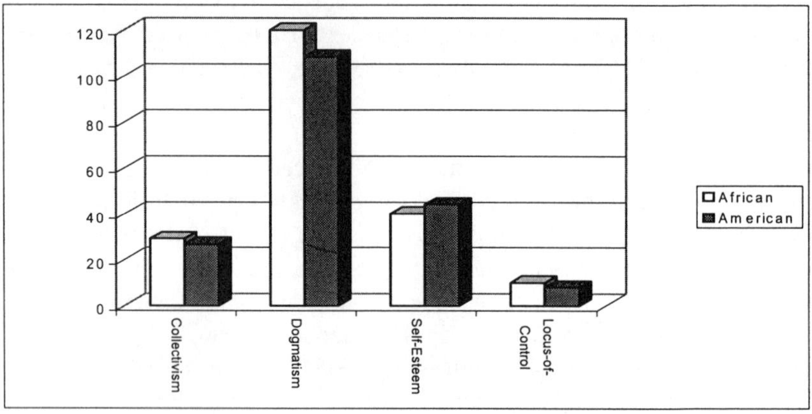

*Significant at 0.10 level.

sure, while lower values represent individualism. Higher values for self-esteem indicate higher or positive self-esteem. Higher values for locus of control indicate an external locus of control, while lower values indicate an internal locus of control. Home country is a dummy variable coded 1 for Ghana and 0 for the United States. Interestingly, dogmatism is correlated with self-esteem, locus of control, and country of origin, but not significantly correlated with collectivism.

Tables 23.2 and 23.3 present results of two multiple regression analyses. In the first model, we regress dogmatism on collectivism, self-esteem, external locus of control, a dummy variable for respondent's home country, and interactions between self-esteem and country and external locus of control and country. As the results show, dogmatism was positively related to both self-esteem and external locus of control. The results did not demonstrate a relationship between dogmatism and collectivism. The results of our tests of interaction effects show that Ghanians with low self-esteem were more dogmatic than Americans with low self-esteem. However, there was no interaction between locus of control and culture.

Since collectivism did not have a significant effect on dogmatism in the first regression, we exclude collectivism from the analysis shown in Table 23.3. The findings are similar in both models.

In summary, we find evidence that self-esteem and locus of control are significantly related to dogmatism and some evidence of the interactive effects of cultural background on these variables. The results of this study should be interpreted with caution given the small sample size.

Table 23.1

Descriptive Statistics

Variable	N	Mean	Std Dev	Sum	Minimum	Maximum
Dogmatism	41	116.18182	14.78271	3834	88.00000	140.00000
Collectivism	41	28.25641	2.77885	1102	22.00000	36.00000
Self-esteem	41	41.86486	4.95627	1549	31.00000	50.00000
External LOC	41	9.36585	3.54793	384.00000	5.00000	20.00000

Pearson Correlation Coefficients

	Dogmatism	Collectivism	Self-esteem	External LOC	Ghana
Dogmatism	1				
Collectivism	−0.022	1			
Self-esteem	−0.547**	0.338*	1		
External LOC	0.433**	−0.053	−0.477**	1	
Ghana	−0.392*	−0.184	0.380**	−0.018	1

*Significant at 0.05 level.
**Significant at 0.10 level.

Table 23.2

Regression Results, Dependent Variable: Dogmatism (including variable collectivism)

Analysis of Variance

Source	DF	Sum of squares	Mean square	F-value	Pr > F
Model	6	2995.35281	499.22547	4.10	0.0061
Error	23	2797.84719	121.64553		
Corrected total	29	5793.20000			

Root MSE	11.02930	R^2	0.5170	
Dependent mean	114.40000	Adj R^2	0.3911	
Coeff var	9.64100			

Parameter Estimates

Variable	DF	Parameter estimate	Standard error	t-value	Pr > |t|
Intercept	1	224.60345	67.95035	3.31	0.0031
Collectivism	1	1.36767	1.21218	1.13	0.2708
Self-esteem	1	−3.71429	1.33094	−2.79	0.0104
Exlocus	1	1.35460	1.72603	0.78	0.4406
Ghana	1	−70.42950	35.11969	−2.01	0.0568
Esteem Ghana	1	1.62946	0.72089	2.26	0.0336
Exlocus Ghana	1	−0.45533	1.07487	−0.42	0.6758

Table 23.3

Regression Results, Dependent Variable: Dogmatism (excluding variable collectivism)

Analysis of variance					
Source	DF	Sum of squares	Mean square	F-value	Pr > F
Model	5	2929.00858	585.80172	4.96	0.0027
Error	25	2953.37852	118.13514		
Corrected total	30	5882.38710			

Root MSE	10.86900	R^2	0.4979	
Dependent mean	114.70968	Adj R^2	0.3975	
Coeff var	9.47522			

Parameter estimates					
Variable	DF	Parameter estimate	Standard error	t-value	Pr > |t|
Intercept	1	258.85705	56.74995	4.56	0.0001
Self-esteem	1	-3.28353	1.18931	-2.76	0.0106
Exlocus	1	0.37198	1.41962	0.26	0.7954
Ghana	1	-74.74153	33.21714	-2.25	0.0335
Esteem Ghana	1	1.53231	0.68441	2.24	0.0343
Exlocus Ghana	1	0.19034	0.88751	0.21	0.8319

Discussion and Implications

In this study, we find support for cultural differences in the willingness to accept new ideas, known as an individual's level of dogmatism. We also find evidence that the relationship between the tendency toward open- vs. closed-mindedness and individual personality characteristics can vary based on an individual's cultural background. Just as these differences may impact the development and exploration of students' self-esteem, they may also have significant implications for educating managers and fostering entrepreneurship.

Appendix 23.1

Selected Components of the ILDA Curriculum

Cultural Orientation

This is especially geared toward American students as a means to transition into being in Africa. The orientation includes what to do and what not to do, health matters, and introductory lessons in a local language. The orientation also creates an environment for African students from different countries to learn and relate to each other.

Educational Tour

One of the lessons that the Inaugural Summit taught was that African students are as miseducated about history as are African students from the diaspora. Therefore, all students would be exposed to historical and cultural sites and information that have particular educational value, such as the slave castles in Cape Coast and the W.E.B. DuBois Center for Pan-African Studies.

Art Exhibition/Concert

The Summit and ILDA delve into education and scholarship. While those are important aspects, they do not represent the totality of African genius and ways to contribute. The Art Exhibition/concert was introduced at the 2003 Summit. It will be an annual component that will celebrate and give students who articulate better through artistic means an opportunity to express themselves. The art exhibition included artists from Ghana and Nigeria. The concert included bands featuring traditional music, contemporary African music, jazz, and more.

Engineering Project

The Engineering Project is a means to specifically contribute to the community. The Summit affords the opportunity to dialogue about what should be done. The Engineering Project demonstrates what can be done. ILDA participants will be involved with a community-based project. Students from Africa and the diaspora will collaborate during the school year through personal interaction and e-mail on the project, and then spend time working on the project during the ILDA. This project brings together professors, students, and engineers in the field not only to learn from each other but also to contribute to a community in need.

Entrepreneurship Project

Summit and ILDA participants are encouraged to submit a business plan for a small-scale project that can be administered through the ILDA. Students will play an active role in reviewing the viability of the project, as well as participating in the execution and, where necessary, administration of the project. Projects can be in conjunction with local businesses or an independent project for the ILDA.

Individual and Group Projects

During the course of the ILDA program, students will be required to do independent and group work. The individual work will be based on their area of interest. Group work will emphasize team building, problem solving, and critical thinking. Final individual and group projects are submitted at the completion of the program.

Career Fair

The organizers want to facilitate matching students with summer and career opportunities with companies, businesses, and nongovernmental organizations seeking students and graduates with an interest in the international arena. We want to have a career fair that will bring interested organizations to the Summit to participate and engage with students. Moreover, we want to develop a database of summer and permanent job opportunities for Summit/ILDA alumni to access and facilitate matching interested students and organizations.

Summit/ILDA Journal

The interest here is in publishing resolutions and proceedings from the Summit, research papers from students in the ILDA, and project summaries and/or recommendations from ILDA group activities.

Partnerships

The Summit and ILDA are presently engaged in discussions with academic organizations in the United States and Africa. We are exploring how to partner to promote our common areas of interest. We are also involved in similar dialogue with businesses and nongovernmental organizations. New established partnerships will result.

References

Azibo, D.A. 1996. *African Psychology in Historical Perspective and Related Commentary.* Trenton, NJ: African World Press.

Banai, M., and P. Katsounotos. 1993. "Participative Management in Cyprus." *International Studies of Management and Organization* 23, no. 3: 19–34.

Bass, B.M., and P.C. Burger. 1979. *Assessment of Managers: An International Comparison.* New York: Free Press.

Bellah, R.N.; R. Madsen; W. Sullivan; A. Swidler; and S.M. Tipton. 1985. *Habits of the Heart: Individualism and Commitment in American Life.* Berkeley: University of California Press.

Blascovich, J., and J. Tomaka. 1993. "Measures of Self-esteem." In *Measures of Personality and Social Psychological Attitudes*, 3d ed., ed. J.P. Robinson, P.R. Shaver, and L.S. Wrightsman. Ann Arbor, MI: Institute for Social Research.

Campbell, J.D. 1990. "Self-esteem and Clarity of the Self-concept." *Journal of Personality and Social Psychology* 59: 528–49.

Fiechtner, S.B., and K.J. Krayer. 1987. "Variations in Dogmatism and Leader-supplied Information: Determinants of Perceived Behavior in Task-oriented Groups." *Group and Organizational Studies* 11, no. 4: 403–18.

Hattie, J. 1992. *Self-concept.* Hillsdale, NJ: Erlbaum.

Hofstede, G. 1980. *Culture's Consequences.* Beverly Hills, CA: Sage.

———. 1983. "Cultural Relativity of Organizational Practices and Theories." *Journal of International Business Studies* 14: 42–63.

Janda, L.H. 2001. *The Psychologist's Book of Personality Tests.* New York: Wiley.

Kluckhohn, C.K. 1951. "Values and Value Orientations in the Theory of Action." In *Toward a General Theory of Action*, ed. T. Parsons and E.A. Shils. Cambridge, MA: Harvard University Press.

Lefcourt, H.M. 1991. "Locus of control." In *Measures of Personality and Social Psychological Attitudes*, 1, ed. J.P. Robinson, P.R Shaver, and L.S. Wrightsman, 413–99. San Diego, CA: Academic Press.

Martin, J.D., L.A. Coley. 1984. "Intercorrelations of Some Measures of Self-concept." *Educational and Psychological Measurement* 44: 517–21.

Owens, T.J. 1993. "Accentuate the Positive—and the Negative: Rethinking the Use of Self-esteem, Self-deprecation, and Self-confidence." *Social Psychology Quarterly* 56: 288–99.

———. 1994. "Two Dimensions of Self-esteem: Reciprocal Effects of Positive Self-worth and Self-deprecation on Adolescent Problems." *American Sociological Review* 59: 391–407.

Oyserman, D., and H.R. Markus. 1993. "The Sociocultural Self." In *Psychological Perspectives on the Self*, ed. J. Suls, 187–220. Hillsdale NJ: Erlbaum.

Palmer, D.L., and R. Kalin. 1991. "Predictive Validity of the Dogmatic Rejection Scale." *Personality and Social Psychology Bulletin* 17: 212–18.

Rokeach, M. 1960. *The Open and Closed Mind: Investigations into the Nature of Belief Systems and Personality Systems.* New York: Basic Books.

Rosenberg, M. 1965. *Society and the Adolescent Self-Image.* Princeton, NJ: Princeton University Press.

———. 1986. *Conceiving the Self.* Malabar, FL: Krieger.

Rotter, J.B. 1989. "Internal Versus External Control of Reinforcement." *American Psychologist* 45: 489–93.

———. 1990. "Internal Versus External Control of Reinforcement: A Case History of a Variable." *American Psychologist* 45: 489–93.

Rumpel, C., and T.B. Harris. 1993. "The Influence of Weight in Adolescent Self-esteem." *Journal of Psychosomatic Research* 38: 547–56.

Shimp, T.A., and S. Sharma. 1987. "Consumer Ethnocentrism: Construction and Validation of the CETSCALE." *Journal of Marketing Research* 24: 280–89.

Silber, E., and J. Tippett. 1965. "Self-esteem: Clinical Assessment and Measurement Validation." *Psychological Reports* 16: 1017–71.

Sue, S. 1999. "Science, Ethnicity, and Bias: Where Have We Gone Wrong?" *American Psychologist* 54: 1070–77.

Taylor, S.E., and J.D. Brown. 1988. "Illusion and Well-being: A Social Psychological Perspective on Mental Health." *Psychological Bulletin* 103: 193–210.

Terpstra, V., and K. David. 1985. *The Cultural Environment of International Business*, 2d ed. Dallas: Southwestern.

Trafimow, D.; H.C. Triandis; and S. Goto. 1991. "Some Tests of the Distinction Between the Private and Collective Self." *Journal of Personality and Social Psychology* 60: 649–55.

Triandis, H.C. 1989. "The Self and Social Behavior in Differing Cultural Contexts." *Psychological Review* 96: 506–20.

———. 1994. *Culture and Social Behavior*. New York: McGraw-Hill.

———. 1995. *Individualism and Collectivism*. Boulder, CO: Westview Press.

Triandis, H.C., and M.J. Gelfand. 1998. "Converging Measurement of Horizontal and Vertical Individualism and Collectivism." *Journal of Personality and Social Psychology* 74, no. 1: 118–28.

United Nations Development Programme, www.undp.ghana.org/pages/country01/2.htm (accessed December 12, 2004).

Wells, L.E., and G. Marwell. 1976. *Self-Esteem: Its Conceptualization and Measurement*. Beverly Hills, CA: Sage.

Wylie, R.C. 1974. *The Self-Concept*. Lincoln: University of Nebraska Press.

Part VI

China

24

Distance Learning Education in China

Jonatan Jelen and Ilan Alon

"May you live in interesting times!" is a Chinese proverb that sounds much like a good-luck wish. China's membership in the World Trade Organization may turn out to be just such an ambivalent experience. Committed to a sociopolitically cautious, deliberate, localized, and incremental absorption of market-economic structures into its system, beginning as early as the 1980s, China initiated a multitude of concomitant internal reforms in support of matching up its infrastructure and competitiveness to Western standards of commerce. Particularly cognizant of the impact and leverage of education in this context, the overhaul of the education system, with particular emphasis on academic and higher education, has been and still is among the more pressing initiatives.

Among the various disciplines in turn, China is especially handicapped by a serious shortage of business leadership and a near absence of postcapitalist management-style culture. Chinese Premier Zhu Rongji, for example, a driving force behind the nationwide efforts to revamp the education system, specifically acknowledged that China needs 1.5 million graduates of master of business administration (MBA) programs over the next ten years. Other estimates are in the millions (Southworth 1999). And even though a 2001 Gallup survey more modestly estimated the number at 350,000, this demand still exceeds by far the most optimistic capacity estimates of Chinese universities' business programs despite the explosive proliferation of proprietary MBA education during the 1990s, given more than 284,000 state-owned enterprises (SOEs), more than 428,000 joint ventures or foreign-owned corporations, and about 2,000,000 private or township enterprises in the country (Chinese MBA Web site 2002). But quantity is not the only issue. Of major concern is the different nature and "quality" of Chinese business education with it limitations and shortcomings in terms of tradition, content, delivery, pedagogy, and competitiveness.

This new context has not gone unnoticed by U.S. business education providers. Pressured by domestic market maturity, dwindling subsidies, and slow economic growth at home, and by the need to help China fill the void, domestic universities recognize a tremendous opportunity for expansion into this extremely populous and vibrant area of markets and are ready to respond.

In particular, U.S. business education lends itself well to this type of export. It is the U.S. crown jewel of strategic competitiveness; it is held in high regard throughout the world as demonstrated by the many foreign students and graduates of U.S. business programs; it is portable across nations and increasingly universal; it is politically unobtrusive and almost inconspicuous; and it is a substantial source of revenue for U.S.-based universities.

However, differences in culture, tradition, philosophy, and sociopolitical and economic infrastructure will certainly bring about challenges for American and other Western providers of business education internationally. Providers of business education to China or the services to restructure Chinese business education locally will have to take into account idiosyncrasies of tradition, culture, and environment in formulating their solutions and offerings. Thus, the question is not only one of "adoption" of, let us say, U.S.-based Western business programs by Chinese students and institutions, but also one of appropriate and relevant levels of "adaptation" of such programs.

In this chapter, we take the position that China's interests could probably be served, at least partially, with the adoption of continental European and Anglo-Saxon business education models by students and institutions, respectively. In this context we will explore four strategies employed by foreign and domestic universities in China: (1) education of Chinese students in the United States; (2) local education of Chinese students; (3) adaptation and reconfiguration of Chinese universities' business education departments; and (4) distance education provided to China from overseas, from the United States, for example. Subsequently, a framework is developed to analyze possible deployment by the U.S. education industry, and to assess educational competencies and capabilities of a proper response to the ambitious Chinese educational effort. To that effect, we discuss the following questions:

- Is the Chinese learner receptive to distance education?
- How capable is the Chinese infrastructure of accommodating this paradigm?

- How can the market be penetrated?
- What adaptations need to be implemented?

The chapter concludes with brief comments that attempt to discuss the applications and implications of these educational and technological innovations.

Traditional Paradigms of Educational Transfer

Generally, three mainstream paradigms have been established since 1978 in China to deliver educational content and expose the Chinese to Western methods:

- attracting Chinese students to study in the United States;
- establishing a direct presence in the Chinese market; and
- reconfiguring Chinese business education.

Attracting Chinese Students to Study in the United States

One powerful approach to the Chinese market is to attract more Chinese students and accommodate them in the domestic business school market. This is certainly not a novel approach, but is one adopted by many U.S. universities that have experience with international students. Chinese students, in particular, are able to score highly on the standardized entrance examinations, such as the Graduate Management Admission Test (GMAT), and can improve the admittance profile and subsequent ranking of U.S. schools.

While U.S. colleges and universities have traditionally accommodated increasing numbers of foreign students, with respect to China, this approach could enjoy renewed interest. Chinese gross domestic product (GDP) growth has been robust and accelerating for two decades and, thus, an increasing proportion of the future management elite can actually afford overseas education. Recent research suggests that China has sent over 320,000 students to study overseas in 103 countries between 1978 and 1998 (Shen 2000), and currently around 50,000 Chinese students study abroad every year (Yi 2001). This number is increasing by 20 percent annually (*People's Daily* 2001). English-speaking countries account for approximately 75 percent to 80 percent of Chinese students abroad and the top four destination countries favored by prospective Chinese students are the United States, Canada, the United Kingdom, and Australia (Böhm and King 1999).

The share of Chinese in total international students in these host countries has increased significantly in recent years. In the United States, United Kingdom, and Australia, Chinese students make up more than 10 percent of all international enrollments. Thus, China has become the number-one source country for these host countries. Of these Chinese students, about 30 percent to 40 percent are enrolled in business courses (Böhm and King 1999; *Economist* 2003).

Although cognizant of the new realities, with some relevant exceptions, traditional U.S. colleges and universities increasingly need an injection of a fresh student population following domestic saturation and the end of the Baby Boom impact. Originally conceived as regional monopolies, with little incentive for efficiency and effectiveness, universities are preoccupied with fundraising, campus building, and structures that barely accommodate the occasional self-selected foreign students. This happens with the usual administrative snags in registration, payment, and visa application processes, let alone the enrollment of large numbers of foreign students in a coordinated fashion. Due to the war on terrorism, attracting foreign students has been exacerbated by the recent immigration restrictions including additional interaction with the Immigration and Naturalization Services successor organization U.S. Citizenship and Immigration Services.

But as a politician would say: "There are no problems, just new challenges and opportunities." We see this new complexity best addressed via specialization, performed by a new type of "education intermediary" that will "package" cohorts of students by undertaking the necessary marketing and administrative processing, evaluation, and acculturation efforts. As an example, such intermediation could be established on terms whereby the university stipulates profit sharing with the intermediary and "outsources" a certain selection of core course to be taught by the educational intermediary in an effort to consolidate the foreign students into economically viable cohorts and to prepare them for the typical interactive environment in business schools' advanced courses and seminars. Such courses can then be integrated via traditional waivers or recognized directly if taught with the requisite quality. In other words, universities can deliver course content in the foreign country, say, China, and admit the students for the latter part of the curriculum to the home country to receive their diplomas. However attractive, it remains a "physical" environment, with all its ancillary constraints, especially with respect to the students' financial endowment and logistics related to the students' housing, work, family, and so on.

Alternatively, the host institution can work out with the home institution a matriculation agreement to be used as a contractual framework for a dual degree program delivered entirely in the host market. To do that, the university may need to develop a presence in the host market, discussed below.

Establishing a Direct Presence in the Chinese Market

Some of the renowned and endowed institutions have ventured down a more progressive path. For example, Fordham University's graduate business education entity (to name but one of its first-mover ambitions) maintains its Beijing MBA (BiMBA) in its entirety in China. This is the first foreign MBA degree in Beijing to be approved by the Chinese government. According to Fordham's Web site (www.bimba.org):

> [T]he goal of the Beijing International MBA is to provide world-class graduate business education for exceptional students and executives in China as well as for a small group of foreign students. Profiles of entering students, both full- and part-time, are comparable to entering classes of top U.S. business schools. With all courses in the BiMBA program taught in English, it is possible for students from participating consortium schools like Fordham to attend a semester in Beijing for credit toward their MBA. In this way, the Beijing program supports the internationalization of the university's curriculum. Currently, student population at BiMBA is about 250, a substantial increase from the 80 students enrolled in its first class two years ago. Further, this year marked a special occasion in the program's development, with 22 members of the first BiMBA graduating class traveling to New York to participate in Fordham's diploma ceremonies. In a separate but related development, Fordham has agreed with the China Institute to create a pilot language program in Mandarin Chinese tailored to faculty who are planning to teach in Beijing and to students who wish to spend a semester at BiMBA.

Such comprehensive and involved efforts remain, however, the domain of the world's well-endowed universities. It may be true that the financial and administrative efforts of such an implementation are commensurate with the prestige and positioning that the school will enjoy in the long run, but rarely are such resources readily available. Though we certainly do not dismiss this strategy, we believe that it may not be generalizable enough to benefit the average American college. We would also point out that there is a significant difference between credible, renowned programs and the numerous MBA education or training programs currently underway in Mainland China, that were permitted by the Chinese central government, sometimes in collaboration with regional authorities (Peng, 2003). Peng (2003) further suggests that building alliances with local Chinese educational institutions is one approach to getting around the strict control that the Chinese central government maintains over foreign degrees being offered in China. Other alternatives include cooperating with major multinational companies that need to train their local Chinese employees or selling courses over the Internet with the assistance of a local agent to recruit and administrate students.

Reconfiguring Chinese Business Education

The most robust but also the most intensive approach is direct investment in a distinct and specific Chinese academic business education culture. However, this discussion needs to include additional sociological and political considerations as it goes to the very core of Chinese management education traditions. For the three post–world war decades, a command and planning model became ingrained as China's economic systems, which reduced the enterprise entity to a mere production unit in the national economic system (Newell 1999). Western management theories introduced in the late 1890s were gradually replaced by Soviet-style socialist and Marxist ideology and did not survive except for isolated instances such as at Shanghai Jiaotong University (Li and Maxwell 1989). In fact, Wang (1987) notes that such subjects as organizational behavior or Western-style market economics were considered antisocialist and, understandably, were not allowed to be taught in Chinese higher education institutions before 1978 (Wang 1987).

Chinese higher education institutes emulated the Soviet structure of three types of institutions, that is, comprehensive universities, technological institutes, and financial and economic colleges (Borgonjon and Vanhonacker 1994; Shi 2000), which map to three streams of management education philosophy. At comprehensive universities, management education focused on macrolevel issues to incorporate Marxist economics and socialist theory (Zhao 1997). A second stream stressed industrial management engineering (at technological institutes), largely influenced by Taylorian scientific management theory, and emphasized quantitative methods (Shi 2000). The third stream with a financial management emphasis was delivered at specialized financial and economics colleges, catering to bookkeeping requirements for the centrally planned socialist economy (Wang 1987). Only after the open door policy following 1979, were more qualitative courses introduced, such as strategic management, marketing, human resource management, and management information systems. Interestingly, but not unexpectedly, these patterns also coincided with the dominant ideologies of the day. While the Cultural Revolution (1966–76) stressed Marxist and socialist ideas, Taylorism became popular after 1979, allowing for improved production efficiency without threatening socialist ideology, yet allowing for quick economic reform (Borgonjon and Vanhonacker 1994). Traditional Chinese management education was thus biased toward a quantitative approach and away from a people-oriented one, as observed by many Western scholars (e.g., Borgonjon and Vanhonacker 1992; Branine 1996; Warner 1992).

The post-1979 dramatic economic transition, however, demanded unprecedented levels of new managerial competence, evolving from bureaucratic order-takers to innovative entrepreneurs (Newell 1999), as SOEs were gradually transformed from "government production units" to independent economic entities with increased decision-making autonomy; the inflow of foreign direct investment (FDI) via numerous joint ventures rapidly increased; and thousands of private and rural (collectively owned) enterprises emerged with only limited policy guidance from local governments. Fan (1998) used a vivid metaphor to describe the new attitude toward this competitive, uncertain, and unpredictable environment: A Chinese manager felt like "a nonswimmer being suddenly plunged into the 'sea of market' by the force of reform . . . rushed in desperate search for new management concepts and techniques" (Fan 1998: 203).

In response, the Chinese government implemented several management training schemes throughout the 1980s, taking a "look West" approach (Borgonjon and Vanhonacker 1994). Among them, two are important in terms of influencing the development of Chinese MBA education. The first was a cooperative management training agreement between the Chinese government and the United States Department of Commerce in 1984, culminating in the establishment of the National Center for Industrial Science and Technology Management Development in Dalian (Fischer 1999; Li 1996). This Dalian-based program provided MBA courses from the State University of New York at Buffalo complemented by the then Dalian Institute of Technology for China-specific aspects (Li 1996). The second program was sponsored by the European Commission and the China Enterprise Management Association, with the China Europe Management Institute in Beijing in 1984 (Fischer 1999). This second Sino-Foreign program recruited both MBA and Executive MBA students, and drew teaching faculty from leading business schools across Europe through the network of the European Foundation for Management Development (Southworth 1999).

Although ostensibly successful, these two international cooperative projects had distinct destinies. After ten years and after graduating 241 MBA candidates who were propelled to high-profile positions in the Chinese government (Li 1996), the Sino-U.S. program folded due to the American government's inability to maintain its involvement (Fischer 1999). The Sino–European program on the other hand, after graduating 236 Chinese managerial personnel during its initial operation from 1984 to 1994 (Wang 1999), was relocated in September 1994 to Shanghai and renamed the China Europe International Business School (CEIBS), now a joint venture of the European Union Committee and the Shanghai Municipal Government with its proper facilities on the Pudong campus of Shanghai Jiaotong University (Southworth 1999). CEIBS is now a leading international MBA education institute on Mainland China, and was ranked forty-third worldwide and number one in Asia for its English MBA programs (Economist Intelligence Unit 2002). These two initiatives are credited with laying the foundation for subsequent proper Chinese efforts.

Deng Xiaoping's pragmatism and the dynamism of the new Chinese economy of the 1980s (Clarke 1999) triggered an urgent need for Chinese managers (Borgonjon and Vanhonacker 1994). Consequently, a series of developments resulted in Chinese domestic MBA programs beginning in the late 1980s (Shi 2000; Wang 1999; Zhao 1997). Initial progress to develop Chinese domestic MBA education was made in 1988 when a number of management professors were assembled by the national Academic Degrees Committee to conduct a feasibility study with respect to MBA education in Chinese universities (Li 1996). Consequently, a task force was set up in 1989 to formulate a working plan regarding training objectives, admission criteria, course structure, teaching methods, and degree conferment for MBA programs to be provided in Chinese universities (Shi 2000). Then, in 1990, a national decree was issued by the State Council to legislate setting up MBA programs on a trial basis in selected Chinese universities (Zhou 1998).

Formal MBA education started in the early 1990s on Mainland China. In 1991, a National MBA Coordination Group was organized to implement trial MBA programs, and nine universities were authorized to offer experimental MBA programs with a total of eighty-six admissions (Wang 1999). A further seventeen universities were added to the initial group, totaling twenty-six universities that were eligible to offer MBA education in China in 1993. As Chinese higher education institutes still lacked the necessary expertise and teaching materials for MBA education, many of these experimental universities sought assistance from their Western counterparts: Nanjing University partnered with the University of Missouri-Columbia, Qinghua was assisted by the University of Western Ontario, and Beijing University cooperated with Fordham University. The Chinese MBA providers simply emulated Western curricula (Shi 2000).

To ensure the quality of these national MBA programs, a National MBA Guiding Committee was set up in 1994 to replace the previous National MBA Coordination Group (Zhou 1998) to standardize screening, admissions, and examinations practices (Shi 2000; Li 1996). In 1995, thirty more universities were approved to offer MBA programs (Shi 2000). A mandatory national MBA entrance examination system called GRK and modeled after the GMAT was established in 1997 (Zhao 1997). In addition, efforts were made to compile case materials that were specific to the Chinese business context (Wang 1999). With this increase of officially authorized MBA programs (62 currently), the annual enrollment of MBA students in Chinese universities has grown from 86 in 1991 to about 15,000 in 2002 (*People's Daily* 2002).

Peng (2003) estimates that the annual intake of MBA students will need to be expanded to around 30,000 by 2006 and he concludes that

[M]anagement education in Mainland China has evolved from a political-ideology-dominated model to an economic-function-oriented approach. In particular, the rapid business growth brought about by economic reform and the open door policy has created an unsatisfied demand for professional managers. Differing from those earlier pure policy implementers required in the central command system, the professional managers demanded for the free economy should, first of all, understand the underlying mechanism of a market economy. Furthermore, they should be able to utilize available resources to maintain sustainable corporate development in a dynamic competitive environment. To meet the demand for such professional managers, Western style MBA education was imported into China in the early 1980s and Chinese MBA education has experienced a dramatic growth in the last decade of the twentieth century. (Peng 2003: 23)

Internet-Mediated Distance Education in China

There is an opportunity for Internet-mediated distance education models to be employed in China. The maturing of the Internet as a ubiquitous medium for learning, business, and lifestyles has also spurred an explosive proliferation of distance learning offerings in business, especially due to the "Internet-readiness" of the content. But while we may consider the paradigm ubiquitous in the West, it does not enjoy the same acceptance level elsewhere (Shive 2000). A careful analysis of the antecedents and success factors of Internet-mediated distance education to foreign students is paramount for the evaluation of this medium in the Chinese context. Four factors are evaluated herein:

* the receptiveness of Chinese students to distance learning;
* infrastructure considerations;
* market penetration strategies; and
* necessary adaptations of delivery, content, and pedagogy to the Chinese market.

The Receptiveness of Chinese Students to Distance Learning

From a historical perspective, the United States has advocated distance learning models of education. These were put in place to help disadvantaged students and working students to obtain higher academic qualifications. In China, the model has a significant advantage over other modes because of the increased sophistication of the market and the gap that exists between needed educational services and their supply.

Indeed, "dual mode" correspondence-based learning started the first generation of long-distance education (Yuhui 1988) as early as 1953 at the People's University of China. By 1997, this first generation mode was implemented in 635 conventional universities via their correspondence education divisions/schools, which provide for printed course materials, correspondence tutorials (assignment marking), compulsory face-to-face tutorials, and regular semester-end convocations.

The second generation was marked by the predominant use of the "new broadcast media." Indeed, China was one of the first countries to use radio and television for higher-educational purposes with the opening of its first Radio and Television University in 1960. In a phased approach, the first group of Metropolitan TV Universities also emerged in 1960. Though interrupted by the Cultural Revolution (1966–76), there was heightened interest in these original initiatives after 1976, especially as a consequence of the Open Door policy. This socialist modernization project called for an extensive qualified workforce. Although the general level of primary and secondary education in China was higher than in most developing countries, admission of students to higher education institutes was relatively limited.

In 1975, the rate of enrollment in China's higher education was less than 2 percent, whereas in ninety-two other developing countries the rate was over 4 percent. The number of college and university students constituted a mere 0.7 percent of China's adults above the age of twenty-five. The number of qualified technicians and engineers accounted for only 2.5 percent of the country's workforce in state-owned enterprises and institutes. A turnaround could not be accomplished by relying solely on conventional colleges and universities within a short timeframe. This led to the founding of the National Radio and Television University in February 1978, subsequently culminating in the establishment of the National Radio and TV Universities system in 1979. A Central Radio and Television University was set up in Beijing, initially supported by a system of 28 provincial radio and television universities, 279 prefectural/civic branch schools, and 625 district/county workstations.

In October 1986, TV University (TVU) teaching programs began to be transmitted by satellite every evening from 4:50 p.m. to 11:00 p.m. Forty-nine teaching hours of transmission time were thus added to thirty-three teaching hours per week via this microwave network. All these changes have provided new opportunities for TVUs to develop and expand. (For a comprehensive discussion of Chinese distance learning in higher education up to 1988, see Yuhui 1988.)

We interpret this level of exposure and length of experience of the Chinese learner to distance education and nontraditional forms of delivery as evidence of robust acceptance and receptiveness levels for today's Internet-mediated distance education, especially considering the quickly evolving imaging technologies and video-conferencing possibilities due to rapid expansion of bandwidth, throughput, and capacity.

Infrastructure Considerations

With respect to China's digital infrastructure the following milestones are ample evidence of its capability and quality (Ji'an 2003). At the end of 1994, sponsored by the former Education Commission of the People's Republic of China, Tsinghua, and nine other universities, China completed the China Education and Research Network (CERNET) Pilot Project, the first TCP/IP-based public computer network in China. CERNET consists of a nationwide backbone, regional networks, provincial networks, and campus networks, providing high speed transmission covering thirty major Chinese cities. The system is controlled by various ministries of the government, allowing some room for private-sector participation with ChinaNet and China GBN (Tan, Foster, and Goodman 1999).

In 1996, Wang Dazhong, president of Tsinghua University, led in advocating distance learning. In 1997, Hunan University, in cooperation with Hunan Telecom, established China's first online university. In 1998, Tsinghua University launched its online master's programs. In September of the same year, the Ministry of Education officially named Tsinghua University, the Beijing University of Post and Telecommunications, Zhejiang University, and Hunan University as the first group of educational institutions to pioneer the digital era of distance learning. In August 1999, Beijing University and the Central Broadcast and TV University were added to the list. In 1999, the Ministry of Education promulgated its "Comments on Developing Advanced Distance Learning in China," stipulating the guidelines, aims, and tasks of distance learning in China. The mandate for developing distance learning focuses on approaches that are planned, driven by demand, expand deregulation, and improve quality.

Another significant milestone was reached in December 2000 as the "CERNET High-speed Backbone Project" was completed. In support, in July 2000, the Ministry of Education released the Provisional Administration Methods for Educational Website and Online Schools, stipulating the jurisdiction of the ministry over educational Web sites and Internet-based schools. The ministry also granted distance learning licenses to Tsinghua and another fourteen universities, and expanded the pioneer list to include thirty-one universities and colleges. It also promulgated "Several Comments on Supporting Some Universities and Colleges to Set Up Internet Education Schools and Pioneer Distance Learning," which granted the thirty-one universities and colleges substantial autonomy in their distance learning initiatives, and allowed them to set admissions criteria and determine admissions quotas, to offer programs outside the subject catalogue, and to award statutorily recognized degree certificates.

In July 2000, the thirty-one pioneers formed a consortium called "Coordination Team for Advanced Distance Learning in Higher Education," with the objective of enhancing interpioneer communication and cooperation and facilitating sharing and leveraging of educational resources. In October, the China Advanced Distance Learning Satellite Broadband Multimedia Transmission Platform began operations, which allowed simultaneous transmission of video and multimedia channels at different rates. Moreover, the Internet access service provided by the platform enables high-speed interconnection with CERNET, forming a satellite–land consolidated bidirectional education network. Operation of this platform thoroughly changes the situation of the initial one-way transmission over the satellite TV network in China.

According to the latest estimates of the Ministry of Education, the thirty-one pioneering institutions have accommodated nearly 190,000 degree-seeking students. This vast infrastructural effort clearly demonstrates China's capabilities and readiness for interactive multimedia delivery of programs designed in the West.

Market Penetration Strategies

Potential Western providers of distance education to China must take note of market structural and cultural idiosyncrasies. The American model is characterized by private and competitive initiatives, dominated by concerns for organic growth, and motivated predominantly by *effectiveness* concerns. And to maintain the parallel, in e-commerce terms, it is a quest for *richness*. The Chinese model is grounded in the central planning tradition and culturally motivated by the concerns of a very large collectivist society about universal access to education and thus exploits the *efficiency* paradigm of distance and virtual learning, and, consequently, the *reach*-paradigm of e-commerce. This implies that the Chinese market cannot be approached the same way as the U.S. domestic market.

The cultural paradigm of collectivism demands large-scale levels of cooperation and collaboration with the political superstructure as well as cooperation at individual institution level. Traditionally, to enforce an intimate level of cooperation, the Chinese economy has accommodated foreign investment only in the form of joint ventures with equal ownership. This leaves little room for incremental and experimental small-scale partnerships, but requires potential providers to demonstrate an immediate capacity for large coverage. This commoditization and liberalization of education requires careful unbundling and outsourcing of some aspects of the education process as well as the integration of partners from business and industry. While most college faculty know how to "chalk and talk," the design and production of effective learning tools and activities in an online environment is a distinct skill. Teamwork between content specialists, curriculum designers, and online technicians from both cultures will be necessary, but can significantly complicate the process and progress (Shive 2000). While there is no magic solution to an endeavor of such ambitious magnitude, we advocate a multidimensional strategy that begins with partnership building as a distinct target long before content and delivery are considered.

Necessary Adaptations of Delivery, Content, and Pedagogy to the Chinese Market

From an American perspective, what the e-commerce revolution was for business, distance learning was for education. A fast-paced revolution atop a rather inert body of knowledge issued from several hundred years of evolution and centered around "talk-and-chalk" technology. But, analogous to Peter Drucker's vision of management in "The Post Capitalist Society" as a practiced but widely unconceptualized discipline, in the now almost typical pattern of technological change, distance learning has arrived without much warning and is being practiced without much preceding theoretical development. Especially in the United States it is still treated as a phenomenon with all its experimental characteristics.

As such, it cannot be leveraged to serve the Chinese market. The demands and the size of the Chinese market require standardization, quality control, and the recognition that course production is no longer the private preserve of individual faculty members. Ironically, this approach seems to have failed in the U.S. market, as demonstrated by some recent divestments from New York University, Columbia University, and other reputable institutions that could not recoup the initial investment in large-scale course design. Finally, what attracts students to the American market is the experience of having a program delivered by English-speaking faculty. It is important to recognize that distance education to China will pedagogically involve more than asynchronous posting to bulletin boards and synchronous faceless chatting. Pedagogically then, we suppose that the crucial success factor will be to evolve our own distance learning, using Internet-mediated video conferencing, the mode that made distance education in China successful in the first place. This in turn requires, first and foremost, that we review and revise our own distance learning models. Even if the management discipline seems naturally to lend itself to faceless distance learning for the Western market, nevertheless, its mission expands when provided to China. It must stimulate more than just descriptive and analytical outcomes, it must become generative for an entire culture to change.

Conclusions and Discussions

This chapter discusses approaches that can be used by educational institutions to penetrate foreign markets and capitalize on overseas market potential. In this context, the authors advocate an Internet-based computer-mediated approach to distance education that can work either stand-alone or in combination with traditional instruction to help bridge the space and time constraints of global markets.

Clearly, the potential of Internet-mediated distance education goes beyond teaching via the Internet within the interstate/internation boundaries or within one discipline. A number of examples from the literature can be used to illustrate the broad range of potential applications and implications of these new technologies across the globe:

- *International marketing education:* Alon and Cannon (2000) show how international Internet-based experiential exercises enhance student learning in the teaching of international marketing by linking student teams around the world.
- *E-marketing:* Granitz and Greene (2003) point to the e-marketing capabilities of distance education including personalization, community, disintermediation, consumer tracking, enhanced customer service, and mixing bricks and clicks.
- *Information technology management:* Loebbecke and Wareham (2003) offer a structured framework for strategic planning, using information, communication, and media technologies.
- *Economics:* Leamer and Storper (2001) analyze the economic geography that changes as a result of Internet mediated transfers of knowledge. Their results show that in fact the Internet causes additional agglomeration of economic activity.
- *Library:* Lyman (1996) discusses the concept of a digital library that can balance the needs of markets and polity as well as intellectual property and the public interest.
- *Educational policy:* Selwyn, Gorard, and Williams (2001) claim that Internet-mediated education can help overcome social exclusion in education and lifetime learning practices. Johnson (1997) provides an over-

view of legal, cultural, and technological issues surrounding the effort to develop an international model of distance learning that can be used in both developed and developing nations.

• *Early childhood education:* Ludlow (2003) examines how the use of technology-mediated instruction to offer initial certification training and staff development activities to prospective and practicing teachers and therapists, has enabled internationalists to enroll in West Virginia University to complete the program.

As the above examples demonstrate, Internet-mediated distance education has the potential to revolutionize traditional models of education, learning, teaching, and information sharing. While cultural, linguistic, legal/governmental, and infrastructural differences still exist between countries, the present chapter shows how one may overcome these difficulties to create value for societies and educational institutions alike. There is a pent-up demand for Western-style education in emerging and transitioning markets that can fulfill the educational objectives of these countries and the institutions that serve them in more ways than are currently perceived. It is possible, for example, that delivering (English) language education by broadband video conferencing is a compelling topic across disciplines and that the market for this includes China as well as other developing countries. Conversely, an American student may be able to leverage the Internet and instructors in China to learn Chinese language, culture, history, and so on. Such efforts may be cost-efficient and effective educational tools. While we are not aware of such efforts in China, we hope that educational policy makers, university entrepreneurs, and supporting businesses will continue to break ground in this area.

References

Alon, I., and N. Cannon. 2000. "Internet-based Experiential Learning in International Marketing: The Case of Globalview.org." *Online Information Review* 24, no. 5: 349–56.

Böhm, A., and R. King. 1999. *Positioning Australian Institutions for the Future: An Analysis of the International Education Markets in the People's Republic of China.* Sydney: IDP Education Australia.

Borgonjon, J., and W.R. Vanhonacker. 1992. "Modernizing China's Managers." *The China Business Review* (September–October): 12–18.

———. 1994. "Management Training and Education in the People's Republic of China." *International Journal of Human Resource Management* 5, no. 2: 327–56.

Branine, M. 1996. "Observations on Training and Management Development in the People's Republic of China." *Personnel Review* 25, no. 1: 25–39.

Chinese MBA Web site. 2002. "China Will Speed Up Its Development of MBA Education." Available at www.mba.org.cn/news/old1205/704.html (accessed December 12, 2004; in Chinese).

Clarke, T. 1999. "Economic Growth, Institutional Development and Personal Freedom: The Educational Needs of China." *Education + Training* 41, nos. 6/7: 336–43.

Economist. 2003. "Western Promise: Chinese Students Are Flooding in to British Universities." *Economist* 366 (8317): 53.

Economist Intelligence Unit. 2002. "Which MBA?" Available at http://mba.eiu.com/index.asp?layout=2002rankings/ (accessed December 12, 2004).

Fan, Y. 1998. "The Transfer of Western Management to China." *Management Learning* 29, no. 2: 201–21.

Fischer, W.A. 1999. "To Change China Redux: A Tale of Two Cities." *Education + Training* 41, nos. 6/7: 277–85.

Fordham University BiMBA Web site. Available at www.bimba.org (accessed December 12, 2004).

Granitz, N., and C.S. Greene. 2003. "Applying E-marketing Strategies to Online Distance Learning." *Journal of Marketing Education* 25, no. 1: 6–30.

Ji'an, L. 2003. "Advanced Distance Learning." *China Education Daily.* Available at www.edu.cn/20010830/200786.shtml (accessed December 12, 2004).

Johnson, A.L. 1997. "Distance Learning and Information Technology: Working Towards an International Model." *Law Technology* 30, no. 4: 1–29.

Leamer, E.E., and M. Storper. 2001. "The Economic Geography of the Internet Age." *Journal of International Business Studies* 32, no. 4: 641–65.

Li, G., and P. Maxwell. 1989. "Higher Business Education in China." Working Paper 4–89, Curtin Business School, Curtin University of Technology, Australia.

Li, S. 1996. "MBA: Fast-track to Success." *Beijing Review* (April 8–14): 17–20.

Lin, J.Y., and F. Cai. 1996. "The Lessons of China's Transition to a Market Economy." *CATO Journal* 16, no. 2: 201–32.

Liu, Z. 1998. "Earnings, Education, and Economic Reforms in Urban China." *Economic Development and Cultural Change* 46, no. 4: 697–725.

Loebbecke, C., and J. Wareham. 2003. "The Impact of eBusiness and the Information Society on Strategy and Strategic Planning: An Assessment of New Concepts and Challenges." *Information Technology and Management* 4, nos. 2/3: 165–82.

Ludlow, B.L. 2003. "An International Outreach Model for Preparing Early Interventionists and Early Childhood Special Educators." *Infants and Young Children* 16, no. 3: 238–48.

Lyman, P. 1996. "What Is a Digital Library? Technology, Intellectual Property, and the Public Interest." *Daedalus* 125, no. 4: 1–33.

Newell, S. 1999. "The Transfer of Management Knowledge to China: Building Learning Communities Rather than Translating Western Textbooks?" *Education + Training* 41, nos. 6/7: 286–93.

People's Daily. 2001. "Hot and Cool Thinking over Studying Abroad—Reflections on China International Higher Education Exhibition Tour 2001." February 18 (in Chinese).

———. 2002. "China Will Speed Up Development of MBA Education, the Planned Recruitment for 2002 is 15,000." May 12 (in Chinese).

Peng, Z. 2003. "Development of MBA Education in China: Opportunities and Challenges for Western Universities." *International Journal of Business and Management Education* 11, no. 1.

Selwyn, N.; S. Gorard; and S. Williams. 2001. "Digital Divide or Digital Opportunity? The Role of Technology in Overcoming Social Exclusion in U.S. Education." *Educational Policy* 15, no. 2: 258–77.

Shen, L. 2000. "Thirty-two Hundred Thousands Study Overseas in Twenty Years." *Life Daily*, January 6, Study Abroad Information Section (in Chinese).

Shi, Y. 2000. "A Status Report on MBA Education in China." *International Journal of Educational Reform* 9, no. 4: 328–34.

Shive, G. 2000. "Distance Learning in a Digital Era: Implications for Sino-American Educational Exchanges." Available at www.chinaonline.com/commentary_analysis/intrelations/currentnews/secure/edusample.asp (accessed December 12, 2004)

Southworth, D.B. 1999. "Building a Business School in China: The Case of the China Europe International Business School (CEIBS)." *Education + Training* 41, nos. 6/7: 325–30.

Tan, Z.; W. Foster; and S. Goodman. 1999. "China's State-coordinated Internet Infrastructure." *Association for Computing Machinery. Communications of the ACM* 42, no. 6: 44–52.

United Nations Conference on Trade and Development (UNCTAD). 2002. "UNCTAD Predicts 27% Drop in FDI Inflows This Year: China May Outstrip U.S. as World's Largest FDI Recipient." TAD/INF/PR/63, October 24, 2002. Available at www.unctad.org/Templates/Webflyer.asp?docID=2832 &intItemID=2068&lang=1/ (accessed May 1, 2003).

Wang, Z. 1987. "Management Education in China: Retrospects and Prospects." Management Paper 5, Graduate School of Management, Monash University, Australia.

Wang, Z.M. 1999. "Current Models and Innovative Strategies in Management Education in China." *Education + Training* 41, nos. 6/7: 312–18.

Warner, M. 1992. *How Chinese Managers Learn*. London: Macmillan.

Yi, Y. 2001. "Promotion War in Hot for International Education Market." Available at http://abroad.netbig.com/head/h1/456/20010629/105509.htm (accessed December 12, 2004).

Yuhui, Z. 1988. "China: Its Distance Higher-Education System." *Prospects* 18, no. 2: 217–28.

Zhao, S. 1997. "MBA Graduate Education in the People's Republic of China." *Journal of the Australian and New Zealand Academy of Management* 3, no. 1: 59–66.

Zhou, W. 1998. "MBA Education in China." *Journal of Higher Education in Jiangshu*, no. 3: 64–66 (in Chinese).

25

Educating Future Marketing Professionals in China

Ilan Alon and Le Lu

Every truth has four corners: as a teacher I give you one corner, and it is for you to find the other three.
—Confucius

Market-based business education in China is a discrete field devoted to the acquisition and application of the unique set of knowledge and skills used in commercial or industrial establishments. It develops an understanding of business, technology, and economic concepts; it develops opportunities for the application of basic academic, thinking, and interpersonal skills; it helps in the economic transition, upon which China embarked in 1978. Its study contributes to a student's opportunities to become a productive worker, an economically successful entrepreneur, and a keen consumer. Business education thus defined and described is applicable in the Chinese context today, but the systematic development of education in business-related fields and its nationwide application has a brief history, going back no more than twenty years. Thus, any effort to evaluate China's business education with the criteria used in judging Western business education is essentially doomed. A reasonable evaluation has to be based on the social and historical background of China's business education. This chapter sets the framework for analyzing marketing and business education in China, and aims to provide a macrounderstanding of China's business education, a framework into which anyone who is interested in a more detailed knowledge can add his/her information.

The need for marketing education has become apparent, as China has transitioned from a planned economy controlled by the state to a more capitalistic society guided by free market principles (Alon 2003a). Marketing education in China has followed the general path of business education, which, before the formation of the communist government in 1949, was taught in universities throughout China. After that point, a seller's market developed, one based on resource scarcity controlled by the central government, and there was no need for market-based consumer orientation, distribution, pricing, promotion, or branding (Zhou 1991). Marketing and business education as it is taught in the West reappeared in 1978 when the Central Committee of the Chinese Communist Party called for a market socialist economy, a politically autocratic liberal economy. Because of economic liberalization, a buyers' market has emerged, and marketing, along with other market-based business functions, has grown in importance. A derived demand for marketing and business education followed. It should be noted that the term "business" in China roughly corresponds to commerce, economics, and/or management, and includes marketing as a core component (Zhou 1991). Development aspects of marketing education, business education, and liberal economics education are thus intertwined.

First, a brief look at the Chinese educational tradition and history will foster an understanding of today's education in China in a general sense; more to the point of this chapter, such an overview will reveal a striking contrast between the meaning and description of education and business theory in the past and what they are today in modern China. Subsequent to this discussion, the rapid growth of business education in today's China is surveyed, together with a short introduction of typical modes of business education. Following a discussion of the rationales behind the rapid growth is an examination of the challenges China's business education faces and the questions to which Chinese business educators are trying to find solutions. Many of the illustrations used in this chapter are from Shanghai and Beijing, two major cities representing China's direction of development.

Cultural Development of Chinese Educational Systems

Traditional education in Chinese history is embedded in Confucian culture. The ultimate purpose of education is nothing but moral and cultural cultivation and the cultivation of social and political administrative skills. This educational tradition has the following features:

- It emphasizes the inheritance of knowledge rather than its creation. Teaching is what is passed on from the teacher to the learner for him to copy.

- It attaches greater importance to social and political functions than to skills in economic and productive activities. The focus of education in both public and private schools was Confucian classical models and texts. Moral instruction formed the focus of education.
- It stresses the achievement and reputation of an individual but treats "the mention of profits" as despicable. One was advised to fulfill economic goals through the acquisition of high official positions, rather than through direct involvement in economic activities.

By the end of the Qing Dynasty (1644–1911), when Western culture began to exert an impact on Chinese culture, the Qing government had abolished the Royal Examination System and founded schools in the modern sense. By eliminating the bureaucratic hierarchy that was the centerpiece of all individual career goals, China effectively began a movement toward its present state. Only then did Western educational concepts and methods find their way into China. However, higher education then—in the early twentieth century—was weighted more heavily in favor of social sciences and humanities than engineering and business education. Successive waves of political and economic instability rocked China in this period. As a result, China saw neither the establishment of a systematic industrial and commercial management theory nor a corresponding educational system; however, Western theories of industrial and commercial management as well as practical knowledge, such as accounting and trade regulations, were being taught in some higher educational institutions at that time.

The 1950s saw China establish a planned economy characterized by public ownership, an economy based on a completely different theory from core Western economic theory. The models and patterns of management were imported from the former Soviet Union. One of the most important features of the economic system was the integration of political, economic, and social functions into one economic unit. As a natural consequence, this economy set up a management theory with its own characteristics and its own rules of operation. The *An Gang* Constitution, for example, put forward principles specific to the management of socialist enterprises. As the government controlled the economic activities of these enterprises, the role and force of the market were close to zero. Enterprises did not need to make decisions concerning production according to the demands of the market, nor did they need to do strategic planning in response to market competition. Therefore, the absence of a rationalist economic basis led to the absence of modern industrial and commercial management theories in practice and in education. The dominant economic theory taught in the university was political economics, a theory based on Marxism. Some Western economic theories were also introduced and taught, but not for practical purposes—that is, they were not to be used in "real" economic activities.

During the Cultural Revolution (1966–76), higher education existed in name only; in reality, colleges and universities were battlefields for revolution. Economics courses were among those completely removed from the curriculum as "capitalist products" and the idea of a "business school" had too capitalist a connotation to be allowed to exist. In 1977, the second year following the termination of the disastrous Cultural Revolution, there was a turning point in the history of China's higher education, for that was the year in which the higher-education national entrance examination system was restored. Universities all over China began to enroll students in many disciplines. However, marketing and business were not chief among them for both practical and political reasons. The second year after the restoration of the entrance examination saw the enrollment of business and economics students at Shanghai University for Economics and Finance, but these students were admitted at a lower grade level than the level at which engineering and science students were admitted. Only three specialized courses were initially offered: accounting, statistics, and industrial economics. The economic system at that time did not require very much more of its practitioners.

With the opening up of China since 1978, an increasing number of Chinese universities have set up departments or colleges of marketing, economics and trade, management, and other business-related fields. These departments have little trouble attracting strong students due to increasing market demand by both domestic and international companies for more sophisticated and modern marketing and business skills. The government encourages and cooperates with educational institutions in the training and education of specialists for modern enterprises.

Describing the education system in China, Hu and Grove (1999) suggest that the transmission of knowledge is oriented more toward theory than toward practice and application; great emphasis is placed on details and facts, which are often committed to memory; a key learning objective is to know and be able to state facts and theories as givens; the content of learning is whatever is found in assigned texts or other readings, as books are the sources of authority; the teachers whose classroom styles are most admired are those who give clearly structured, information-packed lectures written on the blackboard (which students copy verbatim).

This educational philosophy contrasts with the American model, which is increasingly based on case studies, discussion, and experiential education. In the Chinese students' view, run-of-the-mill discussions waste precious time that ought to be used by the teacher to deliver intellectual treasures. Therefore, Chinese students often come to the classroom as an attentive, respectful, and passive audience. This pedagogical tradition is, unfortunately, evident even in master of business administration (MBA) education. As a result, China's MBA education has the following features, which are incompatible with the model of MBA education generally found in the West:

- More transmission of knowledge than encouragement of creative thinking
- More classroom teaching than practicum
- More academic research than experience sharing
- More theoretical analysis than case study
- More basic theory courses than courses that develop students' comprehensive abilities as managers and executives

Marketing and Business Educational Systems

The rapid growth of marketing and business education in China's higher education institutions is more varied in form than it is in the Western context, and represents a development over the past twenty years. Three types of educational systems have been developed to teach marketing and business:

- Business-education programs in Chinese universities
- Joint business-education programs between Chinese universities and foreign universities
- University-based government programs

While the first system is found anywhere in the world, the second and third kinds are typical of today's China.

Currently, more than two-thirds of the universities and colleges in the Shanghai area have developed international cooperation programs at different levels with universities from a variety of developed countries. International cooperation is much encouraged and advocated in China for it is seen as one of the chief channels of knowledge. Such cooperation is also seen as an economical shortcut to the acquisition of Western educational resources, educational concepts and models. It also speeds the training of a cadre of educated, specialized professionals for China's market economy. As far as business programs are concerned, most international cooperation takes the form of foreign professors teaching an average of eight to ten specialized business courses in Chinese universities as "foreign experts." The professors are invited to make textbook recommendations, model instructional methods that incorporate Western cultural practices, and to advocate curricular design or modification. A good illustration of this cooperative structure is the arrangement between the University of Shanghai for Science and Technology and the City University of New York, Queens College. Out of the ten courses taught by foreign professors from the United States, three are marketing-related: Marketing, Advertising, and International Marketing.

Another distinguishing feature of marketing and business education in China is government participation. The government strongly emphasizes educating a workforce with specialized market-based knowledge in the expectation that these people will be able to play a role in the reform of the market economy, especially in the reform of the operational structure of state-owned enterprises. It thus encourages universities, through its educational policy, to run and expand business-related programs and it provides universities substantial support. The China Machinery Industry Shanghai Sloan School of Management at the University of Shanghai for Science and Technology is a good illustration of governmental influence. The Shanghai Sloan School is an executive training certificate program involving a collaboration between the Massachusetts Institute of Technology's (MIT) Sloan School of Management and the University of Shanghai for Science and Technology. This cooperative venture was established and is supported through the offices of the former Ministry of the Machine Building Industry. Established in 1996, the program set the objective of training for state-owned enterprises and organizations high-level managers who "not only adhere to the principle of a market economy with Chinese characteristics, but also have the insight of global economics and technological development as well as management competence and expertise" (Administration Report of China Machinery Industry 2000).

The China Europe International Business School (CEIBS) offers another illustration of government participation in business education. CEIBS was set up in 1994 with the support of the Ministry of Foreign Trade and Economic Cooperation (MOFTEC), the Shanghai Municipal Government, and the European Union. With government backing, CEIBS has been able to capitalize on high-end international educational resources and has set the objective of becoming one of the top business schools in Asia. It is a new product of economic reform and the significance of its establishment lies in its being the first of its kind in China. CEIBS occupies a special place in China's higher education sector, special in the sense that it will play a leading role in developing business-education models, and will contribute to the education of first-class MBA students, managers, and executives working in or planning to work in China. It is the leading institution in China. Programs of this nature may seem extremely expensive when one looks only at average income levels in China (the tuition fees for these programs are eight to fifteen times the tuition fees for regular business training program in the university), but two facts work to mitigate a too-easy rejection of such programs due to their cost: first, some of the trainees are financially supported by the enterprises or government organizations they work for; second, they are presently irreplaceable, providing functions that are not available in any other form of business education. While mainstream business programs are mainly aimed at providing business communities with a basic workforce with some specialized knowledge, government projects are geared toward the production of a sophisticated, Western, globally focused upper-level management corps. CEIBS offers MBA education in which several Western-style marketing courses are offered. Other notable examples include Shanghai Jiaotong University, one of the leading universities in China, and the European Foundation for Management Development.

Modern Growth of Marketing and Business Education

The rapid growth of marketing and business education is reflected in the increasingly large numbers of students who opt for this focus in higher education. It was not until the mid-1980s that business schools began to be set up in regular educational institutions in China; the real development of business schools took place in the 1990s with the deepening of economic reform. The late 1990s saw a dramatic increase in enrollment. The number of students enrolled in business programs (including economics) increased from 396,534 in 1994 to 554,569 in 2001 (China Statistics Publishing House 1996, 2002).

The above numbers do not yet include the number of students in language colleges. The growing number of foreign-language colleges is a remarkable phenomenon characteristic of an emerging market moving toward internationalization and globalization. The significance of these students as regards the present topic is that a large percentage of the students in foreign language colleges are those who, in answering the needs of the market, have business-related minors that are usually placed in parentheses in recruitment brochures; for example, French (Marketing), English (International Business), or German (Economics and Trade). This is a unique form of business education that started in the mid-1990s when the market economy had replaced the planned economy as the main feature of the Chinese economy. The number of students who declared English (or English literature) as majors increased from 350,291 in 1994 to 417,604 in 2001 (China Statistics Publishing House 1996, 2002).

One may ask why the number of literature students is increasing in a rapidly developing economy. The fact is that Colleges of Chinese Literature are shrinking and Colleges of Foreign Languages that offer only literature courses are rare. Thus, the increase indicated here represents an increase in the number of language students who minored in business or economics. Therefore, adding the number of language students in strictly business-oriented programs to the number of students in business-related programs, we find, using 2001 enrollment information, that approximately 18 percent of the university students in China are taking business courses. When this is compared to the situation in 1979 when only one university in Shanghai enrolled just a few dozen economics students and offered only three economics courses, one sees a dramatic change, a change brought about by the equally dramatic transition in the economic system.

In the 1990s, Zhou (1991) and Chao (1995) reviewed the state of marketing education in China and found similar results:

- Transition to a market economy has promoted demand for marketing education.
- There is a lack of suitable books and qualified teachers.
- There is a lack of facilities and supporting teaching resources.
- Greater integration with the global economy is needed, and marketing can help.

These conclusions are in general still valid today. However, there have been rapid changes in the market economy of China, a diffusion of foreign ideas and foreign capital, and recent developments in university education relating to marketing and business education in the past decade. The development of the MBA, in which marketing is core, is one such development.

The appearance and growth of MBA programs is worth mentioning. While MBA education started in the United States in the late 1800s, China's MBA education started gaining momentum in the 1990s. However, recent growth, brief though the span may be, has spawned some significant figures relevant to China as a rapidly expanding market. Since 1991, when MBA programs first made their appearance in nine universities, sixty-two universities in twenty-seven provinces and cities have developed MBA programs. Enrollment figures show a marked increase: annual enrollment has increased at a rate of 6–7 percent per year, from a few hundred in 1991 to 12,173 in 2001. The total number of MBA students over the past twelve years approximates to 47,000, of whom 12,041 have obtained their degrees. However, the relative immaturity of Chinese MBA programs, coupled with increases in demand from local enterprises and joint ventures, has several downsides, which will be discussed in a later section.

In sum, modern marketing and business education in China can be said to have really started only in the early 1990s when the concept of "establishing a modern enterprise system" was put forward and when China was entering the age of the "socialist market economy." While residual educational concepts from the old cultural tradition and from the planned economy still make themselves felt in today's education in one way or another, business education in today's China has become a fashionable boom for young people. This trend is expected to continue for a long time.

Behind the Growth of Marketing and Business Education

Behind all the excitement about marketing and business education is the benefit people see and that they think they can harvest if they invest in it. In addition to this benefit-driven motivation, the sociopolitical background offers a more profound explanation for the current enthusiasm about marketing and business education as an imported Western concept.

First, under the policy pursued by the Chinese government to replace the planned economy with the market economy, each enterprise becomes an independent economic entity, the level of profit realization being the true and only indicator of success or failure. This dramatic change has given rise to fierce competition for market share, and, accordingly, enterprises are faced with a completely new situation, one totally at odds with the old economic system. In addition to production, service, and quality, the efficiency and effectiveness of internal management have become a matter of life and death for the enterprise and a prerequisite for its existence. In a crucial shift from the old system, the new system puts the enterprise in direct confrontation with its external environment, forcing the company to deal with issues such as consumer demand, sources of capital, sales channels, raw material supply, employment, product promotion, pricing, competition, and so on. Therefore, great attention has been paid to industrial and commercial education, as different techniques are necessary to navigate in the new Chinese economic system.

Second, inevitably, the opening up of China's economy has led the country into increasingly close contact with the world economy. China's entry into the World Trade Organization (WTO) and the speeding up of globalization make it impossible for the country to go its own way, which means that it has to abandon idiosyncrasy in favor of following generally accepted rules of economic activity. Obviously, economically advanced countries have many decades invested in the development of mature marketing systems, industrial and commercial operations and management, and institutional structure. To be a successful participant in this world, China must familiarize itself with these market-based operational systems and the principles and norms that support them. Without knowing the motivation behind economic behavior and the (sometimes invisible) rules of economic activity, Chinese enterprises can never hope to acquire competitive power in their confrontations with foreign enterprises. Therefore, Chinese enterprises have turned to educational institutions for better knowledge of the business world, especially knowledge imported from the economically advanced West.

Third, the policy of pursuing a market economy and encouraging differing ownership models for domestic enterprises does not necessarily mean the elimination of state-owned enterprises. On the contrary, those state-owned enterprises that play an important role in the national economy will keep their status. In fact, the Chinese government regards it as a vitally significant task not only to preserve the important position of state-owned enterprises but also to develop and expand their economic scope in the Chinese economy. But these enterprises will have to abide by the norms and rules generally observed in the market, while at the same time fulfilling the production or trade quotas assigned by the government to ensure the increase of enterprise value. Because the modernization of state-owned enterprises in China is strategically meaningful to the Chinese economy, the government has established educational bases for training specialists and has developed policies encouraging the management of state-owned enterprises to take business and management courses. The government even sends some managers to economically advanced countries or puts them in important positions in large joint ventures to further their theoretical and experiential learning. These are not random measures, but are an integral part of long-term strategic planning.

A look at the composition of MBA students in Qinghua University, known as a leading university and the cradle of top leaders of the central government, may help illustrate the point being made here (see Figure 25.1). What is especially noteworthy is the percentage of students from state-owned enterprises, which are normally large enterprises that play a pivotal role in China's national economy. A large percentage of joint ventures are ones created between foreign investors and large state-owned enterprises. A special feature of this initiative is the government's expectation that students should introduce Western marketing and business knowledge into government enterprises and into government itself.

Fourth, an increasing number of foreign companies and enterprises have flocked to the Chinese market since it opened up in 1978. These enterprises and companies, running on their own operational rules, need local human capital, and this has created a variety of opportunities in a burgeoning job market. Multilingual candidates with backgrounds in business education are finding that a number of jobs—from interpreter to business manager—are available. As the average salaries in joint ventures or wholly owned ventures

Figure 25.1   **Student Composition in Qinghua MBA Programs**

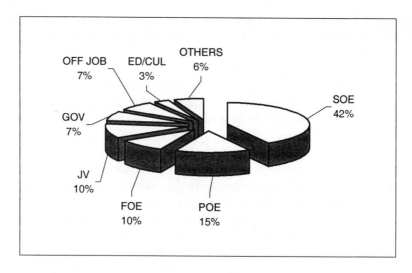

Source: www.sina.com.cn 2003/3/24.

SOE state owned enterprises; POE: private owned enterprise; FOE: solely owned foreign enterprise; JV: joint ventures; GOV: government organizations; OFF JOB: those who quitted job; ED/CUL: educational and cultural institutions.

are higher than those offered in state-owned organizations, especially for highly qualified candidates seeking upper-level positions, young people are highly motivated to take business-oriented subjects and specialized courses, thereby acquiring credentials that allow them to compete for the highest paying jobs. The composition of MBA students in CEIBS illustrated in Figure 25.2 may indicate a strong awareness of MBA education among employees in foreign-owned enterprises and joint ventures.

Discussions of Marketing and Business Education Challenges

While China's marketing and business education, driven by a growing demand, is, on the one hand, an exciting prospect, on the other hand, it is confronted with some problems to which there do not seem to be immediate solutions. Having discussed the growth of marketing and business education at the macro level, and its bright potential for future development, we turn our attention to three daunting issues related to marketing and business education: problems in educational transformation, lack of resources and qualified teachers, and the need to localize business education.

Figure 25.2 **Student Composition in CEIBS MBA Programs**

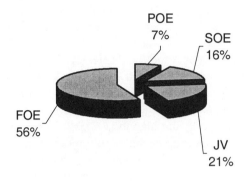

Source: www.sina.com.cn 2002/08/07.

SOE:state owned enterprises; POE: private owned enterprise; FOE: solely owned foreign enterprise; JV: joint venture.

Problems in Educational Transformation

Traditional education in China in the Confucian culture views education as the cultivation of social and political administrative skills. In the planned economy, students were financially supported by the government and were assigned a job after graduation. They were expected to implement the policies of the government. This orientation is clearly summarized by the following dicta, well known during much of the period preceding 1978 and illustrative of the normative, moral goals of all education: "Socialist education should serve socialist politics and socialist construction"; the purpose of education is "to transform the young into people with highly developed social consciences and the knowledge needed to serve the construction of the socialist state." Therefore, the basis of curricular design is not what the market demands; rather, it is what is required by the educational administrative body that represents the government.

Consumer orientation in education is a novel idea in China (to some extent introduced by business educators), threatening traditional relationships between teachers and students. Zhang Weiying, dean of the School of Management of Beijing University, has been quoted by a journalist from *21st Century Economics* on the topic of MBA education in China, "Traditional education is responsible for the government while MBA education is geared to the market. We used to see our students as our products, the products of professors and the college, while MBA education regards students as clients." While it may not be difficult to understand and accept the view of market orientation instead of government orientation, most professors would find it very hard to come to an agreement with an approach that totally changes the teacher-student relationship. The Chinese word for a teacher, *laoshi*, is a term signifying considerable respect and deference, not simply a designation of social rank and function. *Laoshi* and student are viewed to be in superior-subordinate roles, with *laoshi* being expected to take a strong interest in the development of the student as a whole person. Therefore, s/he plays the mentor as well as the parental role and his job is *jiaoshu yuren*, literary, teaching book knowledge and educating people, implying the raising of youth to be socially oriented. *Jiaoshu yuren* is a quality of a good teacher who is able to integrate *yuren* into his pedagogy. Some professors argue that if students are clients, they are analogically customers in a shop and all teachers need to do is supply the commodities sought. This view is equally unacceptable to many students, who were taught from an early age that the teacher is "the engineer of the human soul" and "a teacher for a day, a father for a whole life." It follows that both the educator and the educated agree that the educator provides education that he thinks is beneficial, instead of what the educated thinks he needs. This teacher-student relationship has been the model for thousands of years in a culture that puts much emphasis on writings from the past, writings treated more or less as sacred texts worthy of being committed to memory.

In sum, the traditional educational system is rooted in Confucian orthodoxy. The Chinese economy's emergence into the global capitalistic system requires a new set of skills and abilities, and Western style education is filling this gap. However, in exporting its methods, Western education is challenging the very assumptions on which Chinese education operates, and inducing a transformation in its system that threatens traditional elements. A key question worth studying is how Chinese educational methods, in marketing and business as well as in other subjects, can adapt to and integrate with the global economy.

Lack of Resources and Qualified Teachers

Another problem lies in the lack of qualified and experienced faculty, necessary facilities, and teaching materials and reference books. The solution to the latter two issues is not especially difficult; in fact, some higher educational institutions engaged in business education, especially MBA education, are well equipped, and imported business textbooks are not as difficult to obtain as they were years ago. However, the aspect that concerns teacher resources and teacher quality constitutes a problem that needs to be addressed immediately. The growing numbers of business schools and students do not correspond to the growth of business educators in China, especially in the initial stages of program expansion. This was a problem back in 1991 when Zhou was writing, and it continues to be a problem today.

In universities without coherent business programs, it is not unusual for professors with expertise in a different field, such as engineering or linguistics, to "become" professors of marketing and business just by taking a few related courses. Furthermore, it is still common for MA or MBA graduates to teach business courses right after graduation, even if they do not have any significant business experience to speak of. Unfortunately, the teaching methodology thus used in the classroom is often poor: novice teachers without substantial experience in classroom pedagogy, the business world, or the discipline spoon-feed students from the textbook. The quality of teaching depends too heavily on the teacher's conscientiousness and sense of duty, and too little on those professional qualifications that lead to quality teaching and the transference of skills and expertise.

This lack of qualifications in business educators is magnified by a deficiency in the quantity of business professors. Out of about 7.2 million college students, about 1.4 million majored in business in 2001. There are only about 53,000 business educators to serve this number of students: 5,000 professors; 15,000 associate professors; 10,000 lecturers; 20,000 assistant professors, and 3,000 teaching assistants. Making matters worse is that about 65 percent of these educators are in the area of economics, many trained in Marxist orientations with little training in "liberal" economics (China Statistics Publishing House 2002).

The following numbers show a serious lack of faculty in China's business-education sector. The overall teacher-to-student ration in Chinese universities is 1 : 14. In business-related areas, the situation is worse with a ratio of 1 : 26. It should be noted that these figures do not include the foreign language students mentioned earlier who minored in business. When that number is taken into account, the problem becomes even graver. The surprisingly small number of full professors is upsetting, too: there are about 1,600 business students for each full professor. Considering the number of years that business education has existed in China, it is not altogether surprising that so few have achieved this high rank. However, the issue needs to be raised: While it is easy for the number of business students to grow simply through one year's enrollment, it may take a decade or more for a teacher to be promoted to full professorship, and thus for Chinese business scholarship and practice to catch up.

The general problems of quality and quantity deficiency discussed above are replicated in MBA education. Although MBA programs have the best business faculty of any institution, data show that the annual market demand for people with MBA backgrounds is estimated to be around 30,000, but the total number of MBA graduates so far does not exceed 20,000. This suggests a pent-up demand for MBA education in China, with scarce local skills to fill this demand. The lack of quality and quantity of marketing and business professorial skills may explain why those taking the 2003 MBA entrance examination in both Beijing and Shanghai decreased by 11 percent and 5 percent, respectively, while MA programs, which are more theoretically driven, are in a much better situation.

Western marketing, business and economic models dominate today's globally oriented thinking. China, with its Confucian culture that attaches greater importance to moral gains than to economic gains, and its history of centralized economic planning has a very different theoretical system and operational principles; consequently, China has operated under a different set of "rules-of-the-game" to date. The present scenario is that different groups in China—foreign ventures and domestic enterprises—compete under differing assumptions of business conduct. If this situation continues, the impact of WTO membership on China's transition to an independent economy based on impartial and fair rules may be delayed (Alon 2003). It is widely recognized that reforms in business education are needed for China to meet internationally acknowledged standards. One of the most promising innovations in recent educational history is the increasing number of linkages between Chinese and foreign institutions of higher education in the establishment of progressive business education programs.

Given the lack of faculty as a strategic concern for the development of marketing and business education in China, Western universities may be advised to develop educational programs designed for training the "trainers" of future business leaders who can then strive for better integration within the global marketplace.

Localization of Business Education

Chinese marketing and business students have benefited from the collective knowledge of Western marketing theories, management models, and classroom methodologies. While it is a trend that paves the way for the internationalization of business education and the globalization of the Chinese economy, the progress of global integration is hindered by a number of factors, including an educational system that is still a product of the planned economy, for which the curriculum was created based on government-oriented principles and political correctness. Adapting marketing and business education to Western models has the advantage of infusing much-needed knowledge that will help China to be competitive in an international business arena and to have a broader vision of the global economy. The main sources from which this global perspective is to be derived are foreign books, foreign teachers, and, increasingly, the Internet (although access to the Internet is sometimes controlled). These resources, however, have their limits.

In China, much of the teaching methodology used in the classroom is often based on rote memorization of foreign concepts. These concepts are explained in the context of foreign countries, ones in which most Chinese students have little experience. Adding to this problem is the foreign language in which much of the material exists. It constitutes another barrier to accessing Western knowledge and a wide range of international communications. Since there is too much reliance on translation and interpretation, by the time a translated version of a textbook or an academic work comes out in Chinese, subsequent editions of the book may have been published in the original language. Simultaneous interpretation of a lecture given by an English-speaking business professor in the classroom takes up time and limits the amount of information that can be transferred. There is an increasing need for Chinese knowledge creation by Chinese scholars for Chinese students that fits the global business models.

Because of the traditional concept of education, Chinese teachers and students hold books and written materials in awe and use them as sources of opinions or interpretations. From primary school all the way to postgraduate education, tests are viewed as the absolute determinants of a student's future. Students are accustomed to book-related knowledge, and they are good at taking tests based on the knowledge learned in the classroom and from a few assigned readings. Internships, case studies, simulations and group consulting projects—regarded as integral parts of a business education, especially an MBA education, in the West—are missing from the curriculum of most marketing and business programs, even MBA programs, in China. A key question that arises is how to integrate new Western-style experiential-based and participatory teaching methods to students who are accustomed to the present educational system.

The educational discourse system formed and developed in the Western business academy is being introduced into China, a country grounded in a very different cultural setting and a country that is still economically underdeveloped. China's business educators are now trying to assimilate the system. But how can this discourse system fit into Chinese business culture? Obviously, it involves a long process: accepting and understanding it, and being able to use its concepts in an environment to which the conceptual system of the discourse is totally new, if not alien. Alon (2003b) has discussed the unique nature of Chinese culture and suggested that Western business theories may not be relevant to the current Chinese context. In most state-owned and privately owned local enterprises, there is an increasing awareness of the need to absorb the imported system, but implementation is slow due to key environmental and organizational differences. It is not difficult to understand why some marketing and business graduates are frustrated when they fail to make the necessary adjustments to their working environment.

For this reason, some scholars argue against indiscriminate acceptance of Western theories and models without modifying them to suit local needs. It has been argued that a discourse system should be established, a system shared and adapted to the Chinese business culture, and, at the same time, compatible with the system used in the main stream of the world economy. In a more specific sense, to develop a domestic discourse system of this kind is to develop marketing ideas, economic theories, and management models characteristic of China's economy.

Some preliminary research has been conducted on cultural differences and on the educational approaches that may be appropriate for the unique state of business education in China (e.g., Aguinis and Roth 2003). Using a sample of seventy-six MBA students in Beijing, Thompson (2000) noted that Chinese students are as receptive to case-method teaching as Western students, and that locally oriented cases are more effective than material developed outside of Asia. It is worth researchers' efforts to find out what model of business education fits China culturally, economically, and pedagogically. It is important not only to policy-making government educational administrative bodies but also to those business educators who work at the level of making curricula and who actually stand in front of classes.

In order to address curricular and pedagogical innovation, some related questions need to be addressed. What are the characteristics of China's economy? What are the characteristics of Chinese business culture? What is the direction of development of the country's state-owned enterprises? Does the "socialist market economy" have the same market function as the one that is understood to underlie Western business and economic theories? How and to what extent will the financial, insurance, and legal systems of Chinese society be reformed? The State Asset Management Commission of Chinese government intends to strengthen a "select few" state-owned enterprises (SOEs) by merging 196 top SOEs into about 40 multinational conglomerates (*South China Morning Post* May 24, 2003). But when and how will this take place? Will SOEs be privatized, and, if so, to what extent? Therefore, before these questions can be answered and arguments settled, it is crucial to set up a working discourse system compatible with both domestic and international markets.

In conclusion, marketing and business education, a totally Western concept of education, is burgeoning in China. To equip China to compete as the country's economy becomes fully merged into the world economy, those who teach marketing and business in China have to shoulder the daunting responsibilities of learning, adapting, integrating, educating, and developing. They must engage in a process, and not merely settle for finalized products.

References

"Administration Report of China Machinery Industry." 2000. Shanghai Sloan School of Management at USST, unpublished paper.
Aguinis, H., and H.A. Roth. 2003. Teaching in China: Culture-based challenges. Paper presented at the Emerging Markets and Business Education Conference, The Georgia Institute of Technology, Atlanta, GA (November).
Alon, I., ed. 2003a. *Chinese Economic Transition and International Marketing Strategy.* Westport, CT: Greenwood.
———. 2003b. *Chinese Culture, Organizational Behavior, and International Business Management.* Westport, CT: Praeger.
Chao, P. 1995. "Prospects for International Marketing Education in China's State Enterprise System." *Proceedings of the Seventh Bi-Annual World Marketing Congress of the Academy of Marketing Science*, Melbourne, Australia (July): 86–89.
China Statistics Publishing House. 1996. *China Statistical Yearbook.*
———. 2002. *China Statistical Yearbook.*
Education and Science Publishing House. 2000. Green Paper on Education in China.
Ding Gang. 2000. *Innovation: Mission of Education.* Education and Science Publishing House.
Hu, W., and C. Grove. 1999. *Encountering the Chinese.* Yarmouth, ME: Intercultural Press.
South China Morning Post, May 24, 2003. Available at www.scmp.com
Thompson, E.R. 2000. "International Perspective: Are Teaching Cases Appropriate in a Mainland Chinese Context? Evidence from Beijing MBA Students." *Journal of Education for Business* 76, no. 2: 108–13.
Zhou, N. 1991. "The Revival and Growth of Marketing Education in China." *Journal of Marketing Education* (Summer): 18–24.

Conclusion

The Nexus Between Business Education
· and Economic Development

In transitioning and developing countries, business education is expected to play a more significant role rather than merely to improve the profitability and competitiveness of businesses. It is anticipated that business education will stimulate entrepreneurial spirit and strengthen the capacity of individuals to form new businesses, create employment, and generate income and tax revenues, and, in so doing, contribute to the elusive goal of economic development. Business education will marry the creativity and risk-taking characteristics of entrepreneurs with the sound technical skills and managerial know-how needed to operate businesses in a global economy. Through their lobbying efforts, technically savvy operators can potentially make more meaningful contributions to the formation of government policies that can better serve society's needs.

Although the transitioning economies and developing countries featured in this book have a level of development between that of advanced and underdeveloped economies and they share similar developmental goals, the transitioning countries are in a superior economic position. Both groups want to create jobs, diversify trade, and enter the global market, and both compete for capital flows and the resources of the multinationals, but the two economies face different challenges and issues.

The transitioning economies are formerly centrally planned economies, characterized by open or increasingly open political systems, growing industrialization as well as viable communication, technology, and legal infrastructures, which enable them to participate actively in the global economy (Donnorummo 2000). The countries possess an educated or educable workforce with the capacity to innovate and accept change, and thus have the potential to achieve sustainable economic development. Given their favorable economic status, some of the countries under examination, Estonia, Hungary, Lithuania, Poland, Slovakia, and Slovenia, became members of the European Union in May 2004.

Table 26.1

Quality of Life and Economic Indicators of Selected Transitioning and Developing Country Economies

Selected countries	Population millions 2001	GDP per capita (PPP US$) 2001	Combined primary, secondary and tertiary enrollment ratio (%) 2000–2001	Adult illiterary rate % of people 15 and above 2001	Average annual % growth exports 1990–1999[1]
Albania	3.1	3,680	69	14.7	13.6
Argentina	37.5	11,320	89	3.1	8.7
Armenia	3.1	2,650	60	1.5	−21.5
Belarus	10.0	7,620	86	0.3	−11.1
Bosnia-Herzegovina	4.1	5,970	64	—	—
Chile	15.4	9,190	76	4.1	9.7
China	1,285.2	4,020	64	14.2	13.0
Estonia	1.4	10,170	89	0.2	10.2
Ghana	20.0	2,250	46	27.3	10.8
Hungary	10.0	12,340	82	0.7	8.2
India	1,033.4	2,840	56	42.0	11.3
Kazakhstan	15.5	6,500	78	0.6	4.3
Lithuania	3.5	8,470	85	0.4	2.9
Macedonia FYR	2.0	6,110	70	—	1.2
Nepal	24.1	1,310	64	57.1	14.3
Poland	38.7	9,450	88	0.3	10.8
Russian Federation	144.9	7,100	82	0.4	2.3
Slovakia	5.4	11,960	73	—	12.0
Slovenia	2.0	17,130	83	0.4	−0.5
Turkey	69.3	5,890	60	14.5	11.9
Ukraine	49.3	4,350	81	0.4	−3.6
France	59.6	23,990	91	—	4.9
Japan	127.3	25,130	83	—	5.1
United States	288.0	34,320	94	—	9.3

Source: United Nations Development Programme, *Human Development Indicators 2003, Human Development Report UNDP.* Available at http://hdr.undp.org/reports/global/2003/indicator/index_indicators.html (accessed December 12, 2002).

[1] Data are from the World Development Report 2000/2001 World Bank.

[2] Inward Performance Index Rank UNCTAD (ranks countries by FDI received relative to their economic size, calculated as the ratio of a country's share in global FDI inflows relative to its share in global GDP).

[3] Data are from the International Telecommunications Union (ITU) *World Telecommunications Report 1999.*

[4] Data are from the Global Entrepreneurship Monitor 2003.

Table 26.1 highlights differences in selected quality of life and economic indicators for transitioning and developing countries discussed in earlier chap-

Foreign direct investment (FDI) millions of dollars 1998[1]	Inward FDI performance index rank 1999–2001[2]	Stock market capitalization millions of dollars 1999[1]	Patents granted to residents per million people 1999	Personal computers per 1,000 people 1998[3]	Scientists and engineers in R&D per million people 1996–2000	Number of start ups[4] (1,000) 2002–2003
45	67	—	0	—	—	—
6,150	42	83,887	4	44.3	714	1,991
232	38	25	46	4.2	1,313	—
149	87	—	39	—	1,893	—
873	—	2,584	0	111.6	—	45
4,638	19	68,228	1	48.2	370	732
43,751	59	330,703	2	8.9	54.5	56,325
581	21	1,789	4	34.4	2,128	—
56	77	916	0	1.6	—	—
1,936	53	16,317	30	58.9	1,445	251
2,365	120	184,605	1	2.7	157	85,380
1,158	15	2,260	79	—	716	—
926	60	1,138	26	54.0	2,027	—
118	29	8	16	—	387	—
12	—	418	—	—	—	—
6,365	47	29,577	26	43.9	1,429	800
2,764	108	72,205	105	40.6	3,481	1,160
562	26	723	14	65.1	1,844	—
165	105	2,180	98	250.9	2,181	23
940	112	112,716	—	23.2	306	—
743	88	1,121	12	13.8	2,118	—
27,998	62	1,475,457	195	207.8	2,718	529
3,268	128	4,546,937	1,057	237.2	5,095	1,422
193,373	79	16,635,114	298	458.6	3,161	11,067

ters, with benchmarks against three Organization for Economic Cooperation and Development countries—France in the European Union, Japan in Asia, and the United States in North America. The correlations embedded in the table are indicative of the countries' readiness to provide and use the skills imparted by higher education, including business education, as well as participate in global knowledge economies. In general, the dimensions indicate that the countries reviewed in the book have environments that are amenable to the growth of business and management education, although the developing countries lag behind transitioning economies in educational attainment and the capacity to innovate.

Role of Education

Knowledge Creation and Innovation

According to new growth theorists, increasing returns to knowledge drive economic growth. Education not only provides the technical skills to create and use new knowledge but also serves to empower citizens politically, socially, and culturally and increase the level of independent thought (Mauch 2000). Countries with higher levels of education and research capabilities, as indicated by the number of scientists and engineers in research and development and patents filed, are better able to participate in the knowledge economy. Schumpeter in his classic insights on innovation and entrepreneurship in the capitalist system suggests that innovation—the creation of new products, processes, markets, or forms of organizations—results in the constant evolution of business activities, which leads to new and better ways of doing things. In the process, the old way is destroyed, giving rise to a dynamic process, which he terms "creative destruction."

McMillan and McGrath (2004), writing in a Wharton newsletter, argue that knowledge creation through research and development is insufficient to guarantee growth. Trained managers with competencies in adopting approaches to business building in order to connect technology creation to the target market are necessary. The high levels of competitiveness faced by businesses in the global market preclude the use of strategies focused solely on price. Thus, strategies such as low wages, deskilling, and relocation previously used by businesses to stay in the market are no longer sufficient. Managers need to be able cope with organizational change involving people, processes, and systems and to focus on issues such as standardization, quality, and reliability.

Increased levels of business and managerial skills facilitate access to international goods and capital markets and spur integration in the global economy, which, despite its discontents, provides a channel for growth. Growth in the export base and the development of an export sector reduce dependence on agriculture and move the industrial structures of the countries more in line with those of developed economies and closer to the elusive goal of development.

In order to create a cadre of creative individuals, countries need to emphasize the education of the populace as well as other strategies for the creation of human capital. The economic successes of the Southeast Asian countries of Singapore, South Korea, and Taiwan have been attributed in part to the emphasis that these governments placed on creating a highly educated workforce. The workforce was therefore well placed to make use of externally generated ideas, and then subsequently to transition to the creation of new ideas in their own right. Alliances with large multinationals provided valuable access to markets and attendant knowledge of strategies to penetrate the complex maze of international vendor/supplier relationships. Knowledge of how to deal with international business relations is often missing from the efforts of developing country firms to access external markets.

Donnorummo (2000) suggests that the educational system of the former Soviet bloc is weak in creating an environment of intellectual openness, innovation, and problem-solving skills. The education system should not only provide the technical skills but also impart a culture in which change is acceptable, desired, and sought after. Thus, business education itself has to be flexible, adaptive, and innovative, in order to enable students from different economic, social, and cultural backgrounds to acquire the skills needed to meet the challenges of a changing global political and market environment. Curriculum and pedagogic styles have to reflect the growing importance of teamwork, alliances, problem-solving skills, flexibility, and innovation as integral components of business education.

William Lewis, in a controversial book, argues that "the importance of education has been taken way too far and a high education level is no guarantee of increased productivity" (2004: ix), which in his view is the mainstay of economic growth. Greater levels of competition drive increases in productivity, and a trained workforce, not necessarily a more educated workforce, could achieve these productivity gains. Lewis suggests that the importance of education stems from the insights it provides on how to organize society and from the lessons learned on the primacy of individual rights. What is clear is the complexity involved in the successful growth of businesses, and as Lewis himself suggests, the political environment and business climate are likely to have as much impact as education and other factors.

Capital and Capital Flows

While the emerging markets lack the infrastructure, wealth, and global involvement of developed countries, they are not as poor as developed countries. They are in a better position than developing countries to take advantage of opportunities presented by a liberalized market environment. The highly educated workforce, relatively large numbers of scientists and engineers involved in research and development, and active patenting of new ideas are indicators of the potential for entrepreneurial activity in these countries (see Table C1). Financial capital flows, in the form of foreign direct investment (FDI), are also signals of the positive climate for increases in productivity and output by the emerging economies. Skills imparted in business education are commensurate with the needs of multinationals and lessen dependence on expatriates. These skills enable countries to take advantage of the beneficial impact of FDI, including greater stability compared to other forms of capital flows, its effect on stimulating domestic investment, and the technology transfer accompanying the investment.

New ideas have to be brought to the market place, and this requires not just technical know-how but also appropriate financing mechanisms, whether these are loans at reasonable rates of interest, equity or venture-capital financing, or knowledge of and access to markets. In order to convince the financial backers of the feasibility of the venture, a business plan and marketing strategy have to be prepared. As the authors of chapter 3 in this volume aptly note, businesses founded by individuals with appropriate business education have a greater probability of survival and long-term success than do other types of businesses. In situations where job opportunities are limited, entrepreneurial activity and the resulting start-ups have greater potential to succeed. Higher levels of educational attainment are associated with greater levels of involvement in entrepreneurial firms (Reynolds et al. 2003).

The level of stock market capitalization gives an indication of the propensity to stimulate growth outside of foreign inflows and varies widely across the countries discussed (see table). It provides financial managers with alternative options for securing finance for business operations; however, entry to the market imposes additional demands on the skills of managers as they are faced with other reporting requirements and ownership influences. Managers who are trained in the operation of primary and secondary markets are better equipped to take advantage of the benefits of multiple financing strategies.

Parting Thoughts

It is clear that business education in developing countries has to unfold on different levels depending on the absorptive capacity of individuals in the different countries and the economic and political environment in which they are embedded. Countries with highly educated workforces, such as the transitioning economies of Eastern Europe, are likely to be more significant creators of new knowledge that will enhance and accelerate economic growth. Individuals in these countries are more likely to be receptive to sophisticated financial, marketing, and operational business techniques because of their stronger educational backgrounds. However, individuals from the former socialist states with centrally planned economies are likely to be limited by a lack of experience with market-driven dynamics and the concept of competitiveness. On the other hand, the contrasts within the Indian subcontinent and Latin America, with widely varying levels in the quality and level of educational attainment, highlight the reality that many businesses in emerging and developing economies are unlikely to be able to participate in global markets at the outset and require exposure to simpler business concepts.

The American socioeconomic model, and all that it entails for strategic choices in business education, has been challenged for reasons that are both valid and tendentious. Carl J. Schramm, chief executive officer of the Erwing Marion Kaufman Foundation, however, underlines its jump-starting virtues for growth and states that it "should not be abandoned, as some development economists advocate, but (it) must be improved. The current template is incomplete. In particular, it fails to reproduce a vital element of the U.S. economy: support for entrepreneurship" (2004) and the use of business education as an essential tool to link education to wealth creation and competitive integration in world economic markets. Poor imitations of this seminal model linking business education to job creation and competitiveness should be discouraged, but the underlying educational system that supports it with appropriate business and development policies does offer foundational guidance for thinking through system, curricular, and programmatic reform.

Because transitioning and developing countries are constrained by limited financial resources, they face the dilemma of providing basic educational requirements or higher education, including scientific, technical, engineering, and business education that are more likely to be accessed by the society's elites. Despite the pressures from multiple demands caused by the rapidly changing global economic environment and internal imperatives, developing countries must make efforts to balance resource allocation to competing goals in creating an educated workforce, otherwise they are likely to find themselves in a recurring and downward spiral of low productivity and lack of competitiveness.

Business education will increase knowledge of hard skills in accounting, financial management, international capital markets, just-in-time strategies, lean manufacturing, and total quality management. Knowledge of alternative forms of production, marketing, and organization that go beyond Taylor's scientific management and Fordism, as contributors to this volume have repeatedly stressed, to the so-called soft skills of problem solving, team building, leadership, and motivation strategies will propel the advancement of an industrial structure conducive to the needs of developing economies. In addition to professional training, business education increases levels of productivity in the workforce, helps to create an ethos of service, raises awareness of ethical issues, and reduces the acceptance of corrupt political and business practices.

Business education in emerging and developing economies faces many challenges, not the least of which are the high expectations anticipated; nevertheless, there are opportunities, and the rewards of success are great. Institutions must nurture and develop a cadre of graduates and faculty who can navigate both local and international business environments. In so doing, programs have to surmount the difficulties associated with the absence of technical materials in the spoken language, culture, and context of the population. They have to overcome exclusions imposed by race, ethnic, gender, economic, and social class barriers. As harbingers of change, they serve to promote a culture of tolerance, reduced mistrust, and greater inclusiveness in societies where these may be absent.

References

Donnorummo, B. 2000. "The Emerging Markets and the Process of Globalization." In *The Emerging Markets and Higher Education*, ed. M. McMullen, J. Mauch, and B. Donnorummo, 3–24. New York: Routledge Falmer.
Lewis, W. 2004. *The Power of Productivity: Wealth, Poverty and the Threat to Global Stability.* Chicago: University of Chicago Press.
Mauch, J. 2000. "The Impact of Higher Education on Emerging Markets." In *The Emerging Markets and Higher Education*, ed. M. McMullen, J. Mauch, and B. Donnorummo, 25-44. New York: Routledge Falmer.
McMillan, I., and R. McGrath. 2004. "Does Success in Tech Ventures Follow from Better R&D? Think Again." Knowledge@Wharton. Available at http://knowledge.wharton.upenn.edu/article/1009.cfm (accessed December 13, 2004).
Reynolds, P.; W. Bygrave; E. Autio et al. 2003. *Global Entrepreneurship Monitor.* Executive Report. Babson College and Kauffman Foundation.
Schramm, Carl J. 2004. "Building Entrepreneurial Economics." *Foreign Affairs* 83, no. 4 (July/August) 104–115.

About the Editors and Contributors

Editors

John R. McIntyre is founding executive director of the Georgia Tech Center for International Business Education and Research, a national resource center for the Southeastern U.S. region, and a full professor of international business management at the Georgia Tech College of Management with joint appointment at the Sam Nunn School of International Affairs, Georgia Institute of Technology, Atlanta, Georgia.

He received his graduate education at McGill, Strasbourg, and Northeastern Universities, obtaining his PhD at the University of Georgia, Athens, Georgia. Prior to joining Georgia Tech in 1981, he was research associate for International Management at the Dean Rusk Center. He has had work experience with multinational firms in the United Kingdom and Italy. He has published research articles in journals such as *Osteuropa Wirtschaft* (Munich), *Technology and Society*, *International Management Review*, *Defence Analysis* (London), *Studies in Comparative and International Development*, *Crossroads* (Oxford), *Journal of European Marketing*, *Jeune Afrique*, *Le Moci* (Paris), *Politique Internationale* (Paris), *International Trade Journal*, *Fordham International Law Journal*, and *International Executive*. His most recent books include *Japan's Technical Standards: Implications for Global Trade and Competitiveness* (Quorum 1997) and *Business Education in Emerging Market Economies: Perspectives and Best Practices* (with Ilan Alon; Springer 2004).

McIntyre has had extensive experience in designing and implementing international business education programs at the executive, graduate, and undergraduate levels. He is a recipient of grants and awards from the U.S. Department of Education, FIPSE, and European Union, among others, to further the internationalization of business education and the integration of engineering, foreign languages, and international affairs in the management curriculum.

His professional memberships include Sigma Xi, The Academy of International Business, The Academy of Management, Policy Studies Organization, and The Technology Transfer Society, The International Studies Association, and The American Society for Public Administration. His areas of specialty include international business strategy, export-import management, trade regulation, international business legal transactions, comparative management, international technology transfer, technology clusters as a source of global competitiveness, and issues relating to the globalization of the management curriculum.

Ilan Alon is associate professor of international business at the *Forbes*-ranked Association to Advance Collegiate Schools of Business Crummer Graduate School of Business, Rollins College, which is consistently ranked by *US News & World Report* as one of "America's Best Colleges."

He is the author, editor, and co-editor of nine books and more than eighty published articles relating to international business. Some of his most recent books include *Business Education and Emerging Market Economies: Perspectives and Best Practices* (Kluwer Academic 2004), *Chinese Economic Transition and International Marketing Strategy* (Praeger 2003), *Chinese Culture, Organizational Behavior, and International Business Management* (Praeger 2003). His articles have been published in refereed journals in Europe, Asia, and America. Among the journals that have featured his work are: *Journal of International Marketing, Journal of International Consumer Marketing, Thunderbird International Business Review, Journal of Global Business, Journal of Consumer Marketing, Multinational Business Review, Journal of Business and Entrepreneurship, Journal of Small Business Management,* and *Journal of Consumer and Retailing Services.*

Prior to coming to Rollins College, Crummer Graduate School of Business, Alon taught at Kent State University and the State University of New York. He has lectured at international institutions such as China Europe International Business School, Shanghai University for Science and Technology, Jiao Tong University China, and the University of New South Wales in Sydney, Australia.

An expert in international business, he has been a featured speaker for numerous professional associations, including Academy of International Business, European Marketing Academy, International Council for Small Business, International Society of Franchising, European International Business Academy, Association of Global Business, World Business Congress, American Society for Competitiveness, Association of Marketing Theory and Practice, Midwest Decision Science Institute, Rochester Chamber of Commerce, and others.

Contributors

Raj Agrawal was senior member on the Faculty of Economics and International Business at the All India Management Association-Centre for Management Education (AIMA-CME) prior to joining the Institute for Integrated Learning in Management. He was also officiating director and dean of AIMA-CME. Agrawal received his PhD in economics at Allahabad University. A prolific writer and keen researcher, he has written over sixty articles in leading national and international journals and three books. His areas of specialization include managerial economics, business environments, and international business. His current research interests are the World Trade Organization and allied issues.

Peter Baguma holds a BSC in psychology from Makerere University, an MSC in psychology from Sheffield University, and a PhD in psychology from Vienna University. He is a renowned Ugandan psychologist, researcher, and lecturer in psychology. He has done extensive research in organizational psychology. He is widely published and is associate editor of two international journals.

Serkan Bayraktaroglu obtained his PhD degree from Coventry University and is currently associate professor of human resources management in the Department of Management of Sakarya University, in Turkey. His research interests include strategic human resources management, small- and medium-sized enterprises, and entrepreneurship.

Bijay K.C. is dean of the School of Management, Kathmandu University. He is an accomplished teacher and researcher. He teaches financial management, investment, and strategic management to MBA and executive MBA students at the School of Management, and has been a visiting professor in the Management School, Lancaster University, UK. His research interests lie in the area of corporate finance, capital markets, and strategy. His numerous articles have appeared in journals such as *World Development, Journal of Development and Administrative Studies, Economic Review, Nepalese Management Review, Management Forum,* and *Arthik Darpan.* He holds a PhD from the Faculty of Management Studies, New Delhi University, India, and an MBA from Temple University, Philadelphia, PA.

Earl L. Caldwell II, Esq. is founder and President of A Breed Apart Foundation, a non-profit organization based in Chicago, IL that promotes entrepreneurship and leadership development for youth. In addition, Mr. Caldwell is founder of the International Leadership Development Academy, whose purpose is to foster entrepreneurship and business development in Africa by facilitating partnerships between African and American students.

Scott G. Dacko is a lecturer in marketing and strategic management at Warwick Business School, University of Warwick. He holds a PhD in business administration from the University of Illinois at Urbana-Champaign, and MBA and BME degrees from the University of Minnesota. He has published articles in the *Journal of Marketing Education, Marketing Intelligence & Planning, Benchmarking: An International Journal, International Journal of Advertising, International Journal of New Product Development and Innovation Management,* and the *Journal of Marketing Management.* His research interests include skill development in marketing education and the role of timing in marketing strategy development and success for services and products.

Leo Paul Dana is senior adviser to the World Association for Small and Medium Enterprises and is currently based at the University of Canterbury. He formerly served as deputy director of the Nanyang Business School International Business MBA Program and as Visiting Professor of Entrepreneurship at INSEAD. He is founder of the *Journal of International Entrepreneurship* and the author of 100 articles. His reference volume, *Entrepreneurship in Pacific Asia: Past Present & Future* (World Scientific 1999) has been on the best-seller list for over two years.

Juan Federico received his bachelor's degree in economics from the Universidad Nacional del Sur (Argentina), and is an MSC candidate in industrial economics and development with an emphasis on small and medium-sized enterprises at the Universidad Nacional de General Sarmiento (Argentina). He is a researcher and lecturer in the Entrepreneurial Development Program at the same university.

T.K. Garg is a professor in the Department of Mechanical Engineering, National Institute of Technology, Kurukshetra, India, where he obtained his PhD. He has more than twenty-eight years experience and has advised about twenty postgraduate candidates on dissertation work for the master of technology degree and two candidates on their PhD research work. His areas of interest are CAD/CAM, automation, machine design, and industrial instrumentation.

Kamala Gollakota teaches business policy, international management, and organizational behavior. Her research interests include organizational decline and turnaround and the telecommunications industry.

Vipin Gupta has a PhD (1998) and a five-year postdoctoral senior fellowship (1999–2003) from the Wharton School of the University of Pennsylvania. He was a gold medallist in the MBA program of the Indian Institutes of Management-Ahmedabad (1988–1990). He has been a Japan Foundation Fellow and a visiting researcher at the University of Tokyo (1994–1995). His work has appeared in international journals including the *Journal of Business Venturing, Asia-Pacific Journal of Management, Journal of World Business, Journal of Management, Research in Organizational Behavior, Journal of Case Studies, Multinational Business Review, Advances in Global Leadership, Management Review,* and *Global Business Review.* He is editor of three specialized books.

Serhiy Gvozdiov is deputy director general for Academic Affairs at the Lviv Institute of Management (LIM), Lviv, Ukraine. He received his MBA from LIM and his PhD from Lviv Polytechnic University with additional certificate training from the University of Navarra, Barcelona, Spain. He has directed projects for the U.S. Agency for International Development and Tacis, and has served as an industrial engineer as well as professor at other institutions.

Galen Hull, holder of a PhD from Northwestern University, is currently director of International Business Programs at Tennessee State University. He is a veteran development consultant with thirty-five years of experience in international development, working with U.S. and foreign government agencies, nongovernmental organizations, universities, and small businesses in over thirty African, Asian, Caribbean, and Central and East European countries. His areas of expertise include small and microenterprise development, management education, project design, evaluation and monitoring, and project management.

Donato Iacobucci is a researcher in applied economics on the Faculty of Engineering, Università Politecnica delle Marche, Ancona, Italy. He teaches several courses in business economics on the Faculty of Engineering. His research interests are in the field of entrepreneurship and small firms, with a specific concentration on organizational and financial aspects. Recently he has been working in the areas of habitual entrepreneurs and the formation and development of business groups.

Silvester Ivanaj is associate professor and head of New Educational Technologies at ICN Graduate School of Management, Nancy, France. He received a BS from Polytechnic University of Tirana, Albania, and a PhD degree from Institut National Polytechnique de Lorraine, France. Current interests focus on computer-based new teaching methods, management information systems recently Analysis of Emerging Technologies.

Vera Ivanaj is associate professor of strategic management, human resource management, and organizational behavior at the Institute of Business Administration, University of Metz, France. She received her MS in economic sciences from the University of Tirana and her PhD in management sciences from the University of Nancy. Her current research interests include strategic decision making processes, logistics outsourcing, and new methods of teaching.

Jan-Erik Jaensson, associate professor, was the former head of the Department of Business Administration at Umea School of Business and Economics at the University of Umea. Among other assignments, he has been a reviewer for several international conferences and he has also been a member of several boards. Jaensson and Lettice Rutashobya received the EMERALD's Best Paper Award (2003) at the International Conference of the International Academy of African Business and Development held at the University of Westminster, London, April 2003.

Jonatan Jelen is currently assistant professor of business in the Division of Business and Accounting at Mercy College, Dobbs Ferry, New York. Additionally, he holds responsibilities as coordinator of online learning for the division and is director of the MS in MIS that he is currently creating for the college. He is completing his PhD dissertation on business-computer information systems. Additionally he teaches in South Africa and China. His research interests focus on leadership at large, distance education and pedagogy, information and network economics, cyberlaw, and the management of technology. He holds a doctorate in law from Universite de Pau, France, as well as MBAs from Ecole Superieure de Commerce de Paris, Edinburgh Business School of Heriot-Watt University, and Baruch College, as well as a JD from Ludwig-Maximilians-University, Munich. Germany, and LLMs from Universite de Pau, Universite de Paris II-Pantheon-Assas, and Fordham University School of Law.

Hugo Kantis, PhD, European Doctoral Program in Entrepreneurship and Small Business Management, Växjo University (Sweden) and Universidad

Autónoma de Barcelona (Spain). He is director of the masters degree in industrial economics and development with an emphasis on small and medium-sized enterprises (SMEs) at the Universidad Nacional de General Sarmiento (Argentina), and director of the Entrepreneurial Development Program at the same university. He is a lecturer, researcher, and consultant who specializes in entrepreneurship and SMEs.

Palok Kolnikaj is an associate professor of financial analysis and agromarketing at the Agricultural University of Tirana, Albania. He received his PhD in economic science from the University of Tirana. Former vice governor of the Bank of Albania and former dean of the Faculty of Economics, he has extensive experience in finance and marketing. He is the author of many textbooks and studies.

Rana Ozen Kutanis obtained her PhD degree from Bosphorus University and is currently assistant professor of organizational behavior in the Department of Management of Sakarya University, Turkey. Her research interests include mentoring, gender, work-family conflict, small and medium-sized enterprises, entrepreneurship, job satisfaction, organizational culture, learning, learning organizations, communication, leadership, and behavioral sciences.

Maria-Teresa Lepeley is president of the Global Institute for Quality Education. She has held appointments as professor of business in the United States and Chile, including at the University of Connecticut, University of Texas, and the University of Chile in Santiago. She has been a visiting professor and keynote speaker at universities around the world. She is past president of the Institute for Entrepreneurial Education in Santiago, and author of the book *Quality Management in Education. A Model for Evaluation* (McGraw-Hill Inter-Americana 2001). She has a bachelor's degree in education from the University of Santiago in Chile, and master's degrees in higher education management and in economics, both from the University of Miami.

Romie F. Littrell is an associate professor of international business at Auckland University of Technology, New Zealand, and facilitator of the Centre for Cross Cultural Comparisons. His major research work has been in cross-cultural leadership and management, with engagement in a longitudinal and multicultural project collecting descriptions of desirable explicit leader behavior in various national cultures. Prior to his career as an educator and researcher, he worked for IBM, Xerox, Unisys, and Six Continents Hotels & Resorts. He has lived and worked in the United States, Mexico, the Caribbean, Europe, China, and New Zealand.

Le Lu is professor and dean of the Shanghai-New York International Language Institute, University of Shanghai for Science and Technology, China. Her research covers lexicology, semantics, and cross-cultural communications. She has written numerous academic papers that have been published in prestigious Chinese journals, books, and Western journals. Her books include a translation of *Tradition* by Edward Shils, an American sociologist, two co-edited dictionaries, and a number of textbooks used widely throughout China. She has given fifteen television lectures broadcast nationwide by China Central Television. She and her research partner have successfully finished a project, funded by Ford Foundation, concerning social changes in China and vocabulary changes in the Chinese language. She has recently participated in research funded by U.S. universities, aimed at exploring China's market and has co-authored several reports and articles published in business-oriented journals resulting from this research.

Robert W. McGee is a professor at the Andreas School of Business, Barry University in Miami Shores, Florida. He has published more than forty books and more than three hundred articles in the fields of accounting, taxation, economics, law, and philosophy.

Audra I. Mockaitis is a lecturer in the Department of Marketing at Vilnius University. She received her PhD in comparative management from Vilnius University in 2002, MIB degree from Vilnius University in 1997, and BA degree in Russian and East European Studies from the University of Illinois at Urbana-Champaign in 1993. Her research interests include cultural aspects of international business, comparative and cross-cultural research methodology, and international human resources management issues. She teaches undergraduate and graduate courses in international business, international marketing, and cross-cultural marketing.

Jaime Ortiz holds a PhD from Virginia Tech, an MA from the Institute of Social Studies in the Netherlands, and Postgraduate Diploma and a BSc from the *Universidad de Chile* in Chile. He is director of the Office of International Programs and a member of the faculty of the College of Business at Florida Atlantic University. He has taught and consulted in business and economic matters in thirteen countries, with a particular focus on Latin America and the Caribbean. He is the author, co-author, or editor of two books, nine textbooks, sixty-five research monographs and technical reports, and fourteen refereed journal articles. His work focuses on international business strategy and technological change.

Vanessa Gail Perry, PhD, is assistant professor of marketing at George Washington University (GWU), Washington, DC. Prior to joining GWU, she was a senior economist at Freddie Mac, where she was responsible for housing and mortgage market research. She has published articles in academic journals on the effects of competition on consumers and consumer information acquisition. Her current research interests include decision making and entrepreneurship.

Guy Pfeffermann is director of the Global Business School Network of the International Finance Corporation (IFC), a member organization of the World Bank Group that promotes private sector investment in developing and transition countries. Before joining the IFC in 1988, he worked at the World Bank where he was chief economist for Latin America and the Caribbean from 1979 to 1987. Until 2003, he was chief economist of IFC. He is a French national and has degrees from the Universities of Strasbourg, Paris, and Oxford. A number of his recent speeches and publications can be found at www.ifc.org/economics/.

Sergio Postigo is director of the Karel Steuer Chair in Entrepreneurship, Universidad de San Andrés. He received his PhD from the European Doctoral Program at the Universidad Autónoma de Barcelona and Växjö Universities. He teaches several courses in entrepreneurship at the undergraduate and graduate levels, especially at the Universidad de San Andrés, and in the Master's Degree Program in Economics and Industrial Development at the Universidad Nacional General Sarmiento. He is visiting professor at ESCP-EAP (Paris, France) and Universidad del Desarrollo (Chile). His research interests include corporate entrepreneurship and entrepreneurship education.

Vytautas Pranulis is professor and head of the Department of Marketing at Vilnius University, Lithuania. He received his MA from Vilnius University in 1969, PhD in social sciences in 1977, and Dr. Habil. in social sciences in 1989, both from the Moscow State Institute of Economics. He is the author of five books and 120 publications. His research focuses on marketing theory and practice in Lithuania and the international environment. He teaches undergraduate and graduate courses in international marketing and marketing research, as well as the business environment, supervising several doctoral students. He is editor-in-chief of the international journal *Transformations in Business & Economics,* and editorial board member of the journal *Economics* of Vilnius University.

Galina G. Preobragenskaya is the founding director of Locia, an audit and consulting firm in Omsk, Russia. She has published numerous articles and book chapters on accounting reform in Russia.

X. Dai Rao is a full professor of consumer psychology and international economics, marketing, and business at several universities. She is a former dean. She has more than 150 publications and consulting reports and recently was appointed vice president of marketing at a large multinational corporation. She is co-author of a best-selling textbook on consumer behavior in the Australian and New Zealand markets, as well as one in China. She has published more than seventy articles in many international refereed journals, such as the *Asian Journal of Marketing, Journal of Professional Services Marketing, Psychology and Marketing, Current Psychology, Australasian Agribusiness Review,* and the *Journal of Hospital Marketing.* She was appointed chair of the Business Advisory Council and academic dean at the Kazakhstan Institute of Management, Economics and Strategic Research under the Office of the President of Kazakhstan.

Alfred Rosenbloom is an associate professor of marketing and international business at Dominican University. He has been teaching for twenty years. Before coming to Dominican University, he taught at Benedictine University, Lisle, Illinois, and Lewis University, Romeoville, Illinois. At Benedictine University, he was co-founder and co-director of an Executive MBA Program for Physicians and Senior Health Care Executives. In 2001, he was a Senior Fulbright Scholar in Nepal, where he taught at the School of Management, Kathmandu University. He is a member of the Case Standards Committee and an active member of the World Association for Case Method Research and Application. He holds a PhD from Loyola University, Chicago.

Lettice Rutashobya was former dean of the Faculty of Commerce and Management at the University of Dar es Salaam. A full professor of business administration and entrepreneurship, she serves as director of Postgraduate Studies at the University of Dar es Salaam. Among other assignments, she is vice president for Membership at the International Academy of African Business and Development, Washington, DC. She has also received several awards, including Award Winner, Senior Scholars Research Grant Competition of the Organization for Social Science Research in Eastern and Southern Africa in December 2003.

Liza Rybina is a lecturer in marketing at the Kazakhstan Institute of Management, Economics and Strategic Research (KIMEP). She teaches marketing at all levels. She has served as an internship coordinator helping students to acquire practical skills and develop business networking. As a marketing department coordinator for undergraduate studies, she has contributed to the development of a new "Western-style" curriculum at the institution. She has a diploma in physics and an MBA. Her work as an engineer at the Institute of Hydrometeorology developed her research skills. Under her leadership, an evening program at KIMEP was transformed from a set of courses into an evening, Western-style MBA program. She has consulted for Kazakhstani and Russian companies on sales management. Currently, she is a Junior Faculty Development Program Fellow at the University of Northern Colorado.

S.K. Sharma is a professor in the Department of Mechanical Engineering, National Institute of Technology, Kurukshetra, where he obtained his PhD. He has over twenty-one years' experience and has advised fifteen postgraduate candidates on dissertations for master of technology degrees and eight candidates on their PhD research work in the field of industrial engineering.

Ancheri Sreekumar is presently dean of DC School of Management and Technology located in Kerala, one of the southern states of India. He was dean of the Faculty of Management Studies of Goa University until July 2003, and has been a management educationist in India for the past twenty-seven years. His research interests focus on tourism, education, information and communication technology (ICT) for development, and so on. At Goa University, he was responsible for initiating collaborative research with the University of Aveiro of Portugal in the area of tourism. Currently he is consultant to the government of Kerala for its ICT Programme for Development. He holds a doctorate in management from the Indian Institute of Management Ahmedabad of India.

Maria Fernanda Tamborini holds a master's degree in economics and industrial development, specializing in small and medium enterprises and entrepreneurship at the Universidad Nacional General Sarmiento. She is professor assistant to the Karel Steuer Chair in Entrepreneurship at the Universidad de San Andrés, and her research interests include university entrepreneurs, entrepreneurship in emergent economies, and entrepreneurship education.

Sharon V. Thach is professor of marketing and international business in the Department of Business Administration at Tennessee State University. She has taught and conducted research in Eastern Europe, Mexico, Brazil, Spain, and Africa. Her primary research and teaching interests are distribution, export management, and business strategy. She received her PhD from Michigan State University.

V.P. Wani is a workshop superintendent at the National Institute of Technology, Kurukshetra, India and completed a PhD at that institution in the area of perspectives and prospects of small engineering industries. He has over twenty-two years of experience in the field of project execution, industrial development, and teaching, having guided four postgraduate students in dissertation work for their master of technology degrees. His areas of interest are entrepreneurship development, engineering management, and production engineering.

Index

415

B

Baburao, G., 43
Baguma, Peter, xxiv, 301-319, 405
Bailey, D., 100
Bailey, James, 294-295
Bakshi-Digne, A., 27
Banai, M., 345
Bass, B.M., 305
Baumol, W.J., 256
Bayraktaroglu, Serkan, xxv, 336-343, 405
Beamish, P., 86
Beattie, A., 100
Behrman, J.N., 92
Beijing University, China, 366, 387
Belarus, entrepreneurship training in,
  86-87
Belk, R., 136-137
Bellah, R.N., 348
Belyanova, E., 91
Bender, S., 332, 333
Bendixen, M., 307-309
Bennis, W.G., 305
Berry, M., 191
Bettis, R.A., 166
Bhatia, B.S., 43
Bhaya, A.G., 17
Bhupta, M., 17
Bierschenk, Thomas, 207
Biglaiser, G., 238
Bijay, K.C., xvii-xviii, 69-81, 405
Black, J.S., 313, 315, 316
Blackmail, awareness of, 232
Blawatt, K.R., 88
Bligh, D., 129
Block, Z., 244
Blunt, P., 305, 306, 310, 311, 313-314,
  315
Böhm, A., 361, 362
Bohn, A., 221
Bohn, R., 49
Bologna Declaration, 211, 220, 221, 297
Bolton, P., 85
Booz Allen Hamilton, 3
Borda, M., 100
Borgonjon, J., 364, 366
Boross, Z., 100

Bosnia and Herzegovina
  curriculum reform in, 192-193
  entrepreneurship training in, 87
  translation of texts, 196-198
  USAID faculty training, 193-205
Botswana, leadership behavior in, 311,
  313-314
Bourdieu, P., 22
Boycko, M., 91
BPP Publishing, 185
Braidot, N., 243
Bramson, R.M., 125
Branine, M., 364
Brennan, J., 219
Bribery, awareness of, 232
Britain
  curriculum model of, 338-339
  desirable leadership behaviors in,
    317-318, 319
  entrepreneurship education in, 337
  skill development in, 117-121, **118**,
    120, 121, 143
British Commonwealth countries
  business education model, 143
  skill development in, 117-121, **118**,
    120, 121
Brown, D., 311
Brown, J.D., 347
Brown, S., 30
Brown, W., 242, 256
Buckley, P., 239
*Bulletin of the Association of
  Commonwealth Universities*, 294
Burg, S.L., 198
Burnham, L., 192
Business creation. *See* Entrepreneurship
Business education
  challenge for, 401-402
  economic development and, 395-397,
    396-397
  financial capital flows and, 399-400
  growth of, 3
  innovation and, 398-399
  paradigmatic approach to, 135-137
  trends and practices in, 137-139,
    336-338
  See also specific countries and topics